Conscience & Community

American University Studies

Series XIV
Education

Vol. 43

PETER LANG
New York • Washington, D.C./Baltimore • Boston
Bern • Frankfurt am Main • Berlin • Vienna • Paris

Conscience & Community

The Legacy of Paul Ylvisaker

Virginia M. Esposito
Editor

PETER LANG
New York • Washington, D.C./Baltimore • Boston
Bern • Frankfurt am Main • Berlin • Vienna • Paris

Library of Congress Cataloging-in-Publication Data

Ylvisaker, Paul N.
Conscience and community: the legacy of Paul Ylvisaker /
edited by Virginia M. Esposito.
p. cm. — (American university studies. Series XIV, Education; vol. 43)
Collection of speeches and writings from 1949 to 1990.
Includes bibliographical references and index.
1. Community. 2. Community life—United States. 3. Social action—United States.
4. Cities and towns—United States. 5. Education—United States. 6. Charities—
United States. I. Esposito, Virginia M. II. Title. III. Series.
HN27.Y58 307—dc21 98-40742
ISBN 0-8204-3845-6
ISSN 0740-4565

Die Deutsche Bibliothek-CIP-Einheitsaufnahme

Conscience and community: the legacy of Paul Ylvisaker /
ed. Virginia M. Esposito. –New York; Washington, D.C./Baltimore;
Boston; Bern; Frankfurt am Main; Berlin; Vienna; Paris: Lang.
(American university studies: Ser. 14, Education; Vol. 43)
ISBN 0-8204-3845-6

Cover design by Nona Reuter
Typesetting by Capitol Communication Systems, Inc.

The paper in this book meets the guidelines for permanence and durability
of the Committee on Production Guidelines for Book Longevity
of the Council of Library Resources.

Printed in the United States of America

Contents

Part III
Education: A Generation Too Precious to Waste

Part IV
Philanthropy: The High Estate

 **Foreword**

The speeches and writings in this book provide an opportunity for the reader to spend some time with an extraordinary man. Paul Ylvisaker served as a senior consultant to the Council on Foundations for the last ten years of his life. Not surprisingly, this period paralleled my first ten years as President of the Council. He was a trusted confidant, a wise counselor, an esteemed colleague, and a close friend. But more than that, he was in many ways the heart and soul of organized philanthropy.

Paul Ylvisaker was both a professor and a philanthropist, a man who followed both routes to understanding, the compassionate as well as the analytical. Everyone who accepted his invitation to speak to his class at Harvard came away feeling that they got more than they gave. Each year, he would ask me to help inspire as well as inform his students, to talk to them about not only the rich tradition of philanthropy but also about its potential as a vehicle for compassion and community.

Yet, it was I who came away inspired and energized. The give and take with students was an intellectual challenge I always relished, but it was the time spent with Paul that was the most meaningful. During the walk through Harvard Square, dinner at a local restaurant or time together at his home, we would lay bare our souls; probing the moral underbelly of the craft we had both come to regard as a calling.

Warm, compassionate and engaging, he had an infectious enthusiasm that uplifted and empowered everyone he met. He used his considerable influence not to acquire power for himself but to activate power in others. If he had been a politician, he would have sought power not to concentrate it but in order to disperse it.

The timelessness of Paul Ylvisaker's writings is a tribute to his extraordinary vision. He had the capacity to see connections; the ability to focus on the future, to understand it, interpret it, and inspire others to help create it. Like Thoreau at Walden Pond, he built castles in the sky and then he put foundations under them.

The Frenchman Albert Camus once described a true rebel as one who knows in behalf of what he is rebelling altogether as much as against what he is rebelling. Paul Ylvisaker was that kind of a rebel. He always seemed to know what he was for as well as he knew what he was against.

But Paul Ylvisaker was also a patriot. From the early days of the American Republic, there have been those who argued that the primary passion of the patriot should be the passion for justice. That was Paul Ylvisaker. He was one of the first to see the opportunity to promote civil society in distant countries, but he knew also that the best way to demonstrate the efficacy of our system abroad is to demonstrate that it can work equitably for all of our citizens at home.

Paul was a citizen of the world, one who was at home in every community and every culture. At a time when our world seemed to be fragmenting into "we" and "they" groups, he was searching for the social glue of civil society, affirming the connectedness of humanity. He made the case, whenever and wherever he could, that the fear of difference is a fear of the future. He wanted our organizations to demonstrate that diversity need not divide—that pluralism is a benefit rather than a burden. To borrow a phrase from John Winthrop, he was always seeking to make the condition of others his own.

And that may be the real legacy of Paul Ylvisaker. He liked to describe philanthropy as a salt that cannot be allowed to lose its savor, as a distinctive function that like religion stands eventually and essentially on its moral power. He understood better than most the natural tension between the passion of the moral self and the dispassion of the professional self.

In a memorable speech in Atlanta in 1987, he warned against allowing an alien spirit to attach itself to philanthropy. To foundation trustees, he said, "Guard the soul of your organization, even from your own pretensions. . . . Be willing to open up the black box of philanthropy to share with others the mysteries of values and decision-making."

To foundation managers, he said, "Guard your own humanity. . . . If you lose your own soul—whether to arrogance, insensitivity, insecurity, or the shield of impersonality, you diminish the spirit of philanthropy." To all associated with philanthropy, he said, "Never lose your sense of outrage. . . . There has to be in all of us a moral thermostat that flips when we are confronted by suffering, injustice, inequity, or callous behavior." He warned that the power of philanthropy can indeed corrupt. But conducted in a humane spirit, and with soul, it can also ennoble.

Paul liked to tell the story about when he was asked to work for Joe Clarke, then mayor of Philadelphia. When he asked the mayor what the job was, Mayor Clarke thought for a minute and replied, "To help fight the battle for my mind." There is something of a parallel in the life and legacy of Paul Ylvisaker. He was constantly engaged in the battle for the soul of philanthropy. He wanted it to be a quest for a better human condition, something "reminiscent of the search for the Holy Grail."

The works of Paul Ylvisaker cover a wide variety of crafts and disciplines, but his insights are as meaningful to the citizen trying to make sense of his community as it is to the professional who is a government bureaucrat, a foundation trustee or a business executive. The man portrayed in these pages is one whose professional rigor was disciplined by the capacity to listen and to learn, to dream and to dare. But the reader will recognize him mostly as one who made a difference because he found joy in bringing out the best in others.

When Dwight Allison, Chairman of the Board of Directors of the Council on Foundations, and I went to his hospital room in Boston in 1989 to present him with the Council's "Distinguished Grantmaker Award," we found him, as Dwight put it, "as feisty as ever." But while in his characteristic humility, he sought to downplay this focus on his contributions, we both knew that we were in the presence of a man who epitomized the spirit and soul of philanthropy. In Dwight Allison's words, we "stood in wonder at his capacity to deal bravely with the slings and arrows of time. . . . In the midst of an incredibly active and full life, he never took his eye off the sparrow."

Virginia Esposito has done a superb editorial and archiving job of focusing our eyes on the sparrow. As Robert Kennedy reminded us, "Few will have the greatness to bend history itself, but each of us can change a small portion of events." That is the legacy of Paul Ylvisaker. While others changed a small portion of events, he dared to bend history itself.

James A. Joseph
Washington, D.C.

The Honorable James A. Joseph, former president and chief executive officer of the Council on Foundations, is United States Ambassador to South Africa. Ambassador Joseph has served as Undersecretary of the Interior under President Carter and has been a foundation and corporate executive and trustee.

Acknowledgments

The opportunity to write an "Acknowledgments" section for this volume prompts both profound gratitude and enormous relief. I am deeply grateful to those whose love and regard for Paul Ylvisaker inspired them to devote an extraordinary amount of personal energy and time to this project. I am relieved to have a legitimate venue to confess that the idea for this book did not spring fully formed from my own imagination, bringing with it the plan, the contacts, the material and the overwhelming desire to take on and, ultimately, publish a lifetime of Paul's words. I wish I could claim to have the prescience and the courage that scenario would imply.

What I did have was the incredible good fortune to know Paul Ylvisaker through my work at the Council on Foundations. The Council was privileged to have Paul's wise counsel, predominantly in the building of its educational program, for the last ten years of his life. For eight of those years, Paul and I worked closely together in that effort.

After his death, I began to receive telephone calls from those looking for a favorite essay or speech by Paul. The amassing of his work began in a very small, request-by-request way. And, with the impending sale of his home, his children discovered a treasure-trove of his letters, writings and speeches spanning some fifty years. My search for advice led me to John Collins, the librarian of the Monroe C. Gutman Library at Harvard University's Graduate School of Education. As a former dean of that school, Paul's papers would be archived as a matter of policy.

A plan for an expanded archiving process was worked out, one that would include his personal papers and all others we could gather. The funds necessary for a modest staffing and materials budget were provided by the Boston Foundation, the Carnegie Corporation of New York, the Cleveland Foundation, the Dayton

Hudson Foundation, the Maurice Falk Medical Fund, the George Gund Foundation, the David and Lucile Packard Foundation, and the Rosenberg Foundation. Motivated by their respect and affection for Paul, many of Harvard's faculty and staff, under John's careful and caring leadership, generously donated their time. Deborah Garson, led the research effort, and Patrice Moskow saw each detail through to completion. Their professionalism and talents were matched only by their kindness and patience. I am indebted to all the Gutman staff who made me feel welcome and supported despite many visits, countless questions and more than my fair share of photocopier time.

John, Deborah and Patrice worked with Paul's family to organize his papers in the Hilliard Street house and move them to the library. Elizabeth Ylvisaker, Mark Ylvisaker, Peter Ylvisaker and David Ylvisaker, Paul's children, made the papers available and encouraged me to use those papers in this publication. I came to understand that Paul would intend that the subtitle of this book, "The Legacy of Paul Ylvisaker," refer not only to the words and ideas presented on the following pages, but also to the community of those who were inspired by his words and who carry on his life's work. At the heart of this community are all the members of Paul's family, especially his much-loved children and grandchildren.

In reviewing the papers as they were archived, it became clear they should have a life beyond the file cabinets of Harvard. As I was reaching that conclusion, I heard from the Nord Foundation in Ohio. Paul had been instrumental in advising their family philanthropy and they were looking for a way to honor him for that guidance. They offered to support the editorial development of a book of his papers and I thank Eric Nord, the trustees and members of the Nord family for this generous and timely funding. A remembrance from that foundation is offered at the end of this book by Jeptha Carrell, a former executive director of Nord and one of Paul's Swarthmore colleagues and friends.

While writing and editing "Conscience and Community" were accomplished outside of the normal work day, inevitably the demands and tensions occasionally spilled over. I am grateful to James Joseph, former president of the Council on Foundations, who supported the earliest idea of this project and encouraged my participation in it. Virginia Sullivan, Alberto Rivera-Fournier, Susan Riviezzo and Aisha White helped to keep me organized and on track. My remarkable friends and colleagues on the Council's board and staff, especially Alison Wheeler, Deborah Brody, Jason Born and the members of the Committee on Family Foundations, made my personal and professional passions happily co-exist. I am delighted that my new colleagues at the National Center for Family Philanthropy, including the wise and wonderful Tom Lambeth, enthusiastically offer this encouragement and support.

From the moment the idea for this book began to take form, my dear colleague, Robin Hettleman, saw me through each detail and decision. Throughout the process, Robin offered creativity, criticism and friendship.

With each coincidence in the evolution of this book, when the project began to build up around me, seemingly without architect, my friends saw me through the greatest bouts of insecurity. Wendy Puriefoy, George Penick and I discovered the love and strength that could be found in working on this project, giving some meaningful expression to grief. Judith Healey seemed to know exactly when to call and cheer me on. Lastly, my special thanks to Alice Buhl, a rare combination of intelligence, selflessness, patience and faith. Her inspiration and mentoring are reflected in every page. To the extent that they are not reflected exactly as I would have liked, it just means she has more work to do with me.

Friends old and new stepped forward to serve as readers of the manuscript. Doug Bauer, David Bergholz, Lance Buhl, John Collins, Robert Curvin, Fred Jordan, Louis Knowles, Margaret Mahoney, and Brian O'Connell joined George Penick and Wendy Puriefoy in reviewing various sections of this book, offering key insights and suggestions.

My thanks to Joe Foote, Claude Norcott, Francine Krasowska and Carla Heath who helped to prepare the manuscript for publication. In our rush to the finish, Owen Lancer and the staff of Peter Lang Publishing were understanding and thoroughly professional.

My family has been characteristically supportive through the past five years. When papers, folders and computer diskettes filled the dining room, they (rarely) mentioned that it had been more than a year since anyone actually ate in that room. My brothers and sisters (by birth and marriage) asked just the right number of times how the book was coming, generally keeping any inflection out of their voices that might imply, "When in the heck are you going to be finished?" And, when it all seemed just a little too overwhelming for me, my nieces and nephews provided all the giggles and unquestioning love any struggling editor could need.

Finally, I dedicate this book to my mother and the two people whose inspiration and love must now be remembered only in my heart and will be every day of my life.

To my father, Michael Francis Esposito, who taught by living rather than lecture the values I hold most dear. His generosity, loyalty, intellectual curiosity and love of family, community and God are celebrated and cherished by all who share his legacy.

And, to Paul Norman Ylvisaker, who taught me what is possible when those values direct my priorities and my choices—as in the commitment we shared to the fields of philanthropy and education. More than once I've suspected that Paul's inspiration was guiding me and not a few of the coincidences of the publication process.

Paul used to come to my office from time to time and ask me what I had failed at recently. If I couldn't think of an answer (which wasn't often), he would tell me I wasn't taking enough risks. Well, dear Paul, I have taken a big risk . . . and I've taken it with your work. I thought it was a risk worth taking to share the common sense and uncommon eloquence of your prose. I hope you are proud.

Virginia Esposito
Alexandria, Virginia

Virginia Esposito is currently the director of the National Center for Family Philanthropy in Washington, D.C., a nonprofit organization founded in 1997 to serve individual and family donors.

Paul Ylvisaker: A Biographical Profile*

"From all that he touches—education, philanthropy, politics itself—he has scraped away the encrustation of time with the freshness of his free-ranging mind, the gentleness of his acuity, the relentlessness of his courage, and his compassion for the conditions of men. Untainted by cynicism, he has managed to lift the sometimes tawdry mechanics of government to a moral adventure dedicated to the service of the human heart."

From the Princeton University Citation for Honorary
Doctor of Laws, presented to Paul Ylvisaker, June, 1970

"Day by day we knit this life, this environment, and we're [each] carrying [a] thread that makes the tapestry. If it's going to be a good tapestry—the whole cloth that is your home, your street, your city, your state—you'd better take part in the weaving of it. Don't wait for a master weaver to design your life."[1]

With characteristic artistry and honesty, Paul Ylvisaker accomplished two goals with those 1974 words. He encouraged personal responsibility while hinting at the values that guided his own life choices: respect for the individual, the significance of individual

---

*Editor's Note: This biographical sketch provides a context for the writings and speeches that follow. Wherever possible, Paul Ylvisaker's own words have been used to convey his thoughts about his life's goals and accomplishments. The events of his life are related as he remembered them, with all the subjectivity and insight that one would expect. Some readers may remember these events somewhat differently; the accounts are Paul's personal reflections on these events.

[1] Black, Cobey. "Dr. Paul Ylvisaker: Prophet of Overload." *The Honolulu Advertiser.* January 29, 1974.

action, and the responsibility we carry for one another. The weaving of our diverse personalities and priorities with each act of community creates the tapestry, not just of our own lives. but of a society dependent on acts of selflessness.

Ylvisaker's tapestry is woven of fabrics of rich contrast. Consider the Princeton citation above for just a hint of this contrast:

> his gentle acuity, his relentless courage;
> his fresh thinking, his grounding in the historical references of politics, religion and philosophy;
> his belief that institutions should bow to the needs of the individual, his understanding that only in our interdependency do we realize true freedom;
> his espousal of community action and the power of the local citizen, his early awareness that we were part of a global society;
> his painfully candid and frank appraisals of moral failure, his supportive and nurturing teaching buoyed by an unfailing optimism; and, finally
> his robust spirit in constant battle with the rigors of fragile health.

Though he died in 1992, the triumph of his life is remembered and celebrated today.

The Influence of Family

Paul Ylvisaker clearly deferred to no one in the weaving of his own tapestry, but he was the first to acknowledge that it was the product of many important influences. "I came by [my pioneer spirit] naturally," he said. "My pioneer ancestors came to the Midwest from Norway in the 1870s."[2] On his father's side, he reported, were theologians, educators, ministers; on his mother's were a ship captain and sailors. His ancestry remained a source of intense pride throughout his life, as evidenced by a lifetime of references to his Norse heritage and his own surname.

Difficulty in spelling and pronouncing "Ylvisaker" prompted dozens of humorous anecdotes. But he often referred to his ancestry to explain his personal motivations. When asked about the basis for his environmental concern, Ylvisaker replied, "my name means

---

[2] Black, 1974.

'Field of the Sun God.' My Norwegian ancestors lived in the same place for a thousand years, so concern for the environment is in my genes."[3]

If his ancestors helped define his identity and values, his marriage in 1946 to Barbara Ewing, the Radcliffe student he met while a student at Harvard, and his four children seemed to give meaning and purpose to his quest. Ylvisaker's audiences came to know his children well; he used their childish candor and exploits to introduce lessons he credited Elizabeth, Peter, Mark and David for teaching him. "Parent-citizen" was his favorite self-identification.

A Spiritual Center

Paul's father, Sigurd Christian Ylvisaker, was a Lutheran minister and president of Bethany Lutheran College, a small liberal arts college in Minnesota. Paul charted his involvement with Bethany from age eight, frequently telling audiences that he mowed lawns at Bethany because it was too expensive to hire a gardener. By age twelve, he was writing the college catalogue. He went on to attend the two-year college and return briefly as an instructor.[4]

The influence of Sigurd Ylvisaker and a lifetime of church-related schooling would ultimately lead to an intense, spiritual conflict for Paul. While these influences shaped his love of education and inspired a deep faith in God and his fellow man, they would also prompt him to question both organized religion and religious-based education. In a 1975 speech, Ylvisaker decried those who choose parochial education as an alternative to investing in excellent public schools. A member of the audience wrote to him protesting that most choose church-related schools not out of "democratically unhealthy reasons," but out of Christian concern. Ylvisaker replied,

As one who attended religious schools from third grade through junior college, and taught both in parochial schools and religious academies and college, I know and have gained from what you're dedicated to. It's the nature of this complex life the Lord has put us

---

[3] Black, 1974.
[4] Ylvisaker. Presentation to Eighty-Seventh Annual Meeting of the New England Association of Schools and Colleges, December 15, 1972.

into that there are no single or simple answers. I have seen both the virtues and the problematics of religious education and of public education. . . . I come down on the side of having a pluralistic educational system. I strongly feel that learners ought to experience both, and should be taught to respect the purposes and values of public as well as private/religious education. I know I needed to be 'released' at one time from the prejudices and parochilaism of Lutheran dogma, and to come to respect through wider association the myriads of truths and perceptions of truth that creation has given us.[5]

Paul was expected to follow in his father's footsteps and join the Lutheran ministry, and he came close to doing so. His rejection of that life did not include a rejection of faith. His life would evidence his deep personal spirituality and, upon his death, he would name Bethany Lutheran College as one of two institutions he hoped might receive memorial contributions.

Although he could not find a calling in the organized church, Paul found meaning in the Bible, the teachings of Buddha, and the character of Christ. He used the story of Joseph and the Pharaoh to explain and illustrate subjects ranging from private foundation history to the period between World War II and Vietnam. "Render unto Caesar the things that are Caesar's and to God the things that are God's" became the parable of tax policy as well as social responsibility. (Paul also mused that nowhere in that dynamic of Caesar, God and the individual is the church mentioned.)[6]

Though Paul's spirit was vital and his mind willing, his body could not always serve as a vigorous vessel. He waged a lifelong battle with diabetes and was legally blind for most of his life. When he was thirty-four, a coronary attack contributed to his decision to leave political life for philanthropy. The coronary would also signal the beginning of heart problems that eventually would take his life. But his career and accomplishments reveal a life remarkably little curtailed by physical limitations. It seems reasonable to speculate that Paul's battles with poor health contributed to his talent for living. His breathtaking honesty, his willingness to risk job security

---

[5] Ylvisaker letter to Imogene Treichel, November, 1975.

[6] For one such example, see p. 25, "The Church in Public Affairs."

before sacrificing integrity or ethics, and the joy he found in people may very well have been the traits of someone who knew how fragile his leasehold on this life was.

Beginnings in Teaching and Public Service (1943–1956)

Paul's career began in Minnesota's institutions of higher learning. His commitment to his midwestern roots was strong, and he often referred to himself as a country boy who ended up in urban politics. After attending Bethany, he graduated from Mankato State University. Graduate study at the University of Minnesota continued until a fellowship took him to Harvard. A life in education was well launched.

Political science and economy had been the focus of his education. Paul planned to realize his own dreams for himself and for his commitment to others in the complexities of government and political service. His sense of public responsibility and community drove his dreams and his career. But that career would not begin with an immediate interest in political life or Wall Street.

While certainly possessed of a healthy ego, it can not be said that his ambition was the notoriety of elected office. On several occasions, he resisted pressure to launch his own bid for political office. Nor was he driven by the promise of wealth; indeed, he was not known for his keen sense of money. When asked in 1953 to suggest a fee for a public speaking engagement, Paul replied, "I would suggest $50.00, but please do not hesitate to revise this figure if it is out of line with your budget and with other speakers in the series. I would, of course, be willing to speak without a fee if the situation called for it."[7]

Rather, the university life drew the young graduate student. John Nason, former president of Swarthmore, recounts how in 1948 he asked the Harvard Department of Political Science for recommendations for a tenure track position at the college and received four nominations. Paul Ylvisaker was one of them. Failing to get much information on the teaching ability of the candidates, Nason polled

---

[7] Ylvisaker letter to John Nason, 1953.

recent Swarthmore graduates studying in the Harvard department. Without exception they urged him to choose Paul.

The college never had reason to regret the choice. Ylvisaker was intelligent, articulate and charismatic. He brought to Swarthmore all the promise of a brilliant teaching career. He also brought a number of administrative challenges. Among them, his wide range of interests and skills put him constantly in demand. It was a trade-off the college and his future bosses would have to live with.

"Paul Ylvisaker represented college teaching at its best," Nason commented recently. "Students flocked to his courses and were never short-changed. He was constantly invited elsewhere. I had to work hard to keep him at Swarthmore for the all-too-few years he was there."[8]

Paul took a year off from Swarthmore when he received an appointment as a Senior Fulbright Scholar in the United Kingdom. Letters from England testify that this international experience gave practical expression to the global political theory Paul had studied at Harvard and to the universalist philosophy of Kant that had been an inspiring force in his life since high school. His U.K. experience, his sense of global interdependence, and his understanding of Kant were to be recurring themes throughout his writings.

But the political world was never far away. While serving as Democratic chairman for the town of Swarthmore in the mid-1950s, Paul met Joe Clark, mayor of Philadelphia. Noted city planner Robert Moses had given an uncharacteristically lackluster speech at the Quaker Meeting House after an enthusiastic introduction from Ylvisaker. Angry, Paul "let him have it."

"[I] must have said something that Joe Clark liked," Paul recalled in 1977, "because a few days later, [they] called up and said . . . 'Joe's looking for an executive secretary . . . and he'd like to talk to you.'" Paul questioned his qualifications for the position, but he was intrigued by Clark's description of the job: "It's to help fight the battle for my mind."[9]

"I felt maybe I did have the qualifications for it because I . . .

---

[8] Nason letter to Virginia Esposito, 1996.
[9] Ylvisaker interview with Walter Phillips, November 14, 1977.

could at least argue," Paul said. "It was beautifully put as a challenge to me, and I loved it. I could see myself in that role."

The demands of the position, including maintaining his Swarthmore teaching responsibilities and the task of helping put Clark in the United States Senate, were to take their toll. "I felt inadequate in many ways," Paul said later, "and it turned out that . . . the weight of all this tension and the number of jobs that I was trying to do, got to me . . . Without my knowing it, in December [1956] I had a coronary."[10]

Just before his heart attack, Paul had received an offer from The Ford Foundation. The heavy demands and low pay of his job with Clark loomed large for the young father of three as he contemplated his precarious health and the benefits plan that came with the foundation position. Clark almost talked Paul into staying, but the day after their conversation, a mayoral office colleague died of a heart attack. After two years with Clark, Paul went to Ford.

The security of the Ford position may have been the most obvious and compelling reason for the move, but it was not the only one. More than twenty years after his resignation as executive secretary to Clark, Paul reflected, "I finally broke away from Joe, not because of the coronary, [but] because I recognize what happens when you work as a junior to a man too long. You take on his personality. . . . [Clark's] personality is not my personality. And so I thought, partly to protect my identity as well as my health, I should not go with him."

The Ford Foundation and the Gray Areas (1955?–67)

Paul credited the reasons he came to Ford for his ability to survive the tumultuous environment he found upon his arrival. Unlike many others who came to Ford in the early 1950s, he expected neither a career in philanthropy nor a short-term consultancy with a guarantee of a generous research grant upon his departure.

Paul later characterized the atmosphere at Ford in his early years as "suspicious and paralyzed." Departments competed with one another and trustees seemed to Paul to be "coalitions of very strong personalities and usually of very strong interests."

---

[10] Phillips interview, 1977.

Grantmaking policy during this period seemed unimaginative and risk-averse to the adventurous Ylvisaker. Huge amounts supported academic research and hospitals. In his first eighteen months at Ford, he resigned three times in impatience. But things were not to stay static for long. Out of this same atmosphere, fired by Paul's capacity to see potential and understand what it would take to succeed, the "Gray Areas" program was born.

Paul's public affairs department was involved in the development of programs that continue to have an impact on the lives of millions: Head Start, VISTA, and children's educational television. But it is the Gray Areas program that stands as the greatest example of a private philanthropic initiative that transformed public policy. Gray Areas became the blueprint for Presidents Kennedy and Johnson's War on Poverty, and Paul was the architect.

The term "gray areas" was used by Paul to characterize the section of deteriorating real estate between a city's downtown area and its newer suburbs. The project that came to be known as Gray Areas was The Ford Foundation's response to that deterioration: a multi-year effort on a massive economic and geographic scale, targeting the physical and human problems of urban decay.

In a 1973 interview, Paul would reflect that, while the heroic spirit that marked the early Kennedy era would set the appropriate stage and climate for Gray Areas, a set of internal circumstances would lead to its success. Among these were the ability of two major departments (public affairs and education) to work together, the prestige and good will created by, ironically, the massive hospital grants Paul had dismissed early in his Ford career and the painstaking homework of an extraordinarily talented staff.[11]

While internal and external circumstances converged to create the right time and place, it was the spark of Paul's own commitment that ignited the chain of events into Gray Areas. "I've been working at what you would call community problems ever since I was in graduate school," he said in 1972. "Way before the current interest in the cities, I had the feeling that the American government and

---

[11] Ylvisaker interview with Charles T. Morrissey for the Ford Foundation, September 27, 1973.

foreign governments would have to come to terms on everything from sewage to school problems. The outlook was kind of bleak until the late 1950s. Not many people were interested. At the Ford Foundation, there were just the beginnings of interest, and several of us began making grants to the cities to bring the country to terms with the problems."[12]

In addition to developing a process that included coalitions within and outside The Ford Foundation, Paul learned important lessons about the sensitivity of the program he was proposing. One was language. Phrases such as "civil liberties" and "race relations" were not acceptable in many venues. Even the term "gray areas" came from his search for neutral language.

While the new term may have originated in an effort to make discomfitting subjects more palatable, Paul found it a blessing. A term not tied to the old descriptions of the problems was also not tied to old solutions. It freed his mind to think creatively about the issues.

"I came to [a] sudden perception of the city as the magnet and passage-point of great migrations. . . . It was for me an intellectual breakthrough. I had the sense that we were dealing with people problems, not bricks and mortar and not power structure problems."

Having found both his personal breakthrough and the support he needed at Ford, Paul shaped a grants program unlike anything the private foundation world had ever witnessed. His report to the Ford trustees described

. . . a series of major grants over an extended period which would help a selected number of communities to develop coherent programs of enough scale and leverage to improve the habitat, education, and adjustment of the citizenry of the Gray Area. Specifically, such an approach would aim at creating schools whose location, curricula, and methods were adapted to the needs of these depressed areas. It would mean police and social work, urban renewal and rehabilitation, physical planning, public finance, and governmental policy [that] have at least the virtue of consistency and the ability to distinguish the physical from the human problems of the Gray Area. It would mean private agencies whose energies were

---

[12] Unattributed interview with Ylvisaker, 1972.

harnessed into a constructive rather than a competitive role. And it would envisage these elements as incorporated into a significant demonstration to show that urban growth and change can take place in a climate of hope, respect, and social stability.

The energy and ideas of Gray Areas translated into federal policy in the early 1960s. Many of Ford's key staff and others involved in making the Gray Areas program a reality at the local level found their way into positions in the Kennedy and Johnson administrations. When the War on Poverty was declared, the White House needed what veteran soldiers any sector could offer. Paul served on President Kennedy's Task Force on the City and chaired President Johnson's Task Force on the City. Twenty years later, Paul noted with pride that his 1967 task force was the precursor to the 1968 Kerner Commission and that the Kerner report was a re-working of his own task force's report.

The Gray Areas program had achieved national prominence by the time McGeorge Bundy arrived as president of The Ford Foundation in 1966. A power struggle resulted. As Paul would describe in 1973, he himself had become one of the "feudal barons" he had contended with upon his own arrival. Now he was the baron of the most powerful empire/program of them all. Or so ran the "cold analysis of a leader of an institution [Bundy] who has got a lot of feudal barons. . . . Do you want to go through all the business of having to deal with the baron, or do you deal with it yourself?" Paul imagined Bundy reasoning. "I think he finally decided after some ambivalence he wanted to deal with it directly. And as soon as I knew that, then I knew the thing was done." It was time for Paul to leave The Ford Foundation.[13]

One health crisis had precipitated Paul's arrival at Ford; another marked his departure. At the time he decided to leave the foundation, Paul learned he was going blind. But the promise of good health insurance was not enough to keep him there. In a final gesture that would appropriately close their relationship, Ford insisted that his benefits continue through the transition period.

---

[13] Morrissey interview, 1973.

New Jersey Commissioner of Community Affairs (1967–70)

Following his tenure at Ford, Paul was ready to be "closer to the action," as he would describe it. Democrat Richard Hughes' election as governor of New Jersey provided the call to action. A Hughes promise in the 1961 campaign, a Department of Community Affairs would be established to combine planning, housing, antipoverty programs, and a state review of municipal plans for bond issues. The new agency seemed tailor-made for Paul's interests and talents.

Not everyone thought so. While Joe Clark encouraged him to accept and work with "good guy" Dick Hughes, Senator Robert Kennedy thought Paul had too much to lose. Kennedy thought the future of the interests they shared was in federal, not state, government, and he believed Paul might lose his reputation as a major player in urban affairs. Even John Lindsay, then mayor of New York, thought state government was not the place to be and urged Paul to accept a deputy mayor position in New York City. There were also a number of job offers in private enterprise, with salaries too large to be easily dismissed.

But, as Paul would note later, "it seemed like the right time." On March 1, 1967, Paul was sworn in as the first Commissioner of Community Affairs for the state of New Jersey. Four months later, the Newark and Plainfield riots thrust the new Commissioner into a tragic and dramatic national spotlight.

On July 12, the city of Newark erupted in violence between black residents and police. Some 500 state police officers and 3,000 National Guard troops were called in. In a matter of hours, 3,000 persons were arrested or injured, and twenty-six people, all but two of them black, were dead. Hundreds of small, black-owned businesses were damaged.[14]

Although his years as a judge had prepared Governor Hughes for the law-and-order aspects of the civil disturbance, it quickly became clear that he needed someone experienced and skilled in convening

---

[14] Campbell, Louise. "Paul Ylvisaker: The Art of the Impossible." *City* (a publication of Urban America, Inc.). Volume 3, Numbers 2, 3, 4. 1969.

citizens and convincing community leaders to take part in easing the tensions. Hughes asked Commissioner Ylvisaker to lead that effort.

During the five days of rioting in Newark, Paul arranged for emergency food distributions and worked with U.S. Attorney General Ramsay Clark in an effort to organize federal assistance, including the assistance of the Red Cross. He also helped to organize community assistance in quelling the violence and advanced the work of a group organizing a "release-on-recognizance" plan for the thousands in overcrowded jails.

On July 17, Paul went home to bed confident that the city of Newark was quiet. Two and a half hours later, he was awakened with the news that rioting had erupted in Plainfield, a town some twenty miles from Newark. Paul had been convinced all along that the best way to restore order would be to hold community meetings with a fair hearing of complaints and genuince concern for the issues and people involved. That night, his plan began to yield the results he sought. His confrontation with 400 angry black citizens on a street corner, recently the scene of violence, ended in negotiation rather than further violence.

The next day, state police and National Guard troops were ordered to conduct a house-to-house search for stolen guns. Paul feared the large-scale demonstration of police force in what he believed to be an illegal neighborhood search would prolong and aggravate the violence. Arriving on the scene, he found "armored personnel carriers with tank treads, carrying men with machine guns and bayonets" proceeding down the street. Paul jumped in front of the moving convoy, ordering them to halt in the name of the governor. A scaled-down search ultimately was conducted without violence—and without locating the stolen guns.

While the riots brought the Department of Community Affairs and the Commissioner heightened public attention, they also raised the personal reputation and social capital needed to enable Paul to accomplish much of his agenda. He became known as a fair man, willing to listen and willing to act. A community activist related how she rebuffed the Governor's call to a community meeting, but "Mr. Ylvisaker helped to persuade me. He is a fine man, somebody you can talk sensible to. You can reach him and his staff any time. They sit down and talk to you like good human beings. I like that."

Others shared the same opinion, even those not quite so obviously natural fans of his politics or his values. A Republican assemblyman who tried to abolish the Department of Community Affairs came to appreciate Paul as an honest man and backed off his plan.

"Ylvisaker speaks in the same tone of voice to a welfare mother and to a Senator, and he listens to both for the things that have no words. He seems to have been enough in his own dark closet to find no man an enemy beyond what each of us can see there, and none a stranger. Thus he trusts his instincts, and these give him courage— to act against time and chance, against fears and doubts that paralyze us all."[15]

A political analyst cautioned against believing that Paul's style had no bite: "I have watched Paul Ylvisaker in action on a good many occasions, and in addition to his amazing cerebration he has just enough arm-twister in him to give his urbane persuasiveness a whole lot of muscle."

Riots may have marked the beginning of Paul's term as Commissioner and received the most attention, but other issues had called him to service. He pursued them vigorously—most notably land-use reform and the reclamation of the Hackensack Meadows.

Replacing 20,000 acres of garbage in the Hackensack Meadows with orderly development might seem like a "who-could-possibly-oppose-this" proposition, but there was big money in garbage. Governor Hughes, state Senator Fairleigh Dickinson and Paul barely won enactment of enabling legislation over the opposition of powerful land-fill interests. The art of negotiation to make possible what some thought to be impossible fell to Commissioner Ylvisaker.[16]

Some 3,000 tons of garbage were dumped daily on the Meadows. Many felt that the Garden State, with the help of New York and Philadelphia, was in danger of becoming one large garbage dump. Of the political barriers that stood in the way of the vision for the Meadows, the lucrative business of renting garbage-dumping privileges represented the biggest challenge. Fourteen municipalities were covered by the vast acreage; all would share the ultimate tax

---

[15] Campbell, 1969.
[16] Campbell, 1969.

revenues from the proposed complex. New garbage disposal systems would be needed for more than 100 towns.

Paul would painstakingly but successfully employ the commonsense strategy he had used so well so often—organize the power structure and community action groups. He brought all the Meadowlands participants together—local, city, regional, state and federal—in full view and with the participation of the public.

The vision they pursued was enormous: a sports complex, a hospital, office buildings, a commercial complex, movie theaters, tennis clubs, condominium townhouses, a conservation system, a wildlife management area, and freshwater and salt marshes. When the opening ceremonies for the complex were held in 1976 (after the Democrats had left office and he was no longer in state government), Paul would not be included in the festivities. He eventually toured the site and the saw the vision had become reality. He might have been forgiven if he had indulged in a moment of pride in New Jersey and his own contributions to the immense achievement. But his reflections on that tour indicate a different preoccupation: "What happened to the low-income housing?"

Yet the pursuit of Meadowland reclamation would not represent the most volatile activity of Paul's tenure as Commissioner. In pursuing a role for the state in local land use, Paul would take his most controversial stance. Noting that New Jersey was "devouring open land at the rate of fifty square miles a year," he declared, "We in New Jersey are going to try something that will eject me from office almost certainly." He proposed a state planning commission and attendant regulations that would force local governments to consider their land-use actions' effects on their neighbors. His bill went on to forbid planning and zoning that opposed guarantees of nondiscrimination.

Paul may have been right. His land-use bill was interrupted by the Republican victory in the next gubernatorial election (1970). Shortly thereafter, he was fired. And the future of land use reform? "Sudden death by strangulation seems probable," declared the *Bergen County Record.*

Paul contributed to many accomplishments that helped place New Jersey in the forefront of social reform: an antipoverty program in place before Congress passed national antipoverty legislation;

changes in civil service hiring and training that opened up jobs for the poor; the appointments of a division on aging to eliminate segregation of older citizens and a division on youth to invest in the young; a housing program that included the right to inspect multifamily housing units; and a model cities program.

Paul's final act as Commissioner was to respond to a little girl who urged him to protect the animals and "save the meadows for us children's sake." Paul replied:

> This will be my last letter as Commissioner . . . and I'm glad you've given me the chance to write it to you. I liked your letter—I liked it so much I will keep it with me for a long time [Editor Note: The child's original letter and a copy of the reply were found in Paul's personal files after his death.]. Maybe I won't be able to use this office to help save some meadows for the animals and for young people like you. But wherever I go, I will remember what you asked me and all of us who work in government to do—and your letter will make me try even harder.

Newspaper articles and editorials for weeks decried Paul's firing, noting that his accomplishments and his concern for New Jersey transcended party politics. One *Bergen County Record* editor wrote, "He brought fresh and bold concepts to state government and they were not always embraced. Fresh and bold concepts rarely are. . . . To paraphrase the late John F. Kennedy, [it is] not what Paul Ylvisaker is going to do without New Jersey, but what New Jersey is going to do without Paul Ylvisaker."

Paul's supporters encouraged him to run for governor and for the U.S. Senate. Newspapers carried updates of the offers and awaited the decision. "I know now why guys who are interested in politics are helpless" when asked if they plan to run, Paul told a reporter for the *Bergen County Record* in 1971. "If you say you're not interested, you're a liar. If you say you are interested, you sound hungry, about ready to go." Rejecting all offers, he cited as one factor the $2 million needed to launch a major campaign. He also read America's immediate political future in the ascendancy of Richard Nixon. Nixon had been elected President in 1968 and would be re-elected in 1972. Paul saw a popular groundswell with which he had little in common.

Paul's ability to freely speak his mind was also a prime

consideration. After he left office, the freedom to comment on social need and government responsibility was heady, and he soon realized he made a better gadfly, cheerleader and prognosticator than political candidate. A February 1970 editorial in the *Bergen County Record* encouraged Paul's supporters to look past their dismay to the silver lining:

> There is abundant evidence that he can be most useful to the state and to both parties in the role he has conceived for himself—the role of analyst and commentator and gadfly, beholden to nobody, conscious of no obligation to play anything safe. Brilliant is what Paul Ylvisaker is most often called, and this is not quite fair to him, partly because brilliance has somehow come to be suspect, but mainly because the only peculiarity of his intellectual attainment is his extraordinary common sense.
>
> His easygoing command of the English language sets him apart from statesmen who cannot string together a sentence that will survive honest inspection, but what he says—that this society cannot tolerate, because it cannot survive, fragmentation and balkanization and division into warring peoples called haves and have-nots or blacks and whites or urban and suburban—what he says is the quintessence of the commonplace.

"So I closed the decade [of the 1960s]," Paul recalled in 1972, "by having a chance to go back and look at life from the sidelines again, decide where it was going, and where to jump in once more." He went back to teaching.[17]

Dean of Harvard University's Graduate School of Education (1972–1982)

Education—or more specifically, the university setting—had often provided Paul the opportunity to think about the future course of his life. Teaching may have looked like a refuge after his tumultuous public life of the late 1960s, but it was to be neither a comfortable nor a temporary phase for him.

Ylvisaker considered several options, settling on two: the presidency of Swarthmore and the deanship of the Graduate School of Education at Harvard. Ties to each school were heartfelt. But the

---

[17] Unattributed interview with Ylvisaker, 1972.

opportunity to work with young teachers, to help shape the direction of education and education training, and to advance the role of schools in society captured his imagination and, as he put it, Harvard gave him the next place to "jump in."

Paul discovered his passion for education was as strong as ever. His vision for the schools of the future was shaped by his childhood at Bethany and his experiences as a teacher, at Ford and in government. "I would like to see the schools and the educational system participate much more aggressively and imaginatively in the definition of the future, in scanning trends, so that instead of lagging constantly with an inertial bureaucracy, schools begin to move, to show entrepreneurship, to catch up, to create, to invent."

Paul succeeded Theodore Sizer as dean of the Graduate School in 1972. The early days of his tenure were marked not by what he called "the Harvard penchant to the doctrine of prestigious enunciation," but by a spirit of inquiry that reflected his understanding of the educational process. His gift for listening and discovering that had served him so well was, he believed, particularly appropriate to education. "Education is one of those infinities," he said in 1972, "that gives us plenty of room to search but never the comfort of knowing that you have arrived."[18]

Paul knew what the university expected of him: He was to oversee the downsizing that universities across the country were experiencing in the 1970s. He described his challenge upon his arrival:

> We suddenly are no longer blessed by the proceeds of the outpouring of tax dollars, categorical grants, foundation grants, and all the rest [that] were precipitated in the postwar period by the rising expectations of education and the rise in the number of kids that had to be educated. It will be very hard for people trained in a period of enthusiastic growth to retain a sense of mission and enthusiasm while [these resources] shrink.[19]

The challenge to succeed in such a climate was both painful and generative. The question of morale—his own and that of his faculty

---

[18] Ylvisaker. Presentation to the Eighty-Seventh Annual Meeting of the New England Association of Schools and Colleges. December 15, 1972.

[19] Ylvisaker presentation, December 15, 1972.

and staff, the students, and others in education—loomed large, and Paul knew he had to be unfailingly encouraging:

> It is the strategy of change that may be more effective than the kind of change we used [to obtain] by buying [it] in the last twenty years. Now you have change by saving rather than by spending, change by shrinking in many respects more than by growing, and this leads to an immediate problem, and I place this problem as one of the priorities of education, not simply to go through the act of shrinking, but to do it with the kind of integrity that says what we shrink is less worthy and what we save is more.[20]

What Paul termed the "culture of enthusiasm" was difficult to maintain as more cuts became a fact of life and spirits suffered. "I regard the maintenance of humanity in the face of that temptation as probably Priority Number One in education now."

Having placed humanity, integrity and spirit at the top of his priority list for education, the new dean named four other areas of concern that would shape his tenure at HGSE. The first was the "longstanding one of human development, . . . how the animal learns, and the outburst of that being how we teach, the art of teaching." The second was the environment in which education takes place—the cultural environment, the political environment, and policy. The third area of concern was the allocation and management of resources, both for formal schooling and beyond. Finally, the fourth related to evaluation: Paul cited both literacy and numeracy as key components of that evaluation.

If his first priority—the priority of the spirit—was to give Harvard and the education community some indication of the man he was and the dean he would be, the last component of his program would confirm it. Each area, he announced, would be infused with history and philosophy. While these had been the traditional cornerstones of education, the educational curricula of more recent times separated them from other program priorities. Paul understood that these were integral elements of any endeavor and brought that understanding to the work of HGSE.

The mission and purpose of HGSE were not on Paul's mind alone.

---

[20] Ylvisaker presentation, December 15, 1972.

While he was trying to determine how best to define and pursue a purpose, he knew the administration of Harvard was questioning the purpose of a graduate school of education in fulfilling Harvard's overall purpose. While a school of law or medicine is readily understood, some administrators wondered why an educational institution needed a school that prepared educators.

But the concern for schools in general would continue in the form of attacks on school segregation by HGSE's Center for Law and Education and in pioneering the idea behind educational television programming such as "Sesame Street." Postsecondary education, continuing professional training, and education beyond the classroom would all be part of the Ylvisaker decade.

Paul described HGSE's evolution, including his own tenure, as natural to an institution concerned with learning:

It is not necessarily a mark of uncertainty that a school of education shifts its focus and varies its mix of specializations over time. Quite the contrary, if the fundamental concern with learning remains explicit, and if attention to generic educational roles and processes . . . remain constant, those shifts are healthy signs of adaptation to the rapidly changing demography, technology, job markets, and lifestyles of modern society.[21]

During Paul's ten years as dean, the struggle to redefine a mission, deal with budget crises, maintain faculty and student morale, and make his case (and the case for the school) to the university and the public failed to quell his earliest enthusiasm for the task. Toward the end of his tenure as dean, he affirmed this:

For those of us who directly experienced the most recent chapter in HGSE's evolution, the outcome—a more versatile and challenging instrument for understanding and promoting human learning—seems well worth the struggles we went through.[22]

Despite budget constraints and Harvard's policy of, as Paul termed it, "each tub on its own bottom," which left HGSE to "forage its survival on a shriveling landscape," Paul innovatively and dynamically

---

[21] Ylvisaker. "A Future for Schools of Education?" Presentation to A.E.R.A. April 17, 1982.

[22] Ylvisaker. "A Future for Schools of Education?" 1981.

led HGSE for ten years. He moved it beyond the traditional parameters of education to a commitment to human learning in the most liberal sense and, as he would note later, in encouraging "diversity in [HGSE's] programs, faculty, and student body." He emphasized the role of the schools in the community, counseling teachers and administrators to look beyond the classroom for the influences and learning opportunities that were shaping young lives.

> I can't honestly say that we succeeded at every turn. There is often a lag, and sometimes a discrepancy, between what a faculty will vote for, students will pay tuition for, and funders will finance, and what is arguably or demonstrably needed. Deans live precariously in that hiatus.[23]

In 1982, Paul walked into Harvard president Derek Bok's office for a regularly scheduled briefing meeting. As Paul would remember later, while he had no conscious intention or even premonition prior to the meeting, it became clear throughout its course that he could no longer continue as dean of HGSE. The direction of the university, President Bok's priorities, the fact that his work as dean seemed well on course, and Paul's own "ten-year rule" for effectiveness in a position all came under discussion as the meeting progressed. He offered his resignation, and it was accepted.

Paul retained his position as the Charles William Eliot Professor of Education at HGSE until his death in March 1992, just a few months before he would have retired. The courses he taught reflected the expansive vision for education he brought to his role as dean: education and values, philanthropy and ethics.

The Later Years (1982–92)

Paul's class schedule allowed him to pursue many of the interests that had defined his career. At the time he was resigning as dean, James A. Joseph was assuming the presidency of the Council on Foundations, the professional association of the nation's private and community foundations and corporate giving programs. Joseph was looking for someone to advise him on the evolution of the Council,

---

[23] Ylvisaker. "A Future for Schools of Education?" 1981.

to serve as a personal advisor and to guide the development of an educational programs and services department.

In one of his first acts as Council president, Joseph hired Paul as a senior consultant, a position he would hold until his death. His association with the Council and his service as a trustee of several private and community foundations provided him with both the vantage point and the opportunity to speak and write on the potential of private philanthropy. In 1990, he wrote two pioneering articles on the promise of family philanthropy, calling attention to an area of special—and previously unrecognized—vitality in the field.

He also became active in international grantmaking. His longstanding association with the Bernard van Leer Foundation in the Netherlands was quickly joined by consultancies in Europe and Asia, notably Japan.

These consultancies, combined with other directorships and advisory posts, contributed to the full, often over-subscribed, schedule that was part of his post-dean years. This was not a professor in semi-retirement—and certainly not someone in fragile health—but someone who worked and traveled constantly. It was not uncommon for Paul to agree to give two to three different speeches in three different cities in the same week or to travel to the Netherlands for the weekend to attend a board meeting.

In 1990, he received the Council on Foundations' Distinguished Grantmaker Award, recognizing a life in service to philanthropy. In presenting the award, Dwight Allison, chairman of the Council and a close friend, cited Paul's many philanthropic roles and numerous honors and recognitions:

> . . . the litany of positions, writings, directorships, awards, and degrees only hints at the true character of this man. When his name comes up in conversation, as it frequently does, one hears words of praise for his passion and his concern for others, particularly those who are on the margin of society; words of astonishment at the range of his intellect and his interests—indeed, words of love—for a man who is always ready with a smile, a helping hand, a word of encouragement, an introduction to an opportunity or a friend, and a lively sense of humor.

Allison quoted part of Paul's advice to those engaged in philanthropy, particularly his favorite: "Follow both routes to understanding, the compassionate as well as the analytical. No one can comprehend the universe who does not understand and care for the sparrow." Allison noted that "in the midst of an incredibly active and full life, [Paul] never took his eye off the sparrow."

Paul wasn't present to receive his award. Although only minutes away from the presentation site, he was in a Massachusetts hospital with the recurrence of heart disease that would prove progressively debilitating.

Anticipating his impending retirement as an HGSE professor, Paul took the opportunity to reflect not on his past accomplishment but on how to spend the next phase of his life. The projects he would take on, the time to be spent with friends and family—there were countless possibilities and he joyfully anticipated this time. His "retirement" would include several new consultancies, travel and a new book. But the 1991 death of his wife, Barbara, and his rapidly failing health gently dimmed his enthusiasm and anxiety began to color the anticipation. On March 17, 1992, he died of a heart attack in a Washington, D.C. hospital. It was, perhaps, a testament to his values and priorities that his hospital room was draped not in the well wishes of politicians and educators, philanthropists and international business executives, but in the drawings of his grandchildren. He was seventy years old.

In 1965, Henry Saltzman, a fellow Ford Foundation staff member, wrote to Paul of his intention to resign from Ford and reflected on their close working relationship and the man who had been colleague and friend. He spoke eloquently of his own debt but perhaps expressed the debts of hundreds of individuals who casme to regard Paul Ylvisaker as teacher, mentor and friend:

Very few men possess both a broad outlook and experience along with a soaring creativity.
    Very few men worry profoundly about morality as they wrestle with the realities of doing what has to be done.
    Very few men have protected their idealism while keeping both feet planted firmly in the turbulent stream of worldly affairs.
    Very few men deal with the immediates so well while retaining the capacity to look ahead and dream.
    Very, very few possess a vast capacity for leadership while remembering that those they lead are, after all, human beings.
    These are glistening qualities.

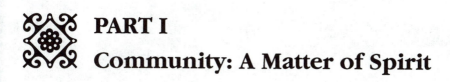

PART I
Community: A Matter of Spirit

*"It's in the law and on your conscience
that you're to have due regard for the
needs of the community you serve."*

—1963

The Meaning of Valley Forge in American History

(Presented to the Valley Forge Boy Scouts of America
Rally, Valley Forge, Pennsylvania, November 14, 1949)

"Valley Forge was the place where American ideals were finally distinguished from selfish interests, and where the first real decision was made to have liberty or else to die."

Any person who attempts to appraise the meaning of Valley Forge in American history owes it to his audience, I think, to show his credentials. In my case, it is somewhat embarrassing according to usual standards. I am afraid it is obvious that I was not around when Valley Forge took place; in fact, my ancestors in 1777 had no intentions of leaving Norway to find out what Valley Forge was or what it meant. Consequently, I have had no [American] grandfather whose knee I could sit on and whose [Valley Forge] stories I could hear; no family relics that tell their part of the story of Valley Forge. Unlike many of you, I have had to get my information third- and fourth-hand; and it is something of an imposition for me to discuss what you might better explain.

It is also true that I am by birth and inclination a midwesterner. While I do not share the views of some of my neighbors like Colonel McCormick, who says that the only thing the east ever gave to the country of any worth was the Colt revolver, or like Roscoe Pound, who claims there's not a red-blooded American left east of the Mississippi, I do have to confess that until two years ago I had never seen Valley Forge or known what it was like. Until I visited it, my impression—which I got from books—was of a brook (only we in the west have rivers), a hundred-foot gully (only we in the west have deep valleys), and a patch or two of winter snow (only we in the west have real snow).

It is also somewhat embarrassing to me to admit I'm a college professor, although I think it would be easier if I were thirty years older and had a beard. Everyone seems these days to want to go to college, but not necessarily to listen to his professors; to have [students] do that, we have to require that they go to classes, and then give them examinations to make sure they heard what we said. The same thing applies to our prestige in the community; I find that businessmen, for example, always treat me well when I pay my bills, but usually shake their heads when I tell them what I think about politics and then say understandingly, "After all, he's a college professor." I don't mean to say they're not right—most of the time they are—just that it's embarrassing.

You may be sure, therefore, that I regard it both as a surprise and as a genuine pleasure to be asked to speak to you on this subject— you who have lived your lives next door to Valley Forge, who know its geography and its history intimately, and [who] are still willing to listen to a rank stranger—even worse, a college professor—discuss its significance. But now that you have seen my credentials, I may as well make the most of them. I would like, therefore, to discuss the meaning of Valley Forge from three points of view, which correspond to elements of my own background: Valley Forge as it appears to a professor of political science; Valley Forge [as it looks] to a midwesterner; and Valley Forge as seen by one who has not always possessed it as part of his national background. Together, I think, they will show how wise you have been in selecting Valley Forge as your anniversary encampment. I hope too that these remarks will encourage you to think through the original purpose of Valley Forge—the securing of liberty and human rights—and to reaffirm that purpose in your own affairs.

The Professor at Valley Forge

First may I apologize if my professorial habits of speech betray me. As a parting word of advice before I came tonight, my wife reminded me that I was speaking to an audience, and not to a class. What she meant, of course, was that a class expects to be bored, but an audience, presumably, does not, and that I should be sure to rise to that challenge. But I am not sure it is a wise thing to attempt new devices.

Valley Forge means two things to the professor of political science. As a fact in history, it represents the turning point of the American Revolution and the first real appearance of the courage and conviction we have come to regard as characteristic of American men and their traditions. Washington came to Valley Forge in the winter of 1777–78 a defeated commander. He had lost Philadelphia to General Howe and his British forces; he had lost the Battle of Brandywine; he had retreated from Germantown; he had practically nothing left in the way of supplies or ammunition; and, during the winter, his army dwindled away to little more than a handful of men—the rest were sick, or had no clothes, or had deserted. It is difficult to say what would have happened to American independence if Howe had been willing to leave the ballrooms of Philadelphia and engage Washington in open battle. But this was not the worst. Each week Washington heard new discouragements. Reed, one of his generals, was negotiating with the British, ready to desert at any favorable moment; Conway and others were forming a secret pact to replace Washington with another commander; and all the while, Congress was divided—if there was any kind of majority, it was one dedicated to self-interest, either for protection or for profit. More than once, Washington himself wondered whether the cause was worth the suffering; whether the signers of the Declaration of Independence had really meant what they said.

Valley Forge was the place where American ideals were finally distinguished from selfish interests, and where the first real decision was made to have liberty or else to die. In this sense, to the professor, Valley Forge is not only an historical fact but a symbol— a symbol of the liberty and protected rights of man, which there became the clear purpose of the Revolution.

The Midwesterner at Valley Forge

I think there is no doubt that Valley Forge in an historical way has proved itself as a worthy site for the coming encampment, and as a symbol well worth recapturing by such a pilgrimage. May I add a few personal impressions from my own first visit to Valley Forge to suggest that the site, perhaps more than any monument I have visited, leaves an indelible mark on one who sees it, and manages in an incomparable way to convey its historical and symbolic meaning. *[Editor's note: At this point, Ylvisaker's notes reflect his intention to offer an extemporaneous "description of Valley Forge, [and] the emotional impact it had on one who had never gone further in his thinking of Valley Forge than the cold pages of a history text."]*

The Alien at Valley Forge

If one reads the historical accounts of Valley Forge, he will be impressed, perhaps more than anything else, with the number of different nationalities and nations that were represented. America's role as a melting pot began early: there were at least ten languages spoken, and more varieties of background. Washington's aides included Baron von Steuben from Prussia and Lafayette from France. The latter [personified] the motive that brought these men together and kept them united during that winter: a dedication to the concept of liberty that demanded tremendous sacrifices. Valley Forge, when it was over, gave us a new definition of liberty: a universal principle that demanded great personal courage and sacrifice to win and to keep.

It is the tendency today to regard liberty as our own product— property that is less to be won than to be jealously guarded. I am not one of those who believes that we have less of an appreciation for what liberty really is than do other states to the east; nor do I believe that by and large we have been shabby in our habits of guaranteeing it. But I do believe that we often become thoughtless, . . . often selfish, and smug. I have been disturbed at hearing reports from our friends in other countries that the impression is abroad that we are no longer defining liberty in this country as a universal heritage, open to all who would desire it, nor do we seem to be active or self-sacrificing in extending its protections beyond our boundaries and beyond our traditional beliefs as to what rights and what groups should be protected. Until we solve the problem of racial discrimination, until we give refuge to the displaced persons of Europe, until we remove every political machine from local politics, we shall not have fully reaffirmed the meaning of Valley Forge.

Commencement Address to Swarthmore High School

(Presented at Swarthmore, Pennsylvania, June 4, 1956)

*"This idea of change, and of change being
synonymous with improvement, is one whose
novelty is difficult for Americans to appreciate,
having lived with it so long. Historically, few
nations have made it a virtue as we have done."*

My main qualification for filling this role as commencement speaker
lies in the fact that as of this year I have now spent more of my life
as a graduate of high school than as one awaiting the day when I'd
[graduate]. I have, if you want to put it another way, done enough
"commencing" so that I can speak with some claim of experience
about what life is like and yet be not too far removed to have some
idea of what high school seniors might be thinking about.

I remember just well enough to know the hazards of not
appreciating what might be on your mind. And so with much care,
I've gone over all the relevant documents of Swarthmore High
School, searching for a clue I knew I'd eventually find. While
looking, I came across certain things which struck some sympathetic
notes: for example, the records of long strings of athletic victories—
twenty-five straight in one case, if my memory is correct. I once
played on a school team that contributed to such a string of
victories—unfortunately, victories for the teams we played. We were
known as the most popular team in the league, which is a
satisfaction coaches and players are prone not to appreciate.

That, however, wasn't what I was looking for. I finally found my
clue in the May 4 issue of the *Garnet*, tucked away in a small note
on the bottom of the page. It read with implications that are bell-like
in their clarity: "Notice to Seniors: Thirty-Two Days Till Ocean City!"

So I do know what's on your mind, and you have my solemn

promise that I will not delay the day of thy going, by the torture of a long address. However, I am here, and will not surrender the platform wordless. So Hear This.

A good fighter should never telegraph his punch. But let me tell you in advance what I'm going to try to do, and how I'll go about it.

Let me confess that I've looked for advice on what to say to you, from a variety of people, who include a high school teacher (who told me to be very brief), a journalist (who said I should say something interesting), my secretary (who killed my first three drafts just by the look on her face when she typed them; she hasn't typed this one), an expert on juvenile delinquency (I won't reveal what he said), a philosopher of history (who wanted to make certain that you be given some reason to remain optimistic and constructive), and a governmental official of an underdeveloped country (who hoped I might "needle you" into an honest appraisal of yourselves as others less fortunate see you).

I concluded that all this could be done by talking for a brief while about the concept of change, and how change in the next twenty years will affect you. My purpose is to needle you, to challenge you, and to leave you with some encouragement. I will not preach a lecture; the answer to the question will be yours, not mine. And there will be no quiz at the end!

You are undoubtedly as tired as I am of the pontifical remarks we hear about the inevitability of change, and the need for every generation to face up to it. Let's turn from these generalities to some facts about the changes that are likely to take place in your time.

It has been said that there are three great determinants of change: population, technology, and ideas. Let's take them one by one.

First, the rate of population change. Between 1650 and 1980, the population of the world will have doubled itself three times. The first doubling took nearly two centuries to accomplish; the second took less than one century; and the third will take about fifty years.

Translating this rate into some concrete figures: When I graduated from high school in 1938, the world's population numbered about 2.2 billion and the U.S. population numbered about 135 million. This year [1956] the world has about 2.7 billions of inhabitants and the U.S. has about 167 millions of people. In 1975, the world's population will number about 3.6 billion and this country's population will total about 220 million.

Or take a look at it this way: Every hour, the world adds to its population as many people as now reside in Swarthmore. Every year, the U.S. adds to its population more than the number of people now living in Philadelphia.

And let me add as an interesting aside: One out of six people who have ever lived, during recorded history, is *now* alive.

Second, technology. Dr. Robert Oppenheimer has recently estimated that we are now doubling knowledge—not just trivial data, but significant knowledge—at the rate of every ten years. In other words, we are now doing in ten years what took one hundred years a century ago, and four hundred years in the time of Galileo.

Third, ideas. The change in population and technology has been one of newness and invention; there is no counterpart, perhaps, of *new* ideas. The significant change has been in the rate at which ideas are spread, are accepted, and become the rules by which men live.

In our day, we have seen the explosive growth and acceptance of the idea of change itself. This idea has been a governing ideal for the U.S. and a fact of its history; it is now the aspiration—for better or for worse—of most of the rest of the world, certainly for the majority of the world's population.

This idea of change, and of change being synonymous with improvement, is one whose novelty is difficult for Americans to appreciate, having lived with it so long. Historically, few nations have made it the virtue we have. The ancient Greeks, for example, feared change as a corruption of what they had achieved. It is not impossible that we may tend toward their conception of change as other nations, to our apparent disadvantage, adopt the idea.

I said I wanted to needle you. [I will do so] in two ways.

First, you are a most favored generation, in a most favored community, in a most favored nation. Change for you has always been to your advantage. It may not always be. You might ask yourself the difficult question, should it be now? On what grounds, besides crass selfishness, do you justify the fact that change should work to *your* advantage, rather than to that of the teeming millions in the less wealthy nations throughout the world? Why should you be overfed, and three-quarters of the world's population be undernourished? Why should you continue to use such a disproportionate share of the world's resources?

Second, you are at the stage in American history and at the stage in your life when you are most sympathetic to change—to the new and the different. Will you become otherwise, increasingly resistant to change and uncomfortable with its results? There is wisdom and humility in the attempt now to project yourself to age thirty-seven. The most difficult part of living with change is to know when to yield and when to resist. This takes a rare combination of knowing what you believe and being tolerant of others. Do you have it? And can you argue without rancor?

I also said I wanted to challenge you. We have a custodial interest in the world's resources, and as stewards we will and should be held to account. It is a problem of first magnitude: how to share the benefits of such resources while using them most efficiently.

There are some other problems:

How to avoid war, not only because of the power of the bomb, but because soon we will have reached the point of no return in our technical civilization. Once disrupted, the machine probably could not get running again.

How to design physical centers for the agglomerations of population. Practically all the net increase in population in this country will fall within the lines of the 170 metropolitan areas. These are already congested and decaying at a rate greater then their renewal.

How to preserve the worth and dignity of the individual in a society that increases in mass. We get to know people in the mass, react to persons as types, explain their behavior as general phases.

How to avoid the loss of the liberal man, in a society in which knowledge is now so vast as to defy the ability of single minds to comprehend or even to survey all of it. Where then the towering geniuses, such as Lincoln, Franklin, Holmes, who saved their community as only an Olympian can?

To all these questions, muscles supply no answers. Our greatest resource, as the Cal Tech scientists have pointed out, is brainpower. Are we wasting it by failing to train it, or [by failing to] direct it, or by our negative attitude toward the life of the mind?

I said I hoped to reassure you. Words in this case are not enough. There are some facts.

The human animal, and the American in particular, has demonstrated in the past decade a quickened ability to accommodate quickened change. There is an optimism not present in 1938 that is written into the new concrete of Penn Center Plaza in Philadelphia, a willingness to look beyond self and self-advantage that is found in the Marshall Aid programs in Europe and the technical assistance programs in Asia.

And we are—though many would refute this—becoming much more appreciative of our greatest resource, brainpower. Planners were a cussword in the vocabulary of the 1930s; today the demand for them in industry and in government has far and dangerously outrun supply. Visionaries are now vice presidents in charge of future operations in the best of our industries.

Change has brought with it an explosive growth in new frontiers. In the 1930s, we wondered whether there were any new frontiers; now your problem is to select which of hundreds you want to attack.

Each year is a better year. These facts may not be persuasive to you, but they are to me. If I had to choose between graduating from high school in 1938 and in 1956, I'd take 1956. And between 1956 and 1975, I'd take 1975. Probably it's only because a boyhood dream of mine was to live to the year 2000.

 # Community Action: A Response to Some Unfinished Business

(Excerpts from an address to the Citizen's Conference on Community Planning, Indianapolis, Indiana, January 11, 1963)

"The awakening of self-respect is the most powerful agent for renewing our cities socially and, for that matter, physically. Partly this must be earned, partly it must be freely given."

I would like to present as straightforwardly as possible some facts, convictions, experiments, and hopes. Whether the facts are correct, the convictions valid, the hopes well founded, and the experiments justified, we leave to the judgment of time.

The relevant facts, as we see them, are the following:

1. We are urbanizing—which means changing our social and economic system—faster than we have been able to adjust our attitudes or our institutions, both public and private.

2. We are still drawing political and cultural distinctions between rural and urban, when the fact is that our whole nation is essentially urban. We are still dealing with central cities and suburbs as though they were separable communities; they are not. We are still dealing with metropolitan areas as though they were local concerns, but they are really national and even international in their reach and character.

3. We are still indulging in the make-believe of two separate worlds: public on the one hand and private on the other. The facts and necessities are otherwise. One blends into the other; one withers without the other. This is genuinely a mixed economy, a society of the middle ground.

4. We are still dealing with cities as though they were bricks without people; still trying with massive programs to perfect

12

physical form and material function while merely dabbling and extemporizing with the city's humane and civilizing purpose, which is to turn third-class newcomers into first-class citizens.

5. We are still practicing nineteenth-century notions of service and charity on a community whose life and aspirations are born of twentieth-century conditions and standards. The day is gone—if it ever [existed]—when gratitude can be earned, consciences cleared, and the *status quo* maintained by unilateral acts of welfare or philanthropy.

6. We are walking into our urban future like crabs, backwards, without the frontal perspective that spots problems before they become impossibly large and immediate.

But these, you will say, are not the facts; they're thinly disguised sermons. Perhaps, but they're not intended as such. Put it this way: these are the facts as we see them, the convictions upon which we have acted and which have led us to the experiments shortly to be described. They invite your criticisms; they obviously beg the many exceptions of communities that have kept abreast of the times.

As long as we're stating convictions, let me complete the list:

7. We are dealing with forces and problems of such magnitude—migration, automation, racial tensions, relaxing moral standards, exploding populations, acceleration of [both] technological progress and obsolescence—that it will take every ounce of energy and imagination we muster, from both public and private sources, to make even small dents, changes, and improvements. This suggests the social application of the art of jujitsu—of exerting smaller forces at points of maximum leverage to capture forces otherwise working against us.

8. A large reservoir of energy, money, and thought exists in the modern American community, but its potential has not been fully exploited, mainly because it has been put to work without benefit of combined strategy and cumulative effect, with no visible evidence or statement of priorities.

9. Ideas and perspectives, not money, are the scarcest commodity—and of all instruments of social action the most powerful.

10. But ideas shrivel for lack of implementation. An essential ingredient of industrial and agricultural progress over the past century has been the capacity for development and experimentation.

Civic counterparts of [industrial research and development facilities] are for the most part lacking. The result being that we research without acting, and we act without reflecting or evaluating.

The City as System

These were the facts and convictions we [at the Ford Foundation] started with. We also had some hunches [with which] to proceed.

Borrowing an analytical technique from industrial planning of recent years, we thought it might be worth looking at the urban community not as a miscellany of people, places, and problems—but as a *system*. Actually, not one system but a series of interlocking systems. We have made some progress, but [we] still have just begun looking at the metropolis as a transportation system, much as AT&T, for example, has long viewed it as a communication system and as countless other businesses have seen it as a system of production, distribution, and marketing. The challenge to us now is to see the metropolis as a social system.

This will take more of an effort than one might first think. We've seen cities and suburbs for so long as a grab bag of separate agencies and experiences and programs that the image and anatomy of the whole [tend] to escape us. You've all had the experience of gazing at a drawing of cubes from one perspective only to have it shift finally, but suddenly, to quite another. Stare at your metropolitan area for a long time, and . . . you're in for quite a surprise when suddenly a new and larger perspective appears.

Try this example: View the metropolis as a continuous system that attracts the newcomer (once the Scotch, the Irish, the Jews, the Italians; now the Negroes, the Puerto Ricans, the mountain Whites, the Mexicans, and the American Indians) and assimilates this newcomer into all that is up-to-date and sought after in urban culture. In the past, it has taken about three generations for a newly arrived group to climb the totem pole of urban culture—by current symbols, to get from central-city tenement to suburban ranchhouse, from menial employment to the university club for lunch, from the sheer necessities of ethnic-bloc voting to the relaxed assurance of nonpartisan elections.

This historic system of producing first-class citizens has worked, but as any production expert could tell you, it's dangerously slow, full of inefficiencies, and in many respects primitive and barbaric. The waste of manpower over the production time span of three generations has been fantastic; if you need current evidence, count the unskilled and unemployed piling up in the population of our central cities across the country. That is, if you have the heart and stomach to do so.

So why not put systems analysts to work on the social production system of the modern metropolis to look for the bottlenecks, to cut waste and reduce time, to speed flow, and to increase social output? Why not make one of our national goals to do in one generation for the urban newcomer what until now has taken three? And as a reminder of the central purpose of cities everywhere, we might ask the French to send us some more Statues of Liberty to be placed at the gates of each of our metropolital centers, and at places where they can be seen by more than passing ships.

This systems approach could easily be mechanistic. Our second hunch—and no doubt yours—[was] that a social system cannot be perfected by clever manipulators, no matter how well trained, nor for that matter by eager philanthropists working alone and from the outside. The toughest problem is that of generating indigenous leadership and the spirit of self-help.

"Community organization" is supposed to be the answer to that problem, and sometimes [it] is. But there are as many forms of community organization as there are organizers, and as many motives and purposes.

The Critical Element

My own personal hunch is that the awakening of self-respect is the most powerful agent for renewing our cities socially and, for that matter, physically. Partly this must be earned; partly—as the saints have taught us—it must be freely given.

The element of spirit is critical; it is not only what we do, but the way that we do it. In our day—with the mind of our communities varying from the reactionary to the liberal, with urban political and social organization ranging from the closed country club to the open door, with leadership ranging from statesmanship to the basest demagoguery—the spirit of urban social change will express itself in diverse, often militant, form. American independence, too, came by fiery patriots as well as by cool-headed generals and far-sighted diplomats. One supplemented the other; one without the other was ineffective; but at one stage, the first had to give way to the second to avoid the negation of every hope by permanent civil war. On the middle ground thus created—neither one of complete acceptance nor [one] of unrelenting hostility—could flourish the domestic tranquility and search for the common welfare which have become the American heritage.

Our third hunch was that [despite the importance of spirit,] certain parts of the urban social system can be perfected by rational means and specific devices with tangible results.

With an eye to the obvious, mayors, governors, and presidents have concentrated their urban programs on physical renewal of the city's urban plant, usually beginning with the central business district.

Our hunch [was] that this is not necessarily the place to start and certainly not the place to stop. Crudely done, slum clearance and downtown redevelopment can actually harm rather than help. What the bulldozer in insensitive hands can mean to the residents of demolished neighborhoods is already painfully evident in the growing record of school transience and residential displacement.

We have placed the Ford Foundation's first bet not on the central business district of the city but on its school system, and more on school outlook and methods than on buildings; on the city and metropolitan area's employment system, on [the] administration of justice, and a growing list of similarly critical "production processes" [that] are currently bottlenecks in the process of citizen-building.

Symbols of Respect

Some of the innovations and improvements [that] suggest them-selves are matters not so much of gadgetry but of spirit. The simple fact that improvements would even be attempted in institutions and neighborhoods long accustomed only to being neglected has peeled a couple of layers of hopelessness off the morale of Gray Area residents. That Detroit would put Negro faces and situations in first-grade primers has been a symbolic act of respect far too long withheld from that growing constituency of our central-city schools. And some day, in some way, the suburban ring of some metropolis will symbolically stop requiring white passports of prospective residents.

But other social inventions can be immediately procedural, physical, and mechanical. For example:

- Building schools to double as neighborhood and social service centers.

- Starting the education of Gray Area children at an earlier age.

- Concentrating on improvement of speech, reading, and other communication skills among Negro children and other newcomers to the cities.

- Adapting techniques borrowed from agricultural extension to the needs and circumstances of an urban clientele—involving health, family budgeting and home management, legal aid, credit use, and house repair and rehabilitation.

- Combining work and study programs for school dropouts.

- Relating (and even subordinating) physical to social planning.

- Pooling local philanthropic funds for common programs—and, I might add, wrenching philanthropy away from many of the easier, more traditional undertakings to which it has become fondly attached, to work at some tougher problems the modern urban community presents.

- Recruiting industry and gearing vocational education to projections of technology and local manpower supply.

- Identifying urban newcomers early.

- Using laypersons in school, recreation, welfare, and other programs.

- Correcting bad practices in arrest, bail, defense, and other links in the chain of administering justice.

- Finding constructive alternatives to [the] present systems of high-density public housing and permanent-dependency welfare payments.

• Widening residential and occupational choice as a way of releasing individuals from the chains of ethnic, racial, and other attachments not freely chosen.

A Need for Inventiveness

Our final hunch was that it would be a mistake to assume that ingenious social inventions could not arise from agencies [that] already existed in the community. The problem was to stimulate such inventiveness within a framework of common purpose and developmental strategy, with reasonable assurance that ideas once conceived could be experimented with and acted upon, and some prospect that the process once begun might carry on continuously. We would have preferred not to have been party to the creation of still another community agency. Wherever possible we have worked through existing agencies. But in three of the four culminating experiments we have helped launch, which are being called the Gray Area projects, the only way open to fulfilling the broad objectives implied in all that has been said thus far was the building of a new instrumentality.

There is some feeling that this decision to establish new instrumentalities is an attack on the present system of community health and welfare councils. If so, it came not by intent nor with malice, but as a commentary on the gap that exists between the job to be done and the capacity of our urban communities as presently structured to accomplish it.

Recall again the requirements as we measured them:

1. The capacity and willingness to see the community and its problems whole, rather than as a collection of agencies and self-interests.

2. The capacity to set common goals, to fix priorities, to develop new approaches, to test them in action, and to evaluate performance against national rather than local standards only.

3. The capacity to mobilize governmental (including federal, state, and local) as well as private resources, and to forge working relationships among agencies of both sectors.

4. The capacity to involve and to affect critical centers of community power, including the intellectual, in order to break the bottlenecks in education, employment, law, health, and other fields.

5. The capacity to finance the considerable costs of research and experimentation and, afterwards, of continuing programs [that have] proved worthwhile, in the growing conviction that governmental budgets will more and more have to carry the main burden of community services and that private agencies will emphasize the critical, the evaluative, and the experimental. We have a growing conviction that more and more governmental budgets will have to carry the main burden of community services.

6. The capacity to convince the people involved—on one level, the industrial, labor, governmental, and civic leadership, and on another level, the man in the Gray Area street—that these programs are "for real," not window-dressing for the *status quo*, not a crumb dropped conspicuously by the affluent few who dine at the community's main table.

Our discussions with governmental and civic leaders across the country have led us to the conclusion that private councils do not, on their own, satisfy these criteria. The reasons most often cited [are] their separation from the public sector, their distance from critical decisions in the private sector, their marginal financial capacity, and their difficulty in setting priorities and measuring performance even among their own participating agencies.

However, in each of the [Gray Area] project cities, the local [Community Funds and Councils of America] organizations have been actively interested and involved. Their participation adds greatly to the strength and potential of the experiments, and my guess is that it will prove of considerable help in raising their status and capacity, and in defining more appropriately [local organizations'] own operations.

Basic Questions

The [Ford] Foundation staff would have to make changes in our own methods if we were to deal adequately with the human problems of urban Gray Areas.

In staffing Great Cities school requests, we combined several separate program interests within the Foundation and employed a device that would start an exchange of ideas going among local officials and agencies in each community. We appointed a team of consultants, which became known as the Gadfly Committee, to ask us and the community representatives with whom we were dealing all the hard questions their varied experience suggested should be asked if grants and projects were to have integrity and meaning.

The committee was one of the most interesting and productive experiments we have ever tried. It included a state school superintendent and a police educator, both from the South; four who knew intimately the Negro life and community of the American city; two equally familiar with the Appalachian, Puerto Rican, and Mexican streams of urban newcomers; an eminent physical planner with urban renewal experience in several major eastern cities; eight Foundation staff members; and the executive director of the United Community Funds and Councils of America.

The committee held sessions in each of the ten cities in which school grants were to be made. Each successive round table with local public and private leaders made it more obvious that broader-than-single-agency programs and policies were lacking, but needed. Schools were central to the health, stability, and welfare of the Gray Areas, and obviously a lead item in anyone's book of social renewal. But until educational planning was related to physical planning, physical planning tied in to social planning, and social planning translated into actions that made a discernible difference in the lives of Gray Area residents, no community could rightly say it was making the most of its resources or doing its civilizing best.

Comprehensive Community Grants

Therefore, when making the school grants, the Foundation indicated the possibility of even more substantial grants for comprehensive experiments drawing together public and private agencies and resources. "Coordination" was a tempting word to use as an objective, but we avoided it as far as possible. The objective was an integrating idea and common strategy, not a concentration of power that would freeze creative energy wherever it might be found in a community agency or individual.

The first community to respond to this informal declaration of interest in a way that met the major tests was Oakland, California. Some time before, tensions had arisen in the schools of the city's changing neighborhoods. Oakland has eased them by the joint action of "Associated Agencies"—an experiment that brought together both top-level and working-level personnel from schools, city hall (manager, police, recreation), the county (health, welfare, and probation), and the state (youth authority).

It was basically on the strength and pattern of this venture in joint action that the Foundation in December 1961, made a $2 million grant for a Gray Area experiment in Oakland. But there were some structural elements added, growing out of the long months of negotiating the grant: a project director's office located within the office of the city manager; a citizen's committee, broadly representative, to give direction and advice; and a committee of executives from the participating governmental agencies and from the Council for Social Planning to plan, organize, and follow up specific experiments.

New Approaches

The grant was divided into several parts:

1. Funds to cover a share of the administrative costs, including the costs of what may prove the most significant element of the experiment—a continuing device for inventing and trying our new and different approaches to Gray Area problems (for example, leave and expense money to permit selected governmental, private-agency, press, labor, business, or other personnel to take time and consult the necessary experts to develop and test promising leads and ideas).

2. Funds to finance projects already developed and identified, of which a major part has gone to the Oakland schools.

3. A "developmental reserve" of $750,000, available on application by the citizen's committee to the Foundation for new experiments [that] are ready for testing, . . . promise to be of more than local significance, and are backed by matching funds pledged publicly or privately within the community or by state and federal grants explicitly for these purposes.

Three other Gray Area experiments have subsequently been launched with Foundation help in New Haven ($2,500,000 in May 1962), Boston ($1,900,000 in July 1962), and Philadelphia ($1,700,000 in December 1962). Basically, the purpose and pattern of [these] grants have been the same as in Oakland:

- Funds immediately released to finance costs of administration, of carrying out specific projects already identified, and of planning new activities of an experimental nature.

- Developmental funds withheld to encourage and partially finance new projects and experiments, as an incentive to continuous planning and innovation.

Halfway Houses

But there is also a significant difference. In Oakland, the city acts as fiscal agent for the grant; governmental agencies have played the principal roles, though with private agencies closely related. In New Haven, Boston, and Philadelphia, special corporations "halfway houses" between the public and private sectors—have been established to plan and direct the experiments:

- In New Haven, Community Progress, Inc. Three of its nine trustees are appointed by the mayor; one each by the Redevelopment Agency, the Board of Education, the Citizens Action Commission, the Community Council of Greater New Haven, the United Fund, and Yale University.

- In Boston, Action for Boston Community Development. Its charter provides for a board of directors of from ten to forty members, broadly representative of the community. The original incorporations (also serving on the board of directors) included the mayor; two senior officers of United Community Services of Metropolitan Boston; the chairman of the Redevelopment Authority; the dean of the Graduate School of Social Welfare of Brandeis University; the chairman of the Boston chapter of the NAACP; and several leading professional, banking, and industrial figures in the Boston community. Subsequently elected to the board were labor leaders [and] school, university, church, and other agency personnel.

- In Philadelphia, the Philadelphia Council for Community Advancement. Initial board members were the federal district judge and former city attorney who took the lead in organizing the project; the mayor, development coordinator, and managing director of the city; labor, NAACP, and business leaders; officials of the United Fund, the Health and Welfare Council, and a local foundation; and the presidents of Temple University and the University of Pennsylvania. Membership of this board is being expanded.

Salient Features

Several other facts about these projects may also be of interest. Local philanthropy has been active in the projects, particularly in Boston, where the Permanent Charity Fund [editor's note: The Boston Foundation] contributed heavily to initial costs of organization and planning and has declared a continuing interest. The Ford Foundation has strongly encouraged joint action with local foundations; without the support of local philanthropy, we doubt whether these experiments can long flourish. To underscore this belief, we have taken an alternative course in two other metropolitan areas—Kansas City and Cleveland—by making block grants of $1.25 million each to associations of local foundations to help them take the lead in experimenting with Gray Area and related local programs.

Each of the projects has been organized also with the objective of helping the community make the most of federal and state grants-in-aid relevant to Gray Area problems. For example, federal planning grants for programs in juvenile delinquency are tied in with the new corporations in Boston, Philadelphia, and New Haven. In all four cities, the matching requirements of our grants can in part be satisfied by state and federal grants for the same general purposes. The hope is that by developing a common strategy and criteria among local public and private agencies, the community will gain a stronger negotiating position with state and federal governments and will be able to use state and federal assistance to better advantage.

Local political leadership, in the form of the mayor, has counted heavily in getting these experiments going. The mayors of Oakland, New Haven, Boston, and Philadelphia have been involved from the start, have made constructive suggestions, and when the going has been rough (these are not uncontroversial matters) have stood their ground. This commitment on the part of elected chief executives has been a *sine qua non* for us in deciding where we would invest our support.

Stimulating Action

The experiments have attracted some of community's very best talent at both board and executive levels; [these individuals] in turn are showing independence and initiative in charting their course of action. As a result, there promises to be a wide variation among the several projects in emphasis, approach, and techniques. As persons interested in experimentation, we could ask for no better response and climate.

While these new instrumentalities are becoming focal points of thought, their governing philosophy is to stimulate action rather than to monopolize action, to work through and alongside existing agencies whenever possible rather than to replace them. If these projects have no effect on the *status quo*, they will be an exercise in the useless and/or unnecessary; it can't, therefore, be glibly said they offer no challenge to anyone.

The challenge of these projects, we hope, will be in the best tradition of American community leadership—which is to allow a mirror to be held up to reality, and to appraise what is being done in the light of an objective assessment of what needs to be done to give new ideas the benefit of trial and experimentation.

The Church in Public Affairs

(Presented to the Conference on the Church and the
City, General Convention of the Episcopal Church,
St. Louis, Missouri, October 13, 1964)

*"The church's shepherds have been meadowed with
their suburban flocks, preaching the message of
comfort to those to whom comfort is already a way
of life."*

My topic—the church in public affairs—builds on a Biblical text:
"Render unto Caesar the things that are Caesar's."′
I have long puzzled over the meaning of that statement of Christ's.
You recall, [it] was in answer to a question, a trick question, posed
to him by the Pharisees. Was Christ being an artful dodger? Was he
giving a political answer to a political question? Or was he saying
that beyond taxes, there really wasn't much that one should render
to Caesar? That matters secular and political really are of small
importance? I'm not certain. (And this is when perhaps a layman can
preach when a minister cannot.) I really don't know what Christ
meant. But what he said, much like the smile of Mona Lisa, has
remained a puzzle to me ever since, and I notice that Mark recorded
that when he said it, those who listened marveled.

Let's take a look at Christ's response in our current setting. In the
last 2000 years since Christ spoke, a lot has happened to Caesar—at
least to our Caesar. Ours is no longer a state [that] claims divine
rights, or exacts total obligation and loyalty. It is extraordinarily
sensitive to rights, tolerant of differences, and protective of freedom.
As a matter of fact, some of us are beginning to think it is too
permissive. In short, Caesar has become the creature and servant of
his people. But the mythology of Caesar, of the tyrant apart and of
the dictator over all, is dying harder than Caesar himself. This myth,
when believed, builds a no-man's-land of indecision and inaction

25

between church and state and creates a void that our society may find to be its fatal defect.

Now what's the present answer of the church to the question put to Christ, posed now not by men who are seeking to beguile, but by people searching for help? "Vigilance, eternal vigilance," the church might reply. "Watch out, be skeptical, let's keep behind our lines." Yes, caution is all right. But isolation? I hope not. The reply by the church, judging from many of its present actions, may be more meager in its tribute to Caesar than even Christ recommended. For the church is not even paying taxes. The irony is complete when we recall that this offer of Christ to pay taxes came from an impoverished man to an established Caesar. Now the church is what is established, and the state is what is becoming impoverished.

What are the needs of the state [that] the church as an institution can appropriately fill? The state, now faced in our society with ceaseless and accelerating change, needs in all of its parts foresight, flexibility, and the capacity to adapt. By long, arduous evolution, the state has developed techniques and instrumentalities all its own for advanced thought and warning. Witness, for example, the [President's] Council of Economic Advisors, which looks far into the future to spot problems on the rise. Look at research and development programs in defense or in agriculture. Long ago, government developed the agricultural experiment stations. It's learned how to adapt, and now urban renewal is one of its methods. It's learned the techniques of feedback and evaluation. And here it's perfected the vote, the election, and similar avenues for consumer complaints.

Industry, too, has developed these techniques for change and adaptation. Less so have the universities and the schools, and even less so has labor. And what about the church? I know it's wrong and mistaken to generalize either among denominations or within denominations. But I sense that Rome, for example, is just beginning to go through in its evolution what King John experienced with the Magna Carta, dealing not with nobles but with cardinals. The ecumenical movement, which is new to the church, is about as politically advanced and sophisticated as America was before Federalism!

The institutional church has not been quick to adapt, nor to foresee, nor to evaluate, nor to innovate. It missed—until tragically late—the urbanizing trends of modern society. First it stayed rural in all its thinking and actions and wound up with all of the compromises of suburbia. Then it became absorbed with real estate—using the tests of the market to know when to abandon its old churches and where and when to build its new. But the market's purpose is to tell what is, not what ought to be. What ought to be is the job of the church—and the most vital need of this society.

Now, by default, it [is] the state [that] has declared war on poverty, and not the church. It is the state [that] has declared war on crime, not the church. It is the state [that] in the last two years has declared war on injustice and intolerance and discrimination and extremism. The church is joining the ranks, but I think more in recognition of a draft than as volunteers. The church is needed in these wars, and these wars are its business.

But is the church prepared? One of the most significant developments of our times is that the state has become an ally, not an enemy, in wars and campaigns of this kind for human dignity and social progress. But more than that, the state is admitting now that it cannot do the job alone and is seeking help. Our society is far too diverse, too large, its problems are far too complicated, its talents too diffused to admit of a monolithic approach by a central government. To win wars on poverty, crime, deprivation, and injustice on the streets of every one of our towns, we need, the state needs, the help of all institutions—public and private, religious and secular. National legislation now concedes this and actually builds on it. The recent housing act allows nonprofit corporations (including churches) to become partners in a national housing program. So do programs of manpower training and vocational education. So will the Poverty Program,[1] and so will, I predict, every major piece of legislation for the rest of this generation. Is the church prepared to accept and implement this partnership?

There are some encouraging trends. [Clergy are engaging] in the experiments now going on, private and public, in cities like New Haven, in Oakland, in Washington and the rest, where society, both

---

[1] Ylvisaker is referring here to the Federal War on Poverty, the group of federal programs launched by President Lyndon Johnson in 1964. "The Poverty Program" and "The War on Poverty" are used interchangeably throughout this book.

public and private, both religious and secular, [is] declaring war on these evils that have walked free in our society. These experiments under pilot programs and under foundation grants are talking and acting broadly and boldly, and I invite your attention to these efforts.

I might also mention that an example of the church [that] goes beyond anything else I have seen, and which raises my enthusiasm for the church as an institution, is the Zion Baptist church in North Philadelphia, in the middle of what is known as "The Jungle" in that city. Its minister is the Rev. Leon Sullivan, six feet five inches tall, who beats the delinquents in basketball so there's nothing they can do but join him. He has taken the church from [a congregation of] 300 to 6,000. You go there only to listen to him on television in the basement of the overflowing hall, so crowded is that church.

Leon Sullivan has, along with 400 ministers in Philadelphia, led the selective patronage system and given force to Negro protest. It "helped" when 500,000 Negroes did not buy the products of [industries that discriminated]. But by Monday morning after his sermon was out, after the patronage started, and when the industries capitulated, Leon Sullivan was not there to brag but to receive in partnership those whom he had had to fight, and to produce a center for vocational training. He started the program in an old abandoned police station. It attracted 5,000 Negro applicants—when federal and state and local programs had not been able to attract more than scores, and at most a couple of hundred. But this is an example of the church as an institution alive and vibrant—and interestingly enough, in a part of the community [that] we had thought needed help but is now showing us what the church can do.

Not all churches have led or even adapted as well. If you want a picture of the opposite [of success], go to Action Housing Inc.'s recent study of three churches in Pittsburgh, which will tell in a devastating way how unprepared the institutional church was when challenged by change and urbanization.

So far I have referred to the church as though—in Christ's words about Caesar—it were on God's side of the equation. But was it? And is it?

In Christ's statement, there were only three central figures. One was Caesar, one was God, and one was the individual. The church was not there, not mentioned. In one critical respect—startling as it may be to say so—the church is more state than it is God. It is not a person but an institution. As a human institution, it is subject to the same propensities and behavior patterns as the state. It has its politics, its cliques; it has its conservatives and its rebels, its instincts and necessities for survival; it has its managerial and revenue needs and responsibilities; and it has the same propensity to the common denominator, to social lag, to the safest course, to the most prudent decision—and the same temptation to sacrifice the individual and squelch the maverick.

To the extent that all social progress requires group or corporate action, the church is needed by the state as an institution, among many institutions. It may be, however, that the church is no better or no worse an instrumentality than any other in society. As an institution, I suspect that Caesar—and I am sure God—could get along without the church [as an institution]. City plans will be made and executed (or voted down) whether or not churches are involved; so will housing for the aged. The poor, the sick, and the maimed will march on Washington with or without benefit of clergy.

But there is one respect in which the church has a unique role on both the secular and religious sides of the equation—which it fills to the extent that it strengthens rather than stultifies the direct relationship between the individual, his Caesar, and his God. This role is neither safe nor secure, and as Christ recognized long ago, it means living intimately with the poor among men, and with the poorer side of every man. For the Christian church, it means the imitation of Christ. When I go back to the Gospels to find the rele- vance of Christ to contemporary society—and the tribute the church can pay both to God and Caesar—I find it in seven extraordinarily difficult norms of individual behavior.

1. Christ's genius of the simple, symbolic act that cuts through the complexities and reveals truth rather than obscures it.

The Gospels are full of examples; let me mention one. When Christ came upon the woman accused of adultery, He curbed the mob by one simple statement, "Let him who is without sin among you cast the first stone." Having restored sanity to the group and dignity to the woman, He spoke directly to her condition: "Go and sin no more."

That was an immensely complicated situation—and in our modern, sophisticated way, we probably would have complicated it more. My guess is, we would have assembled a panel of experts to debate the pros and cons while the stones were falling. And then, in the words of Hilaire Belloc, "The doctors said as they took their fees, 'There is no cure for this disease.'"

Ghandi, [like] Christ and other great religious leaders, had the same genius for reducing the complicated to the simple—yet not the simple-minded. When the British said that the Indians could not have salt, Ghandi led a march to the sea and touched his hand simply to the brine.

In the last two years, we have seen this genius emerge among our own downtrodden; some simple truths are being marched and demonstrated before us. But only a minority of the church's order have joined that march, and this time it is the walls of the church [that] are being shaken by the trumpet.

2. Christ's dedication to the lost sheep: "To the one He left the ninety and nine."

This dedication is increasingly rare in our urban and impersonalized society. What response would Christ be given today if He went on such a mission? "Why waste your time and endanger the rest? Find that lost sheep, and it will probably run away again. Besides, it wasn't very strong anyway. And if you multiply the cost of going after that one by 100, obviously such dedication would be a dangerous precedent and too costly to establish as general policy. Sheep who run away don't deserve to be helped. The return on an investment of time spent with the ninety-nine is bound to be higher."

But Christ's concern for the single lost sheep—in the face of strong arguments to the contrary—is a great part of His relevance to our society. We need that concern, and the example should be increasingly before us. The institutionalized church of recent years has not been the main carrier of that challenge. For the most part, its shepherds have been meadowed with their suburban flocks, preaching the message of comfort to those to whom comfort is already a way of life.

3. Christ's giving of respect and dignity rather than material things.

Nowhere, except in His feeding of the multitudes with five loaves and two fishes, do I recall Christ having given material things to those He wanted to help. His gift was of the spirit. To those of comfortable conscience He brought reproach; to those who suffered He brought comfort; to those ground under the heel of others, He gave respect and restored dignity. All three He accomplished in one sentence when He encountered the woman being stoned.

In sharp contrast, our favorite formula . . . relies on charity and material giving. We have bureaucratized our charities so effectively we don't have to get personally involved. But charity is no substitute for equality; dependency is not the breeding ground for dignity; institutionalized action is hardly the way to make sacrifice or to pay respect.

Mired in charity as we are, we could use the saving example of Christ. But it's a difficult one: equality, dignity, and respect can't be given impersonally, can't be fully converted into programs or discharged by checks, can't be trafficked in only on Sunday. This is the only argument I have for turning you down for the Ford Foundation grant.

4. Christ's subordination of institutions to purpose. "God is a Spirit, and they that worship Him must worship Him in Spirit and Truth."

Christ's answer to the woman of Samaria—caught in an ecclesiastical controversy over the rightful place to be with God—said powerfully what He was to say and imply many times. Form, jurisdiction, real estate, organization, status—all the trappings of institutions—were not the essential matters. In fact, it is questionable whether Christ even thought them necessary at all. Only in the assembling and dispatching of the apostles did He show any signs of interest in organization, and even in those cases the institutional touches were held to a minimum.

The present establishment of the church contrasts so sharply with the simplicity of its origins that one wonders whether its substance and purpose could possibly remain the same. Parkinson's Laws apply to the church as neatly as to any human institution. Machinery becomes an end and a preoccupation in itself. The agenda of congregation and synod become crowded with matters of real estate, procedures, and internal negotiation, and the message and mission of the church are more and more obscured.

5. Christ's confrontation of every man with himself and with the effect of his actions upon others.

No one who encountered Christ was left believing that any man could be isolated either from himself or from others. Christ held up a mirror of painful reality to the wealthy young man who hoped there might be a comfortable route to Heaven. He confronted the rich with the poor—and with the prospect of suffering and sacrifice. With the parable of the Good Samaritan, He confronted each of us with the same. In the contrasting monologues of pharisee and publican, He forced every man to face himself. No one was omitted in His answer to the question, "And who is my neighbor?"

"Greater love hath no man than that he lay down his life for another." What a motto for our time! Yet what a contrast to the social isolationism, self-deception, and caution we have all made into a way of life, not least in the institutionalized church.

6. Christ's lonely acts of courage.

Peter's calculated denial of Christ—succumbing to his fears in the presence of his peers—is an oft-told tale in our contemporary society and in the contemporary church. Yet this was hardly the model or message of Christ. He did not duck the tough ones, dodge the difficult moments, bob and weave with the politics of the moment, or avoid controversy. Or balance the advantages and disadvantages before adopting a course of action then rationalized as right.

Someone has said, "I'd have the courage, if only I had the convictions; and in such a complicated world, to have simple convictions is to be simple-minded." It doesn't take much living with present-day imponderables to sympathize with this comment. Yet again, consider the model and relevance of Christ who, in the quagmire of living, found solid ground of principle and reasons worth the display of courage. In the social and spiritual inequities of today, pointed to by the Negro protests of 1963 and 1964, lie many of the same reasons. What good would be the establishment of an ecumenical order if that united church became even more the passive expression of the lowest common institutional denominator?

7. Christ's willingness to die.

At some point, Christ came to the lonely realization that His work would not be finished nor His mission secured, short of His own sacrificial death. In the greater agony of His decision in Gethsemane He accepted the lesser agony of the cross. Similar anguish has been experienced by other great historical figures: Socrates, Joan of Arc, Jan Hus, Thomas á Becket. In each case, what they represented gained strength through their sacrifices.

Their willingness to die for their convictions has become a fable for most of us, hardly a model. We have perfected instead the art of survival: minimizing risks and maximizing advantage. This is human enough. But is it to be the motto of the church, which was born with Christ's death and has been reborn with each of the martyrs?

These seven symbolic acts and guides to action are what ought to be the church's tribute to Caesar. The church should never forget this mission of producing and motivating the individual in our society to accomplish the short-run goals of the state. But I fear that what we may do is make of the church another institution substituting for, or competing with, the state on the state's own terms—not providing the salt that gives our lives and our society its savor, nor the yeast that leavens our personal and public affairs.

Conscience and the Community

(Originally published in *Television Quarterly*, November 1964, Volume III, No. 1)[1]

"The greatest need of the community for which the broadcaster should have due regard is to have its diversities regularly brought face to face, to find the ties that bind, and to make permeable the membranes that separate. Without this civilizing process of regular confrontation, this evocative but healing act of dialogue, the communities can be jungles."

It is in the law and on his conscience that the broadcaster has to have "due regard" for the "needs of the community he serves." These phrases are about as vague and elastic as the due process and the general welfare clauses of the American constitution, but that's their genius. For it is the uncertainties of the constitution, far more than its fixed meanings, that have prodded the nation to think, to question, and then to quicken its pursuit of a happier and more perfect union.

Therefore, I would argue first—and last—that broadcasters stretch their minds and resources to explore the uncertain and the unspecified in the open-ended charge they have been given. The words "due regard," "needs," and "community" are far-flung territories with infinitely elastic frontiers. If the broadcaster has any conscience and curiosity, he can keep exploring them until his franchises have been taken over by his competitor's grandchildren,

[1] *Television Quarterly* is a publication of the National Academy of TV Arts and Sciences (copyright 1964, National Academy of TV Arts and Sciences). Reprinted with permission.

and still not have exhausted the room for growth and invention these words allow.

That the broadcaster search—and search continuously and creatively—is what this nation of listeners, I think, is asking in the name of the law and the Federal Communications Commission. At least that's what I would try to impress upon him, using the word "community" as a launching pad for a few sample explorations.

If America's radio and television owners want to follow along, they must leave their lawyers behind. This new community we live in has no precedents; it is changing faster than any executive, legislature, or judge can keep up with it; it admits of no final governing code; its social particles are so subtly fused and transmutable they can't be isolated long enough even to classify; and its future is so immediately caught up in its past and present that we don't know what tenses to use when describing it—except we do know that whatever the time, it's imperfect.

The broadcaster needs first to take a closer look at this phenomenon. He might begin by dividing his community into four concentric rings. The core can be labeled the central business district; the next is that growing wasteland between the last new office building and the first new ranch house, aptly titled "the Gray Area"; the third is suburbia; the last we will simply call "and beyond." I would caution again that we have to keep these frontiers infinitely elastic.

Admittedly, such a map may not look exactly like a given community. For example, Cleveland—stopped on one side as it is by Lake Erie—could only grow as a semicircle, not fully in the round. Another community may not have a "Gray Area," which simply means the city fathers zoned or gerrymandered it into some neighboring community, and a broadcaster will have to cross some local boundary lines and *verboten* signs to locate it. Or he may say his signal—and therefore his community—doesn't reach into more than one or two of the rings, certainly not into the "and beyond." But remember, the human particles of this community are constantly on the move. In the tiniest segment of this community come and go every possible type of listener: maid, merchant, commuter, thief, Negro, Texan, Arabic chief.

We could stop to argue these and other miscellanies, but let us recognize at once that I'm cutting as quickly as I can into the diversities—and the generalities—of American community. It happens that as communities grow, these diversities tend to get localized. Wealth and status tend to congregate in the core and outer rings; poverty and disadvantage usually get caught in between, or find pockets of shelter next to the walls of affluence, whether as slum dwellings a block behind Central Park West, or as shantytown on the rim of Fresno, California.

Now here is where the human animal—the listener is one and the broadcaster another—is at odds with himself and his place in nature. Anyone who has studied ecology knows that each species of plant and animal finds its own special sector of the environment to live and hide in. If we were to take a vertical cross-section of the air in a tropical jungle, we would find hundreds of horizontal layers into which the area's variety of insects have segregated themselves. And where they meet, they eat each other.

Man (who is supposedly different from the rest of God's creatures in being social, adaptable, and humane) is tending to live like the insect—stratified, routinized, and defensive—in his own communities. I wonder whether newspapers and broadcasters have abetted or aborted this tendency.

I would argue that the greatest need of the community for which the broadcaster should have due regard is to have its diversities regularly brought face to face, to find the ties that bind, and to make permeable the membranes [that] separate. Without this civilizing process of regular confrontation, this evocative but healing act of dialogue, the communities can be jungles. Authors have grown rich and citizens cynical describing them in precisely that language.

What about the broadcaster? Like most of the educated and better-heeled members of the community, has he, too, hemmed himself in to the blindered existence of central business district and suburb? Does the ribbon-cutting ceremony for a new bank building or the commercialized unveiling of a downtown renewal project get more of his attention than the failure to rehabilitate a run-down school or to reduce the number of bars in the Gray Area?

What faces in what context appear in his spots and commercials, his serials, his newscasts? Or should we only hold him publicly to account for what appears in his "public service" programs?—all of which may be another form of the lower animal kingdom's tendency to survive by segregation.

Incidentally, an example of courage and constructive action along these lines is revealed in what the Detroit public schools have done with their reading primers. Late as the rest of us, they awoke to the fact their schoolchildren were increasingly Negro and low-income, but the books given these children to read were written and illustrated [for the] nineteenth-century white middle class. So Detroit rewrote and recolored, and once-discouraged teachers are finding that the schoolchildren respond as would be expected. Reading is for real; they're inside the books and no longer outside the system.

Sensitive matters? Loaded? Controversial? Maybe. But well within the range of the law and the broadcaster's conscience. He is already deeply involved: his signal, even though it may emanate from one safe corner of the community, is being received in all others. His almost exclusive attention to the white face, to middle-class ways of doing things, to suburban culture, is not being missed in the opposite corners of the community. His impact is various: in some, it breeds hostility; in others, a further breakdown of pride and self-respect; in everyone, a wish—bordering on a compulsion—to share by hook or crook in the spoils of the dominant system.

If broadcasting could choose only one community need to serve in this decade of the Second Emancipation, it should be to fan the small fires of self-respect [that] have been lit in the breasts of the community's neglected and disadvantaged citizens. This year it was the Negro; next year, it may well be the Spanish- and Mexican-American; the year after, perhaps, it may be the American Indian or the mountain white; and who knows, the year after, we Norwegians may become Vikings again.

Broadcasting can lead; it does not always have to follow. Its means and its impact are much more powerful than broadcasters care to admit when accused by intellectuals of negative social influence, almost as powerful as they claim when making a pitch to sponsors and advertisers. The public media can pay public attention—and it is neglect that has been eroding the self-confidence and capacity for self-help in the Gray Areas of American communities.

Broadcasters can interpret and explain—and it is ignorance that has helped breed the contempt [that constitutes] the stifling air in which the kids of our Gray Area have to grow up.

Broadcasters can differentiate—and release individuals from the bondage of group identification in which the inhabitants of our slums and ghettos are caught.

Broadcasters can go behind crime, to indicate causes. They can go beyond arrests, to hold up the mirror to the faults in our administration of justice. They can go beyond relief scandals, to ask why we still substitute charity for equality. They can go beyond protest and show the civic tasks that remain after the marchers go home. And they can bolster by the simple act of understanding those who, in the midst of the Gray Areas, begin to walk tall—the Negro father in a matriarchal society, the lone mountaineer in an urban society he wasn't born to, a kid on the street corner who passed by his first rumble to hunt for his first job.

What is done in commercial programming has as much, if not more, meaning and impact than what is done under a public service label. Because listeners from both sides of the tracks—the ones who vote for Presidents who appoint Federal Communications Commissioners—have an unerring instinct for judging a broadcaster's character from what he does when the chips are down, when his money's on the line. They're not persuaded by how he behaves on Sundays. If his sponsored time doesn't reflect his entire community's needs and tastes, nobody's fooled when he preaches differently during the sanctimonious hours. If broadcasters do not know and live with every part of the community—on the job and off—they will hardly be duly regarded as serving its needs.

Also, as the broadcaster has found, when it comes to public service programming, not everyone is tuning in. Here I'm on his side. How does he attract a heel-dragging, sofa-bound citizenry to the sober mood and long-word-listening requirements of public service broadcasting? It is hard to put questions of foreign aid and local taxes into the language of Chester and Marshal Dillon, without limping on both legs and winding up on broadcasting's Boot Hill. And tough, too, to liven a roundtable to the pace of "I Love Lucy." (Though, to be fair, my kids have learned as much about science from Walt Disney as they have from school; and as for sociology and human relations, well, let's simply say that TV has made them precocious.)

Controversy has been the solution generally adopted by newspapers for "educating the public" and is now slowly making its way into radio and TV. The principle is so old and tested that its coming will be welcomed. But not as panacea. Controversy may open the way to understanding, but it is no substitute—and it is too easily come by. Any ingenious reporter or programmer can find or invent it. But what more?

The answer, I think, lies in distinguishing between conflict and confrontation. Conflict usually develops when confrontation is overdue. Whether broadcasters or politicians or citizenry are to blame, confrontation of the diverse parts of the community has not and does not occur regularly and thoroughly enough, and we are in serious trouble in our communities because it has not. We have tried to find cubbyholes where we can safely deposit each of our own interests and concerns: ghettos for Negroes; shantytowns for migrants; suburbs for middle-class schoolchildren; shopping centers and downtown plazas for business; tax havens for industries; circles and centers for culture; and cars, bars, and airplanes to get away from it all.

We run around the corner to get away from our neighbor and end up colliding with him as he runs around his corner from us. There's no escape. No man is an island. There cannot be passers-by—only the inevitable face-to-face between the Samaritan and the man he might easily have been.

Again, the crying need of the community—and the charge the broadcaster has been given—is to ensure the timely confrontation of its diverse and diverging elements. Most often, perhaps, through controversy: not avoiding conflict, when conflict is a fact.

But people are fascinated by differences, whether or not they are in conflict, and eternally curious about how differences may be resolved. "Harvest of Shame," "Walk in My Shoes," "Superfluous People"—these are visual adventures that have dramatized the point. There are in broadcasting's creative capacity a thousand and one other ventures that can be tried—and many [more] that have been devised—to show and explain the diversities that make up our communities, and in doing so to pave the way for resolving differences other than through neglect or civic war.

We cannot underestimate what efforts like this can do to ease the growingly impossible job of the community's civic and political leaders. They stand at the crossing point of the community's differences, but [they] are judged and harassed by citizens who can indulge the luxury of single standards and simple solutions. It is time we took our citizens into the community's kitchen, where they too can feel the heat; they will [then] be more sympathetic with the political cook and may even be induced to help him serve. All of which makes me wonder why we have not built a dramatic program around the mayor, who up till now has been caricatured as a buffoon. I do not mean a public service program where the mayor is given free time to tell of his accomplishments—essential as this may be—but a series which in fiction can show fact. "The Defenders" has done this for law; when does City Hall get equal time and compassion?

Not, I suspect, until broadcasters have themselves lived long and intimately with the community they are to serve, have acquired the confidence and roots that enable them to confront what the rest of us may avoid, and have suffered their way through to understanding and acceptance. I can sympathize with a Boston broadcaster who said that only after twenty-six years is he being listened to in that community. We cannot all wait that long. But neither is the community something to be understood by passing interviews with men on the street or brought to salvation by itinerant preachers.

Serving the community's needs is not an assignment to be given or taken lightly. It requires a commitment [that] should be measured in years of living and learning in every nook and cranny of the community, and at every level of income and status.

It also means detachment. Among other things, [detachment] from the community as it exists in favor of what it will or might be. Time in our generation is moving so fast that the present is fifty percent future. Yet the human animal finds it hard to set his watch ahead. Someone has to help keep future time. After watching Hugh Downs erase the difference between time zones by taking the hour hand off his clock, I am encouraged to think broadcasters may be the ones to wipe out the barriers between the present and future and to confront the community today with its emerging tomorrow.

Let me be specific. We live today in the straitjacket of past governmental jurisdictions; the average community is severed by hundreds of yesterday's boundary lines. The broadcast signal can cross these lines; it might even take today's voters along and ease their passage from a fragmented metropolis into a united community.

Or microphones and cameras can be taken into our schools, to evoke from the manner and mind of our children the problems and potential of tomorrow's society. A lot can be found, more can be projected, and some will have to be imagined. But the broadcaster's mind and the community's will be stretched from present trivia to the significance of a future that is already with us.

Why not a regular presentation of what the community's tomorrow already is or may be like, or should be? It's been a long time since Socrates provoked Athens to greatness by confronting it with perfection and goading it with The Question. Baltimore has been anticlimatic since H. L. Mencken. Will broadcasting produce the equivalent? Our communities could use some gadflies, and they cannot all be working for foundations, newspapers, and the FCC.

The broadcaster, then, is asked to search, to confront, to agitate, and to understand; to make a commitment, to do his homework, to look ahead, and to remain detached. And when will he know whether he has done his job and discharged his obligations? Like the rest of us dedicated to the public interest, never. His frontiers and obligations will always stretch or be stretched beyond him. It is frustrating, but challenging and never dull.

And as long as America's broadcasters can see bricks being thrown at them from every side, they can be sure they are not far from the place they are needed.

Quality of Life in 1980

(Adapted from *America, 1980*, the William A. Jump–
I. Thomas McKillop Memorial Lectures in Public
Administration, 1965)[1]

"Any present moment is fifty percent future."

Legend has it that a printer's devil one year found himself alone at press time with the *Farmer's Almanac* set up with all weather predictions complete except for July 4. Somehow, the editors had left the forecast for that day blank. So with heroic abandon, the young apprentice cast up a prediction for "Snow, rain, sleet, and hail." That year, in one hapless section of North Dakota, the heavens obliged; and a lucky devil was made into an honest man.

After a month of brooding about today's assignment, my sympathies are with that daring young man. But I don't have his courage, and I doubt if I'd have his luck. Today, you'll have to be satisfied with a less colorful escape from an impossible predicament.

No one can speak definitively about the quality of American life— neither as it is now nor surely as it might be fifteen years hence. Quality involves taste and perception, and where these are concerned, the Romans told us long ago you can't expect final answers or agreement.

But if you'll be satisfied with less, I'll make a stab at the questions before us.

Granted that the America of 1980 will be bigger by just about every statistical index we measure it with, will life in America be any better? Or really any different?

---

[1] Edited by Robert L. Hill. Washington, D.C.: U.S. Department of Agriculture Graduate School, 1965. This presentation was a speculation about life fifteen years in the future. Reprinted with permission of the Graduate School, U.S. Department of Agriculture.

You can find hints and fragments of answers to these questions of quality by consulting the statistical oracles of our society and the numbers they preside over. The advancement of their art of projection is itself one of the emerging and significant features of American life. Within the last generation, we have changed from a society [that] regarded the future as a mystery at once so distant and so impenetrable that it fell more under the bailiwick of the gods than of men. Attempts to sift it through scientifically and with an eye toward rational control were met—especially in government—with corresponding skepticism and moral outrage.

Compare those times with today. The pace of change has so accelerated that any present moment is fifty percent future. Long-range planning has by necessity become a working unit in any public or private organization worthy of its salt. Even the organized church is doing it. And these are not idle probes, limited to research and confined to the production of livestock or the construction of public and private works. They are directed at policy, designed to influence decisions and move assertively into the realm of social planning.

The deficiencies of the art are many—and I will come to some of them in a moment. But consider how far that art has developed in such a short time, how much of a foothold it has gained, and what place it will have by 1980. Whatever the margin of its errors, this continuous forward probing robs the future of most of its surprises, reduces the risk of society walking blindly into booby traps and ambushes, and contributes a good deal to equanimity and stability in society's handling of its affairs. Fortunately, it has not become a monopolized mystique. Long-range forecasting and planning have become suffused throughout our society, making it possible for lesser as well as larger units to assert a place for themselves in the sun of tomorrow.

By 1980, we will probably see considerable advances in the state of the art. But more important than any narrowing of the margin of error will be the further spread in the practice of forecasting and planning to institutions now barely touched but needing it badly, especially state and local governments, private health and welfare agencies, local philanthropy, labor, and education. And we will have become far more sophisticated and systematic in the translation of these probes into policy, through advance analysis of probable consequences and carefully devised experimentation.

This smoother feeding of a future of accelerating change into an ever-complicating present was anticipated—at least for the benefit of the private sector—a quarter-century ago by Joseph Schumpeter.[2] What he pointed toward then was the "routinization of progress." 1980 will have brought us far in this direction, in public as well as private affairs. Or [it] may have. Our capacity to deal with society's future depends upon the mastery of arts far more complex than the amassing and manipulation of data. Until we have addressed ourselves to some questions and problems of social change, we had better not use the words "will" and "shall" to describe the quality of life in 1980. The modesty of "maybe" and "perhaps" is far more appropriate and becoming.

Again, the longevity of 1980's Americans may be extended past the present threescore and ten—*if* agreement can be reached among hostile sectors on ways and means to remove bottlenecks in medical services; stop pollution of air, land, and water; increase highway safety while reducing violence and addiction; and achieve as much progress in the general analysis of health and the allocation of remedies and resources as we have in combating particular diseases. And how sanguine can one be of such progress, judging from the agonies of achieving Medicare, or of controlling automobile exhausts, or of mastering the economies of medical services and insurance, or of stemming the use of cigarettes, [or] of previewing and preventing the harmful effects of new drugs and pesticides?

Again, the entire net increase of the American population between now and 1980 may settle among the inhabitants of our major metropolitan areas—or a growing share may not. What they do will depend on whether these communities have managed to achieve enough physical renewal and social justice to remain at least livable. Maybe they will. Maybe they won't.

---

[2] Schumpeter (1883–1950) was a free-market economist and Harvard professor who originated the term "creative destruction" to describe how competition improves the economy even as it destroys obsolete firms and ideas. He believed that the strength of capitalism was the continuous appearance of new products and processes. He is credited with expanding the narrow scope of economics to include interdisciplinary dimensions of politics, history, and social science.

But we might as well face it: to venture any projections of a qualitative sort, we too are going to have to make certain assumptions. For me, the most important set grow out of differing answers to the question of whether the United States will grow more resistant to challenge and change; or whether it will remain about as pragmatic and flexible as it has in the past; or whether it will step up its capacity to adapt, invite, invent, and anticipate? Each of the three answers one might select provides an alternative assumption on which to rest some forecasts of the form and quality of American life in 1980. These forecasts would provide a range crudely analogous to the statisticians' low, medium, and high. In this case, the labels I'll use are "America in Decline," "America—More of the Same," and "The America I'd Like My Children to Help Build—and Inherit." [This] exposes my prejudices, but leaves the odds and likelihoods still to be determined.

The American Capacity for Qualitative Growth

Before translating assumptions into forecasts, let's take a longer look at current indications of how this country is responding to change. Call it, if you will, America's marginal capacity for qualitative growth.

First, give credit where credit is due. This country has been extraordinarily responsive, flexible, and inventive; these, in fact, have been the hallmarks of its character. With such historic momentum, one could normally presume these traits would persevere through the brief span of another fifteen years. The odds are they will—and I will shortly cite evidence to believe they are becoming even more fixed and vital a part of the American character.

But this happy outcome is by no means certain. With accelerating change and complexity, the American capacity for [three]-dimensional growth will have to expand merely to keep even with the times. And there are some disturbing signs that it may not. One [is] the fact that we have got along in the past with only part of the American system growing at full capacity at any one time. For example, it has been characteristic of the federal system that while one level (say, the states) has been dynamic, the other has been

static—and to that rule could be added the intermittent responsiveness of local government. Fits and starts and missing engines will
hardly keep us abreast of the challenges of the next fifteen years.
The requirement will be full power all the way.

Another cause for doubt is the wearying of the human animal,
battered by conflicting interests and frazzled by the rat race of
constant change. His cry goes up: "Stop the world, I want to get off!"
Recent research suggests that the lemming is driven to the sea not by
want of food brought on by periodic overbreeding, but by nervous
exhaustion and breakdown from having to contend with the social
complexities of so many fellow rodents. [This] isn't so far from
Richard Maier's contention that the major problem of 1980's
megalopolis will not be such graspable nettles as food and water
shortages but an overloading of the human communications system—its capacity to absorb infinitely proliferating signals and still to
respond rationally. The rise of social ailments—mental illness,
juvenile delinquency, alienation—have long been admitted as part
of industrialization and urbanization in the western world. This year,
the Soviet Union ended its futile efforts to define the problem away
by Marxist doctrine and conceded that alienation (and presumably
the other social ills) was a growing characteristic of modern socialist
society. It's at least reassuring to know that we won't be suffering
alone.

If it is increasingly difficult for the citizens of this complicating
world to remain rational and responsive in the thick of things,
consider the lot of the man thrust into the hot seat of governmental
or social responsibility. The spreading diversity of the present and
imponderables of the future press in upon him relentlessly, whether
he is the beleaguered chairman of the local zoning board, the
superintendent of an urban school system crucified by the politics of
de facto segregation, or an American president trying to fit the single
bridle of consensus on millions of political horses riding in every
possible direction. The temptation to delay, to finesse, to dissemble,
and to dodge is as old as politics itself; yet it grows with the times.
A more dangerous tendency is to rage against the future and raise an
army of rednecks and mossbacks to repress those dedicated to
bringing in the new. There is still another [tendency]: the final act of
exhaustion and disgust that drove the marshal of "High Noon" to

throw his badge of office at the feet of his fellow citizens and quit the town.

All of these and other foibles and frustrations conceivably might accumulate to produce an American rigidity [against] change and the beginnings of decline. But the dominant mood now is one of stimulating change and invention. We are going through one of the liveliest and most creative periods in American history, at least with respect to domestic affairs. Witness the signs and the product:

- Three Supreme Court decisions within a decade that have forced fundamental changes in education and race relations, in the structure and functioning of state government, and in the administration of justice and the profession of law.

- Major legislation at all three levels of government [that] has roused the conscience and resources of the nation into an attack on the physical and social ills of our local communities.

- Executive leadership in the White House and in growing numbers of state capitols, county courthouses, and city halls [that] has burst the traditional confines of politics and bureau-cracy to enlist science, industry, arts, and academia in the formulation and execution of public policy.

- Private recognition that ours is an age of public purpose and affairs, reflecting itself in a massive shift in interest and employment toward government and nonprofit sectors (which now account for one-third of all employment, thirty-five percent of the Gross National Product (GNP), and two-thirds of all jobs created over the past five years).

- Pride and protest among the minorities and the young, which in a decade brought social changes that had eluded the grasp of earlier centuries.

- The rise of research and development into a universal, multibillion-dollar activity and the emergence of philanthropy as a built-in incentive to social reform.

- A renaissance in the arts, pointing this time toward the public's rather than the patron's interest.

- A revolutionary change in social outlook, which has removed the *verbotens* from the earlier untouchables of social engineering and family planning and is converting the church from negative to positive.

This promises indeed to be a golden age of American social and political development. It builds on a broad consensus provided by the resolution of the old debate between liberals and conservatives. The conservatives admit that social engineering has not [brought about] and need not bring about tyranny and disaster; that it has in fact helped keep us alive and prospering, and opens more markets for business than it closes. The liberals concede that the system is too complex and has too many advantages for drastic changes to be effective; that the public interest isn't necessarily synonymous with governmental action (in effect, America this past generation has adopted the theory and practice of competition in the public interest).

This rapproachment between former foes has produced a powerful alliance, which so far has outvoted every coalition of discontents brought together to oppose it. It has provided a climate of pragmatism extraordinarily favorable to a melding of public and private interests and toward large-scale efforts at social engineering. What's more, it is building, or riding with, an economy that can afford these efforts and [can] write them off or gloss them over when they fail. Not all will fail. Already there have been some notable successes (not least the stabilization of the economy), and [there will be] more of them as this new breed of public entrepreneurs acquires experience and sophistication.

But this consensus, too, is vulnerable, and an even newer breed of American radical is uncomfortably close to finding its Achilles' heel. [Just] as Keynes once argued that the old guard had stabilized the economy at less than full employment, the new critics have identified social engineering and consensus with an "Establishment" that has achieved political equilibrium at a level well below full social justice. These new critics are in the minority, and many of them are too young to vote. But they are precociously adept at making an overwhelming majority listen and step lively; and they have an uncanny ability to tie their charges to demonstrable social failings and inequities. Negroes and hyphenated Americans *have* been discriminated against; Big Education *has* become isolated, impersonal, and irrelevant; adults *have* become prone to preach one set of morals and practice another; organized and white-collar crime *has* bought and inveigled its way to acceptability; the church *has* abandoned its concern for the lost sheep in favor of suburban life with the wealthier ninety-nine; the individual *has* been cast adrift in modern urban and industrial society. These new rebels know all this. And so do we.

For a while, these criticisms were voiced only by those who wrote successful books and were listened to as raptly and as innocuously as hired preachers on Sunday. But the newer breed of critics don't write books. They picket, they march, they boycott, they challenge, they shame, and they make life uncomfortable for those who were formerly secure. They influence the results of elections; they force Presidents to speak and legislatures to act; they evoke violence though seldom initiating it. Like a column of marching ants, they devour every cause and gnaw at every institution they come across on their way.

They are a novel form of an old American tradition, that of social protest. As with other irritants before them, deposited in the body politic, pearls of social progress are molded about them—or, hopefully, will be.

There are two reasons to wonder. One lies in the split personality of the new rebels. [Although] they are united by their abhorrence of injustice and their readiness to risk lives and reputations in frontal assaults upon it, they are at odds with themselves over the kind of victory they will settle for. The majority are akin to the Populists, farmers, and laborers who preceded them: they want acceptance of themselves and their ideals in an improved American society. But there is a strain, small but endemic, that is different and disturbing. It may sometimes speak the language of foreign doctrines, but it is hardly the tool of anyone. This special kind of rebel is sounding the cry of the alienated and the disillusioned: the whole system smells to high heaven, and basically he doesn't want any part of it, except nihilistically to harass it to death.

In fifteen years, the chances are almost zero that nihilism will inherit or scorch the American earth. But there are enough things going for it that its potential for growth can't be ignored. For one, it can capture and sour a mass of idealism which America has nurtured but not exploited, and can appeal to a mass of alienation which is piling up in every class, age group, and walk of modern life. For another, it feeds upon the failure of more moderate groups, including the new brand of social engineers, to find solutions to problems of social injustice that [will] really make a difference before the available time runs out.

These have always been the challenge of nihilism to the human effort to master nature and its own destiny. We enter 1965–70 with the odds strongly in favor of a successful response.

But let's consider all three possibilities.

Looking Backward: Alternative #1, "America in Decline"

It began to be apparent in the late 1960s. Imperceptibly at first, there was a shift in the pH of the American soil: things went slightly more acid, then more so, and what was highly creative became progressively more barren.

A thousand historians have a thousand and one theories about why it happened and whose fault it is. I'm no historian, but I saw it coming when the congressional committees began their investigations of the Poverty Program three years after it was enacted. Disillusion, hostility, and discontent had been gathering for months. Costs of the program had been soaring; the job corps turned out to be more corps than jobs; community action programs had erupted into bitter factional and political fights; and by then, the minority groups had seen too little benefit to risk their remaining equity in support.

And their equity was dwindling. The public—and worse, their membership—had tired of marches and demonstrations. Those who had "got theirs" gradually withdrew to their own comforts; those who had not either joined the orthodox pressure groups or talked more and more of abandoning the idea of nonviolence—and sometimes they *did* [abandon it].

Life stealthily became less secure. And the more insecure it became, the more people spoke loudly and certainly about what it should be and how it should be lived. Men of moderation and outreach and with a penchant for trying something new got caught in the freeze. Lines hardened. Those in established groups survived. If the groups were big and powerful enough, they prospered. Life for the unattached was rough. But the unattached became fewer. They were absorbed into a growing assortment of military and public work corps and were fully occupied by the increasing requirements of defense and the burgeoning attention to the public infrastructure needed to assure and absorb industrial output.

The arts flourished—or rather, the building of arts centers and cultural facilities [flourished]. Universal education from ages four to twenty took most of the kids off the streets and reduced the unemployment rate. More millions than ever in 1980 are watching more TV stations than ever longer than ever. For a while in the 1970s viewing fell off. People got bored. But there wasn't much else to do; and now that we've made it to the moon and the Russians have made it to Mars, things are back to normal again.

Except for increasing viral infections and automobile casualties, our communities are safer. The crime rate began dropping in the mid-1970s as we doubled the constabulary and the courts turned away from protecting the rights of the accused to ensuring the rights of the citizenry. Delinquency dropped even more abruptly, as the birth rate fell off, teenagers were moved off the streets, campus riots were brought under control, and censorship was applied to TV, movies, and magazines.

Our cities have spread out even farther along the new highways, and we have all the automobiles and buses they said we'd have back in 1965. The old slums and gray areas have been pretty well demolished by now. We gave up on rehabilitation [and] moved the lower-income groups en masse into the old FHA suburbs, and they seem pretty happy living there by themselves.

As a matter of fact, except for a few malcontents here and there, the population seems rather content. Or passive. The mass-produced suburban houses and apartments they're living in don't cost them very much; and they have three weeks' vacation with pay.

Our GNP and family income are well within the minimum range projected by the economists of 1965. Although there was that young professor they fired the other day who argued that you really couldn't tell, because the government had changed the method of calculating the GNP. . . .

Looking Backward: Alternative #2, "America—More of Same"

Considering the primitive statistical tools, computers, and electronic data processing equipment they were using back in the 1960s, it's remarkable how close the forecasters came to anticipating the shape and quality of our life in 1980.

They missed a few things—and some of them they might have caught if they had tested more carefully the internal consistency of their projections. For example, they were so tied to the historical inelasticity of their governmental systems and political folkways that they failed to project certain major shifts [that] sooner or later were bound to result from accumulating increments of change in public management and social behavior. Thus we don't have any such things as "central cities" any longer—at least not in law and public accounting. They're all dissolved into the larger urban regions of which they're a part. The same applies to suburbs and to a few of the smaller and/or depopulated states. You won't find Rhode Island, Connecticut, Montana, or Nevada on any of our maps or separated in our public accounts. Like a number of others, they've been absorbed.

Missing these events, the forecasters of 1965 also were trapped into exaggerating some of the social problems and political trends of their times. Since we no longer have "central cities," the problem of Negro and other segregation is not nearly as acute as the earlier prognosticators feared. If they had fed *Baker v. Carr* into their computers, they would have been less timid in their guesses about the staying power of certain states and the social lag associated with states' rights.[3]

Even if they had exercised more statistical care and used some of our latter-day machines, they couldn't always have been sure which

---

[3] This 1962 Supreme Court ruling addressed primarily the question of whether certain matters were issues of local politics, and therefore outside the court's jurisdiction. Ylvisaker is referring here to the original issue in the case, which was how voting districts were divided up and state legislative seats apportioned. Originally, the states were divided into districts based on land area, which gave an increasing clout-per-vote advantage to citizens of less-populated rural districts. By the 1960s, this imbalance of representation was keenly felt by urban citizens, a group of whom brought suit to the federal courts on the grounds that the *status quo*

of several contradictory trends in 1965's events they should have chosen to project. It was anybody's guess—then and for some time afterwards—whether the bars to immigration would be lowered (which they were); whether the postwar baby crop, when it came their time to form families after about 1965, would choose to have as many children as their parents [had] (and they did not); or whether the death rate would be pushed up by accumulating mortality from certain practices—like smoking, spraying with insecticides, air pollution, etc.—adopted before their dangers were known (and it was). As a result of these understandable errors, and an underestimate of the success of family planning, 1965's projection of our total population was a bit on the high side. And thank the Lord for that.

Because they've proved right about nearly everything else. Automobiles, for instance—they're coming out of our ears. During the past fifteen years, they've been outnumbering our baby crop by a ratio of [more than] two to one. And the end isn't in sight, despite all the thought and money we've put into possible alternatives. We built that high-speed transit tube from Boston to Norfolk, and it did better with sightseers than the World's Fair. It also cleared some of the air traffic over the dangerously crowded east. But it didn't take people out of cars.

They were also right about the continuous growth and sprawling of our metropolitan regions. You can't tell where one leaves off and the other begins, nor one from another; they all look like Los Angeles. But we've gotten used to the life, and in many ways we've improved it. Scattered as we are, none of us lives more than safe walking distance from an elementary school [or] a short riding distance from medical stations, shops, and a cultural center.

Some of the ghettos, unfortunately, are still to be seen—not so often in the old sections, which have been largely replaced by attractive row-housing and apartments for the middle- and upper-incomes, interlaced with parks. [They are] much more [visible] in the postwar FHA developments. But not a one without social service centers, good maintenance and lighting, and neighborhood schools.

---

infringed on their Fourteenth Amendment rights to equal protection under the law. The federal courts ruled that they had no jurisdiction over such a matter. It was this ruling that the Supreme Court overturned.

The quality of life? We get along. A thirty-five-hour week; three weeks' paid vacation; schooling for our kids from age four to twenty; a job change because of automation every five years or so, but retraining and placement almost immediately; full medical protection; and enough of a paycheck to cover expenses and even all those taxes—which, by the way, your forecasters also underestimated. But by and large they're worth it. It took some doing to stop all that rising crime and delinquency back in the 1960s and 1970s, and we're also breaking the back of the welfare costs we had accumulated. Streets are a lot safer and cleaner. TV is pretty dull.

I just wish they could do something about all those cars, and then maybe build a golf course a man could get on to without waiting for three hours. . . .

Looking Backward: Alternative #3, "The America I'd Like My Children to Help Build—and Inherit"

The last fifteen years have been uncertain every step of the way. They've been tense sometimes, rugged sometimes, wild, woolly, but creative—and I wouldn't have missed a day of it.

To the comforts and the freedom of mid-century America, we've added *concern*. We care. If there were two things that started us on our way, they were the protests and the Poverty Program of 1965. One woke us up, and the other put us to work.

Let me tell you first what happened to those marches and demonstrations. You left off with those cliffhangers at Selma and Berkeley. The hang-ups lasted for a while, and so did the marching. The authorities in both cases proved willing to negotiate, but both sides got caught not knowing quite what ought to go into the long-range bargaining package. When they finally got down to fundamentals (and it helped when Negroes and students were given the vote), they began producing the reforms and conditions [that] stimulated economic development in the Deep South and broke the grip in which that strange combination of medievalism and mass production had held Big Education.

From that point on, "The March" became an American institution. Some people argue [that] it's the fourth branch of government. Because whenever the other three branches, and the power structure of society, tend to let things slide, The March begins.

Of course it wasn't that predictable or acceptable in the early years. The March came close to being discredited on a number of occasions when it was used simply to badger and harass, and when some fairly untidy characters got mixed up on both sides of the picket line. But some very able leadership emerged, reminiscent of the Sidney Hillmans of the labor movement, dedicated to the nonviolent tactics of Martin Luther King and capable of dealing both with intrigue and radicalism on their own side and with intrigue and resistance by their opponents.

And so, during the 1960s and 1970s, the parade of new reforms began and the drumbeat picked up. After the South and the universities came the turn of practically every soft spot in the system. No institution was exempt, and the reforms never came faster. First it was vocational training, then the labor unions, then philanthropy, then the arts, then the penal system, then the welfare and charity arrangements; they even went after the rackets and the hoods, beginning in the respectable places they hurt most.

After a while it became fun—or at least the thing to do and be done to. Signs began appearing—"We have been successfully marched against"—and Madison Avenue had a field day. (One company topped them all by claiming: "Our products have been *demonstrated!*") Orders and rank of merit appeared on lapels, students got college credits for taking part, and Ph.D. theses in the social sciences finally spoke the language of the people. By the time the new reformers remembered the Department of Agriculture, the President and Secretary had already worn a path around the building.

The high point came actually in 1976, when the longest parade of all broke up the Yankee monopoly on the World Series. The victory came when Mickey Mantle Jr. was traded to Atlanta.

If The March got things going, it was the Poverty Program, as I said, that got things working. It was protected during those fumbling first years by the angels the Lord must have sent to watch over it, because some of those early beginnings were real lulus. But basically most Americans *wanted* the program to work. It stood for the things the country had waited too long to do or have done. Its very looseness gave every new and unorthodox idea and approach in America's pragmatic reserves a chance to test its merits.

For every bumble (let's be honest, for every third or fourth bumble), there was a ringing success. Mayors and governors and cabinet secretaries who had pioneered in this new business of social engineering, and were lucky enough to bat over .500, became heroes and the measure of those chosen to join and follow them in office.

Their bureaucrats after a while caught the spirit too, although many of the more worldly-wise and skeptical waited too long, and their agencies were left out and then cut back.

Business got into the act, first when prowling for contracts to take up the slack of lagging defense and space business. Then, when involved, they were swept along by the energies and enthusiasms of their younger executives who had long languished for a sense of public service and recognition.

An extraordinary lot of good things got done in American society, and in unexpected and ingenious ways. For example, young architects, volunteering for public service, began designing low-income housing and neighborhood facilities and street furniture—and you've seen the difference they've made in the urban landscape. Along with young economists and engineers drawn from business and the universities, they've also managed to put all the utility lines underground (though they had to conspire a March on the power companies to do it); they've redesigned highways and brought back walkways and bikeways; and a number of them have broken away entirely to form R&D labs, working under contract with public works departments at all levels of government. Lawyers and systems engineers have practically done over the administration of justice and have revised zoning and land tenure and municipal tax systems.

For a while, the theorists of public administration and private management had nervous breakdowns trying to fit these maverick types and procedures into old schools and concepts and salary scales. They even tried a few reprimanding lectures at Harvard's Littauer and Business Schools. Then they gave up altogether and left to write their memoirs. But some theories and regularities are emerging; at least the public entrepreneurs are succeeding in recruiting more and more associates in teaching them the art of breaking social and political bottlenecks. They've even developed standards by which to measure the efficiency of public services and expenditures—but I'm personally leery of this latest wrinkle. It smacks of a new orthodoxy. The genius of the movement has been that it has never been doctrinaire except in its insistence that things get done and the public gets served. If things can be done without going through the laborious route of government, so much the better. If government is needed, so be it. But the closer to the job and the people to be served, the better.

I've gotten ahead of my story. From poverty, this new frontier of social concern and engineering moved out in every direction, usually but a wave behind the last march, and sometimes ahead of it. The educational, juvenile, and welfare fiascos of earlier American society occupied most of the energies [of the social activists]; these were the toughest problems to crack. But the new effort to lick them constituted a massive Hawthorne effect. Soon enough, those who had been, or might have been, the alienated found themselves drawn [into] the society by the concern that was shown.

The effort to improve the urban habitat picked up, too, as the agenda for action was finally pulled away from its limiting concern with what bricks and mortar could be provided on the slim margin of consent among banking, construction, and supplier interests. The legislative programs of 1963 were landmarks.

The arts and humanities? They're alive and active in every community, age group, and income level. Not so much because of all those governmental and foundation grants (although they've helped), but because the country's alive. So much so that the productivity teams other nations used to send here during the Marshall Plan days have been replaced by missions to see how we're handling our social concerns and public affairs.

You ask about those statistical projections of 1965 and how they turned out?

I don't really know. We're not sure numbers really matter.

Except maybe for all those students and those cars and those taxes. . . .

Approaches to Comprehensive Planning for the Human Environment

(Presented to the Symposium on the Impact of
Urbanization on Man's Development, sponsored by the
United Nations with the International Trade Union of the
United Automobile, Aerospace, and Agricultural
Implement Workers of America, Onoway, Michigan,
June 14–20, 1970)[1]

*"Livable solutions to environmental problems will
not emerge until nations individually and together
make the commitment symbolized by the attempt to
devise urban policies—the commitment to try, and
in the very act of trying, to ensure an integrity that
augurs well for human survival."*

The principal benefit we have gained from man's voyage into space
is a perspective on ourselves and our environment. In the mirror of
that vast distance, we suddenly see who we are and what we've
become: a species fast growing toward the limits of our environment, and perhaps tragically beyond. Our globe is tinier than we
thought, its livability more precarious, and our time much shorter.

We have acquired that perspective in the suddenness of a single
decade. The effect could be exhilarating; it could also be shattering.
We now realize that in our efforts to prosper, we have set loose genii
who won't easily be recaptured and subdued. We have developed a
momentum that leaves us more directed than directing, and a
complexity that saps our will and wit to remain in control. We have
divided and redivided our territories and our capabilities and our

---

[1] Reprinted with permission of the International Union, United Automobile,
Aerospace & Agricultural Implement Workers of America—UAW.

purposes into so many fragments that even to talk about planning comprehensively sometimes seems an exercise in self-delusion.

Yet we also know now that we have no alternative but to try. This paper therefore addresses the topic with that sense of realism and in a constructive spirit. It presumes the urgency of our condition; it interprets "comprehensive planning" not as a term of art but as man's continuing struggle to assert rationality; and it goes directly to questions and issues that currently make that struggle so difficult and its outcome so problematical.

Some Hard Facts, the Problems of Change, and the Riddle of Complexity

The urgent need for planning man's relationship with his environment stems from three rugged facts. First, if present trends continue, the world's urban population will grow from 600 million to three billion over the next generation. Second, the world's urban facilities are already overloaded and the environment dangerously polluted. Third, each increment of urban growth as [now] constituted has imbedded within it a further assault on nature, a further deterioration of the environment.

Thus the problem we deal with is not one simply of stretching the *status quo* to accommodate growing numbers. More basically, it is one of changing structures and lifestyles and technologies—the very systems by which we have prospered, or at least survived.

Comprehensive planning during this next generation will therefore be an uphill struggle all the way. To be effective—to avoid the extermination of man—it has to engage in a constant effort to change the behavior of institutions [that] have the power of their establishment and of a general public whose habits are entrenched in majority votes.

Beyond this problem of "changing the system" looms the haunting riddle of complexity. Like those who built the Tower of Babel past a level they could sustain, we are building an urban civilization [that] threatens our power to fathom it. It is hard to plan comprehensively when you no longer are so certain that you comprehend.

The Conventional Wisdom of
Comprehensive Planning

The conventional formula for gaining mastery and understanding of a system is to climb the hierarchy and reach out for wider perspectives and broader jurisdictions. Urban planners have come a long way in this respect since they were first professionally heard from a generation ago. Emerging from their almost singular preoccupation with microphysical concerns, they have arrived at the highest levels of decision-making and the farthest reaches of every discipline. The most encouraging sign that comprehensive planning has "arrived" is the effort that has appeared spontaneously throughout the world to formulate national policies for urban growth. Canada, the Netherlands, and Japan are only three of the many nations currently engaged in that effort.

But the experience of these and other countries, even before the intricacies of ecological relationships were fully discerned, had begun to show that the conventional formula for comprehensive planning—higher status and wider scope—were slender reeds to lean upon. Even with [the benefit of] cabinet rank and sprawling jurisdictions, certain nagging questions and stubborn facts remained. Despite wishes—and sometimes laws—to the contrary, cities continued to grow and automobiles continued to proliferate. Affluent nations, no less than poorer ones, continued to starve their public economies and underfinance their urban infrastructure. Efforts to redistribute urban populations and decentralize industrial development met with indifferent success. Mountains of assembled data still did not adequately [reflect] reality—and even the most sophisticated of systems engineers, fresh from the conquest of space, admitted their inability to comprehend the subtleties and the infinities of the urban complex.

Statements of national urban policy have therefore tended to become rhetorical; only in a very few cases could tangible results be found in stouter urban budgets and tidier landscapes.

It was at this critical juncture in urban planning—with its practitioners simultaneously acquiring power and humility—that the full force and complexity of our environmental predicament struck. Even where planning was thought to be comprehensive, it now seems parochial; a whole range of new variables has to be added to the matrix. Powers [that] had painstakingly been assembled now turn out to be inconsequential when compared with the leverages needed to bring man into harmony with his environment.

Questioning the Unquestioned: The New Frontiers of Comprehensive Planning

Confronted by global pollution, we have no alternative but to press planning past the familiar problems [to which] we [have] had no certain solutions to more monumental questions [whose] answers, at least for the present, almost entirely escape us.

The most basic of these questions is whether the human race can any longer afford the luxury of continuous and accelerating growth; whether the point has been reached where—like the ancient Greeks and medieval Japanese—we adopt a deliberate polity of stasis. Given the momentum of present growth, we would be hard put to effectuate such a policy; few of our experts would have much to offer a city or a nation that decided to restrict its growth. Yet the environmental crisis suggests that we can no longer ignore the logic of such a policy.

Even if we beg the question of continuous growth, we will have to deal with a related one: whether we [currently] have valid and satisfactory ways of evaluating growth. For the past generation, most nations of the world have followed the fashion of using the Gross National Product as their measure of growth and their guidelines for planning. Thirty years of accumulating social costs by the legerdemain of statistics have now taught us how disastrously short-sighted that fashion has been. We have converted every form of economic activity into presumptive social benefit. Anyone now planning comprehensively will have to challenge that calculus. Even economists who once spoke approvingly of "external economies" [are becoming] chastened by rising social costs and are now talking neutrally and even negatively about "externalities."

But what will replace the GNP as the measure? Encouraging progress is being made in the development of social indicators that simultaneously and more accurately assess both social costs and benefits. This development still has a long way to go, especially in converting data that are less than reliable and always subjective into monetary values that find general public acceptance.

For now—and merely by raising these questions—comprehensive planning for the environment will find itself powerfully confronted by economic planning of the more familiar vintage, which has dominated policy at every level of government. Given the scarcity of resources and the elemental need to stay alive, economic growth by almost any measure has been the *sine qua non* of public policy. Calling into question the hitherto unquestioned, at least until we have settled on ways to measure social costs and environmental degradation, will toss many a public authority into a frothing sea of official uncertainty and stormy public debate.

Taming the Tiger of Technology

Technology has been on the loose, and more explicit measures are needed, first, to curb its ravages of the environment and, second, to put it to more constructive use in monitoring, restoring, and improving the environment.

Placing technology on this shorter leash will prove both more and less difficult than we might think. More difficult, in that the consequences of innovation are sometimes too subtle and delayed to be anticipated; less difficult, in that much environmental degradation as a result of technological innovation can be spotted early in its development and [counteracted]—often by the manufacturer itself. Public policy [has been] too lenient, and the public itself conditioned to demand innovation; controls have been slipshod, tardy, and too easily avoided. Comprehensive planning will have to be accompanied by tighter enforcement and more systematic procedures for early testing and surveillance.

More important than the negative is the constructive use of technology. We [may] see a lot more benign technology cropping up spontaneously as both the public and product manufacturers place a higher value on such results. But the major breakthrough along these lines will occur only when the public aggregates enough of a market, and underwrites a sufficient demand, to [stimulate] technological innovations less degrading in their effects. Military and space programs have demonstrated the capacity of governments to set the agenda of technology.

This need to aggregate markets is an additional argument for regional planning of human settlements. It also adds weight to the argument for new towns, which bring together a market of sufficient size for technology to follow a schedule of (hopefully) enlightened demand. But we need not wait upon the emergence of regionalism or new towns. Already the governments of existing communities command sizable markets of their own. If they were to follow industry's example of spending a sizable share of their total revenues in research and development, that would constitute incentive enough for constructive technology.

Reducing the Overload on Planning

The net effect of what has been said and recommended so far is to impose even greater burdens on planners who are already suffering grievously from overload. We are seeing the emotional effects of this overload in the quickening exodus from public life of ever-more-harried officials. We are seeing the steady clogging of the process of public decision-making. As a result, many a government is lagging farther and farther behind in its urban and environmental efforts.

Ways must therefore be sought—ingenious and, if need be, unconventional—to increase the power and scope of environmental planning while at the same time reducing the tensions and the clutter that increasingly gather around it.

Clearer Standards as a Tidying Device

Ironically, much of the tension and clutter comes from the fact that [although] we *have* recognized the urgency of environmental problems, neither our planners nor our scientists are certain or agreed enough to promulgate clear and uniform standards—standards of toxicity and tolerance, standards by which officials and citizens alike can more simply and quickly get about the business of enforcement and compliance. A good deal of research in this field is going on, and considerable progress has been made. However, much of this research is specialized, having to do with the effects of a single substance on a human cell. What seems to be needed is a set of standards focusing on the cumulative effects of varying mixes of toxins and pollutants on individuals and specific environments.

All of which is easier to say than to do. The time periods are long, the variables infinite, and the interrelationships fiendishly subtle and complex. But it is perhaps better to act arbitrarily than to wait overlong, better to set these standards more conservatively than research may later show to be necessary.

Regional Planning as a Tidying Device: Some Conventions and Some Realities

For reasons which one suspects sometimes are more historic than valid, regional and comprehensive planning have been thought of as mutually reinforcing, if not actually the same. They are, if they are defined that way. Regional planning is then presumed to blot out the incongruities and inadequacies of more localized plans, in favor of its own greater rationality and that of the more global planning going on at successive levels beyond.

In that harmonic version, regional planning eases the burden on the overall planning process, adding rationality and subtracting from the workload at other levels. But the realities of regional planning are not always that easy to synchronize and the results not always that efficient. A compliant region may double the paperwork without doubling the output. An assertive region may double the tensions while halving the product. Simply taking a regional approach is no guarantee that planning will be comprehensive enough to preserve the integrity of the environment: TVA has had its fishkills, and the Aswan Dam has already if unwittingly violated the ecology of the Eastern Mediterranean.

This is not to argue against either regions or regional planning. It is simply to warn that we ought not too easily assume that words are the same as solutions.

Toward More Manageable and Effective Planning: The Search for Longer Levers

The planning process—like the human condition—is constantly and perhaps inevitably one of contending with forces [that] are more powerful than the ones we have at our command. The way out of that dilemma lies in the art of leverage.

Greater leverage is also the answer to the problem of clutter and frustration: increasing output for any given amount of input is the formula for efficiency and satisfaction.

Where to look for these more powerful levers? The remainder of this paper describes four areas where such a search might pay off.

Economic Leverages

One of the reasons for the dominance of economic over physical planning has been the sure instinct of economists for finding and manipulating the most powerful of levers: pricing arrangements, tax policy, monetary policy, etc. The use of these instruments by economists for other purposes has already—for better or for worse—played a major part in shaping our urban environment. It is time to use these powers expressly to improve the environment. A number of such uses have already been proposed, and some have been adopted: leaded gas to be taxed and/or priced higher than non-leaded gas; taxes to be placed on industrial firms in proportion to the amount of pollution they generate; a price to be charged for air, and higher prices to be charged for water; surcharges to be added to the price of automobiles, bottles, and other articles to cover the cost of their disposal.

Perhaps the most powerful of these leverages has to do with the pricing and taxation of urban land, to minimize if not abolish the exploitative consequences of land speculation.

The use of any of these mechanisms will be bathed in controversy. Any powerful instrument is a many-edged sword, and its use ought to be carefully calculated and jealously guarded.

Economies of Scale

Much of the clutter and frustration of planning can be attributed to the small scale at which we customarily work, forced to do so not only by the fragmentation of planning jurisdiction but also by the mindsets we fall into.

The value of regional planning and new towns is that they encourage us to work at proper scale and, in doing so, to raise the productivity of our planning efforts. As the builders of new towns have discovered, it is only when one deals with large sites that the value of land under development can be maximized and then recycled into the costs of infrastructure and social facilities.

There are other advantages: one has already been cited, viz., the aggregation of markets large enough to control the agenda of technology. Another advantage of working at larger scale is that it forces us to include enough of the social, economic, and political variables to be at one with reality. Still another is that only by assembling and developing larger sites will we be able to induce the modernization of the building industry and in turn produce the volume of construction that the world's urbanizing population will need.

But scale should not be thought of in geographical terms alone— one can still be small-minded about large territories. Scale is measured by the job to be done and the powers needed to do it. The character of environmental problems is that they override all our boundaries, and their solution requires strategies and powers that transcend the territorial.

The Energy of Participation

A reality no planner can escape is the growing insistence on citizen participation: government by negotiated consent. As numbers increase and citizens become more insistent, the chain of these negotiations stretches on, and emotional fatigue becomes the occupational hazard of those involved. Also, the more comprehensive that planning becomes, the longer the chain of consent and the wearier the planners.

But that is only one side of the coin—and not the one that shows the value. There is power in participation, a power that cannot be matched by any amount of bureaucratic imperialism.

This is doubly true with a problem as pervasive as the environmental, which has its roots so deeply set in the everyday habits of individual citizens. A program or policy based on fiat alone becomes an exercise in futility. Those who plan for the human environment should therefore be spending major shares of their time mobilizing and releasing the energies of the public through as rich a variety of devices as possible, ranging from education to direct citizen control. Especially important (it could well be the most important thing planners could do) is to create a climate of opinion that will not tolerate violations of the environment. The place to begin is in the schools, to make environmental sensitivity as much a part of the culture as literacy and numeracy.

The Power of Protest

One of the greatest powers available—although the harassed planner may not be inclined to recognize or believe it—is the power of citizen protest and complaint. Generally, systems work best when they are under continuous pressure to perform. Some of our more conventional means for exerting that pressure (legislative oversight, executive control, and judicial review) have not always sufficed for a massing society that is properly impatient to get things done and put things to right now, rather than some bureaucratic time later.

A wise and ingenious planner will benefit from that pressure. He too knows the urgency of the problem; and if he is skillful in responding to valid protest, he will be able to turn its energy from negative to positive.

The ombudsman of Scandinavia is a sophisticated model of constructive complaint.[2] In the United States, Ralph Nader has fashioned what is fast becoming an institutionalized grievance mechanism. Almost certainly, equivalent forms of channeled protest will emerge in most other countries, and hopefully planners will learn to live with such protest to their advantage.

The most abundant source of this kind of energy will of course be the youth. It has been interesting to watch the young of nearly every nation respond to the environmental crisis. It is at once a confirmation of their negative views about *status quo* and the chance they have been looking for to make a constructive contribution. If there is indeed any lever long enough to move the world, an Archimedes of comprehensive planning would probably find it here.

An Administrative Note: The Place of Planning in the Governing Structure

The planner has discovered what the beleaguered citizen has always had to live with: everything these days relates to everything. Which raises the question many a city and many a nation is puzzling over: "Where in the structure of government do you place

---

[2] Particularly in Scandinavian countries, an ombudsman is a government official tasked with investigating citizens' complaints against government ministries, agencies, or officials.

responsibility for comprehensive planning, whose responsibility is supposedly to relate everything to everything?" A lot of structural solutions have been tried and found wanting: departmental status, interdepartmental committee, cabinet secretariat, executive staff. The underlying reason may well be that comprehensive planning is not so much a differentiated function as it is—or should be—a general state of mind. The same can be said of the systems approach, which essentially is systematic thinking brought up to date.

If there is any art that is crucial to comprehensive planning, it is the art of the question—the question that starts with a restless probe of relevant (and sometimes seemingly irrelevant) information and then proceeds with equal restlessness and some impertinence to ask whether any given or proposed decision will, on balance, enhance or further degrade the livability of our environment.

This art of the question cannot be lost in the confinement of one discipline, one guild, or one department. It should be practiced on every level and [in every] sector of the governing structure and throughout the entire society.

A Concluding Note on National Urban Policy

The current move toward the formulation of national urban policies is an encouraging response to the crisis of man's environment. It will not be an easy task, for all the reasons cited above. But livable solutions to environmental problems will not emerge until nations individually and together make the commitment symbolized by the attempt to devise urban policies—the commitment to try, and in the very act of trying, to ensure an integrity that augurs well for human survival.

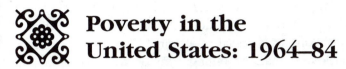 **Poverty in the United States: 1964–84**

(Presented to the University of Colorado Conference on The Great Society Revisited, Boulder, Colorado, June 10, 1984)

"The War on Poverty had its failings, but it was not a failure. Calling it so has become a partisan excuse for calling it off."

My purpose is to trace the long journey this country has taken in its dealing with poverty, from 1964 when the War on Poverty became a high Presidential priority to 1984 when it seems to have no significant place on the White House agenda. My mood is that of an unrepentant poverty warrior, still persuaded that what was launched in the 1960s was essentially noble and successful and that a continuing commitment to develop this nation's wasting human resources is a pragmatic and moral imperative.

The journey has been a long one, from the euphoria of that early period when decimal points in budgetary proposals could be moved blithely to the right, to the melancholy of retrenchment, with decimal points moving inexorably to the left; from the rather quaint conviction in the 1960s that we were mopping up the last vestige of poverty within an affluent nation, to the chastening awareness that we are today coping with a global flood.

Despite those shifts in environment and perception, I still view both past and future with optimism. The War on Poverty was essentially a success: it helped convert the powerful social forces breaking suddenly upon the United States during the 1960s—surging energies of the young and the minorities—into constructive elements; it built bridges between ghettos and the establishment over which an extraordinary percentage of contemporary leaders have passed; it released the creative potential of indigenous populations through the novel vehicle of community action; and it left a remarkable residue of innovative techniques (early childhood

69

education, advocacy and legal services, employment training, foster grandparents, etc.) [that] have tenaciously survived and become respected parts of America's social repertoire.

The War on Poverty had its failings, but it was not a failure. Calling it so has become a partisan excuse for calling it off.

Having confessed those beliefs, let me proceed in a more measured way with an accounting of poverty in America over the course of the past two decades.

Contextual Changes, 1964–84

In many respects 1964 was a different time, a different world. It was an age when the nation was feeling its power; a time of military, industrial, and scientific hegemony; a mood that reflected the optimism of a flourishing suburbia and the exuberance of a swelling generation of youth.

Poverty was a potent political issue. Kennedy had given a promise to West Virginia; big-city mayors in that same 1960 campaign had exacted another Presidential pledge to address their graying area concerns. The urban poor were growing restive; the civil rights movement was in full cry; both the [long affluent] and the newly affluent were feeling a mixture of guilt and altruism. Young turks in the church had seized upon poverty and civil rights as the twin handles of ecclesiastical reform. Burgeoning philanthropies were breaking out of conventional patterns and daring to move at street level. And then Lyndon Johnson suddenly became President, determined to match and exceed the social dedication of his predecessor.

Concepts of poverty and what to do about it also bore the mark of the times. Without sophisticated analyses to go on, there was a tendency to think and deal in undifferentiated terms. There were easy references to "the poor" as though they were a homogeneous and near-permanent cohort of the population; [there were] exaggerated expectations of mass support, as though the poor were a solid constituency. With the administrative expansionism of the New Deal and World War II so close in history, there was an almost automatic resort to "programs" and bureaucratized delivery of services as the way to proceed. Even the refreshing heresy of community action soon carried the conventional labels.

Nor was it measurable at the time how much of the force of the War on Poverty was linked to, and stemmed from, the civil rights and Black (minority) power movements that were simultaneously stirring, as well as the fear generated by urban violence. And since the 1960s? American hope and hegemony have been seriously eroded. Sophistication has brought skepticism, even passivity. There is a perception of impotence—in citizen action, bureaucracies, [and] economic and social engineering. There has been a slackening and even a reversal of allied forces: religious fundamentalism replacing church reform, the civil rights movement placed on the defensive. Old institutional stalwarts have departed the scene: the Office of Economic Opportunity, Area Development, and even HUD, left only with its Cheshire smile.

Demographics have changed, society dividing into aging majorities and youthful minorities. Distance is also growing between minorities of higher and lower socioeconomic status, with former leadership having difficulty crossing the gap. Signs of an underclass have begun to appear. Individual isolation has increased with the rapid disappearance of the two-parent family and the multiplying numbers of latchkey children.

Changes in the economy—most fundamentally the shift from manufacturing with its familiar ladders of advancement to a service/information society—are powerfully influencing the patterns of poverty and the chances of moving into and out of it. A re-stratification appears to be taking place—the relatively few "good jobs" becoming the prize of select professionals, the more numerous "so-so" jobs giving static prospects and insecure tenure to an ever-enlarging fraction of the work force, with increasing numbers of older workers and minority males being consigned to no jobs at all.

Perhaps the most significant shift over the two decades has been in American attitudes: from a perception of continuing economic growth and affluence to one of diminishing prospects and economic instability. "The poor," it turns out, are not so much what we once thought: an identifiable group set apart as "they." There's much more of a flow in and out of poverty, involving a quarter of the population over a ten-year period. In this rapidly changing world, "we" can at any time become "they." And so the ambivalence: a resentment at having to spend dwindling resources on a safety net for others, a chilling second thought that we may need one ourselves.

Changes in Scale and Incidence

Not least of the legacies of the 1960s is sophisticated research on poverty and its measurement, stimulated in those years and steadily maturing ever since. Which is not to say that current data and analyses don't still leave room for differing numbers and interpretations. Scholarly and partisan debate still continue. What I have attempted to do in the generalizations that follow is to distill a reasonable consensus from what the various data and interpretations suggest.

- The incidence of poverty declined over the period 1965–78 and since then has been on the increase.

- Minorities remain the most vulnerable.

- Children are especially at risk.

- Poverty is [becoming concentrated] in female-headed families.

- More and more of the nation's poor are [becoming concentrated] in the central cities.

Some Reflections: Good News, Bad News

Reflecting on experience and inquiry over the past twenty years, one moves through light and shadow. Among the brighter spots:

- First, research suggests that for many Americans who became poor, their stay in poverty is not a long one.

- Second, there's also hopeful evidence that income supplements (in tandem with service programs, as Sar Levitan[1] properly keeps reminding us) have proved effective in reducing poverty.

---

[1] An economist, public servant, and educator, Sar Levitan has worked to develop U.S. social policy. His books include *A Proper Inheritance: Investing in the Self-Sufficiency of Poor Families* (with other authors), *Working but Poor: America's Contradiction* (with Isaac Shapiro), and *Uncle Sam's Helping Hand: Educating, Training, and Employing the Disadvantaged* (with Frank Gallo).

- A third source of reassurance is the tenacious way in which the issue of poverty, the determination to do something about it, and an ever-regenerating supply of institutions and ideas, have persevered—despite the cold water of skepticism, self-centeredness, budget-cutting, and Presidential indifference that have latterly been doused upon them. Such apparently neutral processes as the gathering and publication of time series data have prevented the issue from being ignored. Philanthropy, even when spending at the margin, has helped keep con-sciences alive; so have the innumerable nonprofit agencies [that] somehow manage to survive and proliferate; so have the surprising numbers of community-action agencies still alive despite the loss of federal parentage and patronage; so have the scholars, program designers, and think centers [that] keep evaluating and inventing formulae for legislative and voluntary action; so has that hardy American penchant for fairness that keeps cropping up, particularly now with the specter of the homeless, the hungry, and the jobless looming larger on the streets of Everytown.

But the bad news is still writ in bolder type. Poverty is on the increase in America, and it is impacting most heavily on those least capable of mounting an economic, social, or political defense: minorities, children, and generally those at the bottom of the ladder.

This nation resolved in the 1960s to share its affluence more equitably. Presidential leadership now seems intent on distributing the hardship of the times more inequitably. The general rule seems to be to take from the have-nots and to give to those who have. There has been a direct correlation between the amount of benefits that have been cut and the voting power of those affected: the elderly, for example, have been handled with political respect, [while] the children of the minorities and the poor have had their votes counted and come up wanting.

This is the saddest of all commentaries on current Presidential leadership and on that fraction of the American nation which goes along. Contrast that indifference with a criterion set by the United Nations as the mark of a good society: i.e., that a child is born into that society immediately and continuously feels wanted, needed, and nurtured.

That posture toward our poor and minority children is the more incomprehensible when one checks the demographics and contemplates how much our future depends upon these very children. The number of adolescents and high school graduates in the United States will be falling sharply over the next decade; the most rapidly growing proportion of that diminishing cohort will be minority and poor. The nation will become dependent upon them in every facet of our life: keeping the United States economically competitive; providing a skilled and reliable work force; replenishing our scientific, educational, artistic, athletic, humanitarian, and political sectors; maintaining our national defense; ensuring the viability of our Social Security and other mutual support systems. Why, then, the withdrawal of support, the failure to invest in this next generation? From a War on Poverty to a war on poor children?

One could cite some other ominous signs: the reduction in nutritional programs and health care; the reluctance to provide adequate day care; the allowed deterioration of schools and housing in central cities where so many children of the minorities, the immigrants, and the poor are concentrated. All within the political frame of an aging majority population voting its more immediate self-interests, of parents of public school children outnumbered four to one by other voting adults, of a dwindling generation of youngsters none of whom [has] access to the ballot.

Seemingly bleak the prospects—and one can the more appreciate and applaud those who against the odds have taken up the cause of poor children: the network of child advocate groups across the nation, and most notably the Children's Defense Fund headed by Marian Wright Edelman.

Further backing will come with the rising political activism of the minorities, especially black and Hispanic, whose children and families are immediately at risk and whose swing vote will be more and more cultivated and respected.

My guess is that we are not far from a national burst of interest in America's children as a precious but wasting resource. If so, I hope that it does not come primarily as a political and bureaucratic concern, but as a moral imperative. And while recognizing the pragmatic need for sophisticated mechanisms—"programs that work"—I would be looking first for Presidential leadership to promote a national climate of respect for those whose potential goes far beyond their present status and voting power.

The Changing Concept of Public Service

(Keynote address to the National Academy of Public Administrators, November 19, 1987)

"It is no accident that we have recently come to recognize the independent sector as a precious part of our heritage—in the very decade when self-centeredness and cynicism have reached their apogee. I do not relish the prospect that that recognition will disintegrate into turf wars over who should claim this new territory."

The theme of this talk is taken from a proposition by Gregory Bateson:[1] that every growing organism must simultaneously and correspondingly miniaturize. I suggest it as a cue to understanding recent trends in the nation's efforts to accomplish its public purposes.

First, let me flash back over a century of public administration. Formal study in this field was born of two parents: municipal reform and industrial efficiency—a unique combination of idealism and business management. A critical juncture came with the era of Franklin Roosevelt: public administration went national. It did so with the advent of an assertive federal government, responding to two national emergencies: first, the Depression, and second, World War II. Both required large-scale operations; both were backed by a broad national consensus.

During that era, reform and efficiency were grafted onto humanitarian ideals. During that same impression-fashioning time, the

---

[1] Gregory Bateson (1904–1980) was an anthropologist, philosopher, educator, naturalist, and poet. He was noted for his study of the social forces that bind and divide individuals and groups.

ideology of public administration was powerfully articulated: enlarging mechanisms of an expanded and centralizing system.

Assumptions and legacies linger past their time. President Johnson attempted to replay the heroics of earlier successes, and note his resort to "war" as the banner under which major public ventures in assertive national administration were waged: the War on Poverty, the Vietnam War. Both wars encountered the resistance of a growing, complicating society which was building up its organic need for miniaturization. Neither of the two wars could rally or rely on a monolithic national consensus. Both had to contend with the logic that Bateson had perceived: the dispersion and diffusion of authority and initiative. A generation of advancing growth and complexity had produced a countervailing demand for miniaturization that neither the presumption of single-purpose national policy nor the centralizing legacy of administrative theory could deal with or even articulate.

In retrospect, one can now appreciate the force and implications of that demand. They were inherent in the exploding cry for freedom: the civil rights movement; the liberation movements for women, the elderly, and others; the "War on Washington" engaged in by both Republican and Democratic Presidential candidates; in the shift from social reform to self-realization. And it was becoming institutionalized: in the community action programs of the 1960s; in the successive "New Federalism" ventures of the 1970s and 1980s. Even more, in the shift from public bureaucracies to private instrumentalities: government by contract and the burgeoning of nonprofit agencies. Fritz Mosher,[2] I understand, has estimated that less than ten percent of federal programs are implemented through governmental employees.

This demand for miniaturization was first articulated and politically captured by Conservatives. Their antipathy to Washington and

---

[2] Frederick C. Mosher (1913–1990) was a professor of government and foreign affairs at the University of Virginia. Mosher's study found that "considerably less than one-tenth" of the federal budget was allotted to domestic activities that the federal government managed itself. Details of this work were published in the *Public Administration Review,* November/December 1980, Volume 40, Number 6, under the title, "The Changing Responsibilities and Tactics of the Federal Government."

"Big Government"; their cry for a new federalism; their emphasis on "mediating structures" (family, church, neighborhood organizations, etc.); their push for privatization—all touched an emotional chord in the general public. And, admittedly, with some positive results: for example, the stimulation of greater responsibility in smaller units of government and decision-making. One has only to cite what has happened in education and state/municipal finance.

But conservative expression of that demand has also fallen short in several crucial respects. It has spoken attractively of freedom, but given it only to the privileged. It has shortchanged the American instinct for compassion and fairness. It has identified national unity only with defense; note the neoconservative, intellectualized refusal to recognize the premise of a national community needing to be served for social purposes. It has fostered a self-centered perspective: "I've got mine, now you get yours." It has created a mood of cynicism through flagrant scandal and abuse. It has downgraded the civic service. And strangely, as Lester Salomon[3] had pointed out, it has missed the opportunity to strengthen the very nonprofit institutions and voluntary tradition its rhetoric has always championed.

Nor have those of us in the field of public administration systematically addressed or clearly articulated the need and demand for miniaturization. Beyond, that is, our conventional concern with state and local government. We have tended to be preoccupied and enamored with the intricacies of policy (and increasingly with the intimacies of politics) at central levels—and with the manipulation of power. Similarly, with analytical techniques addressed to impersonalized handling of human problems at mass scale—witness the fascination with quantitative methodology. These concerns and techniques have their place, but they do not address the needs and logic of miniaturization. They are still working on the tenets and agenda of growth and centralization.

---

[3] Lester Salomon is currently Director of the Institute for Policy Studies at Johns Hopkins University. He was one of the first to study nonprofit agencies as a single sector, first in the United States and later on a global level. When Paul Ylvisaker gave this address, Salomon had recently (1982) come out with his book *The Federal Budget and the Nonprofit Sector*.

That is not the driving agenda of contemporary America, nor the need for diversification it is looking to satisfy. The qualities being searched for are flexibility, elbow room, enterprise and diffused initiative, versatility, creativity and risk-taking, shared authority, and a transcending appreciation of the public interest and at the same time of multiple instrumentalities through which that public interest can be served.

Bateson's theory would predicate a creative burst in thought about training for the public service which is already taking place: viz., the rising concern about training for nonprofit management.

The nonprofit sector is now the fastest growing of America's three sectors. It accounts for 17 percent of the nation's service employment; it employs more [people] than federal and state governments combined; it constitutes nearly 10 percent of all economic activity; and it includes hundreds of thousands of independent agencies. Some of these are already doing their own training: e.g., health, educational museums. These multifarious organizations are doing much of the government's business; they are also setting the pace for much government policy.

Predictably, there is now a crescendo of talk and debate about how and where to train managers and administrators of nonprofit agencies. Is there a generic set of skills? Is this field distinguishable from government and business administration? Where on campus (if at all) should this training be located? There are now—interestingly enough—schools of government and business, but none for the nonprofits. Should there be? Or should the training be entrusted to existing schools of business and/or government?

Quite frankly, I would not entrust it to business. The culture of profit is too powerful and antiethical. The experience of Yale's School of Management is hardly encouraging: most of its graduates, inclined toward public service when enrolling, end up in business.

Nor am I entirely happy with the prospect of training for the nonprofits being subsumed under public administration and government. Are they too imbued with the culture of large, authoritative structures? Too involved with the political process? Too distant from the world of the one-to-one?

Yet I'm also not entirely happy with isolating the training for nonprofits from those more familiar environments. Not so much for losing what public administration and business have to teach (and that's a lot). More so for losing what this sector and those devoting themselves to its purposes have to give: a sense of the intimate human encounter and a skill in working at that scale. And a set of values: a reaffirmation of the humane, an antidote to the preoccupation with profit and power, and to the impersonality of the mass and macro.

The nation and its public service need those values badly. As Robert Bellah and his co-authors have so eloquently argued in their recall of de Tocqueville's warning and his phrase "habits of the heart," American individualism is constantly straining the ties that bind.[4] Some transcending sense of community and idealism has to be instilled and given pervasive expression.

What we call the "independent sector" grows out of that ideal, that urge. It is no accident that we have recently come to recognize the independent sector as a precious part of our heritage—in the very decade when self-centeredness and cynicism have reached their apogee.

I do not relish the prospect that recognition will disintegrate into turf wars over who should claim this new territory.

What I do hope for are two things:

First, a provocation to assess again (as in the 1930s and '40s) the nation's needs for recruiting and training managerial and administrative talent into the public service—this time through a lens that focuses on the micro as well as the macro, and on the humane as well as the impersonal.

Second, a signal to the nation's pool of talent that public service—whether in the large or the small, whether governmental or nongovernmental—is indeed a noble calling.

I have emphasized the inevitability and the value of miniaturization. But as Bateson perceived, it is an essential concomitant—not an alternative—to growing larger. It would be fallacious and even tragic to deny the parallel logic of growth and the need for centralizing systems that make an enlarging system cohesive and

---

[4] *Habits of the Heart: Individualism and Commitment in American Life*, Robert N. Bellah, Richard Madsen, William M. Sullivan, Ann Swindler, Steven M. Tipton. University of California Press, Berkeley, 1985.

viable. What happened when public administration "went national" was inevitable and overdue.

My point here is that we have overlooked and underemphasized the simultaneous social process of miniaturization—except as we have attended to its governmental expression in the conventional realm of state, local, and regional authorities. The nation has filled the vacuum spontaneously with myriads of novel and largely nongovernmental instrumentalities.

It's time we attended to the significance of that sector as a complementary form of public service, worked to satisfy its managerial and other needs, and benefited from its inherent and insistent reminder of the human values and purpose that public service is really all about.

I've worked long enough with young people to know the immense appeal of a public service [that] is so broadly and spiritually defined.

PART II
Cities: Mirror to Man

*"Men may find God in nature,
but when they look at cities they are
viewing themselves."*

—1965

**Metropolitan Government—
For What?**

(Presented to the Conference on Metropolitan Problems,
Berkeley, California, July 24, 1958)

*"It is the elastic clause and the possibility of
simultaneous action . . . which we ought to be
stressing in our metropolitan charters. In the give
and take between borough and metropolis lies the
vitality of the system."*

The first, and basic, point I want to make is really quite simple. We
are moving—I think wisely—toward some form of metropolitan
government, not because we know what we should do about the
many problems of urban life and the city, but precisely because we
do not. To resolve our many differences and uncertainties as to how
we ought to live in an urban environment, and to come to some
workable decisions in what is now a sea of indecision—this is what
metropolitan government is all about.

Unanswered Questions

I have been struck, as I'm sure most of you have been, by the
sudden shift of thinking in the United States [that] makes the idea of
some kind of metropolitan government not only palatable but
popular. As a longtime friend of the cause, I should be entirely
pleased. But to a degree, I'm uneasy; in the rash of speeches and the
raptness of attention we all have lately witnessed, metropolitan
government has been treated with a touch of magic—or is it naïveté?
The same touch, whatever it is, [that] one remembers from the old
refrain: "The more we get together, the happier we'll be."

I suppose that if metropolitan government, like marriage, is to be
made attractive to those otherwise reluctant to enter into it, an
unthinking glow of this kind may be needed.

But there is no reason in an audience such as this to promote or perpetuate the myth that, once married, the disparate elements of the metropolis will automatically live happily ever afterward. Metropolitan government is not the same as a program of government; it does not come magically endowed with solutions or answers to the problems and posers of urban life. Lest we be tempted to think so, consider for a moment the more obvious in the long list of great questions [that] await our answering, and on which we can find no certain agreement:

1. What pattern of urban living do we want—the more concentrated, as represented by the historic image of the city, or the less densely settled ("sprawl," to use the current generic term)?

2. Which of these two patterns is the better and/or the more economical? Speaking for sprawl, one might argue the advantages of free choice of location, mobility, and—to mention a new one—the possibility that a gangliated city like Los Angeles may be less vulnerable to massive economic depression and physical deterioration. Speaking against it, one can offer the traditional advantage of the city as the womb of culture, or invite a hardheaded cost analysis of sprawled as against concentrated development.

3. Do we actually have a choice between the patterns, given the vast preponderance of the centrifugal forces [that] beset us? By what cultural revolution are we to reverse the outward pattern of social movement and aspiration? By what bureaucratic fiat are we to retard technological developments in communication and transportation, which propel so constantly outward? And by what catharsis is the American mind to be purged of its preference for semi-rural living?

4. What, in the short and long run, do we do with that growing range of deteriorated real estate between central business district and suburb? Three and four times we have used this area—without rehabilitating—for the "citifying" of our immigrant populations. Now, if we are to believe our economists, this area will be of no further economic use except to harbor the lingering and less happy remnants of the immigrant parade. Shall we—and with our economic arguments against us, *can* we—make of this area anything other than a Pompeii-like memory of a passing stage of civilization?

5. What do we do with our tendency to segregate—socially, economically, culturally? The search for homogeneity has given us

not only white suburbs and darkening central cities; it has also given us two and three-class suburbs—and, I think, is losing for us the thrust and stimulation of that social variety which was to be America's genius and promise.

6. What relevance does the city have to the problem of allocating scarce economic resources or to the process of stimulating economic growth? I am not as optimistic as Chancellor Kerr[1] that Americans will grow ever more prosperous (we are too vulnerable, a rich nation in a poor and increasingly assertive if not hostile world) or, if we do, that patterns of increased production and consumption will naturally favor the renaissance of the city. They have done precisely the opposite in the past; what heroic twisting of trends will change the future? Differences apart, the question remains: can we bring about a consistency between the requirements of economic growth and general increases in the standard of living, and the needs of the city, or do these give evidence of conflicting values and drives?

7. Are we inexorably committed to urban bigness, or is there a more decentralized, small-city way of achieving maximum economic growth and all the advantages [that] now seem peculiarly a function of the large metropolis?

8. And finally, what do we do about the flight from controversy which gives rise to the vacuum in local politics and leadership?

These are prime questions and, as I said, there [currently] is no consensus upon which to rest a set of answers. However we might wish otherwise, one cannot bring together the various geographical pieces of the metropolis and find assembled the jigsaw of a completed program. Not even "the experts" can do it—they are as divided in their answers as the electorate, and perhaps more so. Their visions of "the city" are as diverse as the nine descriptions of the legendary elephant: economists (usually conservative as well as pessimistic) see "major forces"; architects (usually heroic and optimistic) see buildings and articulated spaces; political scientists (usually critical and manipulative) see groups and pressures and

---

[1] At the time of this speech, Clark Kerr was Chancellor of the Berkeley campus of the University of California. A few years later he became president of the entire University. He lost that job in part because California's governor Ronald Reagan was displeased about the Free Speech Movement, which was born at U.Cal–Berkeley.

elections. Add six more disciplines and multiply by the number of men who must make speeches or write articles, and you may get metropolitan government—but you won't by that step alone get an agreed-upon program of action.

What We Don't Get with Metropolitan Government

Then what are we getting, when we get metropolitan government? If your patience allows, let me add a few more "what we won't automatically gets."

We won't automatically get tax savings because of greater efficiency and economy—in fact, I doubt whether any metropolitan government will, over the long pull, ever show a tax decrease. The trend of the times is against it; the backlog of necessary replacement and new service expenditures is too great. Also, we have no clear evidence that efficiency increases with scale; only that effectiveness of service *may* increase and expectations or service *will* increase.

Second, we're not automatically going to get a more beautiful city. Not simply because no two architects or laymen seem to agree on what civic beauty really is, but because aesthetics have been assigned to the agenda of private rather than public action, and the advent of metropolitan government can at most only nudge ahead the still small trend toward legislated beauty.

Third, we're not suddenly going to gain mastery over the great forces [that] shape our urban environment, no matter how many heroes in City Hall. We're not going to be able overnight to produce changes in the structure and growth of our population; we're not going to change the Arabs, the Russians, or the Chinese; we're not going to hold back the technological revolutions now taking form on the drawing board of a Bell Laboratory engineer or in the machine shop of a latter-day Henry Ford. These avalanches of change are always hanging about us, and we can keep them from falling only at the cost of remaining motionless.

Fourth, we're not automatically going to get the political leadership or the technical know-how with which even the most unwieldy governmental mechanisms can work and without which even the best will fail.

What We Do Get with Metropolitan Government

What are we getting? Why does it seem a good thing to be moving toward some system of metropolitan government?

First and last, we are getting a process of government: a formal, legitimate means through which we can not only argue our differences about how to live in and with the city but can also resolve them. We are creating an instrument [that] makes our arguments meaningful—which leads to a decision and to a modicum of agreement, not to continued uncertainty and drift.

To put all this in historical perspective, we are—in establishing metropolitan governments—completing some unfinished constitutional business. The Founding Fathers failed to mention local government in the constitution—which is not too surprising, since they were concentrating on the vacuum in *national* affairs. Had the same deliberate consideration been given to local government by Madison and his colleagues, would it have been likely that the same general principle would not have been applied—i.e., that communities within communities, local as well as state, should be given political identity and nearly equal shares in the nation's total power to govern?

In a haphazard way, local government in the United States has fought its way over the intervening years toward full partnership in the power to govern, as given the states and national government in 1787; it has never fully acquired it. Now urban, the United States in creating metropolitan instruments may—and I think should—extend the federal principle to a third general level of American government, and in so doing, help local government in this country to come of age. One of the greatest benefits will then be to exploit fully at three levels what so far has worked well at two: the continuous stimulus of overlapping communities acting simultaneously, sometimes in conflict, always competitively, withal in concert.

Why the metropolis as the principal instrumentality of this third general level of American government? It is not enough to say that we are now all urban. Nor is it enough—or even accurate—to say that the metropolis is now the expression of the "most natural" urban community—for we know that in many a real sense, the metropolis is no community at all. Nor can we retreat to the mystique of "a region" (which too often has no meaning except as a semantic escape from problems we can't seem in real life to find answers to).

The justification [for metropolitan government] lies in the fact that we have found in the metropolis a potential unit of local government that represents the full range of [opinions] that exist among Americans as to how the city is to be built and life in an urban setting is to be lived: rural and urban, suburb and central city, white and nonwhite, rich and poor, provincial and cosmopolitan. It offers the one means we have, short of the state and nation, to bring back into the play of general debate the questions [that] have been tucked away in our segregated jurisdictions to bring to decision questions which, when answered only by fractions of the community, limit debate and sacrifice the wisdom and stimulus of diversity.

It is, then, nothing short of a process of government that we are creating, and a system of government that we are perfecting.

At that level of enterprise, what criteria and commandments should we observe? I have a Scotchman's dozen to suggest:

1. To create this instrument, we will need for a time a coalition in each community: a latter-day Constitutional Convention of all sectors of the metropolis, to agree on the ground rules by which thereafter they will express and resolve their disagreements. These coalitions already exist. The danger is that they will not be recognized for what they might be and that they will form and disband before their essential purpose has been fulfilled. Some of them will never get off the ground, or serve otherwise than [as] window dressing, or make pious proclamations of great civic deeds that ought to be done; and too many of them will squander their opportunity on the development of projects rather than institutions. But the nobler role of these coalitions as constitution-makers for the metropolis should and will not escape notice of an essential number of communities perceptive of historical development and necessity.

2. The nature—or certain destiny—of this instrument we are creating should be general in purpose and power. We are establishing a process of government, not merely an administrative convenience. Since I can find no historical instance of a single-purpose agency evolving into a general government, my own bent is to press for an immediate step into a fully designed system of metropolitan

government. But if the decision is to try the gradualist device of functional authorities, the least one should learn from the dogged refusal of such authorities in the past to "evolve" [that it is wise to stipulate] that after a given number of years the question should automatically be put to a referendum vote [as to] whether the special unit should then be translated into a more general process of government.

3. The metropolitan system of government, as I've already hinted, should be federal in character. It's rather ironic, isn't it, that it took the Canadians of Toronto to remind us of a technique of achieving unity within diversity which it was our genius once to have intended? But there is still some further room for invention. To adapt federalism to the metropolitan scene is going to require some devises yet unfashioned—for allowing new constituent units to be added as metropolitan growth continues (especially across state lines) and obsolescent jurisdictions gracefully to disappear; for avoiding ponderous systems of representation and duplicative administrative machinery; for tolerating diversity of service and tax levels with a given range of standards.

4. The grants of power to the metropolitan government and to its component units should be broad and generous. The first criterion of this—as I think of any organization system—should be to release power rather than to constrain it. What we are trying to do is to generate and exploit the creative energy [that] local government represents; this can only be done when every unit feels the power to act and has access to "the big issues." In our small-minded way, we have already begun to write into our incipient metropolitan charters the very reverse of the principle by attempting to identify and assign exclusive jurisdictions for metropolitan and constituent governments. The moral of Article I of the constitution seems to have been lost on us; its genius lay not in establishing exclusive jurisdictions but in encouraging a mutuality of concern.[2] It is the elastic clause and the possibility of simultaneous action at both levels which we ought to be stressing in our metropolitan charters.

---

[2] Article I of the Constitution sets up Congress, how its members are to be elected, what its powers and limitations are, and how those powers and limitations relate to those of the states.

In the give and take between borough and metropolis lies the vitality of the system. The more the better; and the more it will be, if both levels are given competence to act on a broad range of the community's problems.

5. The structure of metropolitan government should encourage strong political leadership, by providing for an elected chief executive. To get acceptance of metropolitan government, the system will have to give aspiring politicians something to shoot for. To work, the system will need a focal point of action. The American presidency is abundant proof of the virtues of elected executive leadership; strange if we should neglect its advantages in the constitutions we build for the metropolis.

I would argue this "strong metromayor" plan for another reason: the need in the United States to build a much broader base of positions upon which to rest a career in politics, and a training ground for high executive office in the United States.

6. Adequate staff should be provided. First for the executive; here one can turn again to the American presidency, whose Executive Office represents only a larger version of the kind of institution [that] needs to be developed at the metropolitan level. Second, for the legislature; what has been done in the way of staffing for Congress needs also to be done on a junior scale for our urban lawmakers.

7. There should be a system of checks and balances as effective (though not necessarily the same) as those in the federal constitution, to keep a faction or single interest from capturing this instrument of metropolitan government. There is danger now, that the lopsided coalitions now emerging in our metropolitan areas—the most familiar of these alliances being the ones concerned with commuter transportation and the central business district—will form metropolitan governments preponderantly in their own realm and image.

8. In addition to staff, metropolitan governments should be able to count on a continuing stream of basic and applied research. Industry has come to know the value of research; community government has been almost totally deprived of it. Startling as it may seem to suggest it, industry's ratio of two to seven dollars of research for every $100 of gross income would not be too bad a figure to

shoot for. That much of this governmental research would be done by nongovernmental agencies should go without saying.

9. Given the scale of metropolitan government and urban populations, a whole repertoire of new civic processes needs to be developed, for sounding out public opinion and for encouraging discussion, debate, and participation. We have little more now than the devices of eighteenth-century rural democracy. In public opinion research, in the neighborhood councils of Kansas City and Philadelphia, and in the electronic media of Pittsburgh's WQED and San Bernadino's Metroplex may lie the prototypes of tomorrow's machinery of urban government.

10. An accounting system should be devised [that] will facilitate longer-range calculation of social costs. [Such a system] would reflect the blending of public and private accounts that—whatever our political doctrine—is more and more in evidence in the modern urban community. [Such a system would quantify] the "costs" to the community and to the firm of neighborhood deterioration and the "benefits" of renewal.

11. With as much system and commitment of resources as we devoted to agricultural extension, metropolitan government will have to work at improving the adjustment of the immigrant groups of urban life. It is not enough to turn over the heartland of the metropolis to the untutored use of successive generations of urban newcomers. Whether at the source of the migrant streams, or at the urban delta onto which they spill, or both, a program of habilitation must be developed. Public housing, we now know, was a abortive and ineffective first attempt. Far more thought and commitment are needed.

This is my Scotchman's Dozen. The twelfth I have kept from you is what the more generous Irish have long ago contributed to the urbane tradition of politics: "Keep your sense of humor."

Now that I look back over the miracles I've suggested as historical necessity, I think I'd not only add that twelfth commandment, I'd start and end with it.

The Deserted City

(Published in the *Journal of the American Institute of Planners*, February 1959)[1]

"Where and what is the City of the Myth? It is the intimation of perfection and principle [that] is always just ahead of us, barely discernible, and never within reach. Search for it, and you will achieve not the city of your dream but a city of continued life and steady progress. Quit the search, and the jungle closes in."

I

My topic, and my concern, is the Deserted City. If what everyone is saying is true, that the City is being abandoned, then this is the central fact for planners to think about in an age of change. I agree there is danger that the City may be abandoned. But I doubt if you and I are thinking about the same city. Not the least of our troubles is that no two of us ever do.

What is this City which I fear we may turn our backs on? Let's begin to identify it by reviewing the cities that some say are being deserted.

The City of the Central Business District

One is the City of the Central Business District. This city has very few citizens; its proprietors don't generally think in those terms. So we measure its abandonment by reference to dollars lost—sales, property values, profits, and taxes. Yet despite such quaint variance

---

[1] Reprinted by permission of the *Journal of the American Planning Association*, Volume XXV, No. 1, February 1959.

from civic tradition, this city, of all the cities in distress, seems least in danger. It is showered with attention, and the likelihood is that no expense will be spared to save it. Its defenders are legion, though somewhat oddly diverse. They include, of course, the holders of downtown properties, many of them absentee landlords who long ago moved to the suburbs and who have realized nearly too late the stakes they left politically unguarded behind them. Allied with them, as needs be, are the politicians and administrators of the central city, who must save this last remaining stronghold of a dwindling tax base or surrender their empire. But joining them of late are some unexpected though interesting faces: for example, the artists and patrons of the arts and, more recently, the academics who have discovered to their bargaining advantage that culture-in-the-downtown has a dollar value which the threat of demise has taught businessmen and city officials to appreciate.

I sometimes wonder why we ever worried that this city might be deserted. There are too many interests involved and the value of the city's heartland is too great for that area to be permanently forsaken. If it is deserted, it will be because of a surfeit of attention: too many superhighways driven into the heart of downtown, suffocating rather than reviving the patient, and a diet of investment expenditures so rich that the community around succumbs in the effort to support it.

The City of the Gray Area

Another is the City of the Gray Area, that growing wasteland which starts at a moving point uncomfortably close to the central business district and extends to a moving point uncomfortably close to the better residential suburbs. "Mice Country," as former Louisville mayor Charles Farnsley has so compassionately named it. This city, too, is being abandoned; but that in itself is nothing new. It has been abandoned two, three, and in some cases four times before, by the successive waves of migrants who have come looking for the City only to be told that it was still a suburb or two ahead of them. Certainly, the City of the Gray Area, the Mice Country, is being abandoned; but that is its function. For this is not really a city; it is a social process wrapped up in an appropriately shabby form. It is a process of transition and aspiration and self-improvement—for the immigrant from abroad, for the rural uprooted, for a wide assortment of human beings who are at the bottom rung of their life's ambitions. The irony is that we are abandoning the process but preserving the form. By restrictive national legislation we are cutting down the intake of those immigrants we have been historically willing to assimilate. At the same time we are blocking the suburban exit for the increasing numbers of immigrants whose humble services we want but whose company we would prefer not to keep. Now we have tenements without a trail—mile after growing mile of tenements, shabbier by the year, a wretched form that has lost the saving grace of a noble function. And where are the friends and favorable economic forces to renew this city, the City of the Mice and the Gray?

The City of the Suburbs

The latest City to be abandoned is the City of the Suburbs, though not yet on an overt or wholesale basis. Plans to leave ship are already being prepared by the more perceptive and somewhat sleeker descendants of the species who earlier emigrated from Mice Country. They still don't know where to go, but they're on their way. Some will move farther out, to the City That Soon Will Be; some are going back to the City That Might Have Been, where they will build islands of comfort snugly close to the citadel of the central business district, or a bit more daringly distant but still safely near some remaining outpost of an academic or cultural institution. Some will go to the splendid isolation of the critic's pulpit, or, like me, will on to the safe retreat of philanthropy. Yet most of these half-country cousins will not have the prescience or the means to remove themselves physically from the City of the Suburbs. Instead, they will flee it by withdrawing deeper and deeper into the tight private sector of the home. There they will maintain their own city, and on their half-acre plots will operate their own parks, playgrounds, and swimming pools; their own transportation systems, with two or three automotive vehicles, each designed for a different use; their own cultural and recreational programs, with TV, radio, and hi-fi; and, if the paths of Governor Faubus[2] and the electronic pedagogues

---

[2] In September 1957, Arkansas governor Orval Faubus called out the National Guard to prevent black students from entering Little Rock's all-white Central High

continue by weird coincidence to merge, their own private school systems. Not to mention a computer system of machinery, maintenance, and warehousing to go with it.

In short, the abandonment of the City of the Suburbs to the anarchy of do-it-yourself.

Cities of Low Orbit

We have been discussing fragments of cities. But whole ones, too, will be deserted—the Cities of Low Orbit. Signs are that these cities will not survive the forces set in motion by the massive competition of the age of economic growth into which we are now being drawn by the Cold War, by the internal logic of our own development, and, one would hope, by a selfless national determination to speed the economic progress of the less developed countries in the world about us.

Unless it becomes nothing less than all-out governmental policy to rule otherwise, this economic competition is almost certain to favor those urban areas which either reached a critical size before the economic race began in earnest or, by force of leadership and some accident of location, had managed to assert a gravitational pull of their own.

Deserted cities are not new; what is new is the size of those [that] have lately become vulnerable. In the emerging universe of urban constellations, not just the Small Town but even some Standard Metropolitan Areas will encounter competitive gravitational pulls they cannot counteract. At best, their fate will be that of satellite communities, with borrowed life and captive will; at worst, [they will have] no life or will whatsoever.

The City Beautiful

There are still other cities being forgotten, and they are not just pieces of real estate.

You know well the retreat from the City Beautiful; your profession, I will be ungracious enough to say, fought nearly every inch of

---

School. A federal court, citing *Brown vs. Board of Education*, ordered Faubus to remove the National Guardsmen, and later that month President Eisenhower had to send in federal troops to enforce the court's order.

that road as a rear guard unit. And there are evidences that as a profession you're still occupying the offshore islands, spending much of your substance and time wondering whether the City Beautiful ought to be reoccupied. The conversations and curricula you seem naturally to fall into are still about architecture and design; the heroes of your profession are those who have built great buildings or done other wondrous things in three dimensions; and you seem still to welcome each new wave of super-buildings (offices, schools, mass housing, and industrial parks) as the long awaited D-Day of re-entry. But cities have more than three dimensions; and people, especially architects, have conflicting ideas of beauty.

The vision of the City Beautiful I hope we will keep. The myopia of so many of its designers is, I think, well forgotten.

The City Politic

We have also made our exodus from the City Politic, but here you would not expect a political scientist like myself to be quite so content. Frankly, neither am I content with the way some of my colleagues have defined that city and the supposed means by which they say it can and ought to be resettled. If the prescription for that city runs three parts efficiency, two parts economy, one part metropolitan government reorganization, and no part for anyone but the political scientist, then I [say] let this city go the way of the City Beautiful.

But there is more to the City Politic than that, and I genuinely fear the signs of its desertion. Its main institution [has] always been a common legislature with all segments of the urban population represented; and where today do you find such an institution, either within the metropolis or at state and national levels? Its mode of operating had traditionally been to formulate major issues and argue them through to decision; and where today do you find a statement of the great urban issues, or the breadth and vigor of argument and decision which the scale of these unstated but very real issues suggests? Urban renewal, that iceberg of an issue whose submerged mass we have still to measure, is one of the very few great questions we have begun to identify and debate. But to get it debated and just barely recognized for action nationally, which means city by city, state by state, and above all in Congress, has already exhausted a full generation of urban specialists and statesmen.

The City of History

Finally, we are leaving the City of History. If planners were not so much the picked-on group—the beaten profession—I would be tempted to call it the City of the Physical Planner.

By the City of History I mean the physical model we have inherited from the Greeks, the Romans, and the Middle Ages and the set of visual images by which that model controls our thinking long past the time of its obsolescence. The City of History builds in dense and concentrated patterns around a single core. Into its monumental style of building, into its mode of planning by detailed prescription, and into its zoning tradition of segregated land use have been frozen that city's major premises: an immobile and class-bound population and a glacial rate of technological change.

Against all the forces [that] now set us in motion and propel us toward the periphery, I cannot see that the City of History can prevail. However much some of us with romantic memories of that city may hope that it be not so, these forces amount almost to an Iron Law of Outward Movement. Like the universe, we seem to be racing perpetually into the space around us. The thrust of technology seems persistently toward high-speed facilities [that] will drive us even farther outward. The canons of defense argue for cities [that] are deconcentrated, not walled in. The search for privacy and status still draws the population toward open land, and of open land we still have an abundance. So does our penchant for being pioneers and farmers, even if this be but a fading expression of cultural lag. So do the tactics, the economics, and not least the psychology of the automobile, that mechanized symbol and means of our release from slavery to the single place. And as we move outward, we destroy the option of reverse motion by building one-way systems of technology and communication: streets of concrete, to which we are tied as securely and for as long as we were once tied to rivers and railroads; patterns of production, distribution, and consumption tailored to the way of life and needs of a sprawled population; systems of politics and investment in social capital, which add the lingering effects of inertia.

[Entering] The City of Accelerating Change and Unstable Form

As this new form emerges, one sees not the city of the single cell but the metropolis of many. I think the biologist would more quickly recognize and more easily adapt to this new organism than the planner or the social scientist. The biologist has already come to expect of nature the process of metamorphosis, the process by which a given creature develops into a different and more complex form of being and, who knows, perhaps into a better one. Better or not, this new City is adapting to the function it is expected to serve, in this different world which nature, in its wisdom or folly, has obliged it to enter.

But further than this the biologist has nothing to offer; for this is a process of creative evolution in which the organism, at least according to the philosophers of free will, has a modicum of choice in determining the nature of its next form and way of life. Nowhere in the literature of political biology will you find a description and therefore a model for this next stage in the development of the city—for the simple reason that it has never existed before, and in many of its essential parts it is still to be created.

One thing we do know about this future city, enough to give it a title: it will be the City of Accelerating Change and Unstable Form. Its main problems will be the ever-exaggerating ones of personal and civic adjustment to social mobility and of economic and administrative accommodation to rapid obsolescence of function and physical plant. Almost certainly, this will be the era of the discardable building, the movable utility system, and the landscape [that] can be changed overnight.

From there on, your guess about this future city will be as good as mine.

But this is the city we are entering, not abandoning. My purpose was to describe the city I fear we may desert.

II

This city of my concern is in a sense all the cities I have mentioned, yet none of them. The planner worth his trust should feel deeply the demise of any actual city, yet have a vision of a city beyond all of them, even the city of his immediate future.

The city I'm referring to (let's not play cat and mouse any longer) is a myth; and the planners we look for are those sensitive enough, farsighted enough, and hardheaded enough to appreciate a myth and to work toward at least some small measure of its realization. If you must have a name for it, call it the City of the Common Life and Noble Aspiration.

This city is always being deserted, and sometimes in ways so subtle that not even an acclaimed figure of civic life may be aware that he has departed its state of grace. If you will permit me the escape into allegory, which all social critics have honorably resorted to, let me allude to some of these new entries into the book of civic sin. In the tradition of Dante, descend with me into my Inferno and visit one by one the graduated levels of urban culpability.

The Infernal City

To give you the general design, there are three major levels, and on each of these levels one finds those who in life had abandoned the city unwittingly, thinking rather that they were still loyal subjects within the realm. The largest grouping of these (they are so relatively innocent they can be named) are the well-meaning suburbanites who took to heart what the planners of their day had told them: viz., that open green plots far from the madding crowd were the first essentials of the good civic life, and that population density bred bad civic manners. (I might add that the planners who told them that will be found several infernal stages below, along with those other consultants who are now telling suburbanites that all they need do to save the City is either to forsake their half-acres and move home and way-of-life back downtown, or at least to do more of their shopping there, by automobile.) Being myself a citizen of the suburb, I'll confess I've taken the same liberty Dante did, and have assigned my kind of people to the nicest part of Hades.

On the same general level with my suburbanites, but on the ledge just below them, are those who with the best motives missed the boat in distinguishing the long- from the short-run interests of the City. The results were prodigal amounts of wasted energy and resources, wasted in trying to hold back the inevitable, or to build against nature, or to preserve monuments of the past [that] did nothing but dam the streaming future.

Next below is the group [that] unwittingly confused [its] own special interests with the general interests of the city, or admitted no other: capital improvements for my neighborhood but for no others; I'll skim the cream off the urban renewal potential and you take what's left; better schools but not better neighborhoods; better neighborhoods but not better schools; socialized highways but not socialized transit. You can provide your own damnable list. (By the way, if you should be wondering why the special interests are set down below the short-run interests in this hellish arrangement, it's because the job of discerning the general interest of the present is doubly easier than that of discerning the general interest of the future. All around you in your city, if you will only look for them, are the living reminders of other concerns and other problems than your own.)

One tier farther down is reserved for those who thought the answers to the city's problems required no thought, no adaptation, and no specifics: the patent medicine boys of the urban world. You will understand if I identify them no further; suffice it to say there are quite a lot of them, and they're now selling remedies for the ills [that] beset their companions down below.

On the next nether shelf are those who have acted to break up the city into unrelated parts, destroying the ties [that] keep us one; ties that when broken prevent us from enjoying the benefits of diversity which the city, and especially the American city, has always symbolized. This sin of segregation, not only of color but also of class, of taste, of way of life, and even of economic function and land use, is a sin against the spirit of the city, and as such the worst.

We have still two more general levels to visit, but the heat would probably be more than you could stand. So let me just give you the rough outlines of the remaining design.

On Level Number Two are arranged the same categories of sinners as above, in same descending order of succession. The groups found on this second level are distinguished from their less miserable counterparts above by the simple fact that they sinned knowingly and, indeed, willingly. They are not placed lower in Hades because at least they gave a kind of life to the community.

At the lowest level and spilling on into the Pit are those who did nothing at all. Their motto on Earth was, "Let everything go to hell."

And, appropriately, they were the first to be dispatched—and all the way to the bottom.

I have said nothing about researchers and philanthropoids in Hades, but there is an ugly rumor going around that they are concentrated on this lowest level. There are no facts to support this rumor, but I was given some clue when I searched the upper levels, looking for someone who could organize a research project on the subject. I could find only a handful of competent candidates to do the job, and not a single lost soul to finance it.

III

Let's come back to earth. What good is a myth to a planner who has to live with reality?

Number one, he can use the myth as a prod, to his own further growth and to the leavening of the special interests he must work with. There is no individual performance that can't do with improvement, and no proposal for action that couldn't profit from having its sights raised. The city of the myth can always be defined properly and safely as what has been done, or as what is being proposed, *plus*. The value of that elastic and undefined extra is the powerful incentive that has always shown the way to refinement and progress.

Number two, the planner can use the myth as a measure of scale and proportion and equity and as a critique of goals and techniques and progress. Let me cite some specifics. In the perspective of the city of the myth, what will it avail if the central business district is saved, suburbia made to flourish, and the gray area left to rot? Or if aesthetics are confused with welfare and economics, and zoners are assigned to achieve for the gray area what only politics, justice, and social and economic engineering can accomplish? Or if we spend too little on urban renewal in those areas of the city where some bolder expenditures might generate a continuing flow of private funds, and in the realization of that failure proceed to waste more substantial outlays on other sectors of the city with no such potential? Or if we accept business leadership as the equivalent of political action, and in our ensuing enchantment with "real power" minimize the role of the politician? Or if we submit abjectly to the

Automobile Vote (surely the most unique and massive coalition of single-minded pressures ever to have hit the American political scene, including as it does both consumers and producers), and let the city become but the sorcerer's apprentice of the highway? Or if, in the short-term interests of the central city, the suburb, and all manner of scared or aggressive communities, we go off on a mercantilist jag and wind up with a Balkanized economy (the professionals in the trade might rather say, a system with very substantial external diseconomies)? Or if we continue to welcome, as we do by feeding the fires of economic growth, the massive in-migration of low-income and predominantly nonwhite additions to the urban labor force, but refuse to offer them the historic reward of the opportunity for social advance and assimilation?

Nothing short of our myth of the [City of] Common Life and Noble Aspiration can fully measure the inadequacy and shortsightedness of these approaches.

Number three, the myth is the most potent weapon the planner has in the rough and ready game of power politics to which he is properly and inevitably committed. But it takes a planner with the practiced eye and bargaining skill of a politician to recognize its full strength. Despite all talk to the contrary, the Great Seal of the City, the declaration that this is in the general interest of the community, is a prize for which the mightiest will not only contend but will also make major concessions to secure. True, the Great Seal is not the planner's alone to dispense, but he is strategically placed in the chain of the official decision as it is developed. Indeed he is uniquely placed, because his job is to phrase the agenda of the future, and to draw the first draft—and sometimes the last—of a program to deal with it.

I know it has been popular play among political scientists to ridicule the planner for his political ineffectiveness. But the prescription which usually follows is even more ineffective: viz., if the planner and his office could be moved closer to the mayor, he would automatically gain more influence over public policy. Organizational status may well be irrelevant. The question I would stick by as a prod and, where deserved, as a criticism is: Have you exploited the full bargaining power of the asset you command, the leverage of the myth?

Number four, the myth can be a constant stimulus to the construction of new ideas, for the myth is by definition the symbol of the new and undiscovered. Not new ideas just for the sake of novelty and intellectual gamesmanship; new ideas because they are badly needed and because the power of an idea cannot be matched. To this truth there is an additional dimension which again works in your favor: as someone has said, there is nothing so powerful as an idea whose time has come. It is the luck and challenge of your professional assignment to be responsible for developing these ideas in advance of their time.

My comments may sound high-flown. I would have thought so too, before it came my turn—with the brevet rank we hold as philanthropoids—to make the rounds of the councils of the mighty, and to see them as they too often are: assemblies of power, waiting anxiously for an idea of where to go.

Number five, the final function of the myth may well be its most important: to give the planner a full measure of humility and optimism. A strange combination of traits? The more I see of the subtle process of social change and development, the more meaningful to me the combination of those two attitudes becomes. I'm far from ready to become one of the latter-day disciples of Adam Smith, though I've a growing affection for the master himself. Nor am I yet old or wise or patient enough to say as firmly as did the aging Benjamin Franklin of the Constitutional Convention: "I have lived, Sire, a long time, and the longer I live, the more convincing proofs I see of this truth—that God governs in the affairs of men." But I am ready to confess that there is more wisdom in the pattern of our everyday, marginal adjustments to life than readily meets the eye and, distressingly often, more wisdom in that pattern than in many of the grand designs to which the heroic tradition of our civilization disposes us.

As a critique of our actions, the myth can be a cruel taskmaster. As an invitation to search in the detail of our life for the hints and promise of general principle, the myth can be reassurance itself.

You will of course have to be careful with myth. Myths have made benevolent men into tyrants [and] intemperate ones into Captain Ahabs whose compulsions are not to search for the myth but to find it, not to gain sight of it but to possess and destroy it. You'll have to watch out for the slippery folk who will want you to trade in your myth for a model of their own making.

Also, you've got to remember that the myth is no substitute for a program of action. I'm reminded of that escapist tendency in all of us, one expression being our recent enchantment with the concept of the region. When we chant this work with solemn liturgical majesty, particularly as we add the prayerful words "coordination" and "research" and "interdisciplinary cooperation" (I recommend you try all this in the minor mode), we may well be mesmerized in the belief that we have come upon a solution of all the urban problems [that] beset us. At this point, it will help if you phrase some sacrilegious definition of the myth [that] you can recite with a devilish but soul-saving chuckle. I'm fond of one such definition I've come across for the region, which runs thus: "A region is an area safely larger than the last one to whose problems we found no solution."

In this age of scientific and political skepticism, we may be put on the defensive if we do anything so old-fashioned as to adopt a myth as a working device. But every profession has its myth, and none could have achieved greatness without it. The lawyer has Justice; the doctor, Health; the educator, Truth; the social worker, Brotherly Love. Yours is the City, which is all of these and more; and I think you have chosen exceedingly well.

You will ask the final question. Where and what is the City of the Myth? I know only one answer, and it has been given many times before:

It is the intimation of perfection and principle [that] is always just ahead of us, barely discernible, and never within reach. Search for it, and you will achieve not the City of your dream but a City of continued life and steady progress. Quit the search, and the jungle closes in.

The Brave New Urban World

(Presented to the World Traffic Engineering Conference,
Washington, D.C., August 21, 1961)

*"Planning is politics; but it is even more than that.
Politics has the job of reconciling the known past
with the known present; planning has to make both
the past and present compatible with an unknown
future. If politics is the art of the possible, planning
comes close to being the art of the impossible."*

In recent months, a city has been forced by international events to
become the decisive pawn in the present chess game of man's
destiny and to shoulder the eternal problem of war or peace.

As if a city didn't already have problems enough!

But if the issue of war or peace must be faced, I for one am
relieved that it will be posed in the context of the city. The everyday
realities of urban life hold some hope of pricking the balloons of
ideological conflict and of reducing argument to agreement. Anyone
who would argue theory in the context of the city can't go more
than a few hours without getting constructively concerned with such
practical questions as whether the water pressure is adequate and
the sewers run clear.

Because of this earthiness, the city is a steadying influence in
world politics and has already shown a staying power that I'm
wagering will do much to keep the human animal a creative part of
nature's order for a very long time—long past the days of this
generation and its present differences. As you can see, I'm an
optimist—and a poor choice, perhaps, to talk about urban problems,
past and future.

For I've noticed, and I'm sure you have, that the approved way to
talk about cities these days is to speak solemnly, sadly, ominously,

and fearfully about their problems. You really don't rate as an expert on the city unless you foresee its doom. The city must, of course, always be in crisis and on the verge of catastrophe. No speaker should ever give it more than a fifty-fifty chance to survive past tomorrow; as a matter of fact, it probably died yesterday because the "shambles" we see before us can't properly be called a city anymore.

I've preached plenty of these sermons of doom myself. But standing helpless before the misery of the 650,000 citizens of Calcutta who have nowhere else to sleep but on the streets; running for my life in the madness of Parisian traffic; packed like a sardine in the stalled subways of Manhattan; befuddled by the din and density of a barrio in San Juan; left incredulous by the logical impossibility of any tomorrow for Hong Kong; reduced to absolute impotence in trying to find a street address in Tokyo—in the middle of all this, [I am aware of] the simple reality that these cities do exist, that they exist because people have chosen that they exist, and [that they] grow because increasing numbers of people are choosing to live in them. This simple reality has forced me to ask whether it isn't about time we view the city as less a set of problems than as a very substantial human success.

I want to drive this point home, for probably the most dangerous of our urban problems is that we do such a poor job of defining them. As a result, we go riding off in all directions, like Don Quixote tilting at windmills, like King Lear blindly vowing "to do such things—what they are yet, I know not—but they shall be the terrors of the earth."

Consider the city of the twentieth century as basically a success. This is easy enough to demonstrate in the more affluent societies by the simple act of contrast. Take a dissatisfied citizen. Say, a taxpayer of Toronto who has just been given the bill for the new subway system; or a voter from Miami disenchanted with Metro; or an Oxford don fresh from seeing the plans for a new highway across his favorite college grounds; or a pedestrian in The Hague pinned by a twenty-foot automobile against the medieval wall of a ten-foot street; or a Tokyo subway rider, the last to be pushed into a rush-hour car by the [workers whose job is exactly that]. Take any one of these to the squatters' settlements of Karachi or through the slums of Rio, and he will return thoroughly chastened, wondering why he should ever have thought his mother city had problems worth mentioning.

But more squarely, ask the least fortunate in any urban setting, affluent or under-developed—the Negro ghettoed in New York or London, or the *bustee walla* of old Delhi—ask whether he would choose to return to the rural area from which he or his people came, and the answer far more often than not is a revealing No.

The city is his choice, for if it has not given him perfection, it has given him progress; and if not progress, it has offered hope; and if not much hope, it has meant survival.

The twentieth-century city—let us not forget it—has managed to be this symbol and sanctuary for staggering numbers of the world's exploding population. How Hong Kong has done it, no one quite knows; it's a miracle no less than the feeding of the five thousand with but five loaves of bread and two fishes. The American city has served almost as dramatically; it has been the agent of a surprisingly peaceful revolution which has made a nation of farmers into a nation of urbanites, broken up the single ghetto of the Negro South into a liberating diffusion of dissolving ghettos in far-flung cities across the country, and brought the children of backwoods and backwater bondage into the mainstream of American life. Already the European city is breaking its rigidities to admit the first contingents of an international labor force, whose mobility will be an essential of a united continent and a common market. Japanese cities have risen phoenix-like from the ashes; Tokyo, a cemetery of men and buildings only fifteen years ago, has not only been rebuilt but has become the largest city in the world and is absorbing 300,000 new citizens annually.

The twentieth-century city has also survived the staggering impact of modern science and technology. Painfully and imperfectly, yes. But from one logic of the railroad and the workshop in the loft to the radically different logic of the truck and the horizontal factory, the industrialized city has suffered the pangs of an almost complete metamorphosis and survived. An even greater metamorphosis is in store for the cities of the less industrialized nations, and even greater travail. Yet one can see already the emerging signs of ultimate success—though I admit these signs are easier to find in the abstracted statistics of national growth in India and Pakistan than when one stands in the present squalor of their cities and tries to discern it.

By now, recalling all that you have known and heard and seen of decaying and deserted cities, you're probably muttering that I'm not only an optimist; I'm daft.

I'm not. Admit the problems, but don't let them obscure the important fact that the twentieth-century city—or by its new name, the metropolis—has already done what two generations of prophets have said was impossible. It has survived; and in more cases than not, it has prospered.

Frankly, we haven't consciously done much to help the city in its travail. Mostly we've sinned against it. Let me cite our major transgressions.

1. We have opposed and ignored the city and stacked the political cards against it. Rural domination of public revenue and policy has been an almost universal fact of life; whether in West Virginia or in West Bengal, the fact applies and the effects are evident. The city has been the late, lamented, and abandoned child of aging rural parentage. Even now, with the prospect of literally hundreds of millions to be added to the world's urban population in the next generation, public policies of industrialized nations and the five-year plans of industrializing nations alike are weighted heavily in favor of rural schemes and investments. Like crabs, we are walking backwards into our urban future and begrudging every step along the way.

2. We have shackled the city in rusty jurisdictional chains.

Baseball fans are far more realistic than the devotees of municipal law. In the language of baseball, Kansas City means Kansas City—the whole market shed of paid attendance [that] flows in from two states and hundreds of surrounding communities. But try to operate a common sewage or revenue system over that same area, and you'll find yourself far out in left field and in a quite different ballpark.

Nature made one harbor for Hanshin and another in Tokyo Bay; but Japanese politics have divided those single harbors into four and five independent port authorities. Calcutta has one port, one river, one future; but forty municipalities will have to find agreement before that future is made into anything better than another today.

By present standards, Caesar was dealing with absolute simplicity when he found Gaul divided into only three parts. Today's Caesar would find New York divided into 1,400; and I doubt [that] even with the help of Moses Caesar would be able to conquer it.

3. We have set loose on the city the raw forces of technological change, given the city no advance warnings, done little to cushion the impact, and developed no feedback mechanism to adapt technological developments rationally to the city's necessities. Cities have been made to adapt to transportation systems, rather than transportation systems to cities. Housing and public works technology has been developed for the most part in the image of producer interests, rarely by a calculated schedule of community needs. Billions are being spent by nations to send a man to the moon or to his final destruction; it's already got to the point when a cosmonaut can make it round the world in the time it takes a suburbanite to get to work, or a traveler to get from downtown to the airport. Meanwhile, the principal U.S. agency for urban affairs could barely scrape through Congress this year with a research appropriation of $375,000—a Congress, incidentally, that approved $77 million for research relating to agriculture. By comparison—but only by comparison—Americans needn't be ashamed; you won't find more than a handful of the world's nations that are spending even proportionally as much.

4. Most seriously, we have obscured the humane purpose of the city by emphasizing its real estate. "The City is the People": that's a noble charge [that] has been honored more in the breach than in the observance. Examine the literature on the city and the substance of action programs and you will find them dominated by a concern with physical plant. The going criteria of urban success are the beauty and solvency of the city's real properties, not the condition of the people who flow through them. As a result, the civilizing and ennobling function of the city, mainly its job of turning second-class newcomers into first-class citizens, is downgraded into pious pronouncements and last-place priorities. We despair of our wasting city property and count the costs of urban renewal in building values. These are nothing compared to the wasting resources of the human beings who get trapped in these aging buildings and the value of their lost contribution to their own and the world's society.

5. The search for the public interest, the common welfare of the

city, is always an elusive one, but we have done a first-class job of thoroughly confusing it. We have divided the city into pieces, let it become a jungle of competing objectives and conflicting codes of ethics, and then blithely assumed that by some undefined process our several self-interests would add up to the common benefit. This is another case of man seeing a guiding hand that may or may not be there. Judging from the growing disorder about us, I'm not so sure the faith is justified. And the logic isn't so good either: does it follow that if downtown commercial and industrial development is subsidized to help the central city and its business district more effectively compete with suburban development, which is also subsidized, that the general interest of the larger community is thereby benefited?

The stirring arguments for these two pieces of supposed urban progress are best heard separately. As anyone who has had to deal with such competing claims knows, you can define a civic enthusiast as one who has listened to one appeal, and a skeptic as one who has been around long enough to listen to two.

As I say, we have divided the city into the separate realms of our several self-interests. The city has been subjected to a feudalism [that] doesn't even have the saving grace of a central sovereign to bind it together. Berlin is a dramatic and catastrophic example, but the sectionalism which underlies it is everywhere. Travel the Yamata Loop Line in Tokyo and you will find the separate baronies of railroad and department-store developments into which that metropolitan area is divided. Live a day with the mayor of any city and count the beseeching delegations who want the community rebuilt or the veto groups that want it preserved, each in its own image. Or consult the professions, the experts, and you will find that the same feudal instinct has infected the intellect: the architect, the economist, the sociologist, the political scientist—I dare say, maybe even a few highway and traffic engineers—each has staked out his claim to the whole city and, not getting the whole, has claimed a piece and made himself king.

Humpty-Dumpty—and can all the world's horses and the world's men ever put the city together again?

Well, I don't know about all the world's horses (they're probably saying "I told you so" out in the pastures to which you traffic engineers have relegated them), but I do know that more and more of the world's men seem ready to try. From Auckland to Zagreb, from Venice to Venezuela, there's working evidence of concern with our cities that is moving the urban problem toward the top of the public priority list where it belongs. Items:

- The United States is seriously considering cabinet rank for its housing agency, making it a Department of Urban Affairs.

- Japan, as a developed nation, broke new ground last year by asking the United Nations to provide technical assistance in planning the development of one of its major urban regions.

- West Bengal has created a Metropolitan Planning Agency for Calcutta, requesting assistance from the World Bank, the World Health Organization, the government of India, and a full range of technical advisers internationally recruited to help prepare a twenty-five-year development plan for the entire metropolitan area.

- Bangkok has completed a master plan; Brazil and Pakistan are building new capital cities; Baghdad, Athens, Logos, Khartoum, Amsterdam—these are but a few of the lengthening list of the world's cities [that] are taking serious thought for their urban tomorrow.

And let us not forget my own town of Cranbury, New Jersey.

A hamlet of 2,000 people who this year took a last long nostalgic look at a 300-year history of agricultural quiet faced about to read the handwriting which the advancing empires of Philadelphia and New York had placed on their walls, and then stepped gingerly into [its] urban future by appointing a Citizens Planning Advisory Committee. We are now one with the cities of the world and the twentieth century.

Now having created our committee (of which I am a proud member), we must confess [to] not being quite sure how to put our city of the twentieth century together or go about this new-fangled thing called comprehensive planning.

We know we should reserve some green space, but we don't have the money; and if we did, the green space we [bought would] probably be used more to preserve the *status quo* than for outdoor picnics, which is what we can do better in our own big backyards. We know we should tighten up our controls on strip development along the highway, but our adjoining townships aren't doing so, which gives them the roadside commerce and leaves us with the headache of saying no to exceptions. We'd like to keep our farmers and their lovely green acres in business, but the nation's economic system doesn't seem anxious to cooperate. Some of us would like to improve housing and social conditions for our low-income residents (and we've got some who are pretty badly off), but we're outvoted.

We'd like to preserve the white clapboard Colonial style of our main street, but that would mean arguing with our neighbors about matters of taste; and besides, it gets awfully expensive building and rebuilding eighteenth-century houses at rates we have to pay our twentieth-century carpenters. We should be putting in a municipal sewage system, but by the time one of us has trouble with his septic tank and is nearly willing to pay public sewage assessments, two of his neighbors have just fixed and paid for theirs and don't think much of the idea. Besides, we've built our houses so far apart we're not sure a sewage system could be economically installed; and the reason we built our houses so far apart is because we have one-acre zoning; and we have one-acre zoning so we won't get so many people, because people have so many children, and children have to have schools, and schools cost so much money. The state won't give us any more money; some people say because we're the wrong political party, but really it's because no one can persuade 51 percent of the state's voters to agree to an income or sales tax, which my town wouldn't vote for either. If only we had someone who could tell us really what to do, except that we did invite a half-dozen experts in, and each of them told us something different, except they agreed we should plan for our future. I guess what we really need is some strong leadership. Of course, none of us really thinks his neighbor has what it takes to be a leader, and we're all too busy mowing our one-acre lawns and chauffeuring the kids. Besides, you can't really do the job at such a local level because there isn't enough money or power, and you don't have a large enough view of things. We really need planning at the regional level; but there isn't any region; and if the state or national government takes over, everybody says there goes democracy. And if democracy doesn't go, and if the state or the national government did take over, they wouldn't get re-elected; besides they have too many other things to do and spend their money on. Maybe we should have an entirely new system; but that would take a revolution, and ever since we won our own revolution back in 1776, and especially now that everybody has a car and TV and all that, all you can get people to vote for is an evolution. As my neighbor says, we got ours, why should we help the others get theirs—and isn't that really what planning boils down to?

Just as I was getting this earthy education, and beginning to understand why comprehending people might have trouble with comprehensive planning, the governor of metropolitan Tokyo honored our United Nations Technical Assistance Mission to Japan by inviting my colleagues and me to advise him on that great city's future development. It took me an embarrassingly long time to see how Cranbury's planning problems had any relevance to Tokyo's. But after a while I quit trying to second-guess Tokyo's own technical experts (I found that they knew more than I did about their own problems), and looked instead for the imponderables, unknowns, and inconsistencies [that] everywhere frustrate governors and citizens in this business of city planning.

Like my Cranbury citizens, the people of Tokyo do want to bring their urban development and disorder under control and to make their cities and countrysides more livable. Tokyo by common consent is too big and growing too fast, but no one wants a plan that will keep him from living and doing business there, only a plan that will keep the other fellow out. Real wages are higher, transportation facilities are better, markets are bigger in Tokyo than anywhere else in the country. So if you want rising national income and production, doesn't it logically follow that migration of labor and capital to this prospering metropolis ought to be encouraged, not discouraged? Especially since the national government of Japan has promised to double the nation's income in ten years and to reduce the agricultural population by one-quarter. Except that when you reduce the agricultural population, you weaken the government's strongholds of political support and concentrate the population in the less friendly electoral districts of the metropolis. More industry should locate away from Tokyo to provide catchment basins of jobs more equally throughout the country, but that means building more roads and other public facilities in the hinterland. Since this would mean raising taxes and imposing controls, it wouldn't be very popular with industry. And since it would mean diverting revenue and jobs from Tokyo, it wouldn't be very popular with the local government and voters there—and there are an awful lot of voters in Tokyo.

A lot remains to be done in Tokyo: 80 percent of the metropolitan area is without sewers, and no place in the world has quite the traffic problem. Streets and roads are badly needed, [and] so is parking space. For both these purposes, Tokyo has managed to reserve only one fourth the area provided by most American cities. But Tokyo was originally constructed as a maze to foil the invaders, which it did until the internal combustion engine snarled its way into the city's heart. How do you convert a maze into a grid pattern, or a radial-circumferential pattern, or any pattern that would make sense to automobile traffic? You could restrict use of cars, but I haven't found a politician in the world who was willing to stand between a man and his machine. So Tokyo must have streets, and to have streets they must have the public revenue, and to get the public revenue they must get more help from the national government— and you can finish that sentence. But even if Tokyo had more money to spend, wouldn't building more roads merely induce more traffic?—and you all can complete that sentence, too. Obviously it would, but Tokyo has no more freedom of choice than all the other free cities we know, and will decide to go ahead. But they'll have a deuce of a problem getting rights-of-way; land in the heart of Tokyo is four times as expensive as land in the heart of Manhattan. Also, by law and practice, the government has to negotiate every parcel of land before acquiring it. With few roads, there is much congestion; but one man's problems with congestion is another man's gain. Department stores located at the right congestion points can catch a fine lot of customers—300,000 a day in one excellently crammed choice location. Now Tokyo's department stores have a habit of owning commuter railways, and commuter railways don't always agree that more highways should be built, at least not where there are railroads. Maybe the transportation system of Tokyo should be coordinated, but first you'll have to get about a score of public and private operating agencies to say yes. This will be very difficult, because there is, as the Japanese say, a strong tradition of "sectionalism."

Tokyo, too, would like some green space and has followed London's example of putting large splotches of it on its comprehensive planning maps. If you are a reader of footnotes, you will then discover that at least half a million people are already living and working in this green space, which is a lot of existing uses to have to defend against an application for a new exception. Also, God gave Japan more people than land; as a result, sky-high prices of land make it awfully tempting to anyone involved in a transaction to develop land according to its highest if not its best use. Nor does it help preserve green space to have national housing agencies plant their new developments right in the middle of it; but these agencies are under pressure to provide the most possible homes with the least possible subsidy, which means small apartment units for middle-class and upper-middle-class commuters where land prices are within reach. Which doesn't mean downtown Tokyo.

If Hong Kong is a modern urban miracle, so is Tokyo and every one of its sister Japanese cities. I came away marveling at how the Japanese do it against such odds. Maybe we ought to invite them to send a technical assistance mission to Cranbury.

Meanwhile, a third city of the world has been adding to my education as a planner: Calcutta, which through the government of West Bengal has asked the Ford Foundation to finance the expert help needed to establish its own metropolitan planning agency and a twenty-five-year development plan.

If any city in the world needs a development plan, it is Calcutta. Per capita income is less than $100 a year. The population has grown from 3.5 million to 6.25 million in twelve years; 650,000 of these people call the sidewalks and streets their home. Only two out of 100 of the city's families have homes they do not have to share; the general average of living space is thirty-nine square feet per capita, which is about enough for a man to sleep and roll out of bed in the morning without hitting one of a score of relatives, friends, and strangers sleeping next to him. Typhoid is common; cholera is endemic; dysentery pandemic. The Hooghly River is salting and silting up, gradually destroying the usefulness of a port [that] gives

Calcutta its economic base and accounts for one-half of India's imports and exports. The municipal corporation is bankrupt, and there is only one bridge linking the two halves of a city [that] extends thirty miles up and down the muddy banks. Storm water, sewage water, drinking water, bathing water—why bother to distinguish them? For most of the city's population, they're all the same.

Where do you start planning and rebuilding Calcutta? Obviously, by drilling wells for sanitary water, building storm drains and sewage works, at least one more crossing of the river, roads, schools, factories for jobs, maybe sooner or maybe later some houses—*if* you can scrape up the capital. But to get even some of the capital, you will have to persuade the central government to set aside some of its own development schemes and agree that Calcutta should be given a bigger slice of the Third Five-Year Plan financial pie. But there are other cities in India nearly as badly off, and they all need and want money. Perhaps the government of India can persuade the World Bank to lend Calcutta some money for the bridge; but sooner or later, you'll have to pay back the loan. Maybe you can persuade Germany, Japan, Britain, and the United States to extend credit or to make outright grants, but they have cities and needs of their own— and India doesn't vote in their elections.

To persuade *any* patron, you'll have to convince them that plans made will be implemented. But the Indian Civil Service—perhaps more, perhaps less than other civil service systems—is inclined to move slowly, and there are a lot of agencies to be coordinated. Perhaps then you should create a special authority; but for this you'll need legislative approval, and legislatures have a way of being ornery when it comes to creating special authorities.

But assume you did manage to get that clean water, build that bridge, dig those sewage and drainage fields. More people will stay alive for you to find more jobs for, and if you find more jobs for those already living in the city, the news will carry to the millions waiting in the over-populated villages. And then you're back in the soup again.

Now you're probably muttering that I'm not an optimist, I'm a pessimist. Worse than that, a seductive nihilist who's led you down the garden path to thinking the world might as well quit while it's still behind.

I'm not. I'm still the optimist who began this speech. I'm more than ever convinced that man will have to do far more than he has to plan his urban future. But my experience tells me there's no use dodging the harsh realities, or palming off the art of planning as the sure-fire cure of a new breed of medicine men.

Planning is politics, but it is even more than that. Politics has the job of reconciling the known past with the known present; planning has to make both the past and present compatible with an unknown future. If politics is the art of the possible, planning comes close to being the art of the impossible.

Even closer than that. Because planning must also provide for the person who is affected by your decisions but can't vote in your elections. This may be the generation yet unborn, the unemployed youth of your cities who are old enough to worry but too young to vote, the forgotten neighbors in the gray area whom you have gerrymandered out of your suburb, and such distant and unfamiliar neighbors as those I've described in Calcutta whose circumstance is now haunting the rest of the world with the question whether we will be Pharisee or Good Samaritan.

Close to impossible, yes; but planning in that sense is no different from any of our arts and endeavors that have man and his welfare as their uncertain objectives. The art of planning in the twentieth century is admittedly about where the art of medicine was in the sixteenth. If there is a difference, it is that we are much less naive than the medical scientists who began their rational assault on disease four centuries ago. We know about the intricate web of cause and effect and the subtle process of balance by which nature resists what in man's self-centered view is a total solution.

We can use this sophistication to speed the development of the planning art—not least by perfecting and exploiting nature's process of balance and playing down the childish notion of total solutions. There will never be total solutions to urban problems, for the simple reasons that the future is never finished, there are not enough resources or human agreements to make everybody happy, one man's solution is another man's problem—and traffic engineers and foundation employees would see there would be no further need for their services and throw a monkey wrench in the works.

We ought to be talking about resolving urban problems, not about solving them. I know of no problem affecting cities [that] does not basically involve conflicts, contradictions, incompatibilities, and differences—not so much between goodies and baddies (in fact, rarely so), but between more or less decently motivated persons and groups of persons whose self-interests must be tempered, shaped, and melded if the city is to be anything more than the plaything of the man with the biggest army or the most money or the most capacity for mischief, villainy, or seduction.

This means driving a balance, too, between analysis and action. Cities are caught now between the extremes of contemplation and performance. Judging from the enthusiasm with which research has lately been welcomed by planners and politicians alike, we're in the stage where a study is worth a thousand deeds. The fact is, a study *may* make a thousand deeds unnecessary and another thousand deeds possible, by correctly redefining a problem or preparing the community to accept action that otherwise would be voted down. But that's not always the intent of those who commission studies, and there comes a point where someone must take responsibility and act.

Someone must see to it that Calcutta's millions have potable water, jobs, and housing; these won't come by contemplation. Some way must be found to satisfy Japan's hunger for urban land and her need for better transport and public facilities; her cities cannot grow on research papers alone. And if my Citizens Advisory Committee in Cranbury doesn't get off the ground soon, my town is going to be just another lost battle between experts who know a lot and bulldozers who know nothing.

Please do not misunderstand me; I am arguing for three things— more research, more action, and a better balance between them. So far, we have been dealing with an equation of zero quantities, compared to the size of the problem we have and will have as the world adds fifty million people to its population each year—and most of them in its urban areas.

Another balance, another resolution we have to achieve is between our urban and rural points of view. Too long a domination by one has let to a weakening of the other; the political extremism and the mediocrity of many urban delegations in state and provincial legislatures is the price many countries of the world are now paying for that domination. But fact no longer accords with fiction; there is no meaningful distinction between what is rural and what is urban. And it is about time we revised our constitutions, our revenue systems, and our systems of legislative apportionment to accord with fact.

Next year, the United States will celebrate the hundredth anniversary of its Morrill Act, which established a national network of agricultural colleges and in effect declared to the world that a nation could intelligently plan for its agricultural future. It would be a gesture of worldwide significance if the celebration of that centennial were to be devoted to a resolution of rural and urban points of view and to constructive suggestions as to how a nation in the next century can make its cities as productive as this country in the last century made its farms.

We have also to create a working harmony on urban problems among our several levels and agencies of government. National— even international—policies cannot be effective without being translated into urban programs; and the city is helpless without state, national, and even international assistance. Calcutta will be an extremely valuable experiment in establishing such consortium of interest, energy, and resources; certainly, both the metropolis and the nation would mutually benefit if their development plans were coordinated. Japan will solve none of her metropolitan problems of housing, traffic, and land use until she resolves the conflicting tendencies of local and national policy. And in the United States, practically the whole domestic program of the current administration—and of any future administration—hinges on the problems and the programs of the nation's metropolitan areas. Until now, both urban and national programs have been piecemeal. It would be a dramatic and productive step forward if at least a handful of urban areas were designated for experiments in joint policy and program development—to create more employment opportunities for youth; to improve educational systems, especially in the gray areas of the central city; to develop more effective ways of preventing and treating delinquency and crime; and not least, to begin moving toward the elements of a national urban policy, without which a Department of Urban Affairs will be an empty gesture. The moneys for such a venture in joint action and experiment are already available in a multitude of separate urban, state, and national appropriations. What remains is for someone to take the initiative—and in the interest of local self-government, I would hope the initiative came from our local officials.

There are other resolutions to be achieved, not least between the representatives of the older core and the newer growth areas of the metropolis: call them suburb and central city. Very few nations are strangers to this growing incompatibility [and] to the problem of how to allocate resources between the areas of growth and decay. The United States, as I mentioned, is about to create a Department of Urban Affairs, but its principal political support—and therefore its preoccupations—lie in the older parts of the city. This balance of concern may be healthy, if it simply reflects the greater urgency of the human problems of the core, but it would be regrettable if the immediate political facts of life forced the agency to take the central city's side in the short-sighted battle between downtown and suburban self-interests.

The balance to be struck between mass transit and the private automobile, and between rubber and rail, is old hat to this audience. There will have to be such a balance, though by now the automobile has so thoroughly imbedded itself in the urban systems of the [western United States] that I fear any balance will be a one-sided one. I would guess, too, that the same will eventually happen in Madras and Moscow, when per capita income reaches the point where their residents can make a first down payment. I shall never forget the uncertainty of a Soviet economist when he watched Americans coming to work one-in-a-car and said "We'll never make that mistake—that is, if we can help it." The last I heard, Moscow was building a circumferential highway.

But there is another part of the transportation balance which I hope can still be struck more evenly, which is between obsolescence and new technology. So far, neither the railroads nor the automotive industries have provided a research and development process geared to the developing needs of the urban community; it looks like the airlines will follow suit. Each has [painted itself], or is well on the way to painting itself, into an urban corner. By some device, an urban transportation research and development process will have to be created in this and other countries if we are to have something more than the dead-end evolution which made railroads of the [eastern United States] unable to survive changes in the urban environment.

Another resolution must be found between the physical and human needs of the city. I will risk exaggeration to make a point; my rule would be that we devote most of our available public resources to human improvements within the central city and to physical improvements in the suburbs. From the governmental point of view, the elbow room for producing major physical changes within the older area of the city is very, very small. Money spent in educating children of the gray area, orienting newcomers whose income restricts them to obsolescent housing, providing job skills and opportunities, and the like will have vastly greater returns than money spent on physical improvements. There must obviously be a combination of both, but I would stand fast by the suggested priority.

On the city's periphery, in the growth and open areas, one does have elbow room to create new urban form and exploit new technology. Here one can experiment with physical planning with the prospect of broad effect and wide adaptation. But for the most part, our physical planners have been working downtown, with at best the prospect of changing only 3 percent of the physical plant in any one year. Meanwhile, at the periphery, our new money is being spent by a hodgepodge of investors, largely on the basis of short-range returns and yesterday's standards.

The final balance I would urge is that between self-interest and the public interest. This is the moral question [that] every philosopher of the city has raised, beginning with Plato and St. Augustine. None of us will every fully resolve it, but we will kill the city's soul if we stop trying.

The city's greatest problem is the temptation it holds for one group to better its situation at another's expense. In the vast anonymity of the city, in its confusion of cause and effect, in its capacity to survive and forget and accommodate, the temptation becomes enormous. But nobility dies with each man's surrender, and with it the faith on which the city is built and which it holds as a promise to all who come to live in it—the belief and the hope that there is more to life than the slow, self-centered Darwinian struggle for survival.

As I close with this solemn sentence, an inner smile of mischief recalls a little story that may ease the conscience of you who have to produce this brave new urban world.

A stern Norwegian minister in my native state of Minnesota was going through Luther's catechism with his class of six-year-olds, all overwhelmed by the terrors that might follow if they failed in an answer. The minister came to the question, "Who made heaven and earth?" When no one answered immediately, he called out again in a way that threatened fire and brimstone. Finally, a small thin voice from a frightened boy in the rear, who had been caught asleep and wasn't altogether clear on the question. "I did," he said, "but I promise never to do it again."

A Picture of Regional Planning

(Presented to the Annual State Planning Conference,
Trenton, New Jersey, February 5, 1963)

*"Regional planning [is] the powerful notion that
what you're doing or proposing to do may not be
good enough—that the view you have taken of
things may be too narrow, too provincial, and too
short-sighted."*

There is a street in Atlanta, Georgia, [that] recently become infamous. It's a street with whites on one end and Negroes beginning to move in on the other. Atlanta's solution to that problem has been to build a barricade in the middle of the street—a solution in which both mayor and council have been publicly embroiled. A former mayor of Atlanta, Mr. William Hartsfield—thirty-seven years in office until his retirement two years ago—was asked what he thought of the performance of his successors in this particular case. Bill scratched his head for a while and then said, "Well, I've been in politics for a long, long time, and I've made an awful lot of mistakes, but," he said, "never one that you could take a picture of."

I doubt if there are any mistakes in regional planning that you could take pictures of, for two reasons. One, we are always very careful to say that mistakes are due to the lack of regional planning; and second, no one really knows what regional planning is, so how can you take pictures of what it does—let alone what it does badly?

There are, of course, lots of pictures of what regional planning might do. But these really aren't pictures, they're a kind of dream. Since dreams are easy to come by, we regional planners have one for everyone's tastes. You can also have your choice of color. Most people seem to like green, or at least it seems that way, since that is mostly what we regional planners try to give them. For example, green belts. Now, it is true that everyone may not like green belts.

125

I know one planning critic who defined a green belt as something that separates a white belt from a black belt. But you don't have to worry; even if green belts were a mistake, nobody can take a picture of them because there aren't any. Or at least regional planning can't be blamed if there are, because planners are usually hired when there is great economic competition for land, which is when green belts either change into a developer's red brick or fade into a poor man's gray.

British regional planners came pretty close with their green belt schemes in the United Kingdom. But they forgot how quickly people could get to these distant green belts by automobiles and trucks and how quickly those who held the land could be got to by fast-moving money. So now there aren't many green belts in the United Kingdom. Japanese regional planners put British green on their regional planning maps, too. But by the time they got their spectacles off and went to do their field visits in the Tokyo "green belt," they found over a million people already housed and jobbed on the places where only grass and trees were to grow. In downtown Tokyo, there was also a spot on the planners' map called [a] "green belt"; but if you take a close look (the value of that land is four times the value of land in Rockefeller Center), you will see that it has been turned into a practice putting and driving green on a commercial basis—still green, but not for the public.

The green that counts, it seems, is what crosses palms, and not what grows them.

Now, since we don't get pictures of regional planning's mistakes, but only of its dreams, everybody likes regional planning. Especially since it's usually only advisory and it doesn't cost the taxpayers anything—just high-minded people and sometimes foundations like ours. And if, by chance, some uninitiated planner or some aggressive leader strays from the neutral path to the point of recommending specific action, you can always get out—because regional planning, if it's cricket, is always a voluntary operation, with everybody given the full right of secession and a *liberum veto*.[1]

---

[1] *Webster's Third New International Dictionary* defines "liberum veto" as "a veto exercised by a single member (as of a legislative body) under rules requiring unanimous consent." For example, in eighteenth-century Poland, unanimity was

Now this combination of qualities of regional planning—its dreamlike qualities, its free exit, the fact that you don't have to pay for it—this is a combination that's hard to beat. But there is a final advantage: you can go either way, for or against. If you say you are for regional planning, this is good, because regional planning, like motherhood, is a good thing. But if you're against regional planning, that's good too, because regional planning, like Castro, is convertible.[2] Who wants totalitarian dictatorship telling you what you should do with your land or your township or your whatever, especially *your* whatever?

Does all this make you remember that fabulous invention of Al Capp's, the Shmoo? The happy little bowling-pin-shaped animal that obliged everybody? Eat him, he was delicious, and there were his cousins waiting happily for your next meal—indestructible, easily digested, happy to be killed off, and there would always be more.

Now maybe you understand why there are so many regional planning operations in the United States, with so many supporters and so few pictures of what they do or don't do. Except, of course, for the big picture, which is what regional planning is all about. All of us should have the big picture with the green borders and a dream of your choice mounted inside. It will strengthen your courage and your local government, and you can still do what you want to, if the developer's price is right.

At this point, surely, we ought in fairness to define our terms. Certainly, regional planning can't be all that much of a Shmoo.

And then, again, it may be. One way to be more precise is to define the two component words separately. This gives you *region* and *planning*.

A region is even more obliging a figment of the imagination than the Shmoo, because a region can be anything. You can be sure of one thing: to somebody else, it's not what you think it should be. If

---

required in the parliament, and liberum veto was considered one of the principal rights of the nobility. Each delegate in the parliamentary convocation could prevent a law (or other decision) from passing by voting against it.

[2] Ylvisaker is referring to the advertising slogan and company name of Castro Convertibles, circa 1950–80, an east-coast chain of furniture stores featuring sofas that converted into beds.

you are a twenty-acre developer, the region includes the surrounding eighty acres you can't get possession of. If you are a township, the region consists of three adjacent townships [that] are thumbing their collective noses at you. If you are a county or a state, the region is a frustrating number of other legislatures who don't like your act but want to get in on it. If you are the federal government or the United Nations, the region is something inconveniently smaller, like an unwanted interstate contract or a controversial political bloc or military alliance.

The only agreed-upon definition of a region I have ever heard runs something like this: a region is an area safely larger or smaller than the last one whose problems we couldn't solve.

Now for that other word, planning. That's kind of hard to pin down, too. The same wag who coined that last definition has also come up with one for planning. Planning, he says, is talking more certainly about the future than you dare to talk about the present.

This is delightfully vague. There's a kind of Alice in Wonderland quality to this business called planning, which probably accounts for the following conversation, which is really a piece for the New Yorker. Reporter to planner: "Yours must be the only planning organization in the area, isn't it?" Planner to reporter: "Yes, but not necessarily the largest."

Now let me be honest with you. I came to praise regional planning, not to bury it. But as I thought over what might be said about regional planning, it struck me how open to satire our present use of the term really is.

It has become a kind of bromide, an inducement to sleep when the nervous tensions of real life begin to wear you down, an escape from reality.

It has become a favorite weapon of sterile criticism—a kind of second guessing. "If only you'd taken into consideration a larger perspective—a regional approach—you wouldn't be in the mess you're in." It has become a technician's mystery, something the expert knows how to do, but the layman never. It has grown so pretentious it bears little resemblance to everyday possibilities and everyday problems.

In short, it's become a kind of nothing, wide open to satire, wide open to the devastating honesty of a child who asks whether the emperor, after all, has any clothes on or is wrapped only in his own imagination.

I happen to think that regional planning—or at least the concept behind it—is too precious to become an exercise in futility or a subject for satire. But let's not kid ourselves. To be respected, regional planning is going to have to be for real; to be a source of strength to local government, it's going to have to challenge the *status quo* rather than merely whitewash or amuse it.

What is this valuable concept behind regional planning? It's the powerful notion that what you are doing or proposing to do may not be good enough—that the view you have taken of things may be too narrow, too provincial, and too short-sighted. By this definition, the word "regional" really becomes unnecessary. It's just a convenient way of saying that there is a world [that] is bigger or smaller than the one that you have thought about so far. You can make a lot of mistakes by taking the word "region" too literally. For example, it is easy to get trapped into thinking that there is such a thing as the right or natural region, and then holding up action until the whole shebang gets wrapped up into one administrative package.

Some areas may be better or more economical for certain purposes than others. It would be foolish, for example, to develop a sewage system for half a city. But it would be just as foolish, I think, to wait until three other communities were ready to take action against air pollution before you did something about it yourself.

There is another myth to watch out for: that the larger the area you include, the more power you are going to muster to handle big problems. Power can actually dwindle with size . . . . There is a kind of political and social axiom that if you want inaction, get yourself a big committee.

The point I am trying to make is that regional planning doesn't have to start with a region; it can and should start at home.

It starts with a willingness to see things in a larger perspective. It starts with a readiness to give consideration to public interests that may not have a chance to vote in your own elections. It starts with a decision not to beggar your neighbor, even though you've got a perfect legal right to do so and every economic advantage. It starts with the readiness to act big even on a small scale.

Regional planning, in this sense, is bound to strengthen the local government, because it's a test of character. Particularly in the American climate, where there is very little to encourage or to compel local governments to take a broad view of their own actions. Even more so in New Jersey, where local government has all the free will in the world—all the free will that the great social philosophers have told us was necessary for the building of character.

Character building by free choice is fine, but I have lived too long with myself, my kids, and my neighbors to believe that free choice is enough. Incentives, outside criticism, and occasionally some outright regulations and requirements also have a part to play. New Jersey has given regional planning some incentives. There are about fifty laws on the books in New Jersey [that] permit and, in effect, encourage joint action by local authorities on everything from bridge building to flood control, from housing to port development, from libraries to incinerators. The geographical scope they permit ranges from cooperation by two local townships within the state to those great conferences of local officials [that] are binding together the New York metropolitan community with three states and, in the south, the Philadelphia community also with three states.

In a sense, one couldn't ask for more, but it's my strong feeling that the times require more—far more.

We are getting clear evidence of the need for planning of greater breadth, scope, and impact, and we can be thankful for such stalwarts as the Stonybrook Millstone Watershed Association, the Regional Plan Association of New York, the Meadowlands Regional Planning Board, Penjerdel, and many others for carrying on the sometimes thankless task of reminding us of these needs. We need these reminders. Far from being regional planners by instinct, we citizens of local governments usually take our free choice and, like ostriches, bury it in the sand along with our heads.

Can we deny the need for regional planning when we watch our raw land, underground water, flood plains, and stream beds get claim-staked by twentieth-century prospectors who operate with as much freedom as the Gold Rush boys of 1848?

Can we deny the need for regional planning when we see

explosive gas pockets of race and poverty building up in the older central cities of the state?

Can we deny the need for regional planning when we see the eastern seaboard transportation system evolving itself into a dead end, or a Route 130 chewed up into a continuous jungle of unplanned shopping areas and billboard spectacles?

Can we deny the need for regional planning when we see the housing developments of the postwar period poorly and shabbily put together, more and more being subjected not to delinquency on mortgage payments, but to outright walkaways? People are saying, "It isn't worth it, the community is not worth sticking with, and we'll leave the place, mortgage unpaid."

Left to its character-building system of free choice alone, I can just as fairly predict New Jersey's future as a massive gray area, littered and in twenty years left, as I could wax eloquent over the vigor and health that "going it alone" is supposed to create.

What more, then, than free choice and permissive legislation?

Number one, I'd say some effective outside criticism. You are always on dangerous ground when you play the role of critic. I am fond of remembering a little incident that happened to us on summer vacation in New Hampshire last year. We have three boys who try to preserve our late sleeping in the summer vacation period. They are instructed not to bother us in our cabin, so they go down and amuse themselves catching Freddie the Frog, a bullfrog who for four years has now allowed himself, faithfully, to be caught by my kids. They pick him up, as he lets them do, and then he dutifully escapes. This has always happened without incident. But on this particular morning, my smallest, David, a six-year-old boy, came screaming into our room: "Mark has saved Peter's life!" (Mark is the twelve-year-old and Peter the ten.) I jumped up and said, "What happened?" "He fell in." And I said, "What did Mark do? Did he pull him out?" "No, but he hollered out real loud—'Peter, get out of there, or you are going to drown!'"

Despite the hazards, outside criticism is valuable. I'm not sure that the newspapers have really fulfilled their responsibility in criticizing urban planning in this state or any other state. The reasons are difficult to assess. Partly it is for lack of controversy; partly it is because the newspaper, as an institution, is tied up with the plan in question. But newspapers in the next twenty years are going to have to develop a critical capacity on planning, which until now I [have not seen] displayed across the nation.

I would also argue that we need much better staffing and a less ambiguous role for private organizations, which now are forced to do two things, the mixture of which is not always to their advantage. One is to criticize; and the other, since there is nobody else to do it, is to try to do the job. They end up in the defensive position, having dulled their critical lance and at the same time committed themselves as operators without the necessary resources to succeed.

I know some of the reasons why state agencies do not relish the job of criticizing local governments, and they are sound, particularly at election time. But still, such outside criticism is needed; the state, too, is going to have to play its part.

Number two, we need some real incentives for regional planning, not merely permissive legislation. I know my own community well enough to predict it will not cooperate regionally until either it has incentives or [it] is required to do so. Federal and state governments are beginning to provide incentives for metropolitan cooperation to some of their planning and other grants. I think we're going to have to go much further, so that it is worth a community's while to enter into joint agreements [that] make sense providing a fifty or 100 or perhaps even 200 percent financial bonus for those who plan and operate jointly what common sense says they should.

Number three, I think we need more standards and some outright requirements. State and federal agencies are actually, in my view, too soft, and I am as strong a defender of local government as anybody in this room. We know why state and federal agencies must be gentle for political reasons, why they must use the carrot more often than the stick. But there is no doubt about it: if we are going to enter this world of the twentieth century, we need an agency with at least as wide a perspective as the state to give guidance to what we do locally and to set standards. Local government, I think, needs a stiffer challenge than merely the sermons and the appeals and the lollipops which have so far been handed out.

Number four, we need some staff aids. The 701 planning grants are not enough. The part-time services, usually of a passing consultant, are not enough, and our communities across the nation are just beginning to realize this. A permanent staff and continuous help are needed. If you want to look at what we really need, ask AT&T sometime what kind of staff aids it has for running but one function of a community—its communication system. Executive training, research and development, all these facilities should be available to local and state governments, and to our planning agencies, at least equally in the degree to which they are available to a private concern.

We also need refined data on scaled and scheduled investment in cooperative endeavors. The defeat of proposals for joint action involving, let's say, sewerage systems or transportation systems usually comes because individual municipalities make an intelligent assessment of how much more in the short run it's going to cost them to join others than to go it alone. They may on their own have built a sewerage system last year; why invest in a larger system when the other party hasn't done anything on his own and stands to gain by the new partnership?

Number five, it is about time we face up to it that planning—at the local level, at the state level, and at the federal level—needs some real powers. I've wondered, as I watch my Cranbury Township try to plan a balanced community, how we can do it when we don't have the necessary public capital to take the initiative. Without it, we are forced into a reactive, defensive, and often negative kind of planning. It sounds, perhaps, like municipal socialism to suggest it, but frankly I can't see any other answer if we really want planning in our community than to give us development and proprietary power to acquire land, to develop it, to sell and then to use those returns for the next round of development. I understand this is constitutionally not possible in the state of New Jersey. It would require a great revolution in our thinking. But let's not kid ourselves. If we want planning, a municipality is going to need more powers and capital than it has now.

I have also wondered about the plight of older cities like Camden, Newark, and New Brunswick, as they have been caught in the suburban noose thrown around them. Isn't it about time that we give central cities some extra-territorial powers, or at least a chance to bring counterpressures to bear on the suburbs around them, if we are to ease the problems of race and housing [that] are being bottled up within them? This would be strong medicine, but it is about time that central city mayors have a chance to speak out over the whole area [that] affects them.

I've wondered, too, when we will give cities the powers they need to counter slum profiteering and [give] suburbs and rural townships the powers they need to control land speculation. This may be a long way off, but, again, if we are going to plan, let's start talking about measures with teeth in them.

Finally, I suggest we need a state policy on urban development in New Jersey. Perhaps a State Department of Urban Affairs, if it will produce a state policy. But by all means some aggressive statement of state objectives of where we are going and where we should be.

Again, let's not kid ourselves. Local, state, and national governments do not become strong or communities great by default, nor by self-indulgence. They need challenge as well as freedom. We've toyed with regional planning and the idea behind it long enough. We are no longer building houses and factories, we're building communities. We are no longer citizens of one locality; we've a personal stake in every municipality around us.

I keep remembering George Washington in a piece of correspondence [that] has never been published in textbooks on American government (for what reason, I would like to inquire). George Washington, after fighting the Revolution, turned to a long debate with those who wanted to keep government weak. He said, in effect, "When I fought the American Revolution, I was fighting King George and his autocracy. I was not fighting government." He then went ahead with Hamilton, Madison, and the rest to change the Articles of Confederation into a strong constitution. This is a George Washington not usually quoted. But he needs quoting again in the state he played such a big part in developing. If we are going to plan, let's plan. If we are going to govern, let's govern. Why keep dodging the necessities?

Social and Cultural Goals for the Metropolis

(Presented to the Detroit Metropolitan Area Conference, May 6, 1963)

"'We the people' is one of the most startling and revolutionary phrases ever to have rung out in history. The echoes and revolutionary impact are still rebounding through the extending far corners of our twentieth-century world."

I am not sure that anyone can set goals for as large and diverse a community as a metropolis without resorting to some pretty broad and seemingly pious generalities. Even as extraordinary a group as those who wrote the American constitution—after spending several months in historic debate—conceded as much. They limited their final statement of national purpose to a single paragraph full of vast and undefined phrases:

> We the people of the United States, in order to form a more perfect union, establish justice, insure domestic tranquillity, provide for the common defense, promote the general welfare and secure the blessings of liberty to ourselves and our posterity, do ordain and establish this Constitution for the United States of America.

Generalities indeed, and yet they have served for nearly two centuries as guide and spur to the unfolding of a nation's greatness. If phrases could do this for a nation, why look further for goals for a single metropolis? What would happen if we who are concerned with the American metropolis followed the example of the framers of the American constitution?

I can think of a number of results—each of them as significant and as beneficial to urban progress as the constitution has proved to the extraordinary development of the American nation.

Certainly we would be led to see the metropolis not as a matter of real estate to be bought and sold, or downtowns to be renovated, or suburban shopping centers to be built, or blighted areas to be razed, or expressways to be laid out—but to see the metropolis in terms of the people who are searching for their destinies and pursuing happiness within it.

"We the people" is one of the most startling and revolutionary phrases ever to have rung out in history. The echoes and revolutionary impact are still rebounding through the extending far corners of our twentieth-century world. This is what the ferment in Asia, Africa, Latin America, and Birmingham, Alabama, is all about. Even the communist heresy has paraded under this banner; it could afford to make no other appeal, for it would otherwise have won no converts.

The phrase was all the more remarkable, considering who they were who used it. "We the people" excludes no one. Over our nation's history, it has admitted every conceivable brand of human beings into membership: every race, every religion, every political belief, every level of society, every occupation, every level of income, every nationality.

Remember, the framers said, "We the people." They did not say, "we the businessmen" or "we the lawyers" or "we the engineers," although most of them were men of commerce and the professions. They did not say, "we whites," although all of them were of the Caucasian race. They did not say, "we the rural," although many if not most of them were exurbanites by our present definitions. They did not say, "we the wealthy," although most of them were men of means and all of them men of property. They did not say, "we the elite," although that is precisely what they were. They said, "we the people." And then they added "of the United States"—which is the third revolution they touched off. They refused to say, "We the people of New York, of Massachusetts, of Virginia," etc., even though that is all they were at the time they signed the document.

They declared themselves citizens of a larger community—a community their common sense, threatened pocketbooks, and open eyes told them they were part of, even though the law and fact of governmental jurisdictions had not yet caught up with the reality of their times.

In seven short words the framers had carried off three revolutions:

they had stated national goals in terms of people; they excluded no one from those who might be or become eligible to participate and benefit; and they united local interests within a common government for the nation.

This was nearly two centuries ago, and every succeeding year of that long history has confirmed the logic, the wisdom, and the higher morality of what they did.

Yet we stand timidly today wondering whether we dare do the same in our metropolitan communities, and these are but lesser areas within the nation which the framers united with one bold stroke of the pen.

Why have we been so slow to say, politically and socially, "we the people of Metropolitan Detroit" or "we the people of Metropolitan New York?"

Business does it. Labor does it. Air travelers do it. The Tigers and the Yankees and their fans do it. Even Casey Stengel and the Mets are doing it. And they threaten nobody.

Then why doesn't the general metropolitan public do it? Well, we don't—not when it comes to metropolitan politics and society. "We the people" becomes "some of us people" and "some of you people." "We the people of the united metropolis" becomes "we on this side of city line" and "you on the other side of the tracks."

Maybe that's why so many of us show up in the ballparks of our metropolitan areas and so few of us in the voting booths of our local municipalities. In the ballpark, you've got room enough to play the American game, and you're given a fair chance at any seat in the house or position on the team.

Can we say this of the American metropolis? What elbow room do you have in one of a hundred or more separate governments, with no common authority, to develop a general strategy for metropolitan growth and development? Or even to lay down the necessary ground rules?

What chance does an urban newcomer have, particularly if he has a dark skin, to become a full member of the metropolitan social and economic team when certain positions and places are closed to him? What happens to the general welfare of the metropolitan public if the suburbs play the game of beggar-thy-neighbor and the central city more and more is reduced to the role of beggar?

But what a difference if it were the law of the land to say, "We the people of the metropolis."

What a difference, too, if we were to add as our goals for the metropolis the remaining phrases [that] Washington, Franklin, Madison, Hamilton, and their colleagues included in the preamble to the American constitution: "to form a more perfect union, establish justice, insure domestic tranquillity, provide for the common defense, promote the general welfare and secure the blessings of liberty to ourselves and posterity."

These are not material goals; they are things of the spirit. They are not goals [that] emphasize the self-interests of some at the expense of others; the governing adjectives are "common" and "general." These goals do not give license to the appetites of the present generation; equal voice is given to "posterity."

If we distilled our present metropolitan goals from the muddy confusion of going programs and policies, could we honestly claim they would match the nobility or fulfill the aspirations of the preamble?

Civic improvement in our day has become almost synonymous with upgrading the real estate of the metropolis. But the preamble talks about welfare, not hardware. It sets as our task the upgrading of the condition of human beings, not buildings. It asks that we form a more perfect union, not more imposing monuments; it asks that we establish justice, not just an establishment; it asks that we secure the blessings of liberty, which isn't answered by building a street or plaza by that name and adorning it with a civic or cultural center.

All this is not to say that material things are unnecessary for the good life and the execution of noble purposes. What I am saying is that the framers of the constitution put first things first, and by doing so perfected a nation. The American metropolis—in which now practically all of our nation lives, moves, and has its being—has still to put first things first. It has no preamble of noble objectives drafted in human terms. It is still raw and disorganized; its culture is dissembled; its constitution is unwritten and unformed.

Without these soaring objectives, we become in the metropolis but a collection of warring self-interests concerned with the means rather than the ends of human existence. The greatness of a metropolis lies beyond the realm of means; it waits our identification of ends. And the ends are the first-class citizens we produce.

The metropolis is its people. The measure of its vitality is the energies of its people. The measure of its health is the well-being of its citizens. The measure of its culture is the tastes and talents of its inhabitants. The measure of its future are the pride and prospects of its most humble residents.

A community can have some pretty old buildings and equipment and pass these tests with flying colors. A metropolis can have a shiny new downtown and spanking new expressways and still score pretty low.

Not the least of our problems is that we haven't a known and accepted way of keeping score on the human performance of a metropolis. Statistical series of the sort kept nationally by the President's Council of Economic Advisers might help; but as yet neither the Council nor anyone else has got round to keeping such records on a metropolitan basis. Besides, it isn't certain these statistical indices would tell us much about the kinds of metropolitan performance [that] count.

Figures on crime and delinquency might—if we knew more about what they really meant. Figures on unemployment come closer—if we could have them properly interpreted. Data on mental health and illness, on family income and housing, on dependency, on school achievement and drop-outs—these too might begin to give us a measure of civic performance. And I suspect if these data were to be reported here, the resulting picture would not be an especially encouraging one.

But I would hesitate to leave it with statistics. They have a way of describing only the bits and pieces of life and of encouraging us to respond in bits and pieces of social action and public policy. Try instead to look at the metropolis and its civic performance "whole"; our perspective and our public policy will be the better for it.

Detroit is the symbol of the assembly line and productive efficiency; its genius has been in the application of engineering skills and systems analysis to the processes of production. This community would quickly understand, therefore, if it were asked to conceive of the metropolis as a system of producing first-class citizens and to provide the opportunities necessary for achieving that status.

How efficient is the citizen-building process of Metropolitan Detroit? One way of finding out—and I think the best way—is to do a flow analysis. Choose any youngster in your community and follow his civic course through a lifetime in your system. Or if you are willing to add a bit of stress analysis as well, choose a set of newcoming children from the rural south and observe what happens to them as they move into the production process by which your metropolis turns out its first-class citizens.

How efficient is this system? Or is the first question to be asked, how many of us know anything about it? Where does it begin? Where does it end? What are its stages? And now that we're beginning to get curious, who laid out this process anyway, and what did they have in mind?

Was it intended—and if so, by whom and with what motive—that the least-prepared newcomers to the metropolis get their civic orientation course in the blighted hand-me-down areas of the central city? A pretty rugged first stage in the production process. Possibly a good one for the challenges it offers—provided there were opportunities and countervailing influences proportionate to the challenge.

But are there? Is this the sector of the metropolitan production system where the greatest care, guidance, and opportunities are concentrated? The best schools and health facilities? The most active cultural programs? The most imaginative church work and legal services? The highest level of municipal services? And most important of all, the greatest number of job opportunities?

The highest level of charity and dependency payments, yes. But are these an adequate substitute for equality and opportunity?

By now, I'm sure you've caught the idea and can follow through on your own the rest of the cycle by which we supposedly produce first-class citizens. You can ask for yourself how efficient it is. How much waste it involves in human lives and resources. What bottlenecks there are in education, in law and the administration of justice, in the employment system, in cultural services, in banking and credit, in the methods by which we decide who will manage and who will govern—to mention but a few of the stages along the production line.

In doing this flow analysis, you'd better have a strong stomach and a stout heart. The production system we've jerry-built for our urban newcomers—and for that matter, for our suburban youth as well—isn't very efficient. It is, in many of its parts, downright primitive. I invite you sometime to explore the administration of justice at the lowest level of courts and income, or to join for awhile the society of unemployed Negro youths on the street-corners of our urban gray areas. Or, at a more gilded level, search with your suburban youth for early meaning through the extending years of uncertain responsibilities.

You may find I have exaggerated. I doubt it.

Whatever your findings, your civic perspective will never the same again.

Once you have seen the metropolis as something more than a jumble of buildings and governments and agencies and policies and a marketplace of personal ambitions—have seen it as the system by which we are to produce citizens, the American instinct and genius for turning out a better product at less social cost and in shorter time will inevitably take over. You will find others before you who have seen the system for what it is and who are pioneering in remarkable ways to improve it. I would especially commend those in your school system who are providing models for the nation of new and more effective ways of educating the newcoming children in your central city neighborhoods.

The goal of citizen-building is a noble one, in the best tradition of the preamble to the American constitution. It is right for the metropolis, just as it has been right for the nation.

My own test of the cultural level of any metropolis is not the monumental height of its museums and civic centers, but the plane at which its leaders and its humblest citizens have examined and agreed to improve the human lives of their community. Cultural centers are fine, but they are not always or necessarily the place to start, and certainly not the place to stop.

Let me close with an incident I have found one of the most encouraging signs of cultural awakening and of growing civic maturity on the American urban scene.

The other day, I sat with the publisher of a newspaper in a middle-sized, past-middle-aged city on the eastern seaboard. He was gazing in despair out over the bleak downtown of his community, wondering how by statuary or landscape gardening or a new art museum or whatever his city could build a culture [that] somehow wasn't evident in square miles of parking lots, for rent signs, neon lights, storefront churches, and here and there—the uglier for their contrast—a few new and renovated buildings, their architecture of a style best forgotten.

In the middle of his stare, he suddenly brightened and exclaimed, "Why start from here? Let's start with the kids in the slum schools of our city! And," he added, "I know just the guy to get as our consultant." [It was] a professor at a nearby university who—believe it or not, and let's have more of them—teaches at one and the same time boxing and sculpture.

"There's a man," the publisher said, "who can stimulate culture in this city. You know how he defines culture? 'Culture,' he says, 'is everyman's itch, and the arts are the best ways we've found of scratching it.'"

Not a bad definition. Not a bad formula. The kind of scratch to start from in fulfilling the social and cultural goals of the American metropolis.

The American City: Mirror to Man

(First published in *Life*, December 24, 1965)[1]

"Nothing short of a nation's concern and deliberate policy will build a better environment. Until that concern and policy emerge, individual choices and local decisions will go on missing and sputtering. When they do emerge, the decentralized, spontaneous energies of America will finally have their chance of being harnessed into creating beauty rather than chaos."

Men may find God in nature, but when they look at cities they are viewing themselves. And what Americans see mirrored in their cities is not very flattering. To any of the awakened senses, urban America can be a depressing experience.

Walk the dilapidated streets of Boston's Roxbury section, North Philadelphia, New York's Harlem and Lower East Side, East St. Louis, West Dallas, the poverty-scarred sections of Phoenix, the San Francisco Bay area's West Oakland, and North Richmond.

Travel such corroding arteries as Route 1 through New England, the Baltimore Pike in Delaware County, University Avenue from Minneapolis into St. Paul, Figueroa Street south through Los Angeles to Long Beach.

Look out over the maze of boxes that have been merchandized as suburbs all the way from the Florida coast to Puget Sound.

Inhale the stench of the Jersey "meadowlands" with their oil refineries and open dumps, the steel complex of Gary-Hammond,

---

[1] Published in December 1966 by the Sidney Hillman Foundation as No. 29 in the Sidney Hillman Reprint Series (copyright 1966, Sidney Hillman Foundation). Reprinted with permission.

the smelting towns of West Virginia. Follow—if you have the lungs and stomach to do so—the open-air sewers that clog over Los Angeles and drift as a giant's bad breath all the way from St. Louis to New York. Watch as the great streams and lakes of this nation—the Hudson, the Potomac, the Mississippi, Lake Erie, Lake Tahoe—become the drainage ditches and cesspools of a society flooding in the wastes of uncontained growth.

Scan the spectral web of utility poles and wires that haunt a skyline once graced by trees. Search for a park and fountain in downtown Troy, a pleasant place to stroll at Kennedy Airport, a path for cycling in Detroit.

Trace the city's growing edge: the shack and shanty towns of the outer rim, labor camps converting into year-round slum communities, towns of poverty jerry-built and gerrymandered out of utility and voting boundaries of neighboring municipalities, trailers packed in Everytown's ghetto of "just outside," catch-as-catch-can housing along every available strip of exurban roadway, barns and fences pasted over with the garish advertisements of the urban culture soon to follow. And then contemplate some of the latter-day samples of this emerging urban esthetic, among them the soaring brick piles that promise the city dweller "total living"—if only he can find a place to park.

A Few Clearings

Admittedly, urban America isn't all that bleak. Here and there are clearings in the urban jungle where the eye finds delight, or at least is not offended; that is, given the presence of wealth, or a sensitive builder, or an exacting client, or an advantaged university, or a moment of architectural and civic greatness, an engineering triumph, or some natural feature that overpowers even the mediocrity around it. Beacon Hill and the Boston Common; the planned community of Radburn, New Jersey; Westchester County parkways in New York; much of Washington, D.C.; Chapel Hill, North Carolina; Savannah, Georgia; Boulder, Colorado; remnants of San Francisco.

Sometimes even the gargantuan whole of urban America can be a thing of beauty. By air, and especially by night, our cities are as much a feast to the eyes as any settlement of history. And they are so *because* of their supposed faults, not in spite of them. Gaudy neon lights become flashing gems set against the velvet of darkness. With the flow of headlights along streets and highway they help trace the anatomy of a metropolis in which even the bulldozed monotony of nondescript developments acquires grace and meaning.

The rub, of course, is that only one in five Americans has ever seen his city by air, and the few who do soon return to contend with the grubbier realities below.

Must these urban realities of America be so grubby? Led by the White House, the nation is at last beginning seriously to ask that question. But it is a question that is far easier to wring one's hands over than to solve. There are many concerns, but two stand above all others.

Standards and Restraints

One cuts straight to the heart of our democratic philosophy: Can we develop standards of order and beauty [that] amount to something more than the foisting of one man's tastes and self-interest upon another?

The other challenges our political skill and technical ingenuity: Can we get that extraordinarily free-wheeling and irascible figure, the American citizen-entrepreneur, to accept restraints on his ability to build as he wishes and make money as he can? And can we couple those controls with incentives powerful enough to prod and excite Americans into creating the more attractive urban environment [that] they obviously have the talent and means to achieve?

The Romans, who were no slouches at building cities of their own, were painfully aware of the first problem, and in one of their favorite maxims indicated it was too tough a nut to crack. "When it comes to tastes," they said, "there's not much point arguing."

The pragmatic, I'm-as-good-as-you-are American has tended to agree. Much can be said in his defense. One man's taste is almost certain to be another's displeasure. The higher critics are still debating whether such monumental works as Lincoln Center in New York, or Philadelphia's Penn Center, or Pittsburgh's Golden Triangle are masterly or just mediocre. At a humbler level, the Tennessee mountaineer who moved to Akron, Ohio, may have half-a-dozen cannibalized cars rusting in his shantied backyard, but mixed among them [are] twice as many birdhouses set with poetic concern and tender loving care.

When tastes and attachments can be that diverse, the average voter is bound to be skeptical of any effort at administered beauty. Who's to say what's attractive and what is not? And by an instinct [that] is something more than vulgar, the American has sensed a logic to governed esthetics that is not to his democratic liking. Beauty is related to order, regularity, consistency. Urban beauty—at least as historical examples are cited to us—has been linked to concentrations of power and wealth seemingly necessary to produce it. Leningrad is Peter the Great, ordering the city into existence over the heads of his subjects and with the best European architects working as hired hands. Paris is Louis Napoleon, by whose authority Baron Georges Haussmann could translate design into fact.

An autocrat's wish—and a city of splendor. But the American wonders whether the City Beautiful can also be a city of, for and by the people. To say the least, he's dubious. He becomes even more the doubting Thomas when he sees the sometimes nonsense, caprice, confusion, and malice that can slip in under the banner of urban betterment.

Under the Carpet

How many times have a community's basic faults and problems been swept under a carpet of beautification? Consider the clean-up, fix-up campaigns [that] put brushes in the hands of slum dwellers but not mortgages, paint cans but not paychecks, brooms but not better municipal services. Or the downtown renewal and slum clearance projects that amassed scarce resources under an appeal to the general interest but wound up benefiting a predictable few. Or the reservation of green belts [that] turned out, in Charles Abrams'[2]

---

[2] Urban planning pioneer Charles Abrams (1902–1970) was the first to explore the complex issues of urban housing. In 1963, he was part of a U.N. team that recommended to Singapore an integrated approach to housing, urban renewal, industrial development, and transportation. His books include *The City Is the Frontier*.

wryly satiric definition, to be "those belts which separate white belts from black belts." Or "zoning for orderly development," which has been used by many a municipality to exclude most anyone not already living there. The "Pointe System," by which an exclusive neighborhood rates the suitability of candidates for residence. The creation of parks, but only for those communities lucky enough to have the sites and tax resources available. The adoption of health and building codes, with such standards and enforcement that the poorer family is squeezed from the community.

The first problem of urban esthetics, then, is a problem of philosophy—and not merely one of definition but of values, purpose, and motive. It will avail America nothing if it gains the City Beautiful but by means and intent [that] destroy its own soul.

The Need to Move

Still, it is one thing to be aware of a philosophical problem, and another to be paralyzed by it. The classic puzzler—whether you can ever reach a certain destination when each step takes you only half the remaining distance—is solved not by eternal reflection but by deciding whether or not you want to get there; and if you do, to start and keep moving at a steady pace.

Beauty, order, grace—these are admittedly elusive as the civic objectives, but no more so than the liberty and pursuit of happiness of the Declaration of Independence, or the general welfare and due process of the Constitution.

It is a question of how badly they are wanted. At that point, the politician takes over from the philosopher, asking, as he always must, "How many are willing to fight whom to get what?"

The democratic battles Americans like most to remember are those in which "the people" are pitted as suffering heroes against an entrenched, rapacious few. But in the struggle for more attractive cities, the American people are pitted against themselves, which makes it damnably difficult for any leader who enters the political fray to muster his troops and sustain an attack. He will also have a problem pinpointing "the enemy." The sign and billboard people probably qualify as well as any. They really do mess up the landscape—and in public opinion polls they're rejected by two to one. But their numbers are legion and their faces indistinct—they range from the biggest of business to the smallest of men with the sign reading EAT AT JOE'S.

Therefore, the enemy must be referred to with raised eyebrows but in lower case: "the fast-buck developer," "greedy commercial interests," "the highway lobby," " slum landlords."

There is no doubt that these fuzzy captions match up with some real people who on many known occasions—and heaven only knows how many less-known—have proved themselves to be an esthetic menace. But the categories they cover, the interests they include and, more basically, the human traits they describe, sooner or later implicate just about every American.

Who Is Exempt?

Which property owner hasn't had at least one speculative eye open for the highest bidder, [and] some mixed feelings about zoning regulations [that] stand in the way of re-use or development at maximum possible gain?

Which taxpayer hasn't boggled at the thought of spending those extra sums to add an architect and some amenities to public housing projects, or balked at giving up color television so that his community could acquire some green acres?

Which of us, having just attended a public hearing to stop a public road from coming through our neighborhood, hasn't already rejoined the automobile lobby when snarling our way home over congested thoroughfares? And if the title search is pressed far enough, which major American institution—church, university, bank, insurance company—hasn't been found the owner of slum properties? Which investor hasn't expected the managers of his portfolio and the corporate executives to fetch the largest possible return, even if it means cutting local tax and civic contributions of branch offices or polluting the streams of exurban sanctuaries [that] offered low taxes and a relaxed approach to planning?

These are the untidy qualities found in all of us [that] help mess up our cities. Sometimes they break out into flagrant cases of moral, legal, and esthetic indecency; mostly they remain at the endemic level of individual shrewdness and civic indifference, live-and-let-live, get-what-you-can, and yell-when-you're-hurt.

The city, after all, is a mirror to man. And isn't this the human image one finds, say, in the transition of country road to city street? Trace the familiar process through:

Farmer Smith, who owns half the roadside acreage, needs some extra cash to support his son through trade school. Small-townsman Jones, the eldest son of the corner grocer, is getting married, wants a place of his own, can't find anything in town. His father buys a half-acre lot from Smith and gives it to his son for a wedding present. Young Jones buys a shell house on contract, finishes it after working hours, puts in a septic tank and digs a well. Life gets lonely for his wife—she persuades two other young couples to settle next to them. One more shell house, a trailer, two more septic tanks, two more wells, three cinderblock driveways and a dozen utility poles. Farmer Smith's son comes back from school, gets a permit to convert one of the farm buildings into a machine shop, puts up a six-foot, hand-painted sign, builds on an addition to the old farmhouse with picture window, brick veneer, a television aerial, and aluminum trim. (His wife is very happy.) A buddy of his says, "Let's go partners on a filling station across the road." Then their wives, looking for some extra household money, open up a roadside stand and diner.

Enter the Developer

Soon Farmer Smith, with agricultural prices dropping and his years advancing, starts reading those ads about retiring in Florida, lets it be known he's willing to talk to a developer. The town taxpayers hear about it, calculate the number of schoolchildren the development will bring and the cost of educating them, get all stirred up by rumored versions of the odd ones and barbarians who are moving in, and decide it's time for planning and zoning for the orderly growth of the community. Differences are forgotten long enough to get a federal "701" planning grant. Then, while an itinerant expert puzzles out the jigsaw of a master plan (substituting prefabricated parts for the missing local pieces), they enact a one-acre zoning ordinance requiring paved roads, curbs, gutters, storm sewers, sidewalks, and water connections. With costs raised, the developer isn't interested any more, at least not at the land prices Smith is now quoting.

Farmer Smith starts grumbling. So do those whose second thought is that they might get all that extra work and business [that] comes with town growth and still manage to keep the taxes down. More farmers are reading the Florida ads. While the town debates, Farmer Clark—down the road from Smith and in another township—sells his land to the original developer. A few days later Smith and cohorts start a campaign to amend the zoning ordinance from one acre to half an acre, with reduced road and sidewalk requirements. Pandemonium at the next meeting of the zoning board! The chairman gets mad and quits, his replacement votes for the amendment, and eventually it's adopted. Smith sells his acreage and moves to California.

With or Without Sin

Now you can play this sequence through with or without bribery, corruption, and wicked intent. Farmer Smith may well have been a skinflint. He may have persuaded a few of his old cronies on the zoning board by plying them with favors. He, the developer, and a conniving real estate agent might have promised the town engineer or attorney a percentage of the sale price. On the other hand, the entire cast of characters could have been earnest, God-fearing citizens whose only faults were their limited incomes, choice, and sensitivity.

In either case the esthetic results would be essentially the same—and identical with what has happened to the mass of urban America. Call it by any name—chaos, unplanned growth, ribbon development, social anarchy, slurbs, the decline of American civilization, the resurgence of *laissez-faire*. But recognize it for what it is—a people's *laissez-faire*, which sinks its roots down past any rotting level of corrupt and cynical behavior by the few into a subsoil of widespread popular support and an abiding tradition of private property, individual freedom, and "Every man's home's his castle."

The search for urban policy thus begins with the public's conflicting replies to the philosopher's unrelenting question: What kind of city are you looking for, what kind of beauty, what kind of order?

Merely whisper the question these days, and fifty-seven varieties of answers will be thrust upon you by anxious hands. The one ingredient most have in common is the assumption that other things must change and everyone else conform to the tastes and advantage of one who is doing the proposing. This one ingredient almost unfailingly poisons the solution. *In a democracy the city to strive for is one in which diverse human beings can live freely together, respect each other's varying tastes, and share the immense power of their differences.*

Special-Interest Cities

It is relatively simple to achieve beauty and order, at least of a sort, by building something less than this open city. The ready-mix formula is usually some combination of wealth, homogeneity, and exclusion. Our urban landscape is fast growing with examples of choice suburbs where a more fortunate few manage to find sanctuary from the sorrier conditions of the many. The names of some of these retreats have become hallmarks of American character: Grosse Pointe, Michigan; Winnetka, Illinois; [and] Tuxedo Park, New York, to mention a few.

It is also relatively simple to say what urban policy should be if you are bent on perfecting only that kind or piece of a city you have a special interest in. If you want the automobiled, shopping-center city, go on subsidizing highways, parking, and single-family homes on large lots. If you want the sort of European city American tourists love to visit and downtown merchants want to keep, subsidize mass transit, zone for apartments, and allow taxpayers to deduct rent as mortgage-interest payments on their federal tax returns.

If you are mayor of Central City, charge suburbanites for their use of your facilities and use the proceeds to modernize your public services. If you are the mayor of Suburbia, tell the mayor of Central City to go to blazes and use the money to buy your own water and sewer system. If you are the citizen of Exurbia, tell both mayors to go to blazes, because it is already costing you a bundle to pay for your own well and septic tank. If you are the denizen of Downtown Slum, tell them all to go to hell, join the next rent strike and march on Washington.

If you want a city [that] is tidy and symmetrical, urge the establishment of an architectural review board. If you like your cities a little on the messy side and full of visual surprises, vote "no" on that proposal. And if you like your cities totally spontaneous, cast another ballot against any form of zoning or planning whatsoever. Houston, without either, seems to have boomed, sprawled, and skyscraped as well—or as badly—as any other American city. On the other hand, you might also want to consider the civic damage done to Staten Island during its recent years of free-for-all development.

To repeat, it is relatively easy to decide what policy should be when you have factored America's conflicting tastes and interests into homogeneous pieces of the city—particularly when you keep the other pieces from voting in your jurisdiction.

The Whole City

But what do you do when, as President or as thoughtful citizen, you have to deal with the whole of the divided American metropolis—and simultaneously with all the diversities of that Great American City [that] our nation is fast turning into?

Part of the answer, a fundamental and healthy part, is this division of the whole into more manageable sections. If our system did not allow for some compartmentalization of political, social, and esthetic differences, creativity would be stifled and conflict would become so massive as to be possibly unresolvable.

Another part of the answer is to avoid becoming too solemn and inflexible. A good deal of urban beauty comes, as the beauty in a coral reef, from generations of accumulating individuality and seemingly random growth. Half the art of urban planning is to recognize when to control and when to let alone.

But make no mistake about it—these pieces of urban America, particularly when they are based on the principle of "I've got mine, now you get yours," do not automatically add up to an environment in which the nation can feel great pride or satisfaction. There is, of course, a need for broader vision and direction.

National Planning

If you doubt this, ask the zoning board of a township [that] succeeds in keeping its stretch of road and river uncluttered, only to see its neighboring township spew forth everything from junkyards to raw sewage. Or the city planners who are constantly being asked to crowd a region's economy into the one municipality they are hired by. Or the health officer—paralyzed by the thought of "taking on" the industry that gives his community its jobs and taxes—who quietly prays for the day when state or nation will crack down on those who contaminate the city's air and water. Or that sensitive property owner, forced by straitened circumstances to sell his historic mansion and wooded estate to the highest bidder with the lowest standards, who cries out for a national declaration that *there are some things private money cannot buy but the public must be willing to pay for.*

Nothing short of a nation's concern and deliberate policy will build a better environment. Until that concern and policy emerge, individual choices and local decisions will go on missing and sputtering. When they do emerge, the decentralized, spontaneous energies of America will finally have their chance of being harnessed into creating beauty rather than chaos.

This is not an argument for central domination of local affairs. Quite the contrary. It is a call for elevating the problems of our city to a place on the nation's public agenda—on a par with employment, rocketry, and national defense—and for giving mayors and others who deal with these problems the attention, dignity, and resources they deserve.

Urban policy of this sort will undoubtedly contain stronger elements of control than we have known, and some limitation of choice. There is no longer good reason to leave the trenching of utility lines, or the junking of automobiles, or the regulation of highway billboards, or the guarantee of open occupancy, to individual and local determination.

But for a diverse and free society, urban policy will have to be far more sophisticated than mere regulation and control. Controls are too hard to come by and too easy to get around. They usually are enacted too late and are too often used for purposes other than what they were created for. And at best they represent the common denominator of what we are against, rather than the measures of excellence and public appeal of the cities we hope to create.

Using the Carrot

When developing urban policy in this society, we will have to rely more on the carrot than on the stick—creating incentives [that] are far-reaching enough to express a nation's concern and powerful enough to exert a national influence.

One form of incentive too easily overlooked lies in the reshaping of existing controls [that] now keep local authorities and private citizens from acting flexibly and imaginatively. Antiquated building codes are a prime example. The work now being done with zoning regulations to allow both the municipality and the developer more than one way of satisfying minimum requirements is a welcome instance of how creativity can be encouraged rather than stifled by controls.

Tax incentives are even more promising because they go to the jugular vein of private decisions and have the combined effect of both carrot and stick. There is a long list of possible uses. Both the local property tax and the federal income tax can be adapted so as to reward the man who maintains his property rather than the slumlord who exploits it and the slothful owner who lets it go. Taxes can also be revised to give a break to those willing to add some esthetic extras to the cost of construction. As the laws stand now, concern for beauty will only increase your tax assessment. Another tax break should go to those willing to donate open land or development rights to their communities for public use. Stiff taxes might be imposed on those who pollute air, land, or water—with all or part of these same taxes remitted if the offender agrees to spend equivalent sums to prevent further pollution.

More Tax Reform

Another line of tax reform should start channeling more of our national revenues to our beleaguered municipalities, especially our central cities. Even allowing for that elusive margin of increased efficiency and trimmed services, the financial requirements for keeping American cities going—let alone improving them—have long ago outstripped the capacity of the fiscal system we have grown up with. As a nation, we have dangerously underinvested in our urban plant. We have skimped on maintenance, and what little we have done to establish a reserve for depreciation and renewal would have any private accountant tearing his hair out. Recently, there has been talk of a major redistribution of the nation's tax resources, one proposal being the "Heller Plan" for turning back part of any federal tax surplus to the states. This plan badly needs amending to make certain that urban communities become the prime beneficiaries.

In addition to tax incentives, the nation can also expand its present repertory of grants-in-aid. Such assistance might go to communities willing to invite expert criticism and outside competition in the design of local subdivisions and public facilities. Also, grants could be made available to cities willing to preserve precious land and landmarks from too-eager bulldozers. Grants could be made to states ready to experiment with new forms of municipal acquisition and disposition of land, and also willing to risk the political hazards of moving with help and controls into the vacuum of farmland and metropolitan fringe before these are filled by haphazard development; to universities prepared to train urban experts who are also politically knowledgeable, and then to evaluate performance in words the public can understand; to schools finally ready to expose their pupils to the rudiments of urban esthetics and city planning.

Incentives

Incentives should also go the private sector, extending financial, legal, technical and moral support to those who are pioneering imaginative new settlements on America's urban frontier—men like Robert Simon, the builder of Reston, Virginia, and James Rouse, the developer of Columbia, Maryland. They and growing numbers of others like them are advancing beyond what the public [currently] demands or is content to buy. They could move out further, especially in providing low-income housing and better public facilities, if given more help than is [now] available. These men are representative of the new breed of private enterprisers dedicated to the public interest. They might do even better if prodded by some public competition. There has already been talk of "Oakland East," "Minneapolis South," and "Chicago West"—suburbs built by the mother city, much as the communities of Ancient Greece, when they reached a certain size, spawned urban offspring of their own. We presently have working for our cities mayors and public entrepreneurs clearly capable of such massive endeavors, should the public one day decide to let them capitalize on their experience and try building a few new towns of their own.

And what might be the happy result if governmental agencies like the Post Office were stimulated to try something more than branch architecture and to start matching the elegance—or at least enlightenment—of national industries in the design and layout of local offices and working facilities?

Such "competition in the public interest" could be extended into other areas. American cities are now the by-product of other purposes, the residual of countless decisions made with some other intent than an improved environment for the urban population. Their technology is the leavings from industrial and military research; their officials and personnel the second-class citizens of America's executive establishment. But why should an America [that] has applied its ingenuity with such system and success to lesser objectives fail to provide an equivalent base of research and development for the largest and most important enterprise of all—the building of its cities?

More Research

There is no budget for urban research worthy of the name—though we still appropriate nearly $100 million a year for farm research; no Bureau of Standards dedicated to the needs of America's municipalities; no Bell Laboratory for urban planning; no Rand Corporation for urban transportation; no Brookhaven with resources enough to score breakthroughs in the control of pollution and contamination; no Bauhaus to spur building research and community design; no staff college to dignify and continuously stretch the minds and competence of municipal officials. No single one of these facilities would be enough. The scale of urban development in the U.S. is so immense, and our ignorance of cause and solution so vast, that we will surely need the simultaneous and often competitive probing of many minds in many institutions—

public and private, profit and nonprofit—to catch up with the problem and some day move ahead.

There is obviously a long way to go and much to do. But much has already been done and a number of signs augur well.

We do, after all, have prototypes—and criticisms of these prototypes—on which to consolidate much broader programs of urban renewal, restoration, regional and social planning, new town development, interracial housing, open-space procurement, and even underground wiring. We also have a growing cadre of extraordinarily capable urban planners, mangers, technicians, and researchers.

We have begun—through civil rights legislation and the poverty program—to face up to the moral and human requirements of building better cities, making up much of what has been lacking in earlier efforts at physical and economic planning. Prodded by the poor and by social critics, we have become increasingly sophisticated as consumers of public services—creating new mechanisms for civic complaint and waxing ever more eloquent in expressing our urban needs and dissatisfaction.

We have finally recognized, at least symbolically, the importance of urban problems by elevating the federal Housing and Home Finance Agency to cabinet rank and broadening its title to something worthy of its task: the Department of Housing and Urban Development.

American business has turned increasingly to urban betterment—no longer as a polite slogan but aggressively and competitively as a major new market.

Facing Up

Slowly and not yet surely enough, we are facing up to the harsh realities and deadly hazards of urban neglect. The handwriting on the wall is there to read: the riots in Watts; the long, dark night of the northeastern blackout; the water shortage in the New York metropolitan region; the rising crime rate; the ominously increased morbidity from contaminated air. And if the recent spate of urban literature and legislation is any indication, the American public has finally put on its glasses and looked to see what the handwriting has long been saying.

The most encouraging of all our urban developments is the fact that the preservation of nature's beauty and man's perfection of his own cities have become Presidential themes. This is a certain sign that the nation has become concerned enough for its political leaders to calculate the odds and conclude that there is more to be lost than gained by avoiding the issue, and more to be won by advancing the cause. The President could not risk this commitment until a heroic procession of local leaders had explored the political terrain before him. Especially mayors.

When the record of a more livable America is written, future schoolchildren should be reading the names of Clark and Dilworth in Philadelphia, Lee in New Haven, Collins in Boston, Tucker in St. Louis, Cavanagh in Detroit, Hartsfield and Allen in Atlanta, Daley in Chicago, Lawrence in Pittsburgh, Briley in Nashville—to list some of those mayors deserving of special tribute.

Presidential Resources

Now that the Presidency is finally allied with city hall, the pace of urban progress is bound to quicken. Not only because the White House can command far greater resources and talent, and a far better press, but because the nation at last feels certain that the subject is worth arguing about and that something major is likely to be done.

The argument and the action now can and will begin—in earnest and increasingly with results. The modest proposals placed before Congress this past session, and the lesser legislation that emerged from the usual round of political compromise, will go through the inevitable process of amendment and escalation.

Or should one qualify the word "inevitable"? Remember those verbal games we have played before: the "long levers of great action" that have turned out to be but small bars of self-interest joined to drooping promises and limp excuses; architectural pyrotechnics that ended in large contracts and minor improvements; local action defeated by national apathy?

The answer remains a matter of faith—and perseverance.

Yet, somehow, I believe the American public won't let this new subject of better cities go without a struggle, or let the politicians rest—which means the public will in turn be led and prodded.

Once Americans start seeing examples rather than promises, and are given visions rather than alibis, what is to keep them from working and paying for better cities with all the restless energy they have been spending on faster cars and easier kitchens? A family argument about who gets what, how to do it, and who's to pay? I doubt it. In our history so far, it never has.

Testimony Before the U.S. House of Representatives Committee on Banking, Currency and Housing

(Given on September 27, 1976)

> *"When I closed my eyes to the shabbier buildings of Newark and listened instead to human beings, I found vibrant spirits with more ingenuity in many respects than my suburban folks. And that sturdiness, that sense of common decency, I think are the biggest force our central cities have going for them."*

Mr. Chairman, I am deeply grateful that you have asked me to express my views.

As you indicated, I am a veteran of urban wars. And those of us who have been in the business for a while tend, I think, to be a little bit more hesitant before speaking, not so much about what we are seeing, as what one does about it.

It is extraordinarily hard to reverse the trends we are talking about, and many of us have used up our equities and our wisdom in trying.

I see the decline of the American cities, the central cities, particularly in the industrial areas, as another casualty of the single-entry kind of bookkeeping that human beings and Americans do. We tend to run very quickly after affluence and to duck the cost of prospering. We are looking, therefore, at cities as the unpaid and accumulating costs of the American enterprise. We are also looking at what went wrong in the context of what most Americans think went right.

My concern has to do with the fact that we don't pay all our bills. I have a midwestern puritan's instinct about paying bills and think this nation ought to [pay its bills].

My concern is not so much with the physical deterioration of

160

those central cities; it is far more with those who are victimized by it. I used to go through the exercise in dealing with Newark, New Jersey, of closing my eyes, of walking into that city and "listening to humanity" rather than watching what people live in. And I must say one comes out much more an optimist if one does that. One does because the spirit regenerates; buildings may not.

And I am also concerned about what it says about the American character—a nation I dearly love—that it doesn't pay its bills and allows an accumulated set of unmet obligations do so much damage to so many human beings.

The basic predicament we are dealing with is quite simple. First, most Americans don't want to live in central cities. Second, most Americans don't really have to. Some, yes, some stick or are stuck there for a variety of reasons—often unappreciated. But . . . there is open land out there, and the legal system and other things allow them to go wherever they wish.

What is worse by my reckoning is that they don't have to pay the costs of that choice. They can leave for greener pastures and (for a while) lower costs—whether it is the suburbs or the far reaches of the metropolitan area or the sunbelt or whichever—they can go there without paying the costs of what they leave behind. We have not set up a public accounting system that forces them to pay the full measure of the choices they make.

When the majority of Americans choose not to live in America's central cities, elected state and federal officials are placed in a predicament. And I stress, for reasons I will indicate, elected officials. Elected officials don't relish asking majorities to go against the grain of their wishes. Not only do they not relish asking the majority to do what the majority does not want to do, which is to live in the central cities or pay the costs, they don't get very far in public office if they try.

I am speaking as a bruised veteran. My tenure in New Jersey as a commissioner was cut short with three days' notice and two days' pay when I asked the suburbanized majority of that state to change their zoning law, to change their tax systems, to do the things they had chosen not to do; to change the ground rules by which the central cities and their trapped citizenry were left to suffer the consequences of the majority's exodus.

Therefore we don't have an "urban policy." Those people who use the phrase "urban policy"—including myself and also the Congress—are really talking about a policy that would ask the majority to pay more of the costs of the central cities they have abandoned.

I know that elected officials go in with the best of intentions asking for an urban policy; but they quickly discover they are dependent upon the majority of voters who feel the other way, and shortly they are forced to give up.

I can never forget Pat Moynihan[1] coming into public office, the White House, with a strong statement about the need for urban policy. But after two years of dealing with an American majority headed the other way, Pat concluded we couldn't have an urban policy; at least as he saw it, things were too complicated and Americans were not about to be put into a straitjacket of a set of policies that would go counter to their interests.

So there's been no urban policy. At most, we've been able to squeeze out of the majority of voters what I would call "conscience money." Categorical grants in the 1960s and general revenue-sharing in the 1970s are really conscience money. [It's] like what we give through the United Way: we all feel better for having given charity to a group of people we do not want to get too close to. This sounds like a putdown of what the federal government has done, but really that money is only conscience money directed by a suburbanized majority at a problem they would just as soon leave alone.

What is also wrong about that kind of money is that it is now coming in lesser amounts. There was a mischievous ingenuity in revenue sharing. Washington said, in effect, to local officials: "We will give you less money but let *you* decide how to spend it." Local officials made the trade happily. They had bitter memories of the 1960s when the money went directly to "the folks." They had bitter memories, too, of that money getting out of their political hands and of the loud clamor (but also, I think, the much-needed advocacy) that money produced.

---

[1] Daniel Patrick Moynihan has been a Democratic senator from New York state since 1977. At times controversial for his statements on U.S. demographics and social issues, he advised Presidents Kennedy, Johnson, and Nixon. He served briefly as ambassador to India and U.S. representative to the U.N. His books include *Beyond the Melting Pot* (with Nathan Glazer).

By and large, what revenue-sharing tends to do is give lesser amounts of money in more politically palatable form. What else is wrong with this substitution of money for policy is that the money, when given, gets sluiced mostly to majority concerns. Every time we submitted urban aid legislation in New Jersey, it came out as suburban assistance. If you look carefully at what happens to federal aid, you'll find it similarly diverted from the central cities and their poorer populations to other communities for other and more majoritarian purposes.

Also, money tends to be a palliative; in and of itself, it cannot fundamentally change or correct the problems we are faced with. At best I would guess this money, if it has any visible effect on our central cities, will end up building isolated fortresses of urban livability for a more fortunate few.

I invite you to look at the architecture that dominates the only new construction in the aging industrial cities in this country; it is "fortress architecture." Whether it is the Watergate, whether it is the riverside development in Detroit, or whatever, it tends to draw a wall around itself and to face inward. If you go to Newark, you will see the construction next to the railroad station is just another kind of fortress, designed so that you can come to Newark without ever having really been in it.

What we need to do (and for those who have to contend with majority opinion running to the contrary, it is not a very pleasant prospect) is to change the ground rules by which the system operates.

Let me give some examples to show how complicated the task really is if you seriously intend to change the condition of American city, and particularly the aging industrial cities. If you mean to do that, here are some things you're going to have to get into.

Start at the international level. In your invitation, Mr. Chairman, you asked me to address the federal system and what can be done at the various levels. But the international level may be one of the most important points of leverage. Illustration: our technical assistance in the last generation has been dominated by a philosophy of agricultural mechanization and greater human longevity. The combination of the two has built up a waiting pool of migrants to cities— not least American cities—that is staggering. Literally billions of human beings throughout the world are—or during the next quarter century will be—facing the move from rural to urban areas. And millions of these will be knocking at our doors and/or slipping through them.

Already, because we have increased the survival rate and have found that the only way we can increase agricultural production is usually by capital-intensive rather than labor-intensive means, you will find this pool of migrants increasing its flow. The estimated rate of illegal immigration to this country now is about 800,000 a year, which is double the rate of legal immigration.

There are an estimated eight million illegal immigrants already residing in this country. Where are they? They are filtering like soft-falling snow into our cities along the coastal regions. They are coming largely from the Latin American countries but also from Asia. And I do not count here obviously the legal entry of the middle- and upper-class people displaced by political upheavals abroad; mostly the newer and illegal immigrants are rural and agricultural.

I think the Congress ought to take a look, for example, at what is being done to develop the agricultural communities of the northern states of Mexico. What we did to agriculture within the United States is now happening there; the mechanization that drove millions of southern blacks to our northern cities is now pushing and pulling the legal and illegal migration of Mexicans to our cities, particularly in the southwest.

It is true that rural to urban migration *within* the United States is about over. We have depleted the farm population and there aren't many more left to move. But the flow now is going to come from abroad, and the policies which we have followed in the past, namely of technical assistance, of foreign aid, of international agreements, the Bracero agreements[2] and so forth with Mexico—have served to increase this actual and potential flow.

The premises which underlie our foreign aid policies have helped

---

[2] Beginning in 1942, the Bracero Program (a wartime labor agreement between the United States and Mexico) allowed Mexican workers, mostly agricultural, to enter the United States to work temporarily. The program was closed down in 1964, in part because of media exposés of poor working conditions and other abuses.

set the ground rules for urban policy. Those are some of the ground rules I would argue have to be changed.

At the national level, clearly one ground rule change that is called for is for the federal government to take responsibility for *welfare and health*. That is long overdue. What we have done by localizing responsibility is to force into the central cities the poor, who need both subsistence and medical attention. The cities were the only places where such aid was provided to the poor; they have huddled there, and their concentrations are now bankrupting the cities that gave them aid.

If we were to change the ground rules to say that the nation takes responsibility for basic sustenance and health for the poor and the sick—no matter where they are born and no matter where they may live—our overburdened central cities would have a fighting chance to survive. But more than that, we would have given some mobility to those who have no place else to go than the decaying city.

Youth employment. With current unemployment rates up to 40 percent in some of our older central cities, a culture is breeding true which is a counterculture far more ominous than the counterculture produced by the more privileged youth of the 1960s. This is a survival-by-any-means culture. And we cannot as a nation say that the central cities have the sole responsibility for employing those kids.

The ground rules? It probably means incentive to business. It may mean modifying the wage structure. But a system that drives urban youth and central cities into chronic crime and despair cannot be left intact.

The form and the cost of utilities, especially transportation. We have let the American people have their automobiles, the cities be damned. And Detroit—the city of the automobile—is the city that symbolically and conspicuously is now going to hell. Continue to skew the availability and cost of public utilities in favor of suburban and sunbelt development, and the descent of the cities accelerates.

The ground rules of investment. This particular committee ought to be scrutinizing constantly the investment practices and public regulatory policies affecting banks, insurance companies, and other financial institutions. "Redlining" was but a beginning.

Federal tax policy. The federal government has stabilized, even lowered, its tax rates while forcing, in effect, overburdened central cities to raise theirs. Hardly a set of ground rules that contribute to urban reconstruction.

The states. I would urge that the role of the states be given special attention. States, under our constitution, have the police power which sets the ground rules in most areas of our lives. Let me cite the sorry example of zoning. The states have abdicated their moral and legal responsibility to local communities. The result has been a growing pattern of racial and economic discrimination. That has been even more viciously entrenched by the property tax—another instance of the states' failure to fashion [their] ground rules so that central cities could live on even terms with America's majority.

Fortunately, under minority pressure and judicial duress, state tax systems are being changed, especially to equalize educational resources. I would urge an even broader perspective. Our society has moved to one in which services predominate, not manufacturing. Manufacturing has left the central cities. Their natural advantage—their chance to prosper—lies in their densities, which favor the service economy. But the current ground rules cancel out this natural advantage. Cities rely on the property tax; hospitals, libraries, medical centers all are service-oriented, but they're mostly nonprofit and don't pay property taxes. Yet they require costly municipal services which could be paid for through a municipal (or shared state and/or federal) tax on incomes. But state legislatures and the federal Congress aren't very enthusiastic about changing ground rules along those lines. Result: the cities' prospect of becoming a vital part of the post-industrial society is cut off.

Boundaries are another of the ground rules controlled by the states. Cities *might* prosper if they were expanded to include their more affluent environs; few are.

I would urge the federal government to use its bargaining strength to press for state changes in these and other ground rules. For example, I have never been able to understand why the federal government did not come to New Jersey before it had an income tax and condition federal aid on that state's doing what it should have done, which is to move to an income tax much earlier.

Congress tends instead, by general revenue-sharing and discretionary grants, to give up the bargaining power it has with the states to achieve some of those ground rule changes.

Very little leverage is available at the local level to make systematic changes—yet that is the level where responsibility is being shifted through revenue-sharing and other current devices. Mayors do not have much control over the system, nor do city councils. They need the federal and state governments to work on the fundamental changes that are needed.

One area I haven't mentioned is the working of the municipal bond market. I'd like to see this committee do a thorough investigation of that process. Some of the most damaging and mischievous policies and practices affecting the health of central cities are to be found there.

My plea, then, is to change some ground rules before talking further about appropriating money. The question is, who is going to bell that cat? Central cities are a concern of the minority, not the majority, of Americans. And legislators and congressman, governors and Presidents, get elected by the majority.

It is no accident that the courts are one of the major instrumentalities which are holding the nation's feet to the fire. Elected officials rarely can stand the pressures that favor suburbs and sunbelt. That leaves the courts as the lonely protectors of the minority and the cities. The courts are enforcing the American constitution and preserving a sense of equity. But the courts cannot stand there alone, particularly when they get thrown at them, from this body and the White House, statements that the courts have no business "messing around" in urban finance and education and zoning, and that no one should listen to (and obey?) their rulings. Sad, tragic—because the courts are the primary force holding the system to account.

A supportive force is advocacy—the public interest groups that have lately come into being. We need advocates of the poor and the central city. And thank God many of them have found legal handles by which they can hold us to account.

Mayors, too, but mayors these days have been demoralized. Foundations have joined the fray, but too few. I think the Congress every so often ought to prod the foundations to be more active in urban affairs. Similarly, American corporations: they are allowed to deduct charitable contribution up to 5 percent of pretax income, but actually give only 1 percent. That additional 4 percent could help substantially if devoted to strategic urban problems.

The prospects? One could easily become pessimistic. A counterclass and a counterculture are developing in our central cities. They are dedicated to survival by any means. Unemployment—well, I wouldn't call it that. What's happening is employment in other kinds of human activities—crime, hustling, rip-off. One could foresee the emergence of urban "warlords" who will build their power in trade for guaranteeing personal and job security within deteriorating central cities.

But on the optimistic side—and I have counted on it heavily— there is, down at the street level, a lot of sturdiness, and there is a lot of decency. It is surprising how it has persevered in the midst of urban decay.

When I closed my eyes to the shabbier buildings of Newark and listened instead to human beings, I found vibrant spirits with more ingenuity in many respects than my suburban folks. And that sturdiness, that sense of common decency, I think are the biggest force our central cities have going for them. Certainly it's more immediately to be counted on than the other force that may also bring life back toward the downtown—the shortage of energy, which again would revive the logic of greater density on which our older cities were originally constructed. Though I must admit, having just strolled the revived Quincy Market area of waterfront Boston, I catch a sparkling glimpse of a new urban lifestyle that may appeal to our next generation.

What I would conclude with, Mr. Chairman, is an admonition or a hope that you and this committee will engage the system, its ground rules, and the obstinate way in which they grind out the problems we are talking about, and be willing at least marginally to make a difference; and then to guarantee some kind of sustained effort within those now-depressed areas.

One of the disasters that has occurred has been the break-off of the energy and commitment mounted during the 1960s. The New Town movement and urban renewal—criticize [them] as you will— all of them aspired and ennobled. And then they were dismantled with no hope or idealism left in their place.

I would like to see the Congress make a *minimum* but sustained commitment to every one of these declining urban areas if votes and resources are too few to allow for anything more. Say that this nation—if we can't satisfy all of our housing needs—will guarantee that there will be a sustained effort, despite varying politics and the interest rates, to keep good people working to accomplish set minimums—of housing, employment, facilities. Somehow the rest will get done—if decent people are given your pledge to stay with them.

 # Searching for a
New Urban Policy

(Presented at the Nippon Life Insurance Foundation
Symposium, Tokyo, Japan, April 4, 1985)

*"It is relatively simple for any given champion of a
single city or class of cities to decide what to argue
for in the dialogue over urban policy: more money,
more autonomy, more sharing by others in the
concerns and costs of the communities being spoken
for. What is not so simple is the balancing of those
immediate interests with the competing concerns
and the longer-run interests of the larger society.
The dilemmas of urban policy flow directly from this
intricate and problematic process of balancing."*

The world's cities are within fifteen years of having survived one of
the most turbulent centuries in human history. Change has come
with bewildering speed; the pace has been relentless in each of the
three pivotal areas [that] most powerfully shape the character and
quality of human existence: demography, technology, and ideas.

Urban populations have exploded. Declining death rates and
massive migrations have produced cities of unprecedented size and
diversity.

These same cities have accommodated to four successive revolutions in transportation technology: rail, automotive, air, and space.
They have undergone five revolutions in communications: telephone, radio, television, computer, and satellite. They have seen the
economic base shift from agriculture, to manufacturing, to services
and high technology. They have faced destruction from a progression of military technology from localized armies to globalized
nuclear missiles.

And they have lived through radically changing ideas and
concepts while going through a metamorphosis of their own. The

notion of universal human rights has liberated huge segments of the world's population—women, minorities, and colonialized peoples—and made the cities a symbol of their aspirations to freedom and mobility. Cities have evolved from definable entities to flowing masses of nucleated settlements in which social structures like neighborhoods and families seem to be melting away. Urban systems have developed, linked internationally as modern counterparts of the medieval League of Hanseatic Cities.[1] Increasingly, they are caught up in a befuddling mesh of simultaneous influences, with limited prerogative or means of making autonomous decisions.

Yet somehow the cities of the world have survived. Even those [that] have suffered almost total destruction have regenerated. That simple miracle should be kept in mind as we assess urban policy over the past century and struggle now to find a new urban policy for the century just ahead. What we call cities are probably the hardiest of human institutions, with incredible powers of adaptation and survival.

That perspective provides a basis for optimism; and for the most part, that optimism will be presumed in addressing the essential question of urban policy: Can we find a formula—or a process—that will ensure not only continued survival, but more viable and livable cities than the ones we have known?

A positive answer is by no means certain. We have loosed some obstinate genii from their demographic, technological, and conceptual bottles, and they will not easily respond to our beck and call.

Changing Perceptions and [the] Emerging Nature of Urban Policy

When one looks back over the urban literature of the last century, one sees a steady accumulation of perspectives from which the problems of cities have been viewed. The earliest were undoubtedly those of the engineer/builder, whose domain was urban infrastructure, and the architect/planner, for whom the city has been primarily

---

[1] The Hanseatic League was a medieval association of northern German towns. It arose from mutual-protection alliances among the *Hansas*, mercantile companies with foreign trade, against pirates and foreign competition.

a matter of sculpture and design. To them were added the sociologists, concerned with the way people adapt to urban living and create new communities and lifestyles.

Then the political scientists, attempting to understand and define not only the ways in which cities are governed, but also the place of cities in the governing processes of the larger society. More recently, economists have joined the fray, trying to comprehend the logic of the micro-world of cities and to link them somehow to the macroeconomics of regions, nations, and a congealing world.

The progression has not been as nearly sequential as that, but the undeniable result has been a far more diverse and sophisticated approach to urban policy than was apparent a century ago. The accumulation of knowledge and expertise has undoubtedly helped cities to cope and survive; nevertheless, it has not made the search for an urban policy any simpler or less elusive. If anything, that search is more formidable than ever—more and more reminiscent of the legendary quest for the Holy Grail. Particularly if what we are looking for is a coherent governing statement [that] would make every human settlement into an ideal living environment for all the diverse human beings who are attracted to it.

We now know that such a formulation is impossible; and as one result—in many ways a sad one—there is little in recent literature about utopias, visions of a future that inspire as well as mislead. What we now talk about under the label of urban policy is almost entirely an exercise in coping, accommodating, balancing, and— only marginally—controlling. The early pretensions to the heroic are fading—which is understandable, given the magnitude and complexity of the forces at play, the scale on which they operate, and the massive inertia [that] builds up as our cities and social systems bring with them an ever-lengthening past.

Urban policy thus becomes more dynamic than static, as much process as content—in effect, a continuing dialogue and dialectic between and among differing interests and perspectives. What is essential is the continuous and assertive representation in the determination of all manner of relevant policies (be they macro- or micro-, fiscal or monetary, employment or housing, welfare or education) of what may be called an urban perspective—an insistent voice which does not allow the formulation of public and private policies, or the playing out of social and technological change, without serious and usually contentious consideration of their urban impact.

It has not been easy at either the national or global level to insert an urban presence into the decision-making process. Cities have long and usually been the residuals of policy determined elsewhere, and with other purposes in mind. That is not surprising, since urban consequences are inherently so hard to fathom and politically so easy to ignore; urban constituencies are divided, and [urban] political leaders subordinate in power.

That circumstance may now be changing. As we enter the twenty-first century, there is one dominant force coming into play that suggests a much more explicit and influential place for urban concerns in the determination of national and international policies.

The Emerging Role of Cities in a Changing Economy

Economist Richard Knight has asserted that "the deepening and spreading of knowledge is now the world's dominant activity." As he sees it, the essential change that has moved us from a manufacturing to a service economy is the rapidly increasing share of final product that is knowledge-based and therefore dependent upon the contribution of "advanced services": research, design, computerization, law, accounting, marketing, financing, governmental and public relations, to mention but a few. Actual production of goods can go on almost anywhere; American factories first left the central city for the suburbs, then moved on to non-metropolitan areas, than on to developing nations, and now there is talk of going farther outward into space. But the advanced services on which production and increasingly the general economy depend are concentrating in a hierarchy of urban centers, where there is a critical mass of supporting facilities, intellectual activity, and competitive stimulation.

At the top of this hierarchy are "command and control" centers, the great world-class cities such as Tokyo, New York, London, and Paris, which offer a full range of diversified service of unmatched reputation. Below them are regional and subregional centers with lesser congregations of diversified services—and then another set of specialized service (e.g., government, recreation) and production (e.g., manufacturing, military) centers, many of them vulnerable to obsolescence and decline.[2]

The efficient assembly and continuous nourishment of knowledge-based services are critically important in meeting what is now a global competition among urban and national economies. That competition is fierce and accelerating: 70 percent of my own country's industry now faces foreign-based competition as against 30 percent less than twenty-five years ago, and its share of the world's high-technology exports has fallen from 25 percent to 20 percent within the last decade alone.

The economic fate of nations is now tied inextricably to the performance of their cities. [Nations] will prosper or decline in the degree to which their urban environments provide an attractive and supportive base for the advanced service economy. There are some essential conditions for successfully doing so. One is to make certain that intellectual capital is sufficiently available: a flourishing educational system, facilities for basic and applied research, the capacity for innovation, programs for training and retraining, and state-of-the-art information systems [that] ensure instantaneous networking and knowledge dissemination.

Another ingredient of success lies in the realm of amenities and infrastructure, ranging from high culture to underground utilities. The needs and tastes particularly of those engaged in the advanced services but also of urban citizens generally, make the city an object of consumption, its attractiveness and viability dependent upon its capacity to satisfy the growing demand for an environment of cultural richness and intellectual stimulation.

The linkage between the quality of urban life and the health of the general economy is a powerful argument for a stronger urban voice in the formulation of national policy. But as powerful as the logic is, it cannot dissolve all the complexities, nor resolve all the dilemmas involved in formulating broad policies that promote the general interests of cities.

---

[2] Classification by Thierry J. Noyelle and Thomas M. Stanback, Jr., in *The Economic Transformation of American Cities* (Totowa, N.J.: Rowman & Allanheld, 1984).

Dilemmas of Urban Policy

It is relatively simple for any given champion of a single city or class of cities to decide what to argue for in the dialogue over urban policy: more money, more autonomy, more sharing by others in the concerns and costs of the communities being spoken for. What is not so simple is the balancing of those immediate interests with the competing concerns and the longer-run interests of the larger society. The dilemmas of urban policy flow directly from this intricate and problematic process of balancing. Some of these tension points are described below.

Integrating macro- and micro-policy. National governments find it difficult enough to cope with the aggregate behavior of their societies and economies; an entirely new order of complexity is added when they are asked to fine-tune their fiscal, monetary, foreign, and other policies to ensure the well-being of individual components such as cities. They have understandably been reluctant to do so, except in those instances where the engineering of certain urban consequences is clearly possible and to their advantage. Raising interest rates is a classical example of the dilemma: it may slow a heating national economy but have a devastating effect on the supply of housing in cities which need it.

Deciding between urban and industrial policy. If indeed national policy is to discriminate among subnational interests, the question arises—and is being sharply debated—whether to proceed by industrial sectors or by urban configurations. Stimulating the growth of individual sectors is arguably simpler and more efficient. But it could accelerate the obsolescence of those cities which are judged as poor prospects for economic growth and are consequently bypassed.

Dealing with disparities between prospering cities and those left behind. Not all cities can prosper; and those which do tend to accumulate the political power, competitive advantage, and financial resources that further strengthen their position and increase the disparities between them and less fortunate communities. Urban policy is thus faced with probably its most vexing and generic dilemma: the tension between efficiency and equity. National objectives of economic growth seem most readily advanced by favoring the already advantaged; there are some clear political gains and external economies that argue for doing so. But there are also some longer-term costs: resentment, unemployment, and general decline in the cities left behind, and accumulating diseconomies thought to be inherent in the "overgrowth" of prospering areas.

Dealing with disparities within cities. Every city—whether at its core or at its fringes—has its poorer or otherwise marginal populations: minorities, immigrants, those in passing or long-term dependency. With the increasing rates of unemployment, particularly among youth, in the Western industrialized nations, the numbers of the urban disadvantaged are growing; in the United States, there is increasing concern with the emergence of a more or less permanent underclass. During the last decades, social welfare programs have been expanded to counter these disparities, but dwindling affluence and public resistance are forcing a reconsideration of how much can or should be allocated to income transfers as against other forms of private and public outlays.

Affecting the environment and urban design. Rapid economic development and growth are urgent necessities for nations in today's world, and there is a strong tendency to achieve these goals at the expense of environmental integrity and orderly urban development. Cities themselves will usually make the same trade-offs. Strict requirements for more sensitive treatment of environment and design are seen by the advocates of growth as costly encumbrances. Yet the livability and long-term viability of cities depend heavily on the quality of their air and water and on the attractiveness of their built environment. Again, the challenge of urban policy is to contend successfully for healthier balance.

Allocating responsibility for urban policy. Again there is tension between the need to implant urban concerns into national policies and the pragmatic imperative of allowing as much decentralized authority and initiative as possible. Resolutions will obviously vary with circumstance and time. Nations with limited resources and urgent social conditions are likely to swing the balance in favor of centralized control; others, more affluent and at a more advanced stage of development, are more likely to shift authority and responsibility downward to lower levels of government and outward to private initiative and the play of the market. But whatever the circumstance, the relationships are always volatile; it is difficult to establish a stable and generally satisfying equilibrium. Simply to cite an example, industrialized nations may generally trend toward greater local autonomy, but rising problems of youth unemployment may force policy in a more centralizing direction.

Finding and allocating the necessary resources. No society has the human or financial means to provide optimally for all the contending factors represented in these simultaneous equations of urban [and] national policy. And so there is always the haunting question of how best to allocate the limited energies and moneys that are available. Cost-benefit analyses can be helpful; but without exact measures and indices to go by, they fall short. Who is to say with certainty whether a city of a certain size is or is not more efficient than one either smaller or larger, or that investing a given amount in environmental protection produces a greater social return than an equivalent expenditure for plant modernization? And so urban policy remains fundamentally an exercise in judgment, and matters of judgment sooner or later become items on the agenda of the political process.

Urban Policy as Process:
An American Experiment

When the American Congress passed its Housing Act of 1970, it incorporated in that act a process by which the nation could regularly assess the condition of its cities, confront its urban and national needs, and debate the relative merits of differing proposals for reconciling and responding to those needs: in effect, a planned and explicit consideration of national urban policy. The act required the President of the United States biennially to prepare a report on the nation's urban condition, along with a statement and justification of his administration's policy. That report was then to be submitted to the Congress for its consideration and response, providing an opportunity for a focused and public dialogue.

In its design, the arrangement had considerable merit; in practice, the consequences have been marginal. Richard Nixon, the first President to whom the requirement applied, was totally unenthusiastic, stalled in the preparation and submission of the initial report until Congress threatened legal action, and then presented a document that was little more than a rehash of statistics and vacuous commentary. Congressional response was, as expected, critical; public attention scant. Subsequent Presidential reports by both Nixon and Ford were also tardy and passed without much notice, either in Congress or in the press. President Carter took the assignment more seriously, using the report to express his strong commitment to "targeting" of federal aid and attention to the distressed sections and neighborhoods of urban America. Public response was not particularly receptive, reflecting the growing sentiment against redistribution of resources that were seen to be dwindling, and also against federal intervention. That sentiment prevailed; urban outlays by the federal government began dropping in 1978, and by 1980, the nation was ready for the Reagan philosophy of cutting federal assistance, devolving the responsibility for the nation's cities to the several states and to the generosity of the private sector, and limiting the role of the federal government essentially to improvement of the general economy. President Reagan's 1982 and 1984 urban reports to Congress are a recital of that policy, a repetition of his belief that a stronger economy is the best contribution the federal government can make to the problems of American cities and those of its citizens who are in distress. The reaction of Congress has been equally predictable, a medley of criticism and compliment difficult to hear over the din of debate centering far more on particular national policies than on "urban policy"—an abstraction the public and Congress find it difficult to get excited about. Nor has it become the forum for mayors and other local officials, who prefer to deal with specific issues as they affect their particular constituencies, and on pressure points far more sensitive and responsive than generalized Presidential [and] Congressional rhetoric.

Still, the process has its value. It provides—probably more for scholars than for activists—a continuous recording and assessment of America's urban condition, a more comprehensive view of urban problems and public policy than is available through the fragmentary considerations found in partisan and particularistic debate. And there are signs that the process may mature into something more akin to what the authors of the original [Housing] Act had in mind.

The Congressional subcommittee charged with consideration of the President's most recent report has spent a year and considerable effort preparing for the engagement and drafting a sophisticated response. Its first published statement, prepared with the help of a distinguished group of expert advisers (albeit with a partisan flavor), is entitled "Urban America 1984: A Report Card. A Report on the Widening Gap between the Needs of Cities and Their Ability to Respond." It is to be followed by a second report, outlining in specific terms an alternative to the urban policies presented by the President.

Urban Policy as Content—Some Needed Emphasis

There are several lessons that might be drawn from the American experiment with a focused and comprehensive process of debating national urban policy. One is that it is difficult to gather all the vast assortment of urban and national concerns into one negotiating process and come to a simultaneous set of decisions that will be systematically implemented. The attempt is symbolically useful, but the process of negotiation that actually creates a nation's "urban policy" is inescapably far more discrete and diffuse, a continuous set of bargains struck off by contending local and national interests.

If, indeed, the process is diffuse—or to the extent that it is—it becomes more important to have a guiding set of criteria, a gyroscopic sense of direction, to give some coherence to the accumulating negotiations and decisions that ultimately constitute an urban policy. Formulating such a set is obviously a matter for each nation and society; circumstances and preferences differ, and so must urban policies. But as we move into the twenty-first century with a globalizing economic and urban system, it may be useful to attempt a list of some overarching considerations.

Urban policy will have to assign an ever-higher priority to human capital and the development of human resources. As both the city and the general economy become increasingly knowledge-based, human intelligence and ingenuity will be at a premium. Society no longer can afford the wastage of human beings that has so tragically accompanied industrialization in the past—whether in the form of high unemployment, debilitating poverty, malnutrition, or poor education. Investment in human resources will have a high rate of return, even though it may not be as immediately calculable as investment in physical plant. It is also a political imperative: ignorance, poverty, and unemployment are destabilizing and eventually explosive.

It will be especially critical for cities and urban policy to create and maintain "think tanks" and other facilities for continuous analysis and innovation. Again, as society and the economy find their base in the production of knowledge, the pace of change—and, correspondingly, of obsolescence—will accelerate. Cities cannot risk being left behind; they must continuously invent, adapt, and anticipate. This is true across a whole range of concerns, from a general assessment of social trends and new technology to the efficiency of municipal operations. New partnerships with educational institutions at all levels will need to be formed and new opportunities opened for lifelong learning on a universal basis.

Urban policy and those speaking for cities will have to take a much more assertive role in protecting the urban environment and enhancing the quality of urban life. One of the principal threats to the city, both as an economic generator and as an attractive way of life, is the deterioration of its air, water, utility systems, recreational and cultural facilities, and personal safety. The seriousness of that threat is evident in the loss of population, first by the central cities, and more recently—in countries like the United States where space allows—by the larger and older metropolitan areas as well. There are encouraging signs that the threat is being recognized and that countermeasures are being taken (certainly the curbing of automobile emissions in Tokyo is a happy example). The struggle will not be an easy one; the costs of environmental cleanup, utility replacement, and sophisticated assessment of potential environmental damage will be high. But the city's survival depends on fighting and winning this battle.

A similarly assertive position will have to be taken with respect to technological development and capital flows. A second major threat to the survival of cities is the diffusing pattern of industrial and human settlements that has already begun with automotive transportation and electronic communication. Current innovations such as satellite transmission and distributive processing (i.e., the aggregated use of linked minicomputers with the building of giant computers accessible through fiber-optic cables strung out to scattered locations, and possibly some day the universal availability of fusion energy—all these might lead to a hemorrhaging of urban populations [that] would be fatal to cities as we have known them. Even if such deconcentration is inevitable, it needs to be managed in a way that does not waste the enormous economic, social, and human investment which cities represent. It should be managed, too, in a way that does not remove inordinate amounts of prime agricultural land from active production—certainly not in the circumstance of world hunger we are now encountering.

Urban policy will have to intersect, and often contend, with foreign policy if cities are to remain secure. With the advent of highly sophisticated weaponry, cities have become almost totally vulnerable both at long and short range, from hostile forces without and from terrorism within. With their populations so exposed, cities— and urban policymakers—will have to engage more aggressively in the formulation of defense and foreign policy—and should, in fact, be more visible and audible in international negotiations.

Both actually and symbolically, urban policy should express the aspiration to a free and open society which the concept of a city has come to represent. Cities have broken through the walls [that] once contained them, but nations are still building such walls in the defensive posture of military, economic, and political security. It is unreasonable to expect that the tension between the two approaches will soon, if ever, relax. But in that dialectic, the cities— and the objective of urban policy—should be clear: to survive as forcefully as possible toward a more open, equitable, and opportunity-rich global society.

Trends and Prospects

One wonders what reflections will be shared by urbanists a century from now at another conference like the one we are now attending. Will they be looking back at the transformation of cities into infinitely scattered communities, possibly extending into space, linked instantaneously by exotic systems of communication, relieved of the congestion that today makes them militarily vulnerable and environmentally flawed? Or will cities of an older tradition re-emerge, their citizens having found electronic communication no substitute for intensive human interaction? I choose not to speculate on the third alternative, that cities of whatever form may not have survived. But all three scenarios are possible.

Looking Backward—
And Forward

(Keynote address to the Roundtable on University
Research and Service Centers, Akron, Ohio, April 1987)

*"Your task is to continue your tradition of dealing
with things real and things whole; your challenge is
to shift toward a larger, more complicated whole.
Each locale is now a global microcosm. And the
emerging imperative is to think globally but to act
locally, in a way that makes the two worlds
compatible."*

Looking Backward

Where we are and what we're doing today must always be
interpreted in the light of what has come before.

First, we're part of a tradition of urban reform that has appeared
in cycles. The procession and accumulation of specialists attracted to
urban reform documents the tenacity and continuity of commitment
to the cause. This despite the cyclical downturns in public interest
and political support—not least in the national resting period of the
Eisenhower administration, and now in the Reagan [administration]
dry spell of national interest and finance. This long lineage of
stubborn dedication should be an assurance to all of us, especially
now when we're all scratching an existence from dwindling budgets
and the discouragement from national leadership.

Our urban areas and their problems continue as a challenge and
attraction to rising generations of the nation's talent. And as an elder
participant, [I find] the rising talent I see in this audience a welcome
challenge and assurance.

My theme today is simply this. The changing times make all the
more essential the role you're positioned to play: that of analysts,

change facilitators, and innovators in a system increasingly reliant on local initiative and adaptability.

Let me turn to those changing times and the forces that have shaped and are shaping our present. I would enumerate them as follows:

1. A move from national hegemony to global competition. In the immediate post–World War II period, the United States was dominant in its share of world resources, markets, [and] military and commercial technology. We have subsequently witnessed a far wider sharing worldwide of critical resources, markets, technology, and power. The trend has led to intense international competition and has left each urban area essentially on its own, to thrive or decline depending on its own location, [the] health of its economy, its leadership and ingenuity.

2. A move from agriculture to manufacturing, and then to services and the knowledge-based economy. In 1910, for the first time in American history, the number of blue-collar workers exceeded that of agricultural workers. In 1985, professional, managerial, and technical employees surpassed the total of blue-collar workers. The shift has prompted the development of an entirely new classification based on service employment: "command and control centers," both of national and regional stature; "specialized service centers," including areas like Akron; [and] "subordinate centers," in which services such as military, consumer, and mining predominate.

Within areas so classified, there are accelerating shifts and imbalances. For example, Boston, within a decade, has gone from decline to prosperity; Denver and Houston have gone from prosperity to decline. One of the analyses I have found provocative is that of the Japanese economist Sakamoto; he argues that stabilization and more dynamic development of America's regional economies would increase consumption of domestically produced goods to the point where the nation's international trade would come into balance.

3. A shift from a middle-class [society] toward a stratifying society. This can be read from the changes in both income and wealth distribution. The gap in concentrations of incomes over $48,000 and below $13,500 is now at a twenty-five-year peak. As for wealth, there has been a 10 percent increase in those holding the top

.5 percent, and a 7 percent decrease in those left in the bottom 90 percent over the past twenty years. There have also been geographical shifts, with central cities losing income relative to suburban areas. Another sign of stratification can be found in the nature of jobs. The contrast is particularly evident in the discrepancy between what are known as producer vs. consumer services (the first covering especially the professions: law, consulting, accounting, etc.), the high-paying vs. the low-paying. Between 1979 and 1985, 44 percent of the newly created jobs paid wages at the poverty level; that percentage was twice what it was in the 1960s and 1970s.

Still another evidence is the growth of poverty, homelessness, and hunger in America. The poverty rate climbed from 13 percent to 14 percent between 1980 and 1985. Fifty cities during that time lost 5 percent of their population; but still their poverty rate climbed by 12 percent. The spread of homelessness has caused me to reflect on [my] time working on the problems of Calcutta, where over 400,000 could be sleeping on the streets; I recall wondering if the United States would ever experience a similar tragedy.

And now we're watching the growth of an urban underclass. Richard Nathan, the Princeton analyst, has been persuaded against early doubts that the phenomenon of an underclass is not speculative but real. His data show that the percentage of poor concentrated in urban areas has risen within the last decade from six to fifteen. The number of poor in what he calls extremely concentrated areas has increased by 40 percent in that same 1970–80 period. And the same thing is happening in other industrialized countries: it seems we're witnessing the emergence of a world underclass.

4. A shift from an affluent to a "learning" society. There are still a lot of rich and very rich people in America. But in a recent survey, the United States scored last among leading industrial societies on seventeen indicators of quality of life. Startlingly, there has been no increase in real wages during the last ten years. That static condition has been obscured by a number of factors: the compensating increase in the number of women and family members working, the rising support from Social Security, the diminishing size of families, and the investments from abroad [that] have sustained our financial markets and general economy while the American contribution has lagged.

5. A shift from a predominantly white European stock to a globalizing population of color. The current growth rate of the nation's black population is about twice that of whites. Immigrants, who once came mainly from Europe, are now charting a very different pattern: 225,000 from Asia, 210,000 from Latin America, and only 70,000 from Europe. That does not include the uncounted illegal immigrants.

6. A shift from a young to an aging population. This does not apply to most migrant and minority groups, and that discrepancy represents another major force at work on the American scene. But the aging phenomenon, which characterizes the majority of the population, also describes the condition of the country's infrastructure.

7. A shift from a centralizing to a decentralizing society. For most of the past century, there has been a centralizing trend both in the nation's politics and in its economy. The New Federalism and privatization have begun to reverse that trend.

8. A shift from a liberal to a conservative leadership and electorate. This trend needs no elaboration.

9. A shift from limited access to universal opportunities for learning. No listing of moving forces is complete without including and emphasizing this fundamental change. The opening of formal education to minorities and the general population has transformed the American character; so has the spreading force of the mass media.

Looking Ahead: Where Are Current Forces Moving Us?

First, toward a premium on local initiative and adaptation.

Even national action and national programs reflect the shift; they are increasingly based on local programming and experimentation. The system is too complex to allow for monolithic endeavors. As Gregory Bateson[1] once commented, any organism as it grows larger and more complex must simultaneously miniaturize. The system is

---

[1] Gregory Bateson (1904–1980) was anthropologist, philosopher, educator, naturalist, and poet. He was noted for his study of the social forces that bind and divide individuals and groups.

also too competitive; it demands diversity. Much as we may wish otherwise, especially those of us who are discouraged by present partisan exaggeration and exploitation of the trend, the inevitability of more decentralization flows from the very nature of this complex and competitive society.

The logic of this decentralizing and adaptive mode expresses itself in all four of the processes by which we respond: in the way we analyze problems, the encouragement we give to innovation, the care and complexity with which we approach program development, and the importance we place on continuous adaptation. Not incidentally, it's worth noting what characterized those urban areas [that] have successfully accommodated to recent change. Boston with its superb collection of institutions of higher education and associated research capacities is an outstanding example.

Consider some selected fields in which the response pattern has changed and now reflects the logic of a complicating society.

Economic development. It was once thought that development was simply a matter of attracting factories. Now it's first a matter of sophisticated analysis, starting with an assessment of the general circumstance of a given community and its strengths, liabilities, and potential. Hence the classification system earlier referred to, which helps do precisely that and makes a community come to grips with its realities—not least the uphill struggle facing a community [that] is low on the service economy hierarchy and lacking in the knowledge base so essential to change and adaptation. Job and wage structures have to be scrutinized; so do facilities for retraining and education. I am encouraged by what I see among you of the readiness and capacity to help communities in that kind of self-appraisal.

Programming for economic development is also evolving and adapting. The spread of community development corporations— now numbering over 2,000 nationally—is dramatically expressive. So are the partnerships now flowering in America. I'm proud to say that Boston's Compact, ACCESS, and other collaboratives have set the pace in this respect.

Social improvement. Again, our analytical efforts show sophistication and adaptation. The shift in perspective toward human capital and its development is particularly in point. We have come to realize—I hope not too late—the vital importance of developing the potential of this generation of America's youth, now dwindling in numbers and growing its proportion of minorities and immigrants. And the alarming extent of its wastage is now starkly evident: in the number of school dropouts, in the ravaged environment in which so many of them are raised, in the spreading population of those from the underclass. Within but the space of a few years, educational reform has moved from the unreal concentration on the conventionality of curriculum reform to a confrontation on the reality of an extremely diverse and largely unmotivated urban school population.

Technological advance. This country has lagged in its public utilization of technological progress. Compare our urban conventionalities to the great leap forward of Japan, now building a network of thirty-six technopoli, new cities designed at the cutting edge of advanced communication systems and infrastructure. One can begin to catch glimpses of scattered American experimentation: in Kansas City's use of underground construction and in Otto Silh's resurrection of his earlier Innovative City Project, launched two decades ago in Minnesota and long starved [for] public and private support. But the disparity between military/commercial development and the poor cousin of urban innovation is stark and ominous.

Second, current forces and trends are moving us toward decentralized (and fragmented?) leadership.

The shift is evident everywhere, expressed as one example in the rising activity and importance of governors at one level and neighborhood organizations flourishing at the grassroots. Philanthropic leadership is also spreading out. No longer is the field dominated by the very large foundations; much more is now heard from the rapidly growing community foundations. And the very large are accommodating to the shift by expanding their collaboratives with local philanthropies. Privatization is another expression, with for-profit and nonprofit entities contracting with larger public bodies in implementing otherwise bureaucratized and large-scale programming.

It is still a fair question whether this emerging system of localized and particularized response to problems national and global in scale will suffice without the complementarily of national and global leadership, coordination, and backstopping. My own belief is that it will not. And my optimistic side tells me that the missing link will increasingly be noted and supplied, given the perceptive and pragmatic character of the American public (and, hopefully, world opinion) over the longer run.

Third, we are being moved toward a new consensus.

That long-term adaptability of Americans is already becoming evident. Signs are that the pendulum is already starting to swing from a conservative outpoint toward a pragmatic liberalism—or as Senator Kennedy has named it, a compassionate work ethic. Analysts Hart, Yankelovich, and Harris have already measured and reported this nascent consensus: anti-welfare but pro-children and [in favor of] the investments needed (nutrition, education, housing) to develop the human capital they represent. One can see it in the support given recent innovation in "workfare," in the self-help concept of community development corporations and neighborhood associations, and in the attention given Richard Nathan's formula for "behavioral trades"—the giving of social benefits in return for changes in welfare dependency and other forms of nonproductive behavior.

Fourth, we are being moved toward some new and aggravating divisiveness.

The growing imbalance between the younger and older cohorts of the population is the potential source. Those over sixty-five now outnumber (for the first time since the Baby Boom) those under eighteen, and their voting preponderance adds political power to advocacy of their interests; clearly there is complementarily in employment, as the number of young people declines and the need for the older to take up the slack in labor supply increases.

Another growing cleavage is that between richer and poorer. The numbers involved have already been mentioned; the difference will sharpen as the composition of the growing poor changes to reflect the cultural background of the underclass, immigrants, and long-term dependents. As respects immigrants, xenophobia is a risk and is already showing in the efforts to restrict the use of foreign languages and the rate of immigration.

The fifth direction we are being moved in has already been identified: toward localized and particularized social responses.

I've indicated reasons to understand and still to be concerned: a logic of our complicating society, but is it capable in and by itself to cope with our society's problems? My guess is that there will, with experience, be a countermovement toward national leadership and response [that] will add what I believe to be a necessity: a complementary set of actions simultaneously at local and more general levels.

Your Role [and] Your Agenda

In this future, as always, I would expect you to concentrate on local government and more local concerns, but with an increasing awareness and concern for issues and trends that are national and global in their nature. One of the advantages you bring is what I'd call your "reality quotient": you live well and constructively with real problems [and] real people, and you don't have the ready escape of retreating to the distant and abstract. You are, indeed, one of the few (if not the only) lenses of the university that sees things whole—in contrast to the isolating specializations [that] dominate the life of the campus. Your differentness in that respect may well account for your lack of the kind of traveling reputation that academics develop as the consequence of dealing with specialization skills, problems, and constituencies. Few of you, I notice, are ever called on to appear with Ted Koppel; you may be the keeper of local conscience but are not the keepers of the great mysteries and mystiques [that] attract the wider audiences.

Your task is to continue your tradition of dealing with things real and things whole; your challenge is to shift toward a larger, more complicated whole. Each locale is now a global microcosm. The emerging imperative is to think globally but to act locally, in a way that makes the two worlds compatible. It will help you immeasurably in doing that to participate in larger networks, starting with the kind you've convened here, and extending over national boundaries.

And I'd ask that you constantly remember that your role is essentially educational—not least within your own institution. Higher education is one of the most provincial institutions on the American scene. Its traditions of specialization and scholasticism make it difficult to perceive, change, and respond. And now, just when its thinking and innovative function is most needed by society, it badly lacks the qualities you represent, the lessons from reality that you can pass on.

That educational job is never an easy one, never entirely and only marginally popular. And the more worldly and sophisticated your audience thinks itself to be, the harder it is for it to accept the message from someone hip-deep in the local realities. Recall Lincoln Steffens,[2] who concluded that mayors, mired as they are in the problems of garbage disposal and neighborhood squabbles, rarely are allowed to move on to national office; their identities are too stereotyped, too fixed.

Remember too, that the community is also your student body. You've long ago discovered that your locals won't accept learning by lecturing; a much subtler pedagogy is called for. Your teaching techniques will vary to fit time and place and you'll never have the financial or other resources you need.

But you will have met the test if you—and luckily if others—can say, "The university and the community are the better for you having been around." And after forty-five years of watching you and your predecessors operate, I'm more than ready to say just that.

---

[3] J. Lincoln Steffens (1866–1936) was a reporter and editor whose articles exposing municipal corruption launched the era of muckraking journalism. His book *The Shame of the Cities,* a collection of articles on squalid conditions in major U.S. metropolises, caused a sensation when it came out in 1904.

PART III
**Education: A Generation
Too Precious to Waste**

*"Education is one of those infinities
that gives us plenty of room to search
but never the comfort of knowing
that you have arrived."*

—*1972*

Merging Academic and Urban Affairs

(A report to a National Conference of Educators, Public Officials, and Other Civic Leaders in Detroit, Michigan, as reprinted in *The Educational Record: Special Supplement, Higher Education for Urban America*, June 1964)

"The increasing pace of change in our society is eroding the dividing lines between jurisdictions. . . . It is amusing to speculate that there may soon be a time when, instead of government keeping a check to make certain that competition exists among private institutions, we shall see the private sector of the society moving to make sure that healthy competition exists within the public sector."

Recent discussions of higher education for urban America have helped define many of the problems confronting us and have provided a variety of proposals for coping with them. The aim of this paper goes beyond a repetition of these problems and proposals and looks afresh at the nature of our universities and the representatives of urban government who will be working with them, [hoping] to identify some of the relationships that may be developing between institutions and municipalities. There will probably be no crisp and easy answers to some of the questions raised, but we may arrive at some working assumptions about the appropriate role of the university in an urban society.

One of the major difficulties in a discussion of this kind is the tendency to dichotomize. We persist in thinking about educators as men of intellect and politicians as men of action. And, depending on which group we belong to, we often display another very human trait in trying to justify our own roles by taking a poke at the other group. There are some masterpieces of name-calling rhetoric in the literature from the men of action about the men of thought, and vice versa. Educators today, however, are becoming accustomed to being consulted by the "men of action," and there probably isn't a professor alive who would refuse to accept a call to the White House staff, or to the office of a mayor or governor, to join the action—whether for a brief consultation or for a longer term of service. At the same time, I do not know of a single mayor, governor, or senator who would be unwilling to serve a term as a visiting professor (or, at the very least, to take part in a seminar) at a university. The fact is that fixed institutional roles are disappearing. The increasing pace of change in our society is eroding the dividing lines between jurisdictions. All institutions are changing, and a kind of healthy uncertainty and competition for roles is the rule of the day.

Our search for clues to how we are to operate in the new society will have to go beyond that word "urban." During the past decade, we have come to depend on the word as a label for a new social structure that we are all aware of but cannot really describe. There is a kind of magic sound to it. It can be used in the names of disciplines, in job titles; it works its way into the names of conferences and programs; and slogans built around it have become the rallying cry of the young Turks in just about every institution in our society. There is an urban movement in the church; trade unions are beginning to play with the word; universities and colleges have taken a renewed interest in long-neglected urban studies. "Urban" has become a magic word for the nonprofit agencies and philanthropies, and no one can deny that it is enjoying a great vogue in all branches of state and federal government. We must, however, identify the major characteristics of the new society [that] we label "urban" before we can come up with an accurate description of the role of any institution.

(There is some irony in our current situation, in the fact that the educators on our university campuses who are doing the most up-to-date thinking about urban affairs have largely associated themselves with the oldest political sector of the city: the downtown city group. There is a revival of interest in the central city in the academic community, and the central city mayors have, in turn, been increasingly aware of the universities and have been turning to them for help with their problems.)

Several things about our new society are now clear, and I suspect that we may be moving into the final phase of stage one in the process of definition [that] has been in progress for the past decade. We have had ten years of research, writing, and talking about the new urban society. And while the society has been changing—in a very fundamental way—we have clung to some of our old perspectives in order to get at the truth. Now we are beginning to piece together the results of all this examination.

During his first visit to the United States last year, Willy Brandt paid a call on the Ford Foundation offices and asked five people what they thought the United States would be like in 1980. Their impromptu answers showed wide agreement on the basic outline of the new society, and this agreement helped to crystallize my own thinking on the subject.

I believe that we are now coming to the end of the first period of urbanization and have reached the stage where the ideas produced during the decade of academic analysis are being picked up by political leaders—the men of action. And, having adopted these concepts, the men of action are now asking for programs to cure the ills the analysts have diagnosed.

What we need at this point are a few simple tools that the man on the street can grasp and use in his attempts to manage the new society. But such tools are hard to develop. Adequate programs can be developed only when we get close to where the problems are. While our society as a whole is centralizing very rapidly in some fields—in communications, for instance—there will be marked decentralization in specific action programs. The problems of any one community can, after all, be treated only within that community. There will be centralization in the sense of broad definitions of problems and broad accumulations of resources, with allocation of resources being handled through the larger units of government, but specific programs in individual communities will develop autonomously, in all likelihood.

This process may pose a threat to many of our present social institutions, which have been existing on quite different premises. What we need now is someone to analyze our social system as Lord Keynes analyzed the economic system. As a matter of fact, our present social theory has a great deal in common with pre-Keynesian economic theory. We have assumed that there was a "market mechanism"—an invisible, self-correcting device in social development. But we have learned that this is not true. It is interesting to note that the Council of Economic Advisors was among the first to recognize this fallacy. They discovered, to their embarrassment, that an increase in the Gross National Product was not necessarily accompanied by an increase in employment opportunities; the social market mechanism was not operating to create employment opportunities as it had been expected to; hence the Poverty Program. Our Keynsian social analyst will have to identify the existing social imperfections that stand in the way of achieving equilibrium and full employment, and then we shall have to root them out by determined action—not simply wait for some unknown force to correct them.

I believe that we are now in the process of developing a social theory for this kind of action—action [that] is going to call for strong executive leadership at all levels of society. Strong leadership will be necessary in both the public and private sectors of society, and it seems likely that as much political leadership will emerge from private institutions as from the public institutions. Even a cursory examination of some of our major private corporations reveals how heavily involved they are in the decision-making processes of the government, most markedly in the defense industry, where NASA contracts are so important a factor. Our public and private institutions are, obviously, coming closer together, and some of the methods of private industry may have to be adapted to government. We shall need a kind of research and development department for society as a whole. The prototypes already exist in such institutions as the RAND Corporation and in such community study organizations as have come into being in Kansas City and Detroit, for example. These new social R&D units take many forms, but they are emerging as prototypes for the kind of programs we shall need.

An important factor in developing these programs is the increasing availability of alternative instruments of action. We are beginning to see alternative avenues opened up in the mechanisms of both federal and local governments. It is amusing to speculate that there may soon be a time when, instead of government keeping a check to make certain that competition exists among private institutions, we shall see the private sector of the society moving to make sure that healthy competition exists within the public sector. Nonprofit corporations, too, are emerging as competitors and supplementers of public agencies. And as more and more federal funds are allocated to domestic spending (in urban redevelopment programs, for example), the R&D units of private corporations are investigating ways and means of involving the business world in these endeavors.

All of this promises great flexibility in the public sector of our new society—great flexibility and a blurring of the accustomed tidy lines of authority. Before we reach this point, however, there will undoubtedly be a good deal of jurisdictional dispute on tough constitutional issues; but I suspect that the end result will be worth the struggle.

While public and private institutions have been cooperating in providing leadership and designing programs for social action, the universities also have been getting more and more involved. In recent years we have seen higher education begin to take its rightful place as an instrument of social action and change. Particularly since the launching of Sputnik, our society has come to appreciate the "men of thought," and every meeting and conference called today has at least one Ph.D. in attendance. As competition for entrance to colleges and universities intensifies and more and more public attention is focused on the academic world, we can be proud of the role our professors are playing in the world of action. The scene today is a far cry from that of 1942, when a trustee at a great institution at which I was then teaching could remark that professors really proved themselves during the war: they proved they could drive rivets in a shipyard as well as teach!

Perhaps I should mention that initially the man of thought was called into the world of action not so much because of any special competence, but because he professed a public purpose and because he represented a ready supply of manpower for temporary assignments—he could always be shipped back to the university after a leave of absence without complications to the employment picture. In the beginning, the world of action was not aware of some of the shortcomings of the academician—disciplinary rigidity, for instance. Now, however, elected officials are catching on and discovering that they, too, can set up agendas and raise important questions. In fact, I think that the university, along with other major social institutions, is in for a rough time over the next few years. As attention comes to bear on higher education, some of its flaws will become more obvious. There are already signs of stress. The politics of growth and the problems of leadership within the academic world are quite visible. There is, too, the fact that other instruments and agencies for learning are developing—television, to name one—and as these prove effective, traditional educational instruments will suffer. It would be interesting to know, for instance, what percentage of a young man's knowledge is acquired through formal schooling and how much through other forms of learning.

Although we have not yet arrived at such a point, I feel that there could come a time when the bright youngster might decide not to go to college. He might use those four years for travel, independent reading, apprenticeships, and so on, supplemented perhaps by two or three university courses taken for information he could not get elsewhere. I've watched the high dropout rate among very able students and talked to young people who are bored stiff by graduate school. These young people are beginning to wonder if they can perhaps get equivalent learning even more efficiently outside the university. Indeed, many have found a freedom ride to the south or participation in the Mississippi Summer Project[1] highly profitable learning experiences.

It is time for the academic world to undertake a vast program of self-examination. Are the big questions we raise in the classroom the really big questions of life? Aren't the questions and problems posed by city, state, and federal involvement in the race problem, for instance, the most important questions before our society? What are some of the possible steps universities might take?

At this point I must admit that I have no easy answers, but I would like to hazard a few general suggestions. First, I think the universities will have to serve as a kind of early warning system for society. We could have anticipated the turmoil which now accompanies the Negro's struggle for equality. We could have predicted the problems

---

[1] The Mississippi Summer Project was a 1964 voter registration and education campaign organized by the Council of Federated Organizations. Hundreds of young people, coordinated by civil rights groups, took part.

we now face in educating deprived children in the central cities. We could even have anticipated the great migration to the suburbs since the 1940s and the concomitant problems of urban blight.

Second, I believe that in addition to extending the university into the community, we ought to start thinking about letting the community extend itself into the university. Perhaps we ought to have community agents within the university as well as university agents in the community. Let's bring some of our thoughtful public officials—mayors, congressmen, senators—into the academic world to pose problems of community life and the management of our society. At the same time, the university must continue to engage the community in a dialogue in an increased effort to find the means of making itself relevant to the community.

I spoke earlier of our need for social analysts with the powers and stature of a Keynes; it is up to the university to train such people. We must develop a breed of sociologists and economists capable of deep analysis and evaluation of our society—analysts who will, it is to be hoped for, be much more aware of the needs of deprived citizens than our social critics have been in the past.

The university should develop a counterpart of the cost and benefit analysis employed in the business world. We shall have to learn to identify the most promising means of accomplishing our ends and to eliminate the proposals that are not likely to produce efficient social results. Too often academic people depend on purely quantitative analysis and look for closed systems of cause and effect.

We need, in short, to devise an educational program for the people who will be making social decisions in the public, private, and nonprofit sectors of society. I suggest that such a program may very well cover the entire life span of the individual. This kind of preparation for leadership may take us back to liberal arts, with much heavier doses of education in the early years and periods of re-education for those who show a gift for leadership until, after alternate periods of work and study, we can finally appoint them as professors.

A further need for the new society is the public entrepreneur—a man who can turn a social decision into an effective program. We have a few prototypes for this role in city and state governments today, but we shall need many more of them. They must be men with a pragmatic outlook, neither socialist nor privatist, who can design competent action programs for achieving our social goals.

The university must also turn its attention to the public agenda in the field of technology. I'm not referring to such technologies as are involved in the space and military programs, for the academic world is already caught up in activities in those areas. I am speaking of the kinds of public technologies represented by communications systems, municipal police and fire forces, street and utilities systems, and other aspects of city planning. These fields of public works engineering have been largely neglected since the Great Depression days, when they attracted some of the country's best minds. Our best public works technologists are now reaching retirement age, and the present crop of engineering students will be unable to replace them, having elected to go into more dramatic and exotic fields.

There is also the question of graduate training in the social sciences. I mentioned briefly above the value of participation in such action programs as the Mississippi Summer Project and wonder if the straight line of teaching by the graduate school is the best way. Should teachers, particularly in the social sciences, be the people of least experience? We are now at a point where we can begin to develop a new system of apprenticeship, in which those who are capable of teaching may emerge from the commitments of life rather than directly out of graduate school.

Finally (and this may seem to contradict what I have just said), the university must rededicate itself to the perpetuation of society's ideals and, for this purpose, the young, inexperienced teacher often serves better than his older, more skeptical and cynical colleagues. We need those bursts of idealism, which are more frequent in the young—reminders of a hope untinged by fears of failure. This is the last and the greatest task I would ask of the university, because if there is one need that has become evident to me as I have moved closer to the world of action, it is the need for perpetuation of the ideals and goals of our society—a task of the world of thought.

Beyond '72:
Strategies for Schools

(Published in the *Saturday Review of Education,*
December 1972)[1]

*"The central reality of our modern condition is the
burden of choice and survival that it places on the
individual. Like it or not, we travel alone—
increasingly so, as the ties of family, clan, and
neighborhood are dissolved in the chemistry of a
mass and mobile society. It takes incredible effort
and sensitivity to prepare children (and adults) for
the rigor, perplexity, and loneliness of today's
lifestyle."*

The greatest need in American education today is what it has always
been, only more so: a sense of the importance of education and a
readiness to do something positive about it. That speaks directly to
the mood of the nation, which has been growing more and more
surly about the cost and performance of its schools and colleges. But
it has even more to do with the attitudes and strategies of those in
public and powerful positions who can do and say some constructive things about it.

There is no denying the realities. During the last generation,
Americans loaded two generations' worth of kids and aspirations on
what schools and colleges they had; and, when these weren't
enough, they dug generously into their growing incomes and paid
for more. But the nation didn't really know what to do with all those
kids other than to send them to school; young people were surplus
on the market. There weren't enough jobs or roles for them, and
parents and politicians were so confused about the new culture they

---

[1] Volume LV, No. 46, pages 33–34.

were creating that they couldn't find either the lore or the certainty to tell the kids—or tell the teachers to tell the kids—what the world was all about.

Today, a generation after that bulge of children and affluence and school spending first appeared, all of us have second thoughts. On top of that there's now a spate of reports suggesting that none of that effort, not all the blood, sweat, taxes, and tears were worth it—schools don't really make a difference.

Maybe that's what we want to hear. It justifies our worrying, argues for a lid on spending, and seems to promise some easier solutions. That's where we're tragically vulnerable, each to our own demagoguery and all of us to the expedient tactics of those who court our votes.

I am not blind to the defects in our schools and in our society. I am not averse to some budget cutting; it could conceivably help us to be more efficient and more inventive.

What I fear, however, is that Americans, this time under the flag of the critics rather than the crusaders, will again be led into the trap of the simple solution. And as H. L. Mencken once said, "There is a solution to every problem—simple, quick, and wrong."

The needs and problems of American education deserve to be handled in a more positive way, even if the job becomes far more arduous and complicated. Maybe because it's far more arduous and complicated, since those have been the tasks this nation has traditionally found the most productive and fulfilling.

In that spirit I'd turn to another of our educational needs: the need to nourish the diversity and pluralism of modern life. The real danger in the new conservatism is that it will trigger a reaction against its own real meaning and mission. It will invite further restrictions on individual growth, greater hostility to individual differences, and growing emphasis on conformity, discipline, and security—all of them retreats from the creative individualism that it takes to survive and live decently under modern conditions.

The central reality of our modern condition is the burden of choice and survival that it places on the individual. Like it or not, we travel alone—increasingly so, as the ties of family, clan, and neighborhood are dissolved in the chemistry of a mass and mobile society. It takes incredible effort and sensitivity to prepare children (and adults) for the rigor, perplexity, and loneliness of today's lifestyle.

The culture of our schools, therefore, cannot be either the sheltered comfort of some social preserve or the jungle of urban neglect. Schools need to be secure. They should not be the place where other people for other purposes wage savage battles in the name of law and order. They also should not be a place where kids sense there is a double reality: a supposedly united nation but actually a deeply divided society, a nation prattling peace but making war. Schools certainly should not be a place where kids are told, by political default, scholarly inference, and the sordid circumstances around them that what happens in education doesn't matter.

The fact is that it does—even if our evidence lies beyond the range of our measurements and bias. To read otherwise from the recent and easily misconstrued study by Christopher Jencks[2] is to miss one of his central conclusions. The importance of schools, he argues, does not lie in their capacity to turn poor kids into rich adults. But, Jencks adds, schools are a critical environment. If we really believe in ourselves and our kids, we ought to do far more than we have to improve that environment, to make certain that it nurtures rather than destroys the qualities that make our kids and the society more humane.

James Coleman[3]—another analyst too often read with an eye for the easy way out—has given us some equally tough but constructive advice: Don't expect schools to work on their own. They can reinforce the values of the culture around them. But where those values are negative, schools can do little to soften the tragic consequences.

---

[2] Christopher Jencks is a professor of public policy and a sociologist who studies social mobility and inequality. In 1968, Jencks wrote (with David Reisman) *The Academic Revolution,* which won the American Council of Education's Borden Prize for the Best Book on Higher Education.

[3] James Coleman (1926–1995) was a U.S. sociological researcher who studied the effects of factors like race, income, and parental level of education on children's ability to learn. He performed a study showing that black children learned better in integrated schools, setting the sociological foundation for mandatory busing; he denounced mandatory busing in 1975 as having been unsuccessful, by contributing to white flight from urban public schools.

The remedies that Jencks and Coleman point to don't lie in the direction of splendid isolation or benign neglect. They call for some basic changes and sacrifices, a reordering of values and of social structures to make the school experience more consonant with what it takes to survive and live decently.

Integration—living readily with differences but keeping one's own integrity—is clearly the hallmark of an effective education for our times. There is no magic formula for that kind of integration. But there can be no retreat from it. It has to do with more than race and class. It has to do with the entire range of America's diversity and the diversity each of us feels within himself. In the vernacular, it means getting ourselves together.

What remains to be counted of America's educational needs can be tallied more precisely. One is the need to "cope" with the education of the very young. A second tidal wave of family formation and childbearing is upon us. Those between the ages of twenty-five and thirty-four (the postwar baby bulge) will be multiplying during the 1970s at a rate nine times that of the 1960s. They probably will not be having families as large as the ones they came from. Still, the number of babies soon to be born will be substantial, and the qualitative differences in the lifestyles of their parents will be so great as to give this nation a case of the learning jitters. How do you educate for the unknown in the context of the unfamiliar?

A consensus seems to be growing that the critical stages in growth and learning reach all the way back into infancy and even prenatal periods—involving factors (such as nutrition and early diagnosis of learning defects) that require a synergy of family and public care. So far, the public's response has concentrated on lowering the age of formal education through institutionalized programs such as Head Start and daycare. What is required is probably a lot more complex, perhaps less bureaucratized than that. Whatever is done ought to involve the parents of this second baby bulge, building a concern for the health and nutrition of mother and child.

It also means a far more sophisticated approach to the rebuilding of American communities. Emergence of this new art is evident in the crescendo of efforts to build new towns and recivilize old neighborhoods. The essence of these ventures is their emphasis on communities rather than on structures—communities of neighborhood scale, mixed in race and income, with a bundle of built-in services ranging from security to health and infant care. However primitive these efforts and statements may be, they are saying something that needs to be said, that education has to be intimately related to family and community and to the range of services essential to the growth of whole people and healthy living environments, including personal security.

"Safety in the Streets" has to be listed among America's rising educational needs. Indeed, "Safety in the Streets" has now become "Safety in the Schools." Unquestionably, it is a legitimate issue in itself. But it is also a set of code words revealing the majority's fear of what they see and often imagine to be spreading outward from schools with minority populations. To ignore these fears, and whatever facts they may be based upon, is just as dangerous as to exaggerate and exploit them—and too many of us are doing both. This is the time for something more creative, civilized, and courageous than what is being served up by public figures.

The underlying causes of school disorder and general vandalism lie frustratingly beyond the reach of immediate solutions. But in the longer run they are not intractable to persistent and imaginative concern. We ought to be working simultaneously along two parallel lines. One, a long-range commitment to change the demoralizing environment of the central cities and the poor who are locked within them. The other, a well-organized and steadily financed network of experimentation with a combination of special personnel, parental and community involvement, and alternative learning environments.

In describing another of America's educational needs, one has to be just as realistic; [this is] the need to conserve resources and live within the parameters of shrinking resources—shrinking, at the very least, in relation to rising numbers and aspirations. Education is particularly vulnerable both to cost increases and budget cuts. It is caught in the sticky logic of the service economy, which is inherently resistant to cost-saving shortcuts. The educational establishment is medieval in its origins, feudal in its structure, guildlike and alien to the consumer in its instinctive responses. And the more it opens its services to mass consumption, the more its folkways are exposed to a paying public emboldened to ask harder and harder questions.

If somehow educators and budgeteers could survive these harsh realities with a sense of invention (a sense of humor is probably too much to ask), this could be a creative time in American education. All in all I think it will be. The performances of the states will be critical to the outcome. If one were basing his bets on [the states'] track record, the odds would be long. I'd prefer to wager on some more optimistic prospects that grow out of pressures forcing even the most recalcitrant states to respond.

Obviously, these pressures crowd around the need for more state funding of local schools. They are coming from three directions: from overburdened property-tax payers; from both state and federal courts, which have declared the present system of local support discriminatory and unconstitutional; and from a federal government hoping to shift the monkey of tough public problems onto the backs of state officials (who are hoping to get federal money without being stuck with the problems).

The easy ways out probably will be taken. A conservative Supreme Court may reverse *Rodriguez*.[4] A state legislature, faced even then with a Rodriguez-like decision under state law, may follow the example of Andrew Jackson, thumb its collective nose at the judges, and dare the highest court to do something about it.

Yet it's already evident we will see some major changes in educational finance. State funding will increase, relieving both the local property tax and at least more egregious cases of disparity among schools. State revenue systems will change, moving toward combinations of sales, income, and state property taxes, which in

---

[4] What Ylvisaker predicted did come to pass the following year. In *San Antonio v. Rodriguez* (411 U.S. 1 (1973)), the Supreme Court upheld the Texas system of public school funding. Those seeking reform of public school funding in order to improve disadvantaged children's educational circumstances had hoped for a mandate for equity in public school funding, but the Court held that there was no fundamental right to education under the Federal Constitution and essentially left such matters up to the states. Ironically, 49 states' constitutions *do* expressly mandate state support of education, and many have rejected the assumptions of *Rodriguez*.

the aggregate will be more responsive to growth in national income. Federal aid shared with the states and mailed directly to students and schools will be stepped up.

But even with these assists, education's financial crunch will get worse. Bankruptcy threatens many private and parochial schools. Time bombs of explosive costs are still ticking within a system that during affluence covered the initial but not the deferred and continuing costs of growth. Unionization of teachers and related public service workers is rapidly expanding and consolidating; we are within a few years of the potential of national strikes. In the future, educational reforms will be won only with arduous and prolonged negotiation.

It therefore becomes crucial to exact the best and most courageous response from state leadership during these transitional years when education is being drawn from its former sanctuaries of nonpartisanship into the vortex of public debate, political compromise, and legislative action. Fundamental premises and ground rules are being rewritten; we will have to live with them for a very long time. Most state capitals and educational systems, however, aren't prepared for the encounter. They don't have the perspective, the capacity for research and development, or the negotiating savvy and strength to convert pressures into productivity. And increased productivity should be the name of the game. Wherever there are signs of bargaining savvy on behalf of increased productivity (and in a number of states, governors, legislatures, and departments of education are learning fast), they ought to be given every encouragement. Dollars are fine, but votes are what they need most.

There is still one more of America's educational needs that will remain, even after any miracles we might pull off in our quest for productive and financeable school systems. That need is to release the learning energies and expand the learning capacities not only of young students but of the entire population. There's a vast potential, especially within the new and liberating lifestyles, for educational do-it-yourselfism. It's already happening, and our formal institutions of learning are having to step lively to keep up. I, for one, think we are trying too hard to keep too many persons in formal schooling and for too long—at least in the undifferentiated systems we tend to sustain. What this means is competition. There can be more than one source of education. And competition is the surest means of keeping down the costs.

We can start releasing the nation's self-educational energies by making better use of the media. We can go further by building new learning environments and offering enough of a variety of learning experiences to do justice to the diversity of American learners. We can do still more by pulling down the walls that insulate the guilds from consumers of learning and from each other and by breaking through the medieval encrustations that divert educational effort into a sterile concern with certificates and away from more legitimate goals of learning.

Whatever the route, it is the direction and the commitment to press on [that are] important—toward a community in which learning is endemic, spontaneous, and as much as possible self-directed. Where learning is taken for granted and not neglected. And where being taken for granted means that it is assumed that learning is the most lasting and revered endeavor the community can engage in—a means of fulfillment and a noble end in itself.

The New Freedom

(Presented to a conference at the Center for Black Studies at Wayne State University on "Problems in American Education: The Continuing Challenge of Black Studies," Detroit, Michigan, May 1974)

"It is time that all of us, not just black, not only here, not simply in this country, begin to see and not fear the potential of human growth and development, even if it means evolving at right angles to a social system we grew up with but which may have wandered to its own dead end."

What I have to say—and what concerns me most—goes beyond black studies and the black experience to the common condition of all of us in the longer span of the next three decades.

We already know, from the handwriting on the wall and our deepest intuition, that these decades will not be the years of affluence this country has recently known. They will be a time of shrinking resources. Depending upon our own spiritual response, they may or may not be an era of shrinking hope and dwindling decency.

It would not be hard to paint this future in somber colors—a bleak age in human history during which not only black studies might disappear, but the university itself and the civilization it is built upon.

I think there's a more optimistic way of looking at that future, even if (and possibly because) one accepts the decline of material affluence. And that's what I'll be talking about today. Let me start that more positive trek by sidestepping into a happy reminiscence. Fifteen years ago, Bob Weaver and I were working together in the Ford Foundation, trying to sluice a share of those millions into programs that would address the human problems of the ghetto.

211

Those problems were being malignantly neglected at that time—as swiftly [as] they are being pushed aside again today. Among the many concerns we spent hours and money chipping away at was the insensitivity and inadequacy of children's textbooks—nearly all of them of the "Dick and Jane" variety.

Bob said spontaneously one night, "Hey, let's go on up and talk to Langston Hughes."[1] So the two of us went up to Langston's favorite bar and had an evening I shall never forget. When Langston asked us what we were up to, we said we were thinking about translating elementary textbooks into "Negro," and he roared. He thought that was great. He said he would probably like to spend some time doing that himself. He then asked if we had any way that we could get into the printing business or into the school system. He had been around and fought enough wars himself to know that social change didn't happen simply by thinking and drinking about it.

Our next step was to go to a number of cities, and Detroit was one of them, to get "Dick and Jane" translated. When I look back at that effort (and we did score in getting some new readers published in a different vernacular), I still feel the excitement of a good cause. But I also recognize our own inadequacy and insensitivity—the effort, in retrospect, seems more than a little paternalistic, a bit quaint, a far cry from a serious undertaking in black studies and human understanding.

A lot has happened since then, and generally I find it encouraging. Within fifteen years, black studies [has] become an accepted part of the university (and school) curriculum. This has occurred despite subtle resistance and overt hostility. More than that. Within fifteen years, the black community has moved from the insecurity of having to present publicly a united front on black studies (for fear that internal differences would be seized upon to discredit such programs) to the readiness just displayed here to discuss bluntly and openly what may be wrong with both the idea and its practice. That's a lot of progress for a mere fifteen years, and it's one base for my optimistic look forward.

---

[1] Langston Hughes (1902–1976) was an American poet, novelist, and playwright whose works examined the lives and circumstances of black Americans.

The fear I have is that neither I nor others will hold fast to that optimism—that we will surrender to pessimism and be commanded by the negative. Black studies, we hear, is now "moving to the suburbs." Why? Not because suburban folk have become positive about [its] value, but because they're facing court orders and the prospect of imposed integration and social fire. Elected officials, who should be giving America its positive leadership, have chickened out; it's the judges who are taking on the tough issues, using their leverage to say positive things about land use, property taxation, school finance, and integration. They are declaring for all to hear that the majority can't rule without being sensitive to minority concerns.

Now, whether the courts' answers are the right answers, whether their rulings make as much sense in detail as they do in principle, let's not argue that. Simply be grateful we've got one branch of government [that] is holding America to the commitment [it] made nearly two hundred years ago. But still that is the negative; still it isn't coming with the sense of a positive mission. We're being beaten into it.

It impressed me that some years ago, former Chief Justice Warren refused to go along with the bicentennial suggestion of holding a second Constitutional Convention to reconsider the original document—for the simple reason that Americans are now so hostile to the Bill of Rights they probably wouldn't pass it a second time. Again, the negative.

And more—the prospect of financial decline and social cannibalism. With shrinking budgets, people tend to nibble away at their own decency and devour each other. That is already going on within the universities, with one program pitted against another: athletics vs. history vs. physics, vs. black studies vs. everything. The game becomes one of survival, and the basic instincts get the better of us.

But is that all there is? A scenario for the future written in the negative?

No society can survive, let alone prosper, unless there is that mysterious, elusive, spiritual quality which affirms a positive reason for being. A patient eye can detect that positive force at work in the turbulent odyssey our civilization is making through the last few centuries of violent and seemingly anarchic change. During that time, human beings have been preoccupied with the harnessing of nature and the release of [its] energies. The industrial revolution put steam into a chamber, gasoline into a combustion engine, and the atom into a nuclear pile. We contained natural forces in order to release and benefit from them. In the case of the atom, Einstein calculated the incredible magnitude of the power released: $E = MC^2$. We are now working at the frontiers of that formula, trying to find a container strong enough to harness the full energy of the hydrogen atom. Conventional materials such as steel and concrete have proved inadequate. Interestingly, an invisible force—a magnetic field—seems to hold most promise as an agent for harnessing and releasing the vast energy of the hydrogen reaction.

To repeat: We have been preoccupied by the exploitation of natural energy, and have managed to unlock the power of the physical atom. Meanwhile, a far more significant development has been taking place, without the same awareness or definition: the smashing of the social atom and the release and acceleration of human energy.

In the earlier and more static societies, human beings (particles) had been locked into atomic structures: the family, the church, the labor union, the village, the guild. Call them the social atoms. In recent centuries, particularly in recent decades, and especially with rapid urbanization, we have proceeded to smash those social atoms, releasing the individuals and immense human energies within them. This release has accelerated individual mobility—socially, geographically, economically. And the amount of energy released has been easily that of Einstein's calculus for the physical atomic reaction.

I should not speak too intimately of the black experience, since it is not mine. But I have observed it in the context of the reaction just described. The black migration was not a movement simply from the south but from the social structure that the south represented—a release as traumatic as it was dynamic.

This explosive release of individuals and energies characteristically comes with rural-to-urban migration. Since it inherently involves social disorganization, it is all too easily seen as a negative happening—symptomatic of, if not identified as, anarchy. But viewed positively, this smashing of the social atom signals the multiplication of the human potential and the liberation of the human spirit.

[It is] no accident that we have seen liberation movements cascading onto our recent social scene: first the March to Freedom of blacks; then the student movement; next, women's liberation; then the reawakening of the elderly; and now the crusade for children's rights. Each of these liberations, though [begun] in the name of a class of human beings, has mushroomed from the same explosive concept—that each of us, no matter our category and the groupings and prejudices that bind us, has rights that stem from the simple fact of our being and our individuality.

This same liberating process, the same social reactor, is at work around the world. You can spot it in the growing self-consciousness of the rising generations of countries as seemingly diverse as Japan and the Soviet Union; and if the veneer of either culture should superficially overlay it, one-to-one conversations about personal thought and identity will quickly enough lay it bare.

The sad fact is that contemporary society has not been ready for that sudden release of energy. As a result, a lot of that energy potential has been dissipated as heat. To me, that is what happened in the burning of Newark and in other rebellions within our cities during the 1960s. The buildup of human energy was being dissipated in rage, blinding rage at the society that couldn't deal with all that power that was there. The society could not give a constructive outlet to the power that had been loosed. Our "nuclear reactors" had gone out of control. And the same thing is taking place in other-than black areas of the cities—the ethnic wards are now at flash point, not the waning fires of neighborhood solidarity, but the accelerating chain reaction of changing values. As Yankelovich has just documented,[2] the value shift [that] traumatized the campus just a few years ago has now affected the attitudes of other youth as well. The ethnic twenty-year-old driving a taxi now wears his hair

---

[2] In 1971, Daniel Yankelovich launched his periodic study of consumer social values. The Yankelovich organization now conducts these polls jointly with *Time* magazine about five times a year to assess public opinion on a wide range of issues. Questions are organized into such categories as background or current issues, pairings (the "electability" of various political combinations), the economy, etc.

long and is just as likely to distrust what's established as any other young adult his age, and do his own thing.

Again, the liberated individual, whose growing appetite and opportunity for *lebensraum* is being infinitely repeated throughout a society that is being both energized and overheated by a massive power it hasn't yet learned how to use positively and fully.

I hesitate to use the obvious next stage of the analogy from the atomic reaction, but it does take the insertion of lead rods in the nuclear pile to modulate the reaction in such a way that its energy is constructively used and the reactor does not go out of control. The lead rod is absolutely the wrong symbol to use when we're looking for a social equivalent. But clearly our society, in all its parts, is now going to have to learn how to deal with liberated individuals, how to utilize, rather than lose control of, its social reactors.

This is how we ought to be defining and dealing with the urban problem—that accumulation of an incredible amount of energy that could be developed and expressed constructively. Our cities, no matter their physical condition, are a container of vast potential energy [that] is now being dissipated. But cities are not alone a black experience. They are symbolic of the human condition.

I may be mistaken, but I think I see in Boston the prototypical signs of a community that may learn how to live constructively with the massing energies associated with the emerging values and culture I have been trying to describe. Boston, with its concentration of universities and colleges and the lifestyle of young adulthood and learning that goes with it, [has become] a "universe-city." This culture is approaching critical mass and is breeding by now almost independently of the institutions and conventions that produced it. No one has yet described Boston in these terms, and I have no more than an intuition to go by. Obviously, this emerging culture will have to break out of the chrysalis spun of its former self. The battle over integration is precisely that. It reflects the fear of the new, clinging in fear to the old, that will be the trauma [that] will mark—and may block—the metamorphosis of Boston from one culture to the next.

Fear is one threat to the new; guilt is another. We are attached to the old, often for very good reason, and therefore feel like sinners, or accuse others of sinning, when embracing the new. Our ambivalent feelings about the breakup of the family [are] a case in point. There seems to be an inherent logic to increasing divorce, but [there is] a deep sense of guilt as it takes place.

It may well be that we will destroy the family only to recreate it. I think I detect this happening already, and only by reading the black experience have I caught that hint. Slavery, forced urbanization, and discrimination created a logic of attachments among many blacks that have nurtured a deep spirit of family in other than conventional forms. What for the majority was lost with the disappearance of the extended family (diversity, mutual dependence, "soul") seems to have been saved by blacks through the survival networks of shared suffering and family surrogates. It's in the repetition of this experience that I catch hints of young adult networks that characterize the "universe-city" of Boston—the synthesizing of what the extended family once ensured by birth and blood.

But much of this "communalizing" is unconventional, and we feel frightened and guilty that somehow we are giving way to license, that we are creating not just an open but a wide-open society. Are we not destroying things of value—not just marriage, but any kind of persevering commitment of one person to another, the kind that allows human beings to grow and society to survive and flourish?

I don't know of another single feature of our emerging culture that so fundamentally makes us uncertain we'll feel right about it as this problem of relationships that seem so inexorably transitory.

But by some alchemy, this society will find ways of living with the forces it has released. Genii won't be stuffed back into their old bottles. Ulysses has loosed the winds of change, and they are blowing too powerfully to ignore them. What's more, we'll no longer be able to count on our time-honored remedy for adaptation, which has been to purchase with our affluence a material way out of the predicament or around it. Nor will the old recourse to fascism or totalitarianism be of much avail; like steel and concrete against the hydrogen reaction, they are incapable of containing the impulse toward freedom moving against them. The only means of handling the power of this reaction is to surround it with the strength and subtlety of the human spirit.

Let me refer, in that same perspective, to what has been called the crisis of the university, associated in so many people's minds with the advent of blacks on campus in threateningly large numbers. That wasn't the crisis. The *real* crisis was whether the university could live with free students, students who are mature enough by age or by experience or by instinct to say, "That is what I need to know and this is what I want to participate in." Any hints that the hunger for learning might be stuffed back into an old bottle, or learners forced to make certain choices—any hint of that return to the authoritarian—produces a violent and hostile response. Far from the university having suffered from the invasion of color, class, or mass, this "invasion" was the university's salvation. The university was saved from the presumption that the genii of our age were still dormant within their old bottles and that human energy was something to be administered rather than released. But [has] black studies built on the release or on the inhibition of these same human energies? My biggest qualms about what I have seen and heard is that black studies—far from symbolizing what to me is the black, and human, experience—has frozen in worship at the ancient altars of academic and ideological respectability.

Now I've telegraphed my final punch. It is time that all of us, not just black, not only here, not simply in this country, begin to see and not fear the potential of human growth and development—even if it means evolving at right angles to a social system we grew up with but which may have wandered to its own dead end. We should see that the salvation and only possible maturing of this society, given its founding ideals, is to continue to release and grow the human spirit.

A View of What Education Might Become

(Presented to the Oberlin College conference on *Freedom to Learn*, a book by psychologist Carl Rogers,[1] Oberlin, Ohio, October 1974)

"There is joy in this process of learning, and it's a joy that can be realized only by leaving off the former didactic notion of teaching. . . . I would hope that somehow we could institutionalize [the] learning facilitator and place him, not just in universities and colleges, in a new kind of education there, or just in the high schools and grade schools, but also in those libraries and museums, and in the workplace as well."

I come to you today with a mixture of feelings, and I'd like to share an attitude before I share some thoughts. Thoughts are often wrong, often misunderstood. I want to talk about two persistent attitudes I have, best illustrated, I suppose, by my reference right now to two communities. One is Boston, the other is Newark.

When I went to Harvard, leaving New Jersey, the train I took

---

[1] Columbus, Ohio: Charles E. Merrill Publishers, 1969. Although the Oberlin conference took "Freedom to Learn" as its theme, it was set up to observe the twentieth anniversary of Rogers' 1954 lecture at Oberlin on "Become a Person." This lecture became the basis of his first, widely read book *On Becoming a Person*. Rogers (1902–1987) founded client-centered psychotherapy, one of the most influential and widely employed techniques in modern U.S. clinical psychology today, and his theories on learning further explore this client-centered approach, known in education circles as "nondirective" learning. His hypothesis is that people naturally tend toward fulfillment and growth and that only the individual can tell what is good or bad for him and find the answers to his problems. Thus the doctor, psychologist, teacher, therapist, or parent must not attempt to direct learning if the "helpee" is to achieve self-actualization.

came out of Newark's railroad station, where I'd spent a lot of other nights. During the middle of the riots, it had been my job to see if we couldn't stop [the Newark rioting] fast and prevent its spread. As I sat there, I remembered the 13,000 rounds of ammunition fired in Newark in 1967 and the hopes we had that that city could come alive. I think it has, in a sense that most Americans don't appreciate. Americans go into a city and look at bricks and mortar and feel depressed by what they find in a Newark. What they should be impressed with is that integrity, in the form of a black mayor, has arrived in city hall and kept the faith with kids on the street. I would think that in contrast to what we've seen in the White House, the integrity and dedication that Ken Gibson has would be impressive. If he can't change the bricks and mortar of that city, he can at least keep that faith.

But as I sat among the debris of that railroad station from twelve o'clock at night until six o'clock in the morning, I was thinking what in heaven or hell's name would be the relevance of graduate education at Harvard to this place. I was dropping off to sleep. About three o'clock in the morning, I was interrupted by the arrival of a train crew that had been unfreezing the switches, and they sat down to a desultory kind of argument. Suddenly I was startled into being completely awake—and I have now chiseled the following statement above the Harvard Graduate School of Education, as our motto and motif. One guy was saying to the other, "I've taught you everything you know, and you don't know nothin'!"

If I can approach my aforementioned thoughts with that kind of self-deprecating humor—well, I think it's what all of us are going to need, and need a powerful lot of. It is that basic attitude of being able to take on the tough ones with a sense of reality, with a sense that its bigger than you, with the faith that Carl Rogers has in collective wisdom and collective determination, that brings us through what often seems to be the impossible.

I juxtapose that humorous attitude that I found in Newark [with] Boston. Boston is now very near, not so much to the Newarks and Detroits of 1967 but to the Belfasts of 1974: it is a community where good people are at each other's throats. Sometimes they behave this way for good reasons, but in the historical sense, they follow this pattern of behavior for tragically bad reasons. Boston is a community of communities, of American diversity, but I think that the inhabitants have been insulated in some of these communities, particularly the white ethnic [communities], to the change that dominates our time and will dominate our future. They are very insulated, protective, turning inward; they show a lack of self-confidence, a lack of what Carl Rogers was basically talking about in his willingness to be and become a person.

We're very close in Boston to Belfast, to a division between people becoming permanent. We succeeded in New Jersey in heading that sort of thing off, and as a result I was at one time called to Belfast, quietly, to see if there was anything we knew that could help dissolve that circumstance. And traveling there for just a few days, I realized in my stomach that [that] situation was not tractable to even a sense of humor or even to a historical perspective. A human being can get bogged down. The reason I'm referring to Boston, against the humor I drew from Newark, is simply that as human beings we are now traveling down the narrow channel between hope and despair. It is a journey that Carl Rogers was talking about; it is that journey that I think all of us are taking now. I hope we can all do it, with the legacy of Rogers.

Let me talk a bit about the legacy of Rogers. It was twenty years ago that Rogers was invited out here, and if he didn't enunciate, at least he repeated here, the theme that he has given to our society. In many ways he has planted it so deep into this society that we don't see it anymore, except by contrast. He was really talking, I guess, about the joy of learning.

What Carl Rogers was saying was that there is an exhilaration to the journey that I was describing previously. There is joy in this process of learning, and it's a joy that can be realized only by leaving off the former didactic notion of teaching. It's a freedom, also, that he was talking about. We have been programmed in our society, in many ways, to think other than in terms of becoming a person in our own right. We know that when we talk to our kids. The question we ask is, "What are you going to be?" The answer that they are programmed to give us is, "I will be a judge, I will be a teacher, I will be an administrator, I will be a rebel, I will be whatever." There's somehow the idea that by a process [that] we know as education, they will be converted from what they *are* into a *role*. And when they are in that role, then and only then are they legitimate as people.

My kids and I have spent our summers on an island in New Hampshire, a beautiful retreat. The neighbors have raised their kids there. I've watched those young neighbors going through the crucial period of "after college, what?" One of them—an extraordinary guy, twenty-two years old—left the Cornell School of Engineering and decided to tear down his family's cottage because the carpenter ants had gotten to it, and to rebuild it. But to do that, he had to move the cottage thirty feet. He did it—one individual. He jacked it up, moved it. Then he lumbered his own trees and he scavenged his own equipment from around there. He traded work with people from around there, and he's now building the house.

Now some of the more conventional people up there have been asking, "When is Jerry going to become something and go to work?" And I've thought to myself, all he'd have to do would be go into business as a contractor tomorrow, and do precisely the same sort of thing he has been doing, but he'd be acceptable. The others haven't seen Jerry as a person. There's something about the programming that caused that. This is what Rogers was talking about.

I would like, then, to talk about Rogers in contrast. First, let's contrast him to the person he likes to be contrasted to, B. F. Skinner.[2] (The two men, by the way, have an admiration for each other. They use each other, almost dramatically sometimes, as foils. It is helpful, and I feel sorry sometimes for people who get into theological disputations as disciples of either man.) Skinner is one of those who believe directly in that linkage between stimulus and response. There isn't anything in between but the conditioning. You put the stimulus in, you control the stimulus, and you control the response. Ergo, the best educational philosophy for this nation would be,

---

[2] Behaviorist psychologist Skinner (1904–1990) is best-remembered for his theory of stimulus and response in behavior. His books include *Walden Two* and *Beyond Freedom and Dignity*. In contrast to Rogers' person-centered approach to learning, in which there are few absolutes and the individual directs his or her own development, Skinner saw learning as an input-output process in which individuals could be conditioned to exhibit the desired responses through exposure to appropriate stimuli.

"Let's condition our kids, and condition them right." (And watch out, I always argue, when you condition them right.)

Now, what Carl Rogers does is put a little thing in between "S" [stimulus] and "R" [response]. He puts a "P" there: "perception" if you want to talk about it in scientific terms, "person" if we want to talk in his whole terms. According to Rogers, there are stimuli, there are responses, and often there is correlation between the two. But in between he puts—into that black box which Skinner says contains nothing—something [Rogers] even hesitates to look into because he so respects what is in that in-between process. There is something very basic, mysterious and worthy—and also, by the way, very refractory and stubborn and tenacious—in that process of perception. The animal, the human being, perceives that stimulus even when given to him from the outside by a manipulator. He thinks about it and then responds.

I have already begun contrasting [Roger's outlook to the view of] education as schooling, which is that compulsion to program behavior and convert a human being into a role or something that is expected. We ought to take an historical look at schooling. It's really only been with us in a major public way for the past hundred years or so. It's become much more isolated, as an experience, from work and family, from society. There is an instinctive attempt now . . . to put school or learning back into the flow of activity. By isolating [schooling] from the rest of life, we have even more emphasized programmed behavior, and we have put the programming in the hands of those who themselves have [been] removed, who have been forced to behave by certain role expectations. Rogers [stands] in contrast to this urge to compel and to change and to program.

He also [stands] in contrast to something that lies deep in human beings—strangely, I suppose—which is to treat human beings as means, rather than as ends. In my growing up Immanuel Kant really got into me, during a term paper in high school. In attempting to find out who this mysterious character was, I discovered that simple proposition in which he said, "Treat men as ends, not means." And this again is Rogers. That "p" that he put in between stimulus and response is not to be the object of all these things, but is to be an end in itself. When we treat people as means, are we programming them to certain roles? Do we keep away from that concept of a person becoming something in and of [himself], and becoming an end of [his] own creation? When we do that, we demean the person, and we deny the potential that is there to be what we do not expect, that which we need but which we do not know how to create ourselves. The principle I would try to get across to a teacher is to always remember that what one expects of the student is what one gets.

This is particularly true in the racial breakdown in our schools. There is still implicit in our society a racist philosophy. We have to admit it. There is implicit here an assumption that some people aren't up to others, that we can't expect much from them. I went to Atlanta recently to interview students, along with administrators, on a kind of visiting inquisition that Carl Marberger, the former commissioner of education in New Jersey, has put up. [I talked to] six kids who were dropouts in effect, although they were kind of wandering back and forth. I asked them what was absent from school. Well, "school was nothin'." And I said, "Well, now let me ask you something else. When you duck out of school and you go down to the street corner, it's pretty damn boring down there, too, isn't it?" They grinned; they said, "Yeah, but how do you come off that?" Well, I said, "Would you agree that probably if something was expected of you in school that you would find it more interesting?" And the answer was a resounding "yes."

Now this is an irony in a way, because the punitive nature of high expectations is what has destroyed many a black kid, wiped out many a white kid, in the school system. But those kids still respond, as humans do respond, to an expectation. At Princeton University, when we studied what was happening to blacks, [we found that] in one department—a scientific department that kept its expectations high and worked with individual blacks to meet those expectations—the performance was extraordinarily high. When they were slopped over, where the old tradition of "pass 'em on and don't hurt 'em and don't confront 'em" existed, where they let the standards down and then felt they didn't have to give individual attention, then the performance was low. Rogers, by contrast asks something of human beings, expects something of human beings but respects that individual creative quality that brings something out that one did not expect. That's the legacy of Rogers.

Let's test that legacy, because I don't think any legacy or any theory ought to be let go very easily. For instance, I wonder if the theory itself, to support Skinner for a minute, isn't the result of conditioning. The reason I chuckle over this is because I read Rogers backward, from theory to man. When I finally got down to hearing about Rogers as a man, I said, "I'll be damned. Rogers and I are the same people." He grew up with a strict father—he couldn't smoke, he couldn't dance, cards were out, he said there was even something slightly immoral about effervescent soft beverages. They put him on the farm, and while there wasn't the 4-H when he grew up, there was the prototype of it. He was out there raising little goats and little lambs and all the rest of it, working his tail off under very tough conditions and very high expectations. It was precisely the opposite of what he [now] recommends, I think.

My father was a Lutheran minister, and he was also a college president. He caught me dancing one time, and I had to get up in chapel and apologize. I see myself out there, waiting for my father to announce that Paul Ylvisaker was found dancing and would he please rise and apologize. My brother was also caught, but he was a more stubborn individual than I. He stood up and said, "I apologize for having been *caught* dancing."

At the age of eight, [I had been trained by my father] in the Greek New Testament, and I was down arguing with the Jesuits about "Thou art Peter and upon this rock." It took a little bit to get to that Greek at the age of eight and to be able to do the exegesis.

[My father's college was] so poor at that time, with the Depression, $80,000 in debt and only forty students, [the family] had to do things. My father did the ordering and the painting of things, and I did the writing of the college catalogue. I can still remember writing, at the age of twelve, why a family should send its child for a religious education. When I went there six years later, to the same college, I was testing my own propaganda.

That was as tough and as strict an upbringing as possible. Both Rogers and I arrived at the same theory, which is the release of the human, the lack of programming, and so forth. I therefore wonder whether Carl and I are subject to the Skinnerian kind of conditioning. That is, if you want a free individual, control him tightly while he's young. You give him such an appetite for freedom that he runs for it inevitably. I wonder sometimes if, in our too easy acceptance of Rogers, whether we forget the discipline [that] is needed in the early stages to arrive at the point where freedom is understood and is properly exploited.

I wonder too if there isn't something a bit easy in the Rogers proposition and my own that ignores that the theory came out in a period of affluence in American history. It's fairly easy to talk about individuality and elbow room for the individual when all horizons are opening. This is a remarkable period in human history. Just think about it. During that earlier, that easier time, we were willing to let people be young for a longer period of time. We extended youth up to [age] twenty-eight by the draft (or at least the avoidance of it), by graduate school, by the affluence that allows me to support my kids when they can't find a job and [when] graduate school is the best alternative. That period is ending now. We will not be having that ego room, that growth illusion. Is there something in Rogers that is provincial, that is parochial to its times?

And I would ask about the joy of learning. The joy of learning is easy when the outcomes of learning don't hurt, when they aren't painful. Now take the child as he progresses. We bring into this world protoplasm that instinctively reaches out to test its environment, to control its environment, to enjoy its environment. The happy child, the learning child, as we have seen it, is that child [who] doesn't have such brutal experiences that he is no longer willing to reach out. That is one of the reasons for great care in the early childhood years. As I test it with my experts, it is very important that the child is not exposed to such brutal, or at least un-understandable, hurt that [he] closes in and shuts off [his] learning mechanism. But now we are in a period where the learning is painful. Learning to know the minority in this country is painful, because the minority holds up to us, in [its] mirror, our own failings and fallibilities and shortcomings.

Yesterday, I talked to a bunch of financial vice presidents from the retailing industry who were all against busing and who were, I thought, subverting the U.S. Constitution (along with the American President, [judging] by the message he sent to the streets of Boston, saying, "I don't like busing either"). I reminded them that when I was born, there were 140,000 school districts in this country. Now are 10,000—and the conservative part of this society, including me in my conservative role, welcomed that, because it is far more efficient, [because] we do not isolate the kids, and all the rest. How did we accomplish that miracle of school reorganization in this country? We did it by busing. We bused our rural kids thirty miles in West Virginia and elsewhere, and we have been proud of it. But the moment that black [people are] involved, we are against busing.

I watched twelve vice presidents of finance really sweat that one out. When that mirror of inconsistency is held before us, we find learning painful. One of them from Richmond couldn't take it and walked out of the room. It's the same thing for us: when we get into Rogers' kind of learning experience, our failings are exhibited, our humanity is shown, and the defenses that we've set up are shattered.

But now let's ask more broadly about the pain of learning in the years ahead. This is a time when horizons are closing. We will have three million college graduates unemployed by the end of the 1970s, it is estimated. We are having dropping enrollments, but even those enrollments are too much for the roles [available]. Or put it on a larger scale: the American who insulated his economy for nearly two centuries has now been forced to rejoin humanity.

If you want an image, make your own graph from the year 0 to 2000, and plot the population curve. Put the year 1650 on that graph. There will be a stable line of 300 million to 500 million people up to the year 1650, and then seven billion by the year 2000.

What has happened, if you want to put it earthily, is that the earth has put its straws into our milkshake. Suddenly, incredibly fast, faster than we are going to be able to accommodate, those resources will be shared. Those [resources] which we held most exclusively in our affluence will be shared by a larger world. I'm depressed by the current levels at which we are discussing inflation, when that perspective of limited resources is so clearly in front of all of us. Economic scarcity lies ahead. Our educational institutions are facing it: the drain of school kids in numbers is now hitting the colleges and universities and is producing very acute depression, and trauma, in those places. Learning, for a senior faculty member at my institution now, is going to be extraordinarily painful indeed. Can we survive with a vital, joyful, welcoming learning process, when so much pain lies at the other end?

We're now in a period of incipient anarchy. The fight that I see is not the fight between freedom and authoritarianism, it's between freedom and anarchy. We are more and more incapable of dealing with a massive, complex society through our present methods of government, and what we see now is each person and each group doing its own thing. Anarchy is very much an imminent threat. If you don't believe it, ask any one of the administrators of the nations these days, of if you want to do a very interesting piece of research, do a statistical tabulation of the shortening duration of governments. Whether it's British, American, or Portuguese [governments] or presidencies of colleges, governing bodies and structures have a short tenure, because of the difficulties of dealing with diversity and the centrifugal pull of our society. And we find Rogers saying to us now, increase the centrifugal, increase the elbow room, the ego room of the individual. Isn't it about time for more conformity, for more cohesion?

There's something else coming in, which is interesting in its rhythm in history: the return to what the Greeks called *stasis*. We can't take the change, at the rate that Rogers has said, and what we're doing now is trying to stop the world, in order to stay on. We're going to do what the Japanese did for 300 years, which is zero population growth; we're going to try to stabilize roles; we're going to go to general governmental revenue-sharing, in order to be able to count on things through time. There's a tremendous stabilization urge in this society now. *Stasis*, in Greek, in Japanese, or in anybody's terms, is always "freeze the individual."

The Japanese created the *Eta* group, the *Buraku*, in their period of stabilization, when they said, "We need classes in society, and always a class below, so that everyone else can feel happy." There are three million *Burakumin* in Japan, who are Japanese but were artificially made an outcast group at that time. Only gradually, as Japan is thawing and becoming more "Rogerian," are the *Burakumin* beginning again to find themselves up. The same thing happened with our poverty and minority groups in this country. In the 1960s, we began allowing the migration upward and the mobility of the individual, of the minority. But first the benign neglect of Mr. Moynihan, and then the cynical neglect of Mr. Nixon, has found enough response that we are now beginning again to put in this kind of repression, this idea that somebody should be lower. We can't stand the continual effervescence of human mobility. I put this to you as I put Boston to you: that the theory of the individual, of his becoming a person, getting more and more room and creativity, has to be tested.

But let's confirm the theory. I would argue very strongly that along the axis of personal development lies the only hope for a society undergoing the kind of travail that we are likely to undergo. I'd argue first that the Rogerian movement is irreversible. You will not put the genie back into the bottle once it is loose. I know that if I had written the book that Rogers did, I would have used the analogy of the atomic pile, of how in our society we have put the social atom, which is the church, the family, whatever, into an atom smasher and released the particle, which is the individual. As we have released that particle, we have accelerated it and energized it. There is fantastic energy and acceleration by which, paradoxically, our families and our small ties are being destroyed. We waste it. Newark was an atomic pile out of control. It melted. The energy was converted to heat and dissipated in heat, rather than harnessed. I think society is now at a poise point; will it try to stop the atomic reaction, and the release of the individual energies, and the acceleration of our capacities, or will it learn how to keep the pile going, inserting some very carefully placed lead rods [that] are a facilitation of the process rather than a stopping of it? I think it is irreversible. I think we've reached critical mass in that social nuclear reactor, and the individual is coming loose. The prospect still is there that it may dissipate, but it will not, I think, be stopped. It could just boil out of control.

Another way of confirming the theory is to ask yourself, "Compared to what?" What are your alternatives to realizing the individual? I would argue here that you just cannot run as large and as complicated a society as ours is now without an extraordinary amount of decentralization. If ever Adam Smith were needed to write a social history, he certainly is needed now to talk about the release of the individual so that adjustments and creativity will continue within his or her environs, unattended by bureaucrats who themselves are impotent. This society, if it were to subtract 10 percent of what Rogers has accomplished, would be in deep trouble.

I myself have been a bureaucrat, a state commissioner, trying to deliver better housing to the poor in Newark or better education to those in Plainfield. I know that bureaucrats in this society are impotent and incompetent to perform those services and to fulfill those needs in the time allowed. I must say that the best thing that has happened to me is that thing called naderism, written with a small "n."[3] Sophisticated consumers are keeping the system under pressure and working with the assumption that the "action starts with me." I don't mind at all, therefore, if a demand is made for freedom in that kind of a trade-off.

In terms of change, we will never be able to produce stasis. Built into our population now is an inertial guidance, a gyroscopic inevitability of massive change. Even if you get to zero population growth, which we have right now, for seventy years we're going to have the whiplash of the population boom before that. As the population changes in age, it produces its own ideas and changes. In terms of resources—and this is a strange statement perhaps, but I will make it flat-footedly—we do not have the resources to support bureaucratic solutions to the world's problems. It is impossible. All we have is the hope of resourcefulness and that ingenuity which comes, as the Latin says, out of necessity.

And finally, in confirmation of the theory, is integrity. Society just can't mess around, as we've seen with Mr. Nixon and others, with all that indirection and pretense and defensiveness. I don't have time to wait, before I do something or have something done, for someone to lie to me. It isn't the morality of it, it's simply whether or not one can run a system based on it.

Let me just conclude with a few propositions about education and what this means in our time. I am very depressed by one of my colleagues at Harvard, Christopher Jencks. I've told him so, and we've had some very good arguments, and I happen to think that he is a product of Rogerian thought himself. He is a lovely, creative

---

[3] Lawyer and consumer advocate Ralph Nader is best known as the leader of the consumer protection movement. He founded the Center for the Study of Responsive Law, the Center for Auto Safety, and the Public Interest Research Group. His 1965 book *Unsafe at Any Speed* helped convince Congress to mandate federal controls of automobile design.

guy, but I think he blew it when he made the statement that schools don't count. I think he was writing negatively about an irrelevancy. He was really talking about *schooling* when he asked if we turn poor kids into rich kids by sending them to school. His statistics said no, and I won't argue with statistics, although a lot of them are fallible. The problem with the study was that he didn't put into anything but a footnote that while schooling in that sense doesn't count, *learning* does.

This was the time that Harvard should have used its influence, if it has any in this more democratized society, to declare affirmatively the importance of learning. It should also have declared the importance of people, because according to the Jencks formula, you *became* somebody as a result of education if your income went up because you got to be a lawyer or a doctor or those other things that dominate your undergraduate life here and at Harvard. He was saying, "You make dough out there if schooling counts." That kind of thing, I think, doesn't matter now. What does matter is the value of a person developing, wherever that developing, that learning, occurs.

By 1976—we have about a year and a half left would make another declaration of independence and freedom, saying that we ought to make universal that thing called the freedom to learn. I would put it in with those rights which were identified in 1776 as the inalienable rights of man. It should be said that it is a crime to deprive someone—a ghetto kid, an affluent kid—of the willingness to learn, the joy of learning in that sense, and the right to learn. This country would do well to entitle its entire population to learning.

We have entitled our kids to schooling; at that level, we entitle them to learning. As our population ages, we should entitle the adult population to learning. Five countries in Europe have done this within the last decade. In France, 2 percent of the adult population can, as a matter of right, get further education. Britain this year entitled everyone over nineteen to return for education. I'm finding now a tremendous appetite for learning that is bringing the most extraordinary people in their mid-thirties to our school right now, women and minorities particularly. Twenty-five percent of our community are self-directed learners from the minority community, and 55 percent are women. They have a power that the school is now beginning to recognize, simply by being overwhelmed by such powerful consumers. Many of them are in opposition to the usual kind of professional training which says, "We will teach you to be a teacher and an administrator." Rather, they are training themselves, developing themselves as human beings.

We can do it through mechanisms that are now being worked out. For instance, Senators Javits and Kennedy are now revising unemployment insurance and Social Security so that all of us during our lifetimes can make learning deposits and can withdraw upon occasion. I think, by the way, that this is going to mean the release of our eighteen- to twenty-four-year olds from the feeling that now's the only time you ever get educated, so you can rebel now and forever lose it, or you can stay with it, even if you don't like it, and take it. If we can relax and allow the adolescent population to go to work earlier, and mix education with the rest of life, with the promise that they are not forever lost, past twenty-four, that they can return, I think that we're going to do an awful lot for the education below that level. We're also going to do what I think is even more important in this society, which is to assure and remind the adult population that learning is lifelong. Those schools, those colleges and universities that respond to that kind of a call to learning, and to universal rights of learning, are going to be extraordinarily interesting places in the years to come.

I've found that the community colleges are perhaps the fastest to adapt to this market. Often in ways that we may not like, such as super-vocationalism, although I don't decry that. But they are in the marketplace, and having to survive on that ingenuity of responding to the adult population. Many colleges and universities, including my own, are going to be threatened to the degree that they try to insulate themselves and try to maintain a tradition that is not responsive to the nature and universality of education that we might guarantee.

There will be some very ingenious institutions and techniques adopted during this period. I would guess that libraries and museums are going to come back into their own, particularly if we use that Rogerian tactic of a learning facilitator, of one who deals with a consumer who is entitled to education and who is asking for advice and facilitation of that learning process. I would hope that somehow we could institutionalize that learning facilitator and place him, not just in universities and colleges, in a new kind of education there, or just in the high schools and grade schools, but also in those libraries and museums, and in the workplace as well. I am really a believer in cooperative education, in the business of living while learning, and doing this at an early age. That Rogerian kind of facilitation, that kind of learning, I think, could be an exciting statement for 1976.

It's going to be most difficult on those of us who run institutions. Institutional survival right now is one hell of a job, and one hell of an agony. I can project my own school now, as an affluent institution, and see nothing but despair and agony ahead in terms of institutional survival. I talk to my colleagues in primary and secondary education, and they face legislative cutbacks at all levels and bond issues cutdowns. There is a feeling up ahead of great improbability, that the institution will not survive. I happen to believe that there is no institutional answer for that, no conventional answer that lies in institutional wisdom. Rather, there is only that kind of entitlement that reaffirms in the population the understanding of the need for learning and the right to avail themselves of it.

# Educational Ethics in a Market Society

(Lecture given at Yale University, October 1981)

"The educator I would train, the educator I strive to be, is one who recognizes the interdependence between the one and the many and who is willing to accept individual responsibility, and all the anguish and excitement that comes with it, for the unending task of achieving justice and harmony between them."

It's about time that we talk about ethical issues in the professions, given the dominance of the service sector in the American economy and the emergence of the professions as the dominant elite; given, too, that the professions generally have only embryonic concepts of their social role and responsibility. They have emerged as an elite, still trailing with them their feudalistic origins and orientation: self-regulating, territorial, preoccupied, and insular. All of which is reflected in their codes of ethics; they tend to be pious and protective, a far cry from the universalism of an Immanuel Kant.

Essentially, the professions are active in two domains: the open market and the institutional home. The epitome of the first is the fee-for-service practitioner, with codes of ethics addressed to that environment (e.g., advertising and its rules of competition) and with political activity geared to minimal interference and regulation. During the last decade, as the nation became conscious that the professions were displacing industrialists as the new elite, this autonomy has been increasingly challenged; it would be an interesting historical odyssey to compare this period in the development of the professions with the rise and "domestication" of the robber barons of industry, beginning a century ago.

The other domain of the professions is the institutional: service as staff members of corporations, government agencies, educational and other nonprofit organizations. Bureaucratization of the professions produces crosscutting loyalties, an example being the corporate lawyer, with allegiances both to his guild and to his employer. Within academic institutions, these mixed loyalties become quite diverse and complex: adherence to the rules of the disciplines (guilds), to the claims of Alma Mater and employer, and to the "academic tradition." The last is an oft-repeated, if somewhat mystic, liturgy of free speech and inquiry, reasoned discourse, evenhanded analysis, open access and full documentation, no deception, etc.

Emerging from the separateness of academic guilds, old school ties, and monastic oaths is the generic role of the educator. It is still a weak amalgam of all those facets and traditions. Significantly, it has no written code of ethics.

Why the emergence and significance of "educator" as a generic role and profession? Principally because of the shifting of educational activity from institution to market, the diffusion of learning and teaching throughout society. We know its signs and its causes: the explosive growth of learning demand and the knowledge industry, the demographic shift away from "schooling" ages, the new communications technology and individualized delivery systems, the availability of mass markets and massive rewards, the need for increased productivity and accelerated transfer of technology, the hunger for credibility and for "uncertainty-removing" (professors have taken the place of preachers in praying over American society). Add to this list our preferred learning styles: consumer-oriented, on-site, counseling and facilitation rather than lecturing, at lower cost than implicit in full-time and/or residential study. Similarly, our preferred professional lifestyle: autonomous, entrepreneurial and stimulating, having the best of both worlds (the roving professor with a university base), and financially rewarding (does an educator have to take the vow of poverty?).

Symbolic of this new breed of educators are Peter Drucker, Carl Sagan, Kenneth Galbraith, Kenneth Clark—and to demonstrate the range, I would add Bill Moyers.

It is not only individual faculty but educational institutions and guilds [that] are being caught up in the drift toward the market. The dynamism, the magnetism are too powerful, certainly compared to the dwindling countervailing force of traditional sources of income and clientele. Take for example the public schools: with only 25 percent at most of American taxpayers having children in the public schools (and with the children of immigrants and minorities becoming an ever-greater share of that percentage), they're rapidly losing out in competition with private schools and appealing notions like tax credits and educational vouchers. But not alone the public school. All age-bound institutions of formal learning are in a race for survival, adapting as quickly as they can, and oftentimes questionably, to the imperative of the market. As the old nursery rhyme would have it, it's off to the market or cry and go hungry at home.

The result is a congeries of contending claims on the individual educator: from the market as individual entrepreneurs, from their beleaguered institutions, from the public who as patrons are demanding efficiency and "value added," from learners as sophisticated clients and consumers.

In this changing environment, then, what does it mean to be an educator? There being no explicit role definition or written code of ethics, one has to get inside the evolutionary process to find the touchstones by which opposing claims and tensions are being appropriately resolved. In that perspective, it's fascinating to scan Jane Clapp's 1974 compilation of 205 associations' *Professional Ethics and Insignia*. Some observations:

First (at least as I conclude from the material), to the degree to which a profession is "on the market," it seems more likely to have a written code of ethics—and a more detailed one. Engineers and psychologists, both heavily involved with consulting and fee-for-service, go on for pages. In contrast, philosophers apparently have no written code whatsoever.

Second, all codes are guild-oriented. In the relevant case, there is nothing under the generic title of "educator"; the only educational titles that appear are "teacher" (from two of the unions, the National Education Association and the American Association of University Professors) and "reading." Not even "researcher."

Quite obviously, there's a vacuum—and a vacuum [that] nature will abhor. And there is abundant evidence that the vacuum is being filled. Filled by:

- *Consumer pressures* from the young students of the 1960s, the more mature students of the 1970s and 1980s, and mass media exposés such as "Sixty Minutes" on the exploitation of black athletes by universities and colleges.

- *Government regulation*: affirmative action, the Buckley Amendment, review of research on human subjects, education of the handicapped, and federal guidelines and municipal regulations covering genetic research. (Harvard University recently distributed to its faculty and staff a twenty-six-page compendium of applicable governmental regulations.)

- *The guilds.* Note the increasing frequency of code revisions, interpretations, and supplements. To cite but one example, the recent statement by NCAA [National Collegiate Athletic Association] and ACE [American Council on Education] on "The Coach as Educator" (a significant step, but we still await a consideration dictum on "Athletics as Curriculum"). And the Carnegie Council on Policy Studies and Higher Education (1974)—mark the title: "Rights and Responsibilities of Students and Their Colleges in a Period of Intensified Competition for Enrollments."

Worthy of special note is the American Sociological Association's evolving efforts to articulate its own ethical imperatives. A first attempt at an explicit code was voted down in the 1960s. Later, a mild one was adopted and then strengthened to address the rights of research populations, authorship, the review process, teaching, research, and public policy. Now a new attempt is being made. Titled "Toward Ethical Guidelines for Social Research in Public Policy," the proposal opens with the following paragraph:

> Front-page headlines about economic indicators, voting analyses, national school achievement test scores and a myriad of other topics tell the story. Social science is now taken seriously in public policy. No longer are social science findings and theories of great interest only to those in the discipline. Such work now has the potential to affect the lives of citizens.

The proposal explicitly addresses such sensitive issues as the statement and conceptualization of the problem to be researched, the choice of research method, research design and outcome measures, sampling, data-gathering procedures, analysis and interpretation, statement of policy implications, and publication publicity and public debate. Simply by provoking discussion of these issues and appropriate guidelines, a service has been done; one would hope that debate would proliferate among all the sectors that constitute the profession of educator.

Academic institutions themselves are joining in filling the vacuum left by lack of a generic educational code. Protocols and guidelines are steadily being elaborated by universities and colleges governing faculty behavior in "outside activities." Harvard, to cite one example, has over recent years instructed its faculty not to place themselves in privileged positions within outside granting and contracting agencies and [has] ruled against faculty collaboration with the CIA in covert activities on campus. In a very recent development, the Council of Harvard's Faculty of Arts and Sciences has recommended a quantum change in its policy on conflicts of interest: it has added to that traditional phrase, "conflicts of commitment." In so doing, it has grasped the nettle of conflicting loyalties and said, in effect, that its faculty must choose.

Still, despite all the new entries mentioned, much of the vacuum still remains. A significant and growing part of the educational profession writ large remains outside or on the margin of control. Witness the major research universities' struggle with the question of how to organize their faculties' involvement with genetic research. And those same centrifugal pressures are evident in elementary and secondary education: viz., what about moonlighting by the nation's schoolteachers?

Catching up with the fast-moving challenges and ethical dilemmas of the modern educator is no easy task; there are a number of persevering problems. One, already mentioned, is the tendency of particular groups to be self-serving in their formulation of ethical guidelines; altruism and the generic have to wait their turn. There's also a tendency, when an institution or association does adopt a protocol, to become ever more deeply enmeshed in Talmudic, hairsplitting refinements leading to frustration and litigation. But principally the problem—and, I will soon argue, the healthy challenge—lies in the elusiveness of what we try to pin down as ethical, whether it be in the definition of an ethical dilemma or in the formulation of ethical guidelines. There is a great gap between elegant theory and its application to raw and conflicted reality; [it is] one thing to speak in Kantian or Rawlsean[1] abstractions and another to say what should or should not be done in worldly circumstances. Given that difficulty, I can appreciate the temptation of lawyers to say that what is legal is ethical, or of economists to solve the problem by worshipping the role and outcomes of "the market."

With or without established codes, it eventually comes down to the individual and his/her concept of how to behave in a way that contributes to the general good, characteristically in situations where self-interest is more apparent than that shrouded universal. And I can think of no more acute instance of that dilemma than in our very existence as relatively affluent and secure citizens of a world deep in poverty and turmoil. What are the ethics involved in the simple maintenance of our personal and national standard of living?

I confess that at that scale I begin to appreciate the doctrine of original sin (once born, we're in it) and the gospel of atonement and forgiveness (like the pleading publican, we're closer to salvation simply by recognizing and admitting our predicament and impotence). I appreciate, too, the accumulated wisdom and workable simplicities that religions embody in their moral adages and commandments.

In fact, we resolve these dilemmas by tenacious struggling, by acting and being chastened, and by accumulating self-corrections. Even Moses found, after his first stab at the Commandments, that he had to go back to his mountain drafting board and begin again.

There are some admonitions that help in that growing and coping process. Two I've drawn from my favorite educational philosopher, Israel Scheffler. Meeting with our case-writing workshop in educational ethics, Scheffler stressed, first, the importance of disclosure, the willingness to open not simply one's books but the process and substance of one's reasoning and decision-making. Second, and at

---

[1] Ylvisaker is referring here to the writings of American philosopher John Rawls, best known for his still-evolving theories on social justice, fairness, punishment, and duty. His work continues to spark debate among ethicists and political philosophers.

first blush surprisingly, he added, "Take care of yourself." He meant to say, not to take care of number one, but to nurture your body and soul so as to be able to give the best of yourself to others.

To those, I'd add a couple more. One is to keep your sense of humor and humility. The other is constantly to look for feedback— from peers, from critics, and most of all, as I also interpret John Rawls to say, from the least privileged who are affected by your decisions and behavior.

Let me return more explicitly to the question of appropriate ethics for a modern educator. Allow me to talk from circumstances in which I have struggled with that question over the past decade as Dean of Harvard's Graduate School of Education. For me, the question divided itself into two parts.

The first: How were we to define the scope and mission of the school? Not in one fell swoop, but in sometimes fumbling, always reaching fashion, we broke through the confinement of a traditional concentration on formal schooling and focused instead on human learning—at whatever age it might occur, in whatever environments. Fair to say, this was not entirely a decision in the abstract; we, too, were sensitive to the market and responding to the explosion of careers and job opportunities into every sector of society, every nook and cranny of contemporary demand for places to learn, for chances to grow. But more than that, we were trying to express our own concern that as a leading educational institution we should deal broadly rather than narrowly with the role of the modern educator and with the behavioral norms that that generic profession—in all its variant forms and unregulated frontiers—should be, even if not controlled by, at least troubled by and struggling to improve.

The risk in adopting that broader focus was to accept the conundrums of diversity and ambiguity. The gain was to give, and be given, more room and provocation to grow.

The second question was even more fundamental and far more difficult: What kind of human being do we want to grow, both in our learners and in ourselves? Until we have answered that question, can we really formulate a code of ethics for the educator—or, for that matter, for any of the human-serving professions?

Now—and, revealingly, I hope forever—we're in the process of articulating an answer to that eternal query. A substantial number of our faculty and advanced graduate students have undertaken a global study of the concept of human potential, collaborating with collegial teams in other diverse cultures and tapping the findings and perspectives of every relevant discipline. Emerging from these explorations is the tension between two orientations toward human potential and its fullest development: one, the concept and encouragement of human potential in essentially individualistic terms, the autonomous human being becoming the fulfillment of that potential. [Two,] the contending notion that the individual realizes his/her potential in the context [of], and only in community with, the group of which she/he is a part.

My own feeling—influenced, I am sure, by my acculturation—is that if choice must be made, it would be in favor of developing the autonomous individual. But life tells me that truth not only lies, but is created, in the tension between opposing forces. No man is an island. The educator I would train, the educator I strive to be, is one who recognizes the interdependence between the one and the many and who is willing to accept individual responsibility, and all the anguish and excitement that comes with it, for the unending task of achieving justice and harmony between them.

Anyone fairly working at that task will be found lonely out in front of any written code of ethics.

Reforms—And Whose is This?

(Presented to the Kettering/ECS Conference on State
Educational Reform Movement, Philadelphia,
Pennsylvania, April 1984)

*"What's missing is the positive expression of the
nation's challenge to develop the human resources
of an oncoming generation increasingly immigrant
and minority, a generation altogether too precious
to waste."*

My purpose—or hope—today is to put this current round of
educational reforms in a longer and broader perspective. But the last
thing I want to do is to de-energize this creative burst of reform by
state governments. It's badly needed; it's warmly welcome; my hope
is that it will be augmented, leveraged, and humanized.

We've all witnessed other waves of reform. My first experience at
close hand came here in Philadelphia when Joe Clark after World
War II led the charge against Republican corruption and, as mayor
for a vivid four years, turned this town upside down and around. As
his executive secretary, I was too buried in the everyday excitement
to notice the metamorphosis of that reform. It began with a
preoccupation with the central business district and physical
redevelopment. Tearing down the Chinese Wall (the Pennsylvania
Railroad's elevated tracks spiked into the downtown) became the
symbol. It wasn't until some years later that attention focused on the
plight of the urban minorities squeezed by urban renewal into
unlivable circumstance. Action on one front had led to reaction on
another, and the agenda of reform shifted from physical to human.

There is a rhythm to reform. The movement begins when "the
time has come": public consciousness of a conspicuous social failure
rising to the level where politicians sense a supporting majority.

242

What is critical at that point is who sets what agenda—and usually it will be an agenda of the immediate and the tangible, the most readily votable by the majority. No matter whose agenda, the release of social energy produces its own reaction, a contrasting agenda is posed, and then there is either a workable synthesis or social stymie.

Does this current wave of educational reform fit into such a cycle, and, if so, where are we at this point?

See it first in its demographic context. The cohort of American adolescents is now sharply declining, with the high-school-age group falling off by about 25 percent over the next decade. Within that declining cohort, the percentage of minorities is rapidly rising: 17 percent of the general population, 26 percent of the school population, in 1980, and increasing to [more than] 20 percent and 30 percent by 1990. To those numbers should be added the burgeoning influx of immigrants, whose median age is more than ten years lower than that of the general population and mostly within range of the traditional school age. Most of this growing population will be attending public schools and will be heavily concentrated in the nation's largest central cities.

There's much that's undeniably threatening in that environment, and it's understandable that America's leading politicians would have addressed the nation's educational concerns mostly through the language of fear: falling test scores, school violence, "forced busing," spreading illiteracy, teacher incompetence, inability to compete with the labor forces of foreign nations. President Reagan's resort to school prayer is simply the final link in that chain of apprehension.

And most of these concerns are real. We are, the facts tell us, developing an urban underclass; and urban economies, even with a metropolitan job market hungry for qualified applicants, are burdened by a downtown population unprepared for entry-level employment. Employers used to a generation of youth-in-surplus and low entry wages now face the far different prospect of shrinking pools of qualified youngsters and higher entry-level wages. A nation that is steadily aging has to look forward to the haunting uncertainty whether there will be a large and productive enough younger work force to pay its mounting social security bills or enough recruits to sustain a strong and sophisticated national defense.

Through all the recent reports and talk of educational reform, the dominant note is one of fear, the targeted audience a frightened majority, the agenda centered on a promise that the schools and the youngsters and the educators within them will all be made to shape up.

What's missing is the positive expression of the nation's challenge to develop the human resources of an oncoming generation increasingly immigrant and minority, a generation altogether too precious to waste.

Whose Reform, Whose Purpose?

Much of the rationale for reform has rested on the fear that America will not be competitive in the global race for dominance of a high-tech economy. Again, there is both validity and majoritarian appeal in that line of argument. But before we commit the education of this generation of young Americans to that singular objective, it's worth remembering that while the twenty fastest-growing occupational categories are all "high-tech," the sector they represent in the nation's future work force will supply less than 10 percent of total employment.

The task of educators, now as always, extends far beyond the training of potential employees for a narrow slice of the future job market. It's an essay in human development, carried on first of all in the interest of the individuals being educated. But why are we hearing so little about reform from the point of view of young people and their optimal human development? What an irony that neither parents nor children have been given much voice in the process thus far.

Some Political Facts

The answer lies first of all in the relative weakness of the constituency. The parents of children currently in public schools comprise only 20–25 percent of the electorate. More and more of them are immigrants, minorities, and the poor (in Boston, school parents constitute only 12 percent of the electorate, and over half of all school enrollees come from "the projects"). School children can't vote, and this time in America belongs to older people who do vote and are constantly gaining in numerical strength.

It follows from those simple facts that the only path to political action and reform is to build coalitions of those who are otherwise interested. Judged from that point of view, this current wave of reform has in many respects been a resounding success. Witness the simple fact that governors across the nation are vying for leadership of the movement, that upwards of a hundred study commissions have been created, and that practically every state legislature has educational reform on its agenda.

But there is a cost to every success including this one. Those "otherwise interested" are in the majority, outnumbering parents and children and with much superior bargaining power. The coalitions thus formed are volatile and often ephemeral. It becomes easy in those settings to "blame the victims": parents for their indifference, teachers for their incompetence, schoolchildren for their language, culture, and disinterest in the rigors of learning. Members of the coalition move quickly to their own self-interests, whether it be the political future of a governor, the manpower needs of high-tech employers, or the pent-up demands of underpaid teachers. And since time is of the essence (reform's moment never lasts forever), the agenda of reform is hastily put together out of what is rather conventionally regarded as immediately doable. Witness most of the reforms now being considered by the states.

Compared to What?

Education for any child is a complex, often mysterious and unpredictable human journey. For today's and tomorrow's public schoolchildren, it is and will increasingly be demanding of a quality of human contact that under present structures and political climate is not easily supplied. How does one—in the moment of transition from a broken home or impoverished neighborhood or alienated culture to the morning's first class—break through the inner turmoil of a child and make him/her ready for learning? How does one peer through the barriers of language and seeming passivity or obvious aggression to find and provide for the unique needs and potential of those crowding individuals?

If education is thought of in those human terms, there are, I think, some elemental guiding principles by which we can measure the effectiveness of our efforts at reform.

First, no child shall remain anonymous, or be otherwise impersonalized. I once asked a teacher in a ghetto high school how many students could go through three years and remain in effect unknown. The reply was a disconsolate "Too many."

Second, each child during a given school career should have encountered and been nurtured by at least one ([and this is] asking for all too little) teacher or administrator who believed in him or her. A mentor, a confidant, an encourager, a challenger—whatever it takes to help make the child believe in him- or herself.

Third, each child should have had the experience of social acceptance, earned by the development and use of that child's particular talents and potential. That insight was brought home to me recently and vividly by Archbishop Flores of San Antonio, himself a child of impoverished Mexican migrants who made his way against the odds from working in the fields to a distinguished position of saving souls. "Children," he said, "need applause— earned applause." As a parish priest, he had organized a class of struggling Hispanic kids into a singing and dancing group. The motivation that flowed from their being praised by a visiting bishop and the local community had demonstrated for him an educational imperative that he has ever since adhered to.

A Difficult Agenda?

As tests of the educational reforms we are attempting, these are some pretty formidable objectives. But whether these or some other set of equally humane imperatives, it is the special responsibility of those of us in educational reform to keep the ultimate purpose of reform in sight and intact while negotiating change in the political bazaar. Without such overarching goals writ explicitly in the language of individual human development, the current wave of reform will dissipate into splashes of legislation for the benefit of those "otherwise interested."

An encouraging step in this direction has been taken in Massachusetts. A document emerging from the governor's informal cabinet on education is prefaced by a statement of outcome criteria—i.e., what essential purposes should have been served a decade hence by current reform. Expectations include increasing quality without diminishing access, achieving equity between young and old in the allocation of resources, making certain that excellence does not lead to elitism, [and] producing both a school and a public environment conducive to learning and supportive of those involved.

However phrased, statements of ultimate purpose and expectations should be written in capital letters at the head of every proposal for educational reform.

The Hispanic Experience

I confess that these reflections on education and educational reform—stemming originally from thoughts about my own schooling and that of my four children (as one sage has put it, aren't all theories of education autobiographical?)—have been stirred again by my work with the National Commission of the Secondary School of Hispanics. The commission has been probing the reasons why such a tragically high percentage of our Hispanic youngsters are being "wasted," their educational needs ill-attended-to, their school careers unrewarding and short. In the process, we've visited schools and neighborhoods in [affected] areas, scoured the literature and the data, conferred with educators and community leaders, Hispanic and Anglo alike—and most rewardingly of all, have listened to Hispanic youngsters ranging from discouraged school dropouts to those doing spectacularly as students and human beings.

Our central question to these young people was as follows: "Somewhere the road divides; for some of you schooling is a success, for some of you a failure. Can you tell us what makes or has made the difference?"

Their answer was simple, consistent and unanimous: Whether they had encountered an environment that nurtured and adults who cared.

Will our school reform movement make that happen for this oncoming generation of precious Americans, or will the wastage continue?

Higher Education and Social Justice

(From "Promoting Social Justice: From the Campus to the Community," *The Educational Record*, Fall 1990)[1]

"Higher education will be fairly judged by its effort against the tide to make its campuses empathetic, if not wholly in congruence, with the struggle of the marginal to move into the mainstream."

Higher education has for centuries struggled to protect its freedom from external constraints, and it has done so with considerable success.

But freedom for what? In one way or another, society—as well as needling members within the academy—have stubbornly and persistently asked the question. And signs are that the question will be raised even more provocatively during the years ahead.

Traditionally, the answer has been that the unfettered search for truth demands and justifies freedom. The answer is powerful enough to have persuaded scores of generations to respect the autonomy of academic institutions.

But is it enough of an answer in our times? Indeed, has it ever been?

The conventional triad of academic missions hints that it may not. Research—the quest for knowledge and truth—is the first of these missions; its logic and its claim have stood the test of time. So does teaching—the transmission of truth without intimidation. But the third accepted mission—service to the community, of which higher education is a part—sets one off on a long trail of wondering and uncertainty.

---

[1] The *Educational Record* is a publication of the American Council on Education (copyright 1990, American Council on Education). Reprinted with permission.

And it is that trail of questioning that contemporary society will be exploring ever more insistently. Not least [is] the haunting query [that] concerns us here. What responsibility does higher education have for ensuring, or at least promoting, social justice in the society it is committed by its own profession to serve?

Simply asking the question "What is social justice?" may suggest a rather simple way out. Enough to pose the philosophical and political conundrum—couldn't that fulfill the research and teaching mission of higher education? Given the intellectual excitement that puzzler always touches off, higher educational institutions might pride themselves in that straightforward accomplishment.

But do scholarly inquiries, seminars, debate, and disquisitions suffice to meet the criterion of service? Before responding too quickly or easily, consider some of the complex issues involved.

First, what operational definition of social justice underlies at least this treatment of the topic? Fundamentally, it has to do with fairness and equity in the distribution of opportunity, in the treatment of individuals, in the assurance of personal and economic security, and in the protection of civil and human rights. In a tradition long respected in American culture, John Rawls[2] has added the critical test of social justice—that it be measured from the viewpoint of the least among us.

Second, what is the emerging condition of modern American society that so urgently presses its needs—and arouses its expectations—upon higher education for the unique kind of service it can provide in helping assure social justice?

To begin with, the nation has come increasingly under siege: economically, with global competition and the fading hope and reality of ever-growing prosperity; culturally, as its values and way of life come up against a [changing] world and colliding philosophies; militarily, with regional conflicts over resources and the invasive threat of drugs and disorder; [and] socially and politically, as alien forces within us erode the customary bonds of family, civic associations, and codes of ethics, bringing on the intimation of eventual anarchy.

---

[2] Rawls is an American philosopher best known for his still-evolving theories on social justice, fairness, punishment, and duty. His work continues to spark debate among ethicists and political philosophers.

Siege is bringing on a siege mentality, evident in the growing distrust of the very institutions society has honored and relied upon for the sense of security now being diminished. Growing suspicion, too, and even hostility toward the stranger, whether within or without. Also evident is a growing readiness to curtail the freedoms and a reluctance to sacrifice for the well-being of others less able to fend for themselves, a growing concentration on self-interest over community welfare, and a growing sense that society's problems and problem people are too many and too complex to sustain any sense either of social confidence or competence, let alone the commitment of substantial social resources.

There is no question that American—and for that matter global—society needs the proverbial strength of Aaron to hold up the sagging arm of its wearying Moses. And why not the aid of the academy, so long rested in the nurturing sanctuary of intellectual freedom?

But there is a third conundrum. How does a pluralized, heterogeneous, and inherently obstinate near-nonentity like higher education assert a presence coherent and forceful enough to become a Gibraltar within the storm-tossed sea of modern society?

First by renewing and making explicit its commitment to what is its historical mission: keeping alive the very concept of freedom and social justice within a beleaguered society. Second, by making certain that its campuses model the ideals and practices of a free and just society. Third, by encouraging its own members as individuals, and on well-considered occasions, by acting institutionally to enter directly into the struggle for freedom and social justice in the surrounding society.

The first of these three odysseys may at first glance seem the simplest, but the everyday complexities of survival have proved that it is not. Contrary forces, often of overwhelming power, are at work. How to find a niche in an increasingly fierce competitive academic market? How to salvage a balanced budget out of a sinking set of resources and an escalating load of rising costs? How to keep alive and adapt a curricular commitment to the liberal arts in the face of a felt and real necessity to equip graduates with marketable skills? How to keep up with the student, faculty, and public expectations without steeply raising tuitions?

These and a host of other nettling concerns can become totally preoccupying. One often wonders while listening to the din of academic discourse whether the awareness of a higher purpose for higher education has become obscure or even lost. Certainly, the going impression among legislators and donors is that academic whining has drowned out the more clarion and refreshing voices of social leadership.

And it is that voice that a demoralizing society is badly in need of and is waiting for: someone of courage and integrity, representing the best and the freest from the academic tradition, to reaffirm the faith in and the dedication to the basic values of liberty and social justice. Ironically, it has taken those without the protections of academic freedom to signify with their own blood and loss of freedom just what those values are and what they mean to a troubled world: Martin Luther King, Jr., in this country [and] Nelson Mandela more recently and globally.

My own sense is that the public, even when adding to the load of problems being dumped on the academy, expects more than the complaining it is getting. [Perhaps it expects] another level of response, something more akin to a reaffirming set of declarations of basic academic and social purpose.

The second expectation is no more easily accomplished: to make the campus a model of social justice. In a knowledge-based economy, higher education has become the major gatekeeper of social standing and even financial success. What are known as "producer services"—i.e., law, management, investment, consulting, and the like—are the province of the new aristocrats of society, those most powerful and privileged in an economy in which access at all levels depends more and more upon the availability of postsecondary education. In an ascending hierarchy, higher educa- tion—whether reluctantly or enthusiastically—caters to and builds both the current and emerging elite. But what then of the mission of social justice, the assurance of equal opportunity to minorities and others left by the wayside? The problem becomes even more vexing and complex as the cost of higher education advances and sources of financial aid recede—also, too, as evidences of on-campus prejudice are breaking out throughout the country.

Clearly, the question of higher education's commitment to equal opportunity presents the greatest of its challenges in meeting the expectations of social justice and, more practically, in simply surviving the pluralization of society and the growing polarization of classes. Will higher education become less representative of the larger population it is pledged to serve, in its student body, its faculty, its governing boards, and in its general posture and outlook? [There are] no easy answers, but higher education will be fairly judged by its effort against the tide to make its campuses empathetic, if not wholly in congruence, with the struggle of the marginal to move into the mainstream.

Social justice within the academy poses a host of other challenges to higher education: equity and empathy in relation to students and staff alike, ranging from the assurance of due process to the guarantee of honesty in recruitment and advertising, from the peaceful resolution of disputes through negotiation to the protection of rights such as free speech both of those on campus and guests invited from the outside, from the tolerance of differences to the intolerance of sins against the spirit of freedom and social justice.

Society's greatest expectation of higher education is that its own practices demonstrate its acclaimed convictions. Social justice, like charity, begins at home.

And finally, the third mission of service by higher education to the larger community of which it is a part, individually and as an institution becoming a force for social justice throughout society.

Individually, members of the academy are irrepressible; in one form or another they will make their presence felt in every manner and milieu in which issues of social justice will be fought out. The institutional role of higher education will not be so much to promote that penchant as to defend and protect it. But encouragement is still in order, even when it means risking the peace of the campus and the public standing of the institution. Higher education cannot look with contentment and pride on its record of encouragement; as Ellen Schrecker has documented in *No Ivory Tower: McCarthyism and the University*,[3] the readiness to go along with academic repression has at critical times been as powerful as the instinct to go against it. Nor

---

[3] Cambridge: Oxford University Press, 1986.

has tenure been the guarantee of the freedom to speak independently; the record prompts the query whether it has become more the ultimate fringe benefit than the intended sanctuary for social criticism.

In a democratic and market society, where consensual politics and majoritarian economics prevail, that often lonely voice of social criticism, expressing the cause of the "least among us" that John Rawls has elevated to the first essential of social justice—in such a context, the prime tenet of higher education, the invitation and the right to speak independently, becomes society's most precious asset and its saving grace. Clearly, higher education's chief responsibility and its most valuable service to society is to ensure access to that independent voice.

But higher education's obligation to be of service to society in the cause of social justice does not and cannot stop there. There is an institutional role that lies beyond. Determining that role is admittedly more complicated—not least by the accepted and deservedly honored rule of institutional neutrality when it comes to taking stands on social and political issues. That rule has a powerful logic going for it: taking an institutional stand could well compromise the tolerance and encouragement of individual choices within. But it cannot and does not need to be an unyielding inhibition. There are instances where institutional stands must be taken, in fulfilling both the mission of higher education and the cause of social justice.

Both are evident in the need to combat the wastage of human resources in American—and similarly, in world—society. In the United States, popular votes and the popularity of tax reductions have conspired to perpetuate the deprivations of poverty; the wastage of human talent is of grotesque proportions. [This is even more true] on a global scale, as the prosperity of the industrialized nations stubbornly thrives on or along with the disadvantage of three quarters of the world's population living in underdeveloped nations. Looking at this predicament, former President Jimmy Carter would ask for every university to adopt a forgotten nation. That may be stretching an emotion to an unworkable assignment. But institutions of higher education can, and have begun to start at home, by partnering with schools and businesses across the country in efforts to recast the education and improve the chances of disadvantaged children in our own communities. They can also collectively, as they have through the American Council on Education, state a priority—if a choice must be made—in favor of early childhood education. [Here again is] a merger of self-interest with a voicing of concern and social justice.

A more controversial arena revolves around investment both of public funds and private endowments, as a way of making an institutional statement about social justice. In the name of institutional neutrality, some colleges and universities have withdrawn from making such statements. But the very fact of ownership of securities, and the act of not concurring in shareholders' resolutions either to condition or to divest, is itself taking a stand. And the haunting question remains, what force has the institution been in promoting the cause of social justice in the larger society?

Higher education in many respects will and must live apart from society in order to fulfill its mission of being of service. But it cannot live removed from the turmoil and tribulations of that society. Certainly not when it comes to the struggle for social justice. Equity, not least as seen from the point of view of the least among us, is too much a part of the values and fibre of the academic tradition to allow contrary forces on the outside to go uncontested.

Responding to Political, Social, and Ethical Issues

(As published in "Governing Public Colleges and Universities" and "Governing Independent Colleges and Universities," 1993)[1]

"The irony of pluralism is that it simultaneously demands and resists efforts to reach consensus on values. It sheds light on our diversity, yet resists the imposition of any one code. Anarchy reigns at one end of the continuum, authoritarianism at the other. . . . The resolution lies in nurturing diversity while professing and practicing one's own creed."

It has become a truism to start each decade with a declaration of impending change. Even if a truism, the statement still has to be repeated: each decade of this century has seen the pace of change speeding up. And trustees of colleges and universities will find in the 1990s another dizzying rearrangement of the social and institutional landscape, already nearly unrecognizable.

The most problematic aspects of this change are the causes and consequences of increasing diversity, the onrush of pluralism in every aspect of life and quadrant of the globe. Spirits and voices so long held quiescent by traditional constraints have shaken loose and been given expression and power by today's electronic and photonic magnifications of the printing press. Both globally and

---

[1] Both publications are subtitled "A Handbook for Trustees, Chief Executives, and Other Campus Leaders." Richard T. Ingram and Associates. San Francisco and Washington, D.C.: Jossey-Bass Publishers and the Association of Governing Boards of Universities and Colleges, 1993 (copyright 1993, the Association of Governing Boards of Universities and Colleges and Jossey-Bass Inc., Publishers). Reprinted with permission.

locally, the haunting question is whether the center can hold, whether any known or putative form of governance can contain, let alone harness, the centrifugal genie that modernization has freed from the bottle.

One can therefore expect leadership and decision-making to become ever more precarious and diffuse. The law of negotiated consent within a constantly differentiating constituency fastens itself with titanic force to all social institutions, especially to the academy, where it has so long held sway. A second and possibly countervailing force will also gain strength during the coming decade: the dwindling of resources and the cost-price squeeze. Higher education has become a big and expensive enterprise, with essential outlays needed for physical plant, staff salaries, complicated student needs, and regulatory requirements. Fiscal constraints could invite more decisive leadership, but leadership could also shatter against the call for pluralism and negotiated consent.

Both these contending forces will be intensified in the 1990s. Pluralism will intensify through the swirling mix of cultures, religions, and divergent interests, now global in their reach. It will intensify through demographic shifts within our own and the world's population that will steadily diversify applicant pools, faculties, and student bodies and through the erosion by advancing technologies of the insulating barriers that have traditionally kept academic and social communities as stable enclaves. Fiscal constraints will intensify as societies pay the accumulated costs of environmental damage, poverty, health deficits, and social insecurity [and] as the agenda of the cold war shifts to regional and internal conflicts that are accentuated by struggles over diminishing resources. It is not beyond imagination to see a human race—and the academy—surviving and even flourishing in that contentious environment. But the learning curve and the art of social invention will have to move sharply upward for the continuation of progress and even for survival.

Communications technology and global migration have made all sorts of boundaries permeable and in many ways obsolescent. The boundaries of the campus are no exception. No longer a walled city, the academy is more liquid than fixed. Administrators, faculty members, and students flow outward, and electronic messages, competing values, and social violence gush inward. No longer is the academy a protected and exclusive terrain, and it becomes less so with each passing year.

So far, implosion is more evident than explosion. External forces have had more of an effect on the campus than the campus has had on the culture outside. There are exceptions: scientific and technological discoveries, such as the discovery of DNA, that have radically altered the thinking and agenda of the global community; the ingenuity of "Sesame Street"; and the pedagogical artistry of peripatetic scholars on television. But these are individual sorties rather than collective assertiveness on the part of the academy.

Governance in such a fluid environment, even establishing an identity, becomes all the more a mercurial endeavor. But that is the challenge of the 1990s and beyond. The challenge begins and ends precisely at the point of establishing an identity, a distinguishable and distinctive mission, a forceful statement of what colleges and universities are all about. Trustees bear the ultimate responsibility for ensuring that such a statement is made. The mission statement must be a declaration of the values that the institution stands for, values that must be conspicuously practiced amidst the swirling pluralism of the life surrounding the institution.

The irony of pluralism is that it simultaneously demands and resists efforts to reach consensus on values. It sheds light on our diversity, yet resists the imposition of any one code. Anarchy reigns at one end of the continuum, authoritarianism at the other.

But trustees do not have to adopt either extreme. Pluralism admits of its own resolution. The resolution lies in nurturing diversity while professing and practicing one's own creed. And this is precisely what trustees and their institutions will be called upon to do in the years immediately ahead. The squeeze on resources will not allow institutions and individuals to be all things to all people, but the grounds for making choices—of general mission and particular stands—will have to be explicit and clear. This task will not be easy, but it will be essential, especially as the din of conflicting voices becomes ever louder and the issues to be settled grow even murkier.

The primary thrust will have to be on campus; campus leaders, including trustees, will need to define and model the behaviors they believe are critical. But no such candle can or should be hidden under a campus barrel. Those values need also to be extended into the world beyond.

Guiding Principles

In responding to political, social, and ethical issues, trustees have three essential responsibilities. First, they must discern critical influence in the external environment. Given their growing intrusion, external factors, such as demographic shifts, economic trends, social forces, and cultural tensions, need constantly to be identified and assessed by trustees. All of these factors occupy center stage and require far more attention from trustees than the casual reading of relevant newspaper articles. Trustees need to examine these factors at periodic retreats that feature, at least in part, the scanning of the future and involve faculty members and experts skilled in such assessment.

Second, trustees need to translate an understanding of the significance of external developments into campus policy and practices. Being aware is half the battle; the rest is a matter of making certain the college or university is prepared to deal with what lies ahead. Presidents, administrators, and faculty members need to be regularly questioned as to whether they have anticipated and laid the groundwork for handling selected issues as they emerge.

Third, trustees should monitor the social, political, and ethical performance of the institution through recurrent questioning and discussion. It is one thing to profess the virtues of good citizenship, quite another to live up to those ideals. Trustees bear the ultimate responsibility for institutional performance; their own example sets the tone and the standard. Simply by raising concerns regularly and insistently, trustees can effectively discharge that responsibility.

Values to Uphold

Governing boards, together with campus leaders, should periodically take inventory of their values. What do we and the institutions we serve stand for and strive to advance? There are many possible answers, of course, but here are five to help start a conversation with other board members.

Academic freedom. The signal contribution of any institution of learning is to ensure society access to the independent voice, that is, to be a forum for persons given freedom and sanctuary to address problems and issues—sometimes with detachment, sometimes with passion, but always unfettered by chains of enforced conventionality. That freedom is not simply the function of tenure, which seems often to be more the ultimate fringe benefit than the guarantee of an independent voice. It is, or should be, the value pervading the entire institution and the essential contribution of that institution to society.

In the coming decades, society will badly need the independent voice for its creativity, criticism, advocacy, and challenge. During times of turmoil—as clearly the 1990s will be—society tends to close in on such freedom, just at the time such freedom becomes more essential. So, unfortunately, does higher education. Witness the constricting response to McCarthyism in the 1950s and the current wave of "political correctness" now insinuating itself on so many U.S. campuses. Commandment number one for trustees will be to preserve academic freedom, often against the odds and at heavy cost.

Excellence and equity. In the years ahead, with rapid demographic shifts producing rising proportions of minority members in the actual or potential applicant pool for higher education, the two academic values of excellence and equity will have to considered in tandem. There is evidence of success and ingenuity in dealing realistically with these values. The Algebra Project in Cambridge, Massachusetts, has demonstrated the capacity of minority students to achieve high levels of competence in mathematics, and the relatively new notion of multiple intelligences has challenged the myopic insistence on IQ as the single indicator of human potential. But colleges and universities will have to stretch their imagination and energies to create new approaches to the resolution of tensions between the twin values of excellence and equity. In the process, they must make a greater commitment to K–12 educational reform and improving their own recruitment, counseling, and curriculum.

Tolerance and caring. The decade of diversity will put a premium on the virtue of tolerance. Tolerance has always been considered the cornerstone and product of higher learning. It is the essential capacity not only to understand the human condition that gives rise to diversity but also to appreciate the extraordinary human benefits of diversity. Whether colleges and universities can maintain this tradition of tolerance in the face of expanding differences, challenging so much of the *status quo*, is a central question. Crimes of hate are rising across the country, and tension and violence already abound on U.S. campuses. More tolerance will be required. An atmosphere of caring is needed, to assure those who are different that they and their education are treasured by everyone associated with the institution.

Academic accountability. Academic freedom carries with it the reciprocal obligation of being accountable to the constituencies of higher education and to the general public that has ensured the freedom the academy enjoys. The boundaries of accountability are constantly and progressively being expanded through laws and regulations; [through] an enlarging conception of the social an ethical role and responsibility of higher education; [through] more explicit definitions and expectations of institutional performance, output, and value added; and [through] ever more sophisticated consumer demand. Trustees will often find this complex environment of expectations perplexing. But failing to study it assiduously will place them and their institutions in peril.

Institutional neutrality—a value open to exception. It has been persuasively argued that institutions of higher education ought generally to remain neutral on controversial issues. This argument posits that colleges and universities should encourage individuals within their orbit to express themselves freely and vigorously but refrain from taking institutional stands that could inhibit the freedom of individual expression and mire the institution in prolonged, acrimonious, and divisive debate. Colleges and universities, it is contended, are not public legislatures; they should not become partisan but should seek to enlighten public debate by providing access to the independent voices of individual members of the academic community.

So far, so good. But as a rigid orthodoxy applied to every political, social, and ethical issue, this rule would morally cripple higher education. Too many institutions have hidden behind the rule, dodging the responsibility of wrestling with the knottier and more troubling issues that confront them and of giving force to the ideals they profess. Colleges and universities with religious affiliations and more codified sets of values usually find it easier to take positions on difficult issues. But even they find the going rough, when, for example, campus dialogue centers on such issues as abortion. More and more, they, like their secular counterparts, will find themselves pressed to declare institutionally where they stand on issues such as investments in South Africa, U.S. participation in regional and global conflicts, the implications of genetic engineering and biotechnology, race relations, and the allocation of social energy and resources.

There is no general formula for resolving the question of whether to remain institutionally neutral or to take a stand. But there is the imperative of regularly confronting the question and determining openly whether this is the place, this is the time, to say as Martin Luther once did, "Here I stand; I cannot do otherwise."

The art of defining whether an issue is political, social, or ethical. If one could clearly distinguish between political, social, and ethical issues; it might be easier to sort out which issues should find their way onto trustees' agendas and how trustees should respond to those issues. For example, issues judged to be purely political in nature might appropriately fall under the rule of institutional neutrality and be left to the tug and pull of individual opinion and partisan interplay. But most issues are not so unambiguous. What may begin as one development—for example, the widening of social disparities—quickly takes on the coloration of politics and the suspicion of ethical impropriety.

Weighing the response to such issues is exceedingly difficult. When and how should the debate continue as essentially a matter for individual expression, and when and how should the institution intervene? How a response is arrived at is often as critical as the response itself. Should it be proactive or reactive? Determined in open debate or behind closed doors? Made by the entire academic community or only a ruling segment? Arbitrary or in some way honoring the academy's credo of converting each provocation into a learning experience?

Trustees are likely to face ambiguous political, social, and ethical issues frequently during the next decade. Trustees would do well to anticipate and lay the groundwork for their responses. Their rule should be "no surprises."

Critical Issues and Likely Provocations

Several issues are likely to seriously affect college and university campuses in the next decade. These include globalization, equity and social justice, integrity, due process, and ethics.

Globalization

Driven by technology, especially communications, the world is rapidly converting, as Marshall McLuhan said it would, into a global village. Already we have an instantaneous global market, a global political forum, a globalizing consciousness and response to a deteriorating environment, and a nascent world order evolving through a reaffirmed United Nations. That all this might be undone by a proliferation of isolated tongues, the collapse of another Tower of Babel, is entirely possible. But either alternative will be played out on a global stage. Higher education cannot avoid the consequences nor stand aside as an uninvolved observer.

The consequences of globalization will be both positive and negative. Just as with Sputnik, a powerful set of stimuli will be applied to all of U.S. society, and the responses will be varied: to reach out, to be part of, to compete, to learn, to grow. On the other hand, conflict will be universalized. Disputes outside the campus—whether in adjacent or distant communities—will be replicated within the campus, particularly as campus populations increasingly represent diversities of class, race, and national origin. Curiosity about people from other cultures and backgrounds will grow and produce healthy innovations in curriculum, research, and outreach. Fear of others will also grow, hopefully not apace. This fear will result in tensions and even violence flaring both on and off campus.

Those contrasting trends are already visible. Stanford University and Connecticut College are expanding their curricula sympathetically and constructively to be more global in content and perspective. The campuses of the universities of Michigan, with heavy Arabic concentrations, reflect the tensions of the Persian Gulf War. Brown University and scores of other institutions are scarred by hostility and campus violence inflicted upon them both from within and without. In the swirl of these developments, colleges and universities will be hard pressed to mediate conflicts of culture, politics, and values; to accept differences without surrendering their own distinctive values and rules of conduct; to prepare the campus and surrounding community so that the ground rules for handling disputes and resolving differences are understood and agreed upon; and to make each controversy an opportunity for learning.

In the 1990s, conflict will be especially likely over military operations and service. Another debate may arise over the social role of both higher education and government. What should the response of higher education and government be to poverty, both local and worldwide, [to] environmental degradation, [to] the ethics of competition, and [to] other accumulating dilemmas of moral choice?

Each of these issues will provoke trustees to consider whether to adopt an institutional position or follow the rule of neutrality. If there is any general principle that may help resolve the question (and ultimately there may be none, only personal and collective judgments), it is that institutional stands should be taken when basic values are challenged and the very survival of the institution and what it stands for are in question.

Equity and Social Justice

Higher education will find the century-long tension between elitism and equality exacerbated in the years immediately ahead, for a number of reasons. Demographic shifts are producing a population that is increasingly minority, poor, and less prepared for higher education than [were] students of the last several decades. Harold Hodgkinson, the Paul Revere of educational demographers, has been sounding the warning: "At the moment, over 30 percent of our youth are at risk of school failure when they show up at kindergarten on the first day." A 1989 report of the U.S. House of Representatives Select Committee on Children, Youth, and Families cites the following statistics:

Although the number of children has fallen since the 1970s, the size of the overall population has continued to increase. Thus, children now make up a smaller fraction of the total population—26 percent— than they did in the past—36 percent in 1960. By 2010, children will represent only 23 percent of the population. Minority [groups] will continue to grow as a proportion of all children, comprising one in three children by 2010.

The more exclusive U.S. universities and colleges might be able to conduct their business as usual, comforted by the fact that their applicant pools, even when shifting toward greater proportions of minorities, will always yield enough students to sustain both their present numbers and standards. "There will always be," as an institutional officer remarked to me nonchalantly, "the number we need of our kind of students." But most colleges and universities will not have the luxury of standing aloof, and even those who presume to do so will not be immune to confrontations erupting over the social, political, and ethical issues arising from demographic shifts.

An even more fundamental reason for heightened tension is higher education's inherent identification with the current and emerging elite. Not only are colleges and universities dependent financially and otherwise on the more favored and affluent members of society, but it is also their declared purpose to produce those who will exercise leadership. And now that knowledge has become *sine qua non* for success in this age of information, higher education will become ever more the gatekeeper for entry into and progress in lucrative professions, particularly the professions that are the aristocracy of the service economy. Access to higher education is critical. But access will not be easily ensured for the growing pool of disadvantaged and less-prepared members of the population, not with rising costs and declining student aid and the pressure and need to raise standards to meet the requirements of economic competitiveness and the general sophistication of modern life.

There are some ameliorating influences. The need of many institutions simply to fill classrooms to survive will make entry into college easier. But what implications does this easing of standards have for quality and financial aid? As a result of the Persian Gulf War, another influx of veterans with another GI bill can also be expected, and with greater numbers of minority applicants. One can find encouraging signs of institutional sensitivity, given the determination of leading colleges and universities to be more aggressive in recruiting less-privileged students and making the necessary accommodations in financial aid, instruction, and counseling.

Trustees will need to attend to the issue of equity and social justice, anticipating the effects of the issue not only on institutional practice but also on the larger society. The cause of social justice will be a constant provocation during the 1990s because of imbalances of opportunity within the United States and globally, the reverberating disparities between populations in the northern and southern hemispheres, and the haunting predicaments of foreign populations seeking refuge and a better life in the United States. It would be surprising if trustees were not called upon to engage themselves personally as well as institutionally in these issues.

Integrity

The first victim of increased competition among colleges and universities is likely to be truth. Institutions will be tempted to advertise falsely, misrepresent what they can actually provide, cut corners and engage in cutthroat competition, allow inequities in faculty and staff compensation, tilt financial aid packages toward [a] favored clientele, bury deferred maintenance under accounting covers, profess [a] set of ideals and ignore them in practice, and withhold from recruited presidents and faculty members the harsh realities they will discover when appointed. These practices are, sadly, already in evidence. And if truth becomes the victim, what is left of the soul of higher education?

Above all else, trustees have to be the guardians of truth. They do so, first of all, by insisting on and practicing integrity in their own relationships and deliberations. Second, they need to assure the campus community that truthfulness will be honored rather than penalized. Third, they will have to monitor the institution's performance in every aspect of its work and processes, asking hard questions and being willing to face equally hard answers. Fourth, they need to examine their institution's external relations and communications, to make as certain as they can that the general public's rightful expectation of academic integrity is being satisfied.

Due Process

In recent decades, the public has increasingly insisted on fairness in every facet of institutional life and on governmental response to unfairness through increased regulation of vital academic processes that were long carried out without public scrutiny. For example, the public has become concerned about affirmative action, research on human subjects, facilities for the handicapped, genetic research and engineering, environmental impact, sexual harassment, and financial aid and repayment. The lengthening list shows no signs of shrinking, despite recent moves toward deregulation in the general economy and spreading resistance to regulations within the academic community.

Fairness is a powerful concept. Whether it is realized through governmental action or the voluntary response of colleges and universities, it will continue to be high on the agenda for higher education. Much of the agenda will be defensive, that is, simultaneously resisting the further intrusion of regulation while fighting counterattacks by those who would do away with innovations that on balance have advanced the cause of fairness. Affirmative action will continue to engender debate. So will judicial entry into tenure-granting processes, interinstitutional communication of policies of financial aid, secrecy in standardized testing, and confidentiality in a wide variety of traditional academic practices.

Knottier than any of these issues may well be the growing concern over freedom of expression on campus. Will equal opportunity and equal protection be given to views, either from the right or from the left, contrary to those prevalent (the current term is "politically correct") on campus? What provisions or constraints should govern the appearance of outside speakers on campus? What latitude should be allowed for the unpopular, the unconventional, even the obscene?

Although these concerns involve the substantive aspects of due process, they also directly raise the question of fairness—equity among the various claimants and fairness in the procedures by which policies are adopted and carried out. Trustees will obviously have to familiarize themselves with the law and make certain they have sound legal advice. But they will also have to make certain that their institutions take the initiative in ensuring fairness and anticipating and containing the disputes that are bound to arise.

Ethics

Everything that has been discussed thus far has an ethical dimension. There are other domains in which trustees will increasingly face ethical dilemmas that will demand a constant consideration and restatement of moral standards and values.

Science and technology, particularly biotechnology, will be the focus of many ethical concerns. The possibilities of altering reproductive and emotive behavior, of expanding the whole range of human choice in which divine or statistical law once prevailed, are bringing on a new age of ethical debate. Equally provocative are the exploration of space and consequent issues of priorities; revolutionary developments in communication, raising privacy questions; and environmental research that will force a rethinking of cultural norms and possibly the entire premise of economic development and the social order.

Higher education should be a major forum for such debate, divisive though it will surely be. The fact that the top two campus life issues of concern to college and university presidents are substance abuse and student apathy suggests that the academic forum is far from realizing its potential and responsibility.[2]

Being a trustee is no longer a passive exercise in civic distinction. It is a demanding role that requires focused attention on emerging issues of global scale and consequence. The campus cannot be isolated from the contentious questions that will be placed on society's agenda. It will in all likelihood be center stage, where most of these dramas will be played out. And trustees will bear the ultimate responsibility for making certain that the debate will be conducted openly, fairly, and with enlightenment and reason.

What will be expected of trustees is due diligence, the honoring of higher education's fundamental values and traditions, and a very healthy dose of self-education. One wonders whether there is in Oklahoma's recent legislation requiring governing board members to enroll in continued education an augury of what is to come.

---

[2] Ylvisaker is referring to a survey of college and university presidents taken jointly in 1989 by the Carnegie Foundation for the Advancement of Teaching and the American Council on Education.

PART IV
Philanthropy: The High Estate

*"Philanthropy—in the degree to which it
fulfills the aspirations of its spirit and
tradition—is a rare element in our social
firmament, a salt that cannot be allowed
to lose its savor."*

—1987

What is New in American Philanthropy

(Presented to the Eleventh Annual Conference of the National Conference on Philanthropy,[1] Saint Paul, Minnesota, October 19–21, 1966)

"Philanthropy does what would be risky for others to do. It rarely does what is risky for it to do."

It is a very good feeling to return to a place where people can pronounce both Ylvisaker and Mankato.

This meeting, I take it, is a gathering of the "haves" and "have-nots," with two questions directly or indirectly on the agenda: "How shall we give, and how shall we get?" I admire the courage of philanthropists who come to these lions' dens.

Perhaps we ought to let the askers in on one of the givers' secrets, which is, that we philanthropoids don't know how to get the money either. After twelve years in business, it's still a mystery to me just how one gets a Ford Foundation grant. But I do have one piece of advice for the asker: never mistake the uncertainty of the giver for a "yes." Because the natural condition of a philanthropoid is uncertainty, while his natural response is a "no." And we have a rule when uncertain or in doubt: hire a consultant. Which converts your own uncertainty into somebody else's indecision, and usually—but not always—befuddles the applicant as well.

I remember one very sharp correspondent who recommended that we take the farmers of the cut-over areas of the midwest who aren't doing so well and let them grow kids instead of crops— "adopted" kids from the slum areas of eastern and other cities. Well,

---

[1] In 1980, the National Conference on Philanthropy merged with the Coalition of National Voluntary Organizations to form the Independent Sector, a national coalition of 800 voluntary organizations, foundations, and corporate giving programs headquartered in Washington, D.C.

I thought this was an interesting idea, so I wrote some of my farming friends in the midwest for their reaction. The answer came back, "We'll be damned if we will." I reported this reaction to our correspondent, who by now had gone to Europe thoroughly convinced that the Foundation would accept his proposal. After reading my letter, he fired back a devastating commentary on our society of gifts and foundations, which was that decision-makers don't decide; they just pass the buck along to consultants.

Today, let me not dodge the issues, but say bluntly what's on my mind. The topic assigned me is "What's New in Philanthropy?" Frankly, there is more that's new outside philanthropy than there is inside philanthropy. Which is not to say that we in philanthropy are not changing or that we are not getting better, but, simply, to admit that the world around us is changing an awful lot faster than we are.

Whether it is changing for the better or for the worse is a question that not everyone agrees upon. It is precisely in that area of uncertainty that I'd like to begin, for it is by the perspectives and prejudices and purposes we bring to this point of uncertainty that we basically ought to be measured. Justice Holmes once wrote that a man is to be judged by his basic intent, not by how the fates conspire to order the jumble of the day-to-day around him. And as givers and getters of money, that too is how we are to be judged: by our intent and our motivation and our perspectives. As for our grants, even the best of them become but footprints in the sand. Let me start then with perspectives, and I deliberately want to draw them as wide as possible.

We (and I'll explain the "we" in a minute) are an affluent minority in the world, caught between two guerrilla wars and two jungles— the jungles of our own urban and rural slums, and the jungles of Viet Nam. Now the question to set your perspective and to challenge you is this: "Can the established order that we live in and represent be stretched fast enough and far enough to shelter and to include those who are outside, or who feel outside this system?"

Who's in this *status quo*? There are a lot of "haves," who really think that they are "have-nots." You remember the drumbeats of our revolutionary war? For two centuries, they have echoed so deeply within us that we are conditioned to think of ourselves as the underdogs, mavericks, the "outs." The same carryover of past self-image applies to the depression kids, of which I am one. A depression kid can't quite believe that he's made it to become one of the "haves." But he has. Even our bearded college rebels are among the "haves"—rebels with tuition paid.

The struggle between the "haves" and the "have-nots" will dominate the next two or three centuries. It's going to be a rough struggle. One can easily become pessimistic and conclude that, like the French aristocracy in the 1780s, the "haves" may be overrun by an avalanche so large they can neither comprehend nor contain it. And as a philosopher, one might go beyond to contemplate what kind of culture might then emerge. An optimist might find an analog to what de Tocqueville found in the New World—a refreshing contrast to pre-revolutionary France. A pessimist might see another return to the Dark Ages.

What faith, what commitments, what elasticity, what relevance do we philanthropists bring to this critical stage in human history? What we represent is the resilient margin of the industrial order, the most stretchable part of the world's *status quo*. The program question for us is whether we are stretching our resources and ourselves, as far and as fast as the situation demands. Not our own immediate situation, which is but a cozy corner in the walled castle of industrial affluence, but that universal circumstance which is the growing discrepancies between those inside the system and those without.

Those who get must face the same larger questions as those who give. Jarred by the poverty of Calcutta, I often wondered during my years at the Foundation what would happen to the finer American applications if we threw philanthropy open on a worldwide basis and then drew our priorities on that scale of need, rather than [based] on the affluence of our own system. But even within the confines of our own situation, I wonder whether we miss the chance to tug as often and as hard as we might at the universal problems. It's my conviction that these problems appear in your own backyard just as they do in Calcutta. The question is whether you recognize them and catch hold of them.

My own bent is to read these problems from the major trends and characteristics of our times. One trend is certainly the impersonalizing of our relationships and interdependencies: the closer we become, the more distant.

I will never forget Britain's Labour Minister of Education who in 1951 described to me his own difficult transition from rural to urban England, how it felt to be "near and far." Here is his account:

> I came to my apartment the other night, just when another fellow arrived at the street entrance. We didn't say a word to each other. Got on the same elevator, saying nothing, rode up to the same floor, saying nothing, walked down the hall, saying nothing, and still saying nothing found ourselves fumbling for keys to adjacent doors. Even to reticent Britishers, the silence had become oppressive. My "neighbor," obviously not knowing who I was and caring less, finally broke silence. "When do you suppose," he asked me as he disappeared into his flat, "we'll be rid of this bloody government?"

As our relationships become impersonal (a process otherwise called urbanization), the neighborhood, the church, the village, the guild, are eroding, irrelevant, or at best going through the anguish of reformulating their reason for being.

The problems that result from this impersonalization are easy to miss—they usually crop up on your blind side. It took a Japanese to turn me around so I could see one of them. He was considering establishing a foundation in Japan. When I asked him what his first project would be, he said he would create a marriage bureau. I thought he was joking, but he wasn't. In traditional Japan, marriages have been arranged; but the urbanizing group have to manage on their own—and they could use some help, at least until new traditions are established and understood. That "foreign" suggestion drove me back to look at my own culture, and not until then had I realized how little we had done to adapt our cities to the needs of young people. As Charlie Abrams[2] said in New York, "Where are the trysting places?"

We have renovated our downtowns for office workers and executives, but not for young adults or children. And we're reaping

---

[2] Urban planning pioneer Charles Abrams (1902–1970) was the first to explore the complex issues of urban housing. In 1963, he was part of a U.N. team that recommended to Singapore an integrated approach to housing, urban renewal, industrial development, and transportation. His books include *The City Is the Frontier.*

some of the consequences: a drifting young adult culture with a rising rate of social pathology.

We produced a "baby bulge" and suburbs to go with it. But we neglected to build cities to greet these kids when they graduated from the suburbs, or by the misfortune of poverty and race had no suburbs to graduate from. A lost generation of kids and a lost generation of community building, and where were the philanthropists—we who had the stretchable resources, the resilient margin of affluence to create and recreate the ties that bind, to include rather than exclude the newcomers to our established order? There are many small things we could have done and did not, not least providing for urban newcomers the welcome wagons and information centers and neighborhood services they so badly need. And there are very big things we should not have done but did: breaking up and segregating communities by bulldozers and boundaries, leaving us with problems of communication almost impossible now to overcome.

Are we capable of stretching our minds and resources far enough to bridge the gap our negligence and rigidity have created? A few polite gestures and dainty dabs of money are no longer carrying far enough. Philanthropy has no alternative now but to dare—though in this business, I've found that gambling is usually the safest bet. At least it places you within reach of payoffs on a scale relevant to the problem.

Characteristically, we at the Ford Foundation gambled this past year, inviting some of those who had burned Watts to participate in the management of an employment project we had helped finance. We're not yet sure whether the project will succeed. But we did get an immediate payoff in communication. Behind militancy, we found integrity and concern: people who cared enough to hate included— more than one might have thought—persons ready to build and create. They didn't easily trust, but they came at our invitation to visit with the Rev. Leon Sullivan and his self-help training project in Philadelphia. They didn't come for a grant, they said—self-help was their motto, and they had a program of their own already going. "We've got problems, and here's what we are going to do. We're not going to ask for money. We've got an organization; we're not going to beg—we're a proud people. But we've discovered that burning doesn't do it. Number one, we have formed our own police force. We're encouraging the businessmen to return to Watts and guaranteeing them protection. Since we've organized, only two windows have been broken, and we paid for them out of our own pocket." "You know, we've got communists on every street corner in Watts. We're not going to pay any attention to them—if anybody is going to blow up this system, we're going to do it! We don't need any outside assistance." These fellows were talking a language [that] we on the other side of the community had seldom taken the trouble to understand. . . . Why have we taken so long to listen, especially we who could most afford the time and had the least to lose?

Another perspective [is that from] the age of the free individual. This is the age when people feel equal, insist on being equal, and are very assertive in stating their rights. The right most demanded is equal access—especially to the level and mix of services crucial to a decent standard of urban living. This rise in consumer demand for services is touching off a crisis for each of the trades and professions: health, education, architecture, crafts, even the ministry and philanthropy. None of these have been adapted to a mass market, with each consumer asking both excellence and equal access. The guild philosophy still prevails, with limited entry, limited supply, limited patronage. With the advent of mass consumption, the trades and professions will be under sharp and increasing pressure to expand their numbers, extend their service facilities, and become more responsive to the consumer. The medics, [because of] Medicare, are at the breaking point now. The lawyers in the United States are under the same pressure, but they have been much more adaptive. Recently they have cooperated with the poverty program, have begun creating neighborhood law services and extending their services to parts of the market they had previously neglected.

This principle of equal access will also revolutionize the area and profession of city planning. In the past we have planned our cities with an eye to the mass production: distribution and consumption of physical and manufactured goods and related services. We are now in the service economy, and the city has to become a service city. Look what they are building for our old folks in the leisure and retirement worlds across the country: physical environments built around services and equal and immediate access to them. (The old can vote, the kids can't—and note the difference in the city catering to them.) Now ask yourself about your community, not merely in terms of poverty but in terms of the total market. Is your city being constructed to give access to services that count and that are asked for by this new generation of demanding customers? Have your philanthropic programs contributed to this new trend or to former patterns?

Another perspective [is that from] the age of public purpose. The nation's and the world's first business over the next 100 years is going to be public business. It has to be, because in this kind of society you have to have collective mechanisms to allocate resources and set priorities, whether we like it or not. Yet though ours may be the age of public purpose, it will also be the age of private means. The bureaucratic tradition is growing obsolete. The hierarchically organized public bureaucracy—a carryover from the medieval days—relies on its muscle system. Consider instead a nerve system—a system of quickly energizing the vast resources of the private sector to fulfill a public purpose. At a premium will be the man versed in that emerging art of "the public entrepreneur": the man who can create jobs, get performance, cut through the red tape, and do a job.

I would also argue for competition in the public interest. Why have we believed in competition in the private sector and discouraged it in the public sector? To the public sector, we say "It's overlapping, duplication." It's going to be necessary and healthy to have public definitions of jobs to be done and then private mechanisms, nonprofit corporations, and even contracts to profit-making corporations to do these jobs. [It's] no accident that you see many former government officials moving into the private sector in order to do public jobs, or remaining in the public sector but creating private mechanisms.

We are also going to need social research and development. Take a look at [3M], GE, Ford, GM, or Western Electric. The genius of these has been that they have had research and development [that] lets them stay out in front and adapt and be flexible. The public sector? Where is its research and development? We're beginning to develop corporations such as RAND, to which the government awards contracts for research and development. The Poverty

Program, whether it is known or not, was conceived in this image to begin providing the free money and the good minds to invent new types of activities that would get jobs done [and] to begin adapting the public mechanism to do an efficient job.

From that perspective, government is now our largest philanthropist. You know, it's interesting how government has turned to grantmaking as its administrative device. Even the Ford Foundation has been shrunk to junior size by comparison. In more cases than we'd like to admit, public philanthropy has turned out to be more enterprising than private philanthropy, one main reason being that it's far more representative and has no choice but to be relevant.

But public philanthropy has run its own peculiar problem: the shortage of funds available because of Viet Nam. Whether or not the public well runs dry, the question still faces us in private giving and getting: are we prepared to be relevant to the great issues and trends of our day, and be disciplined by the overriding priorities? With government money in short supply, more than ever we are the system's flexible resources. There are in this country well over 15,000 trusts and foundations. Go into individual cities and begin counting these trusts: the numbers and the amounts will surprise you. But have they responded to the job and responsibility in which they are cast by the times, and to the perspectives demanded by the times?

Even greater than the challenge of relevance or the responsibility of remaining flexible and creative is the challenge to be the keeper of the public faith and conscience. Altruism in our day comes hard, and as the world's growing population presses more heavily on available resources, altruism will come even harder. The choice constantly before us will be to grow and share, or to conserve and protect what we have. The real costs of Viet Nam are not the financial costs. The real costs are what it is going to do to one creative, stretching, and sharing instinct of the United States. I hope it is only a short-term period. But I wonder, when last year [1965] brought the white backlash, the slowdown on the war on poverty, the slowdown on the model cities and housing programs: one wonders, is the United States beginning to close, to conserve, to hoard, not to stretch and grow? It is our function in philanthropy to make sure that that tender instinct continues; otherwise we're in trouble.

We *are* keepers of the faith, the faith that keeps us sharing, growing, risking, serving. It is easy actually to do the opposite while using these words. I talked yesterday with a fairly young observer of philanthropy. "You know," she said, "I've discovered something. Philanthropy does what would be risky for others to do. It rarely does what is risky for it to do." I wish you would think about that for a minute.

If you look at the innovations that our public reports claim and then look at the perspectives and the scale I have given you and the worldwide priorities—remembering that in another generation we will add two billions to the world's population, almost all of them "have-nots"—ask yourself, "Are these innovations we claim *really* innovations, or are some of them window dressing?" Are we coming to doublespeak, to doublethink, the language of *1984*? (Remember, George Orwell's original title was *1948*. The publisher changed it because nobody shared Orwell's belief that *1984* was already here.) The capacity in all of us to say one thing while doing the opposite is ever present. I think it behooves all of us to look at what we do in philanthropy under the easy title, to ask whether we are really keeping the faith or going through the motions.

Now a personal note: I decided this week to leave the field of philanthropy. I've served my hitch. It's been twelve years. I believe in philanthropy; it's a function which, if it did not exist within the United States, would certainly have to be recreated. It helps hold this diverse society together, and it is beginning to show itself as almost the fifth estate in our society—and not only in our society, but also throughout the world. Japan is looking to its tax laws, planning revisions that will encourage the development of philanthropy. Germany and the Volkswagen Company have begun to sort out patterns of giving that they might encourage.

The function of philanthropy is a good one; it's essential, and it ought to grow. But only if it continues to grow in its own special responsibility, which is to keep the system growing. At least that's the philanthropic faith I've tried to keep.

And my thoughts upon leaving? The reassuring one that all those people I've said "no" to over these twelve years will now be able to get another chance.

 # The Filer Commission in Perspective

(Keynote presentation to the Twenty-seventh Annual Conference of the Council on Foundations, Atlanta, Georgia, May 11, 1976)

"Philanthropy will not be free, or open, or accessible, or accountable, or in touch unless it has those qualities of caring and nurturing and persevering. But also [it must have] a sense of humor."

I've been sort of a house radical in philanthropy for some time. Continuously, when you reach out the hand of friendship I bite it. And tonight you may feel is no exception.

But I want to explain my motive in anything that sounds critical. I respect the philanthropic process very deeply. Many have underestimated the place of philanthropy in modern society, too often seeing it in very provincial and parochial ways. Tonight, I have chosen the topic "The Filer Commission in Perspective," in order to delineate more sharply the philanthropic process as I see it evolving in the United States and, significantly enough, in other cultures as well.

The Commission on Private Philanthropy and Public Needs can be faulted. But I think it will stand as a landmark in the evolution of American philanthropy. I speak more as historian than as an immediate critic, trying to see it in the perspective of a century of developing American institutions.

Something happened about 100 years ago. After the Civil War, affluence came to America, and large corporate structures began to emerge. A process that was essentially one of personal benevolence suddenly developed into something more. We began to bureaucratize both the giving and the getting in philanthropy, separating at an increasing distance the original donor from the ultimate recipient. This move toward bureaucratized philanthropy is associated, obviously, with the complexity of American life, with specialization and the industrial model; in effect, we have industrialized philanthropy. Something else happened during this period. The importance and the purpose of the single act of giving began to fade, and other purposes beyond helping one individual began to emerge. Bureaucratized foundations began talking "programmatically," saying that they would like to change this or that feature of American society, move toward new policy, leverage social change. Enough money was put together so that in an organized way we could convert personal giving into social engineering.

This metamorphosis has created something in between, a depersonalized process that to many looks like a mysterious black box. And the ever-quizzical American is compelled to ask, "What's inside?"

Within the last generation, we've had three successive probes into what goes on in that black box. The first was stimulated by McCarthy and Reece in the 1950s.[1] They asked the question, "Is something un-American going on inside?" We went through that decade trying to respond and saying, "No, what's inside is genuine, 100 percent American." And largely we proved it.

The next set of questions came when Congressman Patman[2] persisted in his skepticism, and in 1969 got Congress, speaking for a

---

[1] The Reece Committee of 1953 was one of several congressional groups investigating possible communist activities among foundations, although its original mandate was to study interlocking control of foundations and foundation funds by certain families, corporations, and groups. This shift of focus was part of the national obsession with communism that was both fed and exploited by the "witch-hunting" activities of Wisconsin Senator Joseph R. McCarthy.

[2] Congressman Wright Patman (D-Texas), chairman of the House Committee on Banking and Currency for forty years, waged an anti-foundation campaign during the early 1960s. He believed that wealthy east coast families exploited legal loopholes available to foundations in order to protect their fortunes, thus unfairly competing against emerging fortunes in the south. Ylvisaker often speculated that Patman's intense suspicion and contempt for the wealthy and their foundations stemmed from a childhood experience—Patman's father's small grocery store was forced out of business when a large east coast supermarket chain moved into his Texas hometown.

public curious about that black box, to ask, "Is something illegal going on inside?" So we opened it up and sure enough, there was. There was enough of the illegal and questionable that a very rough law was passed, and we began to isolate what is proper and not proper in this large-scale, organized social process that philanthropy has become.

In 1976, we're beginning a third public dialogue. The question has shifted again. It is now, "Is what's in that black box of philanthropy worth the price the nation is paying for it?" At his point, Filer—I'm using the shorthand—enters the dialogue. It was intended that the Filer Commission, with the consent of both those who asked the questions and those who would be asked, decided to prepare a factual and reasoned background statement so that the forthcoming dialogue would not get out of hand, would not become as hairy as the furor and forensics of 1969. The Filer Commission represents that common determination to prepare for the question.

Now, credit the Filer Commission. It has done more in an accumulative way to define what philanthropy is than any other group [has done] in the past. Certainly, we now have far more data about philanthropy—more, perhaps, than we know what to do with. But even with all those facts that Filer has gathered, what goes on in that " black box" is still elusive, still not easy to communicate.

First, it's become painfully evident that our vocabulary has not kept up with the evolving thing called "philanthropy." It has been the tax lawyers who have developed the terminology and the jargon: "501(c)(3)," "501(c)(4)," "public charities," etc. Foundations are not philanthropy because philanthropy is something more—you have further to distinguish the donor and the donee, the private foundation and the public charity, etc. A lot of terms are struggling into existence to express something that has become extraordinarily complicated—an evolving organism with an embryonic vocabulary.

Filer, like all of us, found this primitive vocabulary frustrating. The more so, as the commission—in one of its most significant strides forward—broadened the concept of philanthropy to include the entire "third sector": i.e., that which is neither profitmaking (business) nor regulatory (government).

But in stretching the popular view of philanthropy, Filer also made the concept more elusive, more difficult for folks to understand. They thought *before* Filer that philanthropy was where you looked for money. Now they learn there are 500,000 and more organizations, all of which are out to *get* that money, that are part of philanthropy, part of a "third sector." That requires a lot more thinking about to understand.

Filer went on to give us all a lot more to think about before any of us can say we really understand, including some quite disturbing facts. A good part of America has been asking, "Is what's in that black box a sanctuary for the *status quo?* Is it a tool for the chosen few?" Filer gave some very disturbing replies. The commission's report and its research papers make it clear that giving in America is a concentrated process: the higher-income people give most of the money that is available for philanthropy. Professor Martin Feldstein's[3] work shows there is also a class pattern in American philanthropy. The wealthier give predominately to hospitals, culture, and education; the not-so-wealthy give mostly to the common man's charities—the church, the Boy Scouts, the Y, etc.

Filer also showed some concentrated receiving of charitable gifts in America. One example: a third of the gifts of appreciated value end up in twenty educational institutions, a fact that is likely to stir some sharp questioning by Congress and the general public.

Credit the Filer Commission: it displayed these facts. But it's fair to say the commission in its recommendations eased away from confronting and trying to change those facts. For example, the commission voted to continue the deduction system. There is a more equitable alternative: the tax credit. But Filer stayed with the deduction system, which perpetuates higher incentives for the wealthier, more concentrated sources of giving, and the class pattern just described. The tax credit as an incentive to giving is more egalitarian, and the Donee Group,[4] as you know, recommended it.

---

[3]Throughout his career, Harvard University economist Martin Feldstein has studied issues relating to taxation, savings, unemployment issues, Social Security, and national economic policy. Six years after Ylvisaker gave this speech, Feldstein was appointed chairman of the President's Council of Economic Advisers.

[4] As the Filer Commission began its work, some were concerned that it was "too elitist" and that the concerns and work of more broad-based or smaller nonprofits were likely to be overlooked. The commission then funded a separate, parallel investigation (the name Donee Group reflects the grant-receiving status of many

But Filer really didn't confront that choice, except to describe its impact and decry its disadvantages from the point of view of established philanthropy (e.g., the fear that tax credits would make gifts to the church more vulnerable and encourage legislators to abandon [altogether] tax deductions and their concomitant advantages to the wealthy).

Filer also went very light on corporations. Corporate giving in the United States, the facts clearly show, is depressingly meager: 5 percent allowable and less than 1 percent given. A debate did occur within the commission about whether corporations ought to be prodded into 2 percent or more, by such devices as a forgivable excise tax. But the argument dissolved into nothing more than an innocuous sermon. Another instance of Filer's skittishness was the commission's exemption of churches from its recommended requirement of full financial disclosure.

My intent here is not so much to judge as simply to report a pattern: an existing system was fully described but not as fully confronted. The gift of appreciated value was kept as is. Charitable bequests were kept as is. And I was disappointed, I must say, that a more forthright position wasn't taken on the minimum tax: saying loud and clear that philanthropy would render what it owed to Caesar, that no citizen could escape paying taxes altogether, even if that meant that the charitable deduction would to that extent have to yield. By the way, the statement would have cost practically nothing; the loss in charitable revenues would be practically nil.

Filer showed other strains of conservatism. The commission talked more about the budget crisis of established organizations than about the emerging needs of a developing third sector. To be fair, it would not have been a simple matter to have made that inventory, unless one were inclined to accept partisan statements at face value. Still, we have enough evidence to know that relatively little of philanthropy's resources are going to causes that affect women and minorities. The Donee Group was emphatic on this point. Again, the pattern of "establishmentarianism" that emerges from Filer is clear.

---

smaller nonprofits) into issues important to such organizations. The Donee Group's report to the Filer Commission recommended—among other things—that Filer advocate open reporting by foundations and add to its membership representatives of smaller, minority-based and female-based nonprofits.

Filer also saw philanthropy more as a matter of money and taxes than of what I shall later argue to be the spirit and essential purpose of philanthropy.

In dealing with philanthropy not simply as foundations but as a third and integral sector of America, Filer did prepare the way for the public dialogue that is now beginning to take shape. I think that this in itself was an historic step. But the inevitable question then follows: "Is that third sector a vital, dependable, and effective instrument of a modern constitutional democracy?" It is not enough to say, "Of course it is," and Filer tended to do just that. There was, and I rather appreciated him, one very strong conservative on the commission who exclaimed one day, "Look, enough of this apologetic nonsense. Let's go down to Congress and pound on the table and say we believe in philanthropy. It's a lot better than anything you can compare it to. Why this hangdog approach?"

Attractive, yes, but also dangerous. Take a look at your own poll of what I'd call the "nodding" American public. Nodding quietly, doesn't know quite what's going on in that mysterious world of philanthropy, knows it's supposed to be good, gives you a favorable rating—65 percent do. But the figure I'd watch in that poll is the 25 percent "no opinion." Constantly, throughout the survey, at least 25 percent are saying they haven't yet make up their minds. That undecided vote is dangerous.

Especially so since the operative attitude in our society is not that of passive assent but of active skepticism. The Filer Report has run into its share of that biting reaction, more I think than it deserved. Reminder enough, if you need one, that philanthropy has some rough questioning ahead.

Thanks to Filer, we're readier for the "Dialogue of 1976" than we otherwise would have been. There are some new elements in this upcoming dialogue. Let me start with one: the vocal presence of the consumer.

When foundations went up against Congress in 1969, they kept looking for their loyal supporters, and nobody showed up. As a matter of fact, grantees were reluctant to go down there and parade their luck, and for every recipient you had given to, there were hundreds of ingrates. This time around, the consumers will be there; their first appearance has taken form in the Donee Group. That is the significant new development in the dialogue in 1976. It is not just the Congress, nor just a few disappointed people who are about to grill you, but a consuming group of American citizens who need the product of philanthropy, need what it represents. They are saying, "We want you to shape up."

So far, this budding consumerism has not gone beyond the first modest appearance of a well-mannered group. They aren't yet into litigation. But universities and the business community—where consumerism has had a decade to flourish—can predict the near advent of "rights hunting" in philanthropy, the restless search for legal handholds that will support increasing egalitarianism.

And be aware, too, of a rising generation of social entrepreneurs, insistently pressing for the kind of financial leverage philanthropy has to offer. At Harvard, one of the subjects most studied now is philanthropy. Why? There is a breed of Americans who don't want to go into big organizations and get hassled by bureaucracies. They are just as turned off by government as they are by corporations. They know that to do interesting things requires funding, and they want entrepreneurial risk money. You should see a class of seventy at the Graduate School of Education, coming from graduate departments all around Harvard, poring over your reports, inviting philanthropoids to speak, interrogating them about philanthropy's role and their own part in it.

But aggressive consumerism and entrepreneurialism aren't all you're facing. There's that general public, saying in effect, "Personal charity—one willing individual helping another—is one thing. Impersonal philanthropy is quite another. We're not sure we want to be raided by do-gooders coming out of an inaccessible sanctuary where we can't get at them through the vote."

There is something else new in 1976. This time everyone knows the republic is in trouble. Anxious rather than confident, Americans are torn between the conservative wish to go back into the comfortable past and a radicalizing premonition that maybe we need to take some bolder leaps into the future. The latter instinct is growing stronger, and it evokes a memory of a prophecy made back in the 1950s: that foundations one day would be questioned not for being so radical, but for being so timid.

This American republic of ours now needs an auxiliary thrust—

not something in place of its government, nor something (as David Hunter[5] said last year) "above the battle." The republic is looking for a vital force that is complementary to government, at times confronting and countervailing, and always providing options.

Foundations in their role as donors represent a private version of the legislative process in America—a deliberative process that selects goals, sets values, and allocates resources. The donee part of philanthropy is the private counterpart of the administrative process in government, an alternative vehicle for getting things done. You occupy not just a little private preserve; you are a precious institution and asset in this country [that] allows Americans to hear and to speak with the voice of the prophet against their own elected officials, and to try things faster and in another way.

To be what the Republic in 1976 needs, philanthropy has to be—and to be seen as—consistent with democratic ideals: it must be open, it must be accessible, it must be accountable, and it must be in touch. Both Filer and the Donee Group have done us a service by listing some of the steps that can be taken to assure those qualities in philanthropy, both in giving and receiving.

My guess is that the country is ready for another round of legislation that will state more clearly, more precisely, how we can make philanthropy more open, more accessible, and more account-able. If put to the vote, many of the changes that Filer recommended I am sure would pass.

But I want to emphasize what I think you want to emphasize as well. There is another quality in demand. We need a philanthropy that is *free*, and I think here is where Filer came up short. Freedom (and Filer made this mistake) is not the same as elitism, not simply the preservation of established "excellence." I wish I could rid our literature and our preaching of that timidifying notion of excellence, the crippling fear that the mediocrity of the mass will overtake the excellence of the few.

What we are fighting for now is the right to be different.

---

[5] David Hunter was executive director of the Stern Fund in New York. He delivered the 1975 keynote address to the twenty-sixth annual conference of the Council on Foundations, encouraging foundations to get down into the fray rather than remain "above the battle."

I don't think Harvard (to cite an example close to home) should claim to have a corner on excellence. We have a right, though, as any other body has a right, to be different and in that very basic sense, to be free. Nor do I think that being free means being tied to the *status quo*, that the only way we can maintain the freedom of philanthropy is, say, by maintaining—or even allowing—tax incentives to those who give. Nor is freedom simply a function of money and taxes, although I don't want to underestimate their importance.

What Filer did, in this perspective, was to pour new wine into old bottles. What emerged, I think, is too clever by half—a recommendation, first, that we keep the present power system that philanthropy represents by preserving the deduction system; and then that we invite a whole lot of other, poorer folk to play the game along with the wealthy. The deduction system remains intact while we encourage another sixty million Americans and more to participate—to get double deductions and 150 percent deductions, depending upon their income.

Watch what this does. Filer asked at one point the most revealing question of all: "How much does the nonprofit third sector spend?" What are the cumulative budgets of hospitals, Boy Scouts, all such enterprises in the third sector? That total comes out to $80 billion annually. Those revenues are derived roughly as follows: one-third private giving, one-third government, and one-third earnings.

Filer then asked the question, "If we gave up all the tax incentives for giving, how much would we lose of the $80 billion?" That loss turns out to be $5 to $7 billion in current annual revenues.

In other words, if we were to extract entirely from the tax system all inducements to giving, we would lose 10 percent or less of philanthropy's current annual income. Now, that is crucial money, and I don't come quickly to the conclusion that we ought to court its loss. But what Filer recommended is that we more than double the involvement of giving with the tax system; if we followed the commission's recommendations, an additional $11.7 billion would be leveraged into private giving by tax inducements. The public question not faced by the commission is this: do we want to involve American philanthropy further, if at all, with tax advantage? Simply asking that question is powerful medicine. It *will* be asked because it is a public policy question that Congress cannot avoid. I have no doubt but that the pressures will be such that we will not abandon the relationship. But it is fair to ask whether we ought to dig philanthropy deeper into tax considerations and into the dependencies and the public doubts that follow on. We may lose—we may already have lost—far more in spirit than we gain in revenue.

The question becomes particularly crucial when tax advantage is tied up with another element of freedom that I firmly believe is more important to philanthropy than financial solvency: the right of free speech. Here I am adamant, and I would ask you, as thoughtful citizens if not as self-interested philanthropists, to think about it hard.

The right to petition Congress, by my reading of the First Amendment, is a right guaranteed to all. But we have allowed the Congress, the legislative body, to condition that right not only for foundations but for the whole nonprofit sector. I believe that free speech—the right to engage the public's mind and its elected representatives—is the most precious cornerstone of a free society— and of any free and vigorous sector within it.

Yet we bargain with Congress over the right. We let them attach conditions to that right; and we think we are doing well when a piece of legislation gives us a couple more percentage points of leeway, or a new formula, basically because we are worried that unless we let that sleeping dog of lobbying lie, Congress will get angry and cut back on the tax advantage it allows.

I feel very categorical about that. In no way should philanthropy be compromising its ability to speak freely and to help fight the battle for this nation's mind. It's that kind of freedom that philanthropy needs if it is to be of any use to a free society. We ought not to be bargaining that birthright away for a mess of tax pottage.

On that most basic point, we can and should be categorical. But we can't on most others. Ours is an incredibly complex time and circumstance, and the Filer Commission has helped us understand how complex and subtle are most of the problems we deal with, the solutions we arrive at, and the trade-offs we'll have to make. A complex society is like a scorpion—come at it from the front and you get stung sharply, quickly, from the rear. It's fascinating to find how counterintuitive the system really is. For example, there is a part of me, a populist instinct born of the midwest, [that] would like to raise the effective tax rate on wealthier people and reduce some of their advantages. The commission, through Martin Feldstein and others, explored the effects of such a move and discovered this delicious irony: government would get more in taxes but less than the amount otherwise given to charity. Charity would get less. The wealthy would be left with more money to spend on yachts or whatever. And the populist would have been confounded because his tax reform would have made the rich richer. Why? Because the tax deduction is "efficient": more is leveraged into—and out of— philanthropy by existing tax incentives than the amount of tax revenue either forgone or recovered.

Another sting from the scorpion's tail: among those of us who feel minority concerns, there is a tendency to threaten philanthropy when it is slow to respond by saying, "Shape up or we'll sic government on you." I believe that minority causes are the natural and appropriate agenda of philanthropy and ought to be explicitly so declared. But we'll have to think twice about using government as a club, because government is run under democratic rules [that] make it basically a friend of the majority; and by definition, that majority would rather ignore those concerns than activate them. Which is not an argument against using government as a prod—but [it should be used] as a caution.

Let me put this into perspective. I said the question this time around was not "Are you Communists?" or "Are you illegal?" The salient question is now "Are you worth it?" Worth the taxes we forgo—obviously that's part of the question. But more than that, what value is there, what return to society, in allowing philanthropy the freedom to bark at our legislators, to propagate [grantmakers'] own concept of the public interest, to engage in social engineering, to court the public's mind whether demurely through research or boldly through lobbying, even to venture the reform of government and the reordering of social priorities?

Both the question and any relevant answer we may give to it moves us inexorably toward the concept of philanthropy and foundations as public trusts, and away from a time when founda- tions and philanthropy could be regarded as a personal affair and a personal prerogative. Go back to the corporation of the late nineteenth century; you can see how it became domesticated, regulated, and constrained because we realized that a corporation, even when declared by the Supreme Court to be a person, was a person with a public responsibility and a public role. We are now watching philanthropy go through the same process of being steadily converted from a personal instrument into a public trust.

Institutional expressions of this change will be difficult to work out. But as we go ahead, trying falteringly to invent some kind of regulatory process that doesn't destroy freedom, some way of moving money—whether by revenue-sharing or whatever—from the public sector into the private sector without contaminating it, we are going to have to rely basically on the spirit of philanthropy rather than simply on our technical smarts. That spirit, as I feel it, has several qualities. One is the patient intelligence that works steadily at what seems unworkable, that chips away at impossibilities, and over time produces at least passable answers.

But patient intelligence is not the whole of the philanthropic spirit. It is also the impatience that constantly tugs at the inertias in our social system. Those inertias are all around us. During this decade, I think, philanthropy should be spending a large part of its energies tugging at one stubborn form of inertia: that of the barons of the post-industrial society—the professions and related magnates of the service economy. They are the ones now whose minds we should be fighting for, they who—though they resist the responsibility of leadership while enjoying its benefits—will have most to say about the quality of life in the generation ahead.

How are you doing with that battle, now that it is 1976 and you've had half a decade to engage the professions and other captains of post-industrial society?

In law, I think, progress has been made. I commend to you a publication just issued by the Ford Foundation [that] reviews the development of public interest law. The difference between current acceptance of the concept by the legal guild and the stubborn resistance encountered when it was first institutionalized a dozen years ago is an encouraging measure of what philanthropy can accomplish.

In medicine and education, I am not so optimistic. These are powerful guilds [that] probably will be bypassed before they can be socially vitalized. It will happen to medicine now that we've discovered the diminishing returns on further investments in medical care and technology and the rising return from self-care, health education, nutrition, and prevention.

Conventional educators are being bypassed by Sesame Street, by lifelong learning in nonformal settings, by schooling within industry, by late-night talk shows, to mention but a few of the burgeoning alternatives to education as we have known it.

And how is the tug-of-war going with the inertias of the philanthropic profession? I asked you four years ago what you were going to do about your own profession. It did not then have a code of ethics; it did not have much of a sense of itself as a group of professionals. Be thankful for the Tax Reform Act and now for the consumer movement: they do you a favor by tugging at you. Neither you nor our needful society can afford to be comfortable with your inertias.

Another essential quality of philanthropy is the spirit of caring, of nurturing, of persevering. These are qualities that don't fare very well in the professionalized bureaucracies of men and majorities, with their heavily technical calculations of whom to help and when. But they are qualities that women and minorities have come to appreciate from life in a different milieu—and philanthropy would be the better for speeding their participation (if indeed they keep the faith they bring with them).

Philanthropy will not be free, or open, or accessible, or accountable, or in touch unless it has those qualities of caring and nurturing and persevering. But also [it must have] a sense of humor. One glaring weakness in Filer is that not once, as you read the report, do you find the cause even to smile. And which of us can do this society any good without a bit of the droll, the whimsical, whatever it takes to see ourselves and what we do in perspective?

Social Justice and the Role of Philanthropy

(Presented at the International Conference on Opportunities for Philanthropy, sponsored by the Josiah Macy, Jr., Foundation, Bellagio, Italy, October 1976)

"Philanthropy [must] move out of fixed and safe positions into more independent, flexible, and far more exposed stances between the contradictory forces that are generating tension, and without the resolving action of some agent such as philanthropy, will otherwise tear nations and neighborhoods apart."

In accepting social justice as one of its goals, philanthropy is inevitably drawn into the philosophical question of who deserves what share of society's power, resources, and rewards. Philanthropy in America—and fair to say, I think, in other nations as well—has yet to engage that question at the totally befuddling level of complexity now apparent in the realities and the paradoxes of urban overload and global poverty.

Philanthropy has been spared the full agony of dealing with the question by the provincialism of its origins and the sheltered workplace within which it has carried on its labors. In its very nature, philanthropy is a product of wealth, a representation of what is voluntarily contributed by those who have enough to give for purposes, however benevolent, that stay reasonably within range of interests and perspectives.

It does not demean philanthropy thus bluntly to describe it, because there is still in the charitable impulse more of a drive to see the universal in the particular than one finds in other social processes—barring, at their best, religion, politics, and academe. No accident this conference nor this assignment; but no excuse, either, to evade the obvious implications of who is asking the question and with preferred outcomes in mind.

Some Historical Perspectives: Where Philanthropy Is Coming From

The philanthropy "we" represent has engaged the problem of social justice in two separate but converging theaters: the domestic and the international.

In both environments philanthropy has operated generally on the same set of values and assumptions:

- That human beings, whatever their social origins, should enjoy a steadily increasing measure of freedom, equality, and security.

- That the processes by which social goals are determined and resources allocated should be made more accessible to all groups and individuals within society.

- That sustained economic growth is the quintessential element needed to achieve these goals.

- That all these gains can be accomplished without fundamental change in the culture and institutions that created and still sustain philanthropy.

Philanthropy could take on the mission of promoting social justice without placing its own assumptions and survival at risk.

American philanthropy has now had nearly a century of experience operating within the comforting framework of those beliefs. It was after the Civil War that burgeoning wealth begat large-scale philanthropy: successively and symbolically, Carnegie and Rockefeller, each in its turn and with growing flotillas in their wakes, ventured forth ever more intrepidly on the quest for greater social justice.

For most of that century, along most of the distance traveled, the odyssey has been not only safe but reassuring. Those were years of rising affluence and hegemony, not only for Americans but for the culture of industrialization and egalitarianism they came so conspicuously to represent. Charitable enterprises shared the same attributes and enjoyed the same success as did business and democracy. They were, when looked at in the large, indistinguishable; not even the profit motive or the political calculus really separated them, since philanthropy was dependent on both and lived well within their constraints. Stated more positively, they were bound together into a single, coherent system; philanthropy acted to reinforce the values of that system, serving as a troubleshooter at home and as a missionary abroad.

The results over time have indeed been impressive, and never more so than during the crescendo of charitable crusading of the past two decades. Domestically, the foundations and the nonprofit service sector became the main incubators of social reform and the war against poverty; no matter that those actively engaged in these missions were such a minor fraction of that vast and otherwise somnolent enterprise called philanthropy. Over that period, the system in all its parts operated at peak efficiency: the economy provided a climate of hope and a larger pie for everyone to slice into; government transferred wealth and opened new avenues to participation; and philanthropy gave haven to nobler purposes and newer ideas. The number of poor in America was reduced almost by half; millions of minority group members and the young were enfranchised and otherwise given entry to the system. The irony of it all is that Americans now look back on that combined surge of social energy as essentially a national failure.

Abroad, the display of concerted energy was equally impressive—not the least being the powers released by philanthropy. The Ford Foundation's position in India until the mid-1960s epitomized the assertive influence of the goals and ideals that philanthropy brought with it, and the Green Revolution provided what may have been a curtain call of concluding approbation. Another miracle had been accomplished in unwavering dedication to the simpler concepts of humanitarianism and social justice. But, like its domestic counterpart, the international war against poverty and injustice seems to have run out of both miracles and acclaim.

Sisyphus Time

What philanthropy and its collaborators have encountered is not failure but paradox: the farther they succeed in lifting their burden, the heavier it gets and the more weary the doers of good become.

Similar forms of the paradox have appeared both at home and abroad. Its cruelest expression is that progress seems inexorably to ensure retrogression. Success in reducing mortality has overwhelmed the capacity of even rapidly developing societies to expand per capita benefits. Accelerated economic growth has been followed not by the closing but by the widening of the gap between "haves" and "have-nots." Raising agricultural productivity has inundated cities with well-fed and ill-housed migrants. Providing adequately for those migrants has helped attract more [of them] and [has] left cities bankrupt of the means to maintain even their current levels of services. Sharing power with new cohorts of the left-out has not reduced social hostility; if anything, it has added a new cleavage between indigenous "haves" and "have-nots." The extension of rights from the few to the many, and from civil to economic, has elaborated political and bureaucratic mechanisms that suffocate as much as they liberate.

Two decades of unparalleled economic development, governmental intervention, and philanthropic initiative have brought us to a seeming impasse both here and afar. Within our society, a sun belt of remaining optimism and vigor is detaching itself emotionally and politically from the older industrial areas, especially of the northeast and middle west; and within those aging industrial regions a culture of permanent unemployment and crime—a counterculture of ominous proportions—is fast developing and breeding true. Forty percent unemployment rates now prevail among urban black and other minority youth; survival by any means is the going imperative; and a [1976] survey by the National Center for Urban Ethnic Affairs of eighty-seven inner-city neighborhoods (twenty-three black, ten Hispanic, and fifty-four white) found nothing but continuing deterioration.

With the proportions reversed—the poor far outnumbering the affluent—the same fracturing is evident internationally. Manouchehr Ganji, in his 1974 report to the United Nations Commission on Human Rights, documented dismal measures of the widening gap.

The stone of Sisyphus has grown heavy indeed.

Philanthropy and the Art of Weightlifting

The last few years have not been easy ones for those practicing the art of philanthropy. What Forrester[1] calls the counterintuitive obstinacy of a complex system has nettled its way into our consciousness, there have been deepening pangs of self-doubt and mounting bewilderment about what to do next, more or differently. Even if painful, some of this pause for reflection has been useful; American and philanthropic idealism have had some growing and maturing to do.

There are already signs of learning—evidence that philanthropy in the relentlessly probing style that justifies its existence has begun to find more sophisticated and effective ways of working through the dilemmas of social reform. One, noted by Adam Yarmolinsky,[2] is the shift in focus from direct relief to social and economic development, a shift encouraged by congressional recognition that private agencies can play an important role in foreign aid programs. Experience has also shown the wisdom of "development from below" that is, a strategy based on labor-[intensive] rather than capital-intensive activity, greater community involvement, and expanded participation of counterpart voluntary organizations.

Much the same kind of learning and inventing has been going on domestically. The War on Poverty, opportunistically maligned by

---

[1] MIT professor Jay Wright Forrester began the field of system dynamics in 1956 as an outgrowth of his pioneering computer work in the 1940s and early 1950s. Working on aircraft stability, Forrester decided that a digital computer was more suited to address the complexities of his problem. He developed a prototype, then a working computer; he helped to invent magnetic core memory and other aspects of computer architecture and storage technology. He has gone on to apply system dynamics theory to such widely diverse systems as economics, social structures, and industry. His papers include "Counterintuitive Behavior of Social Systems," "Christianity in a Steady-State World," "Beyond Case Studies—Computer Models in Management Education," and "Understanding Urban Behavior."

[2] Ylvisaker is referring here to Yarmolinsky's "Philanthropic Activity in International Affairs," a 1976 study for the President's Commission on Private Philanthropy and Public Needs. Yarmolinsky, a professor of public policy at the University of Maryland, served on the Filer Commission (see "The Filer Commission in Perspective," page 280), and participated in the development and implementation of President Johnson's War on Poverty programs. His books include *Private Energies and Public Purposes: Revitalizing the Non-Profit Sector.*

self-serving critics, was a badly needed and surprisingly productive proving ground for new insights and approaches. Development from below was the hallmark of that venture: though splotched with episodes of anarchy, community action succeeded in breaking through the hardened crust of conventional leadership—minority as well as majority—and gave scores of thousands of the hitherto uninvolved and uninvited the preparatory scrimmaging they needed before plunging into the game of regular politics. Philanthropy pioneered that exploratory probe into social reform; it is now sifting through a decade of learning and painstakingly gleaning and polishing the social wisdom that emerged. If I were to designate the most valuable of these insights, aside from the concept of community involvement and development from below, I would honor most the notion of consumerism and the invention of public advocacy. Without sustained pressure from those in need, economic growth and social progress will never flow beyond the elites and the bureaucracies through which they are filtered.

The common element in those and other accumulating hints of how to contend with paradox is the requirement that philanthropy move out of fixed and safe positions into more independent, flexible, and far more exposed stances between the contradictory forces that are generating tension and, without the resolving action of some agent such as philanthropy, will otherwise tear nations and neighborhoods apart. Philanthropy, from one point of view, paid dearly for its adventurousness during the past two decades—not only in the penalties dealt out through the Tax Reform Act of 1969, but even more so in the self-administered penance and confinement that followed. From a longer and more optimistic point of view, however, its confronting of harsher reality paid off. Stripped of some of its easier illusions and alliances—and its improprieties—philanthropy is that much more prepared to deal with the raw dilemmas now standing between our hopes for social justice and their fulfillment.

Those dilemmas are legion, and they dissolve interminably into each other for as far ahead as any futurist can see. But begin with two of the nagging questions and choices that lie immediately ahead.

Can philanthropy continue its preoccupation with
social justice at home when far greater inequities are
rampant and multiplying globally?

Some facile as well as some substantial answers come quickly to
mind: "You have to begin someplace"; "We have an obligation to
give at home"; "We know the problems in our own backyard";
"Everything is relative: an injustice close by is just as iniquitous,
painful, and deserving of attention as an injustice somewhere else";
"We're powerless to do anything in someone else's sovereign
territory"; "We're too small to make a difference beyond our own
neighborhood"; "Try telling Congress, your own constituency, and
the petitioner in front of you that you can't give at home because
you're giving abroad."

If these aren't enough, there's yet another reason for thinking
twice: the amount of time and money philanthropy [now] devotes to
the cause of social justice at home is pitifully small compared even
to a more global assessment of what is needed within developed
nations such as the United States. If giving abroad becomes a mere
substitute for giving that pittance at home, more has been lost than
gained.

More, because the problems of social justice and the process of
achieving it are linked. Take a very concrete example: the problems
attendant on human migration. As development occurs, migration is
a seemingly inevitable concomitant. In our times it has become
massive; hundreds of millions of people are on the move. Whether
forced or free, they are drawn as by the force of magnetism or
osmosis toward places of economic and social attraction.

"Do it unto the least of these, and ye have done it unto Me." That
mixture of challenge and comfort suggests one legitimate way of
resolving the dilemma of whether to deal with the problems of
injustice at home or abroad: do both in your own backyard. If
developed nations were to attend more sympathetically than they
have to the process of migration and the plight of migrants, they
could considerably ease the social frictions that are generated by
increasing global movements, and in much better conscience claim
good citizenship. That mission alone could occupy the major part of
any foundation's agenda in any of the more developed countries. Its

relevance to the current concerns of minorities and the urban and rural poor in the United States is obvious.

It would be too easy to stop there. Accepting only the responsibility for aiding migrants who manage entry into more developed countries merely deals marginally with the global problem of social injustice. Besides, a natural alliance is soon struck between established rich and newcoming poor, which discourages the arrival of any more. The zoning game that bars the urban poor from making it to the suburbs is just another expression of the exclusionary motives that build national immigration barriers. Philanthropy should think long and hard before becoming even a well-intentioned partner in that cabal. Indeed, philanthropy ought to be taking the lead in the opposite direction—of promoting, or at least sympathetically and constructively analyzing, the concept of a universal human right ultimately to move at will. It is hardly consistent to posit that right for human beings who, by accident of birth, have been placed within reach of opportunity but not for others who chanced to be born a boundary's distance beyond.

There is a very direct way in which philanthropy could help close the widening gap between the world's richer and poorer populations: by explicitly and aggressively prodding the more affluent communities [philanthropy represents] into meeting the quite modest quotas of foreign aid called for in the United Nation's strategy for the Second Development Decade.

There are several ways in which philanthropy might take the lead: by a stepped-up program of public and self-education; by a voluntary program of tithing and pooling; and by challenging corporations, which in the United States now devote less than a fifth of what tax laws permit in the way of charitable deductions, likewise to contribute and pool significantly larger sums for independently administered foreign aid or other forms of socially oriented investment. In the United States alone, stepping up corporate giving from the present 1 percent to the allowed 5 percent of pretax profits would yield approximately $4 billion of additional resources. Coming now, that contribution would be a healthy corrective to the foreign bribery that recent disclosures suggest has become a widespread form of international corporate behavior.

If social justice is to be achieved, will more fundamental changes be required than philanthropy is ready or able to be party to?

Philanthropy in America has twice managed to accommodate itself to the massing of social problems: first when it shifted from personal charity to institutionalized giving, and second when it moved beyond the provision of direct services to the notion of strategic expenditures that would induce larger and more continuous spending by others. At both junctures philanthropy was responding to the obvious: if it was going to have any impact on the accumulating weight of social problems, it had to look for the longest levers it could find. That very process of searching was a contribution; philanthropy was freer than most to explore the next dimension.

It now seems clear that philanthropy needs—and is needed—to go searching again. The levers it has been using have proved too stubby. Constricting resources discourage the older strategy of pyramiding expenditures. To make the challenge to philanthropy even greater, the question is now being raised in this country and, even more so, in the Third World, as to whether philanthropy is too tied to established interests to be counted on for a willing spirit and an honest search.

The criteria for such a search—the tests of adequate leverage—are imposed by the nature of the poverty and urban problems, and by the fact that this time the judging will be done by the victims of injustice as well as by the doers of good. Society around the world has grown restive, sophisticated, ornery. The climate for leadership has grown hostile and, for self-appointed missionary work, almost impossible.

Can philanthropy, born of wealth and a set of systems under attack, meet the test and make still another creative adjustment to cultural change? Try answering that question in the context of what is needed to keep America's urban problems and the predicament of world poverty from becoming even more crushing burdens than they are.

After decades of analyzing and suffering the problems of urban demise, we now *know*, victims and experts alike, that we are not dealing with something that went wrong with the system, but with the sorrier side of what went right. Most Americans have got what they wanted: cars, mobility, lawns, elbow room, new lifestyles, fewer constraints. They also got the freedom to escape. But their freedoms became other people's confinements, the more so as the voting power of suburbanizing majorities increased, and as the agendas for legislative bodies—private as well as public—served more and more the interests of the released, less and less the interests of the confined. That left the courts (because of their commitment to the constitution), philanthropy (to the extent it could mesh idealism with sobering considerations of the side its bread was buttered on), and the ghetto members (constantly subject to attrition of their own leadership through success or sell-out) to deal with the intensifying concerns of the urban poor.

We now *know*—and New York city's threatened bankruptcy seems to have been more instructive than riots, simply because the message got closer to most people's homes and pocketbooks—that the only way of easing "the urban problem" is by some fundamental changes in the ground rules by which everyone in the system prospers or suffers: changes in tax laws, zoning practices, income distribution, welfare financing, and the structure and functioning of government, corporations, and philanthropy itself. Fair to say, we have only a freshman's view of the systematic changes that are in order, even less informed a sense of how they can and should be synchronized. But one thing is certain, they all jab at Americans where it hurts: the freedom to go to it alone, to garner the benefits and slough off the costs.

Philanthropy is obviously at risk when it starts dealing with the ground rules of society, rather than with individual cases of injustice. Understandably, most of American philanthropy has not made the adjustment, but there is a growing segment that has. The spate of literature and activity addressed to the question of systemic change—revising state tax systems, for example, to provide more equal opportunity in education—gives reason to believe that philanthropy is capable of another enterprising stage in its own evolution.

Philanthropy's Dilemma

There is no entry point into this third stage of evolution—dealing with the ground rules of the established order—that offers a painless way for philanthropy to ease the pain of others.

One reason has already been made evident: systems in motion generate inertia, acceptance, and the simple fear of trying the unknown alternative. Resistance to redirection accumulates and becomes immense.

Second, it is extraordinarily difficult for philanthropy to act, or, certainly, to be seen as acting, in the neutral role it prefers. I doubt whether that professed neutrality was ever devoid of self-serving or of self-deceiving pretension, and I'm frankly glad that a more exacting social environment is forcing greater realism and self-realization within philanthropy. For it to move independently toward the points of maximum leverage on social change, however, will produce more of a tug with its own moorings than philanthropy has ever experienced.

Third, the emerging effort to deal with the ground rules of society inevitably brings philanthropy deeper into the territory of public policy and the turf that has traditionally been the domain of government and politics. None of the existing fictions, conventions, and protocols are really adequate to cover this entry, which explains the anxiety over the quickening dialogue between Congress and American philanthropy. But the imperative of growing philanthropic involvement in public policy also explains why both parties to that dialogue are sticking at it so tenaciously; why Congress, though lashing out against philanthropy, never destroys it; and why, in fact, even in its most hostile mood, Congress employs language and tactics ambiguous enough to let the evolutionary process move pragmatically ahead—pragmatically, but never comfortably.

Fourth, the closer philanthropy gets to the outer realities and inner workings of political systems, the more tempting it becomes to take on their logic and character and to lose the essential spirit of philanthropy. That spirit is to share blessing and hardship, and to bring together the universal and the particular. Politics, both domestic and international, measures things more by power and feasibility in the shorter run. By getting closer to that calculus, philanthropy takes on a battle for its own soul that will be constant and wearying.

Philanthropy and Paradox: A Concluding Note

Weariness is probably the most debilitating consequence of paradox—and of the humanitarian assignment given philanthropy to make the dividing logics of prospering and suffering more consonant. A set of laws operates perversely against the reconciling efforts of social reform. The first law states that when forces get going in one direction, toward concentrated wealth or accelerating poverty, they keep moving that way with reinforcing effects. The second says that the more complex a system becomes, the more energy is required to accomplish any given amount of social change, the ratio mounting in proportion to the increasing number of consents to be negotiated and consequences to be thought through. The third holds that the more generalized the goal, and the more complex the means to achieve it, the greater the tendency for society to fractionate into competitive, but humanly comprehensible, communities of real or imagined self-interest.

Every one of these laws wears away at the energies of social reformers; their combined effect is enough to make even philanthropy wonder whether universal justice and macroengineering aren't beyond its capacities and any reasonable set of expectations—whether, after all, the best thing to do is to "clean up the corner where we are." One glimpses those signs of retreat in the majoritarian consensus that colored the final votes of the Filer Commission in such a conservative gray. The message was that the dominant elements in American philanthropy were not ready to spend their energies or their equities much beyond the boundaries of their familiar interests. Nor were they ready to make substantial changes in the ground rules—or sacrifice the advantage—that generated, nurtured, and insulated their existence.

What the Council on Foundations has recently done, in adopting a formal resolution calling for renewed commitment of its members to the cause of social justice, is more in accord with the nobler purpose of philanthropy. I saw in that resolution a greater willingness than was exhibited by the Filer majority to preface any reconsideration of society's ground rules with some public-minded rethinking about its own. But even the council's resolution was flawed (I would guess by the same inertial lapse in sensitivity that belies all our best efforts to change). Its wording respected only the human rights of "all *our* people"—italics added. What that phrase needs is a modifying adjective generous enough to embrace the whole world.

. . . And Reflection

The imbalance in resources between developed and developing nations is conspicuous in philanthropy. Modern foundations are the product of Western industrialization; even when they operate altruistically, they remain essentially paternalistic in their relationship to the world's and, for that matter, their own domestic poor. Philanthropy has accomplished a lot and can accomplish a good deal more, within the parochialism of its *status quo*, by illuminating and alleviating the condition of the world's "have-nots." The time has come, however, to raise the question of whether philanthropy itself should pluralize and distribute its resources more fairly on a global basis. The need for and the logic of locally controlled philanthropies within the developing world seem clear. I would propose that the major foundations of the developed nations undertake a systematic and common effort over the next decade to stimulate the growth of indigenous philanthropy, regional and national, within the developing world. The obstacles are formidable, but if philanthropy has generic worth as a complementary social process it deserves universalizing.

Domestically as well. The fatal flaw in Western philanthropy's performance at home is its one-sided character, which has the affluent unilaterally answering the two crucial questions posed earlier in this paper. Far better that our own less advantaged share the responsibility of working through those questions than have them wait passively to hear and then resent the answers given them by an established few.

The Relationship Between Private Philanthropy and Government

(Presented to the Hillcrest Conference on "The Art of Giving," Rockefeller Archives Center, October 14, 1977)

"There is a universal appeal in the nonmonetary values philanthropy represents—the notion of a third force dedicated to values [that] go beyond economic gain and political power."

As some of you know, I keep violating a rule I imposed on myself several years ago never to talk on philanthropy again. I do come here to welcome any sign of philanthropic life that I can spot these days, to try to fan it, because my interest is in a very lively philanthropic sector. This is particularly needful after the trauma of 1969 and after the inflationary disasters we have all gone through.

The topic that was given to me was "The Relationship between Philanthropy and Government." But as I read back through some of the study questions, it became clear that my section also had questions relating to the relationships with business and government. So I have decided to talk about the three arts: giving, prospering, and governing. As most of you know, I have been described by conservatives as mildly outrageous and by radicals as outrageously mild, and tend to wander between those two extremes. My interest this morning is in asking radical questions—radical in the sense that they go to the roots of these three arts, these three social processes, and particularly the philanthropic. Somehow these questions peel away at the excuses and crutches we have, and begin to press very hard at what our essential functions are and what our essential social contributions really can be.

Of the archivists, there are several things I would ask. This is an interesting perspective to view philanthropy from—I do not regard it as "from the tombs" at all, but quite the contrary, if you would join me as futurists who view the future in retrospect. What will you need to provide social historians in the years 2000, or 2025, or 2050? What will you have to contribute to these social historians, who will be asking, "What complementary and countervailing roles did the three sectors play in social development?" Frankly, I would like to see our archivists be far more aggressive than they have been in demanding contemporary records of philanthropy. We have been hit hard by the populist views, the increasing democratization of our society. Our society has forced us to provide records and to do business in the open. I do not remember having heard, except rather mildly, from archivists saying, "We have a legitimate claim on your information." I do know that there has been, for instance, an oral history project in the Ford Foundation. I have watched scholars as they increasingly begin to prowl for philanthropic information, having got the scent of something that is socially significant. But I haven't seen real aggressiveness; and just last week I watched a major foundation refuse a scholar permission to do a case study of its decision-making process.

For the last twenty-five years, we have required this sort of openness on the part of business and government, and I think we should be willing to expose philanthropy, not for exposure's sake, but for learning's sake. The young people I deal with have an extraordinary interest in philanthropy, for a variety of motives. The most popular course taught at the [Harvard] School of Education (barring statistics, which is required) is one on philanthropy, taught by one of our development officers, who responded to the demand and was overwhelmed by the number of people who turned to it.

Reviewing the principal relationships of business, government, and philanthropy, I think it is easy to say historically that the main relationship has been between government and business. This is in contrast to the medieval period, when dualism of church and state characterized society. No one has missed the point that our society is dominated by this dualism and tension between business and government. In a broader perspective, without oversimplifying, the role of philanthropy (the so-called "third sector" of nonprofit institutions) has been more of a pawn than a principal in the triad of social structures. It has been the creature of [business], sometimes the feared agent of some conspiratorial outside force, and mostly ignored by government until recently.

The faults of philanthropy clearly account for some of this subordinate position. I would draw your attention to John Nason's study of foundation trustees.[1] He has a deep spirit of dedication to the private sector and was deeply troubled by what he discovered when he sampled the trustees of American foundations and found they were years behind college trustees (who themselves had a generation of catching up to do) at the point that government made it clear that legal liability as well as honor went along with their appointment.

The virtues of philanthropy also account for this subordination. It is very difficult for this indeterminant, in-between, rather novel sector in American society, as represented by the foundations, to establish its presence. This is true especially [because] pluralism rather than monolithic consistency is one of its main virtues and sources of energy: it is not one thing, but many. And its credo is modesty, or at least a low profile. But I note as we look ahead for prospects of a vital and strong philanthropic third force that there is now the self-conscious emergence of the third sector. The Filer Commission marks and symbolizes that emergence.

One can enumerate the challenges that face philanthropy in trying to establish itself as a major sector. One of these is scarcity in our times, and the dilemma of funding in a period of dwindling affluence. There is a noticeable relationship between the emergence of abundance in this society—especially corporate abundance—and the blossoming of philanthropy. During the Korean War, for example, when the imposition of an excess profits tax gave added incentive, there was a proliferation, especially of corporate foundations. But we are now in a time when the third sector faces scarcity rather than abundance—precisely at the time when philanthropy wants to maintain a much more dominant role, a much more

---

[1] Ylvisaker is referring to Nason's *Trustees and the Future of Foundations*, which was published the same year this talk was given. Nason, who was president of Swarthmore College during Ylvisaker's professorship there, served on the boards of several educational and philanthropic institutions. He revised his look at foundation trusteeship in 1989 with *Foundation Trusteeship: Service in the Public Interest*.

aggressive posture. Inflation, stagnation, and reduced yield from investments are trimming the third sector's resources and its potency.

Another challenge comes from the public sector. Tax reform is a conspicuous example—not only the restraints imposed in 1969, but the continuing efforts to expand the coverage of the standard deduction, the net effect being a steady lessening of the incentive to give. [Another example is] tax reform in the sense that loopholes will be closed and those sources of business and personal funding shut off.

Moreover, there is the question of governmental takeover. Government from the 1930s on has not only outspent private philanthropy and established financial dominance, but it has also appropriated the philanthropic function. There are governmental philanthropies like the National Endowments of the Arts and Humanities, the National Science Foundation, the National Institute of Health, and so on. More than that, the governmental process has become more philanthropic in character: faced with a complex society and the inability to finance and solve everything, categorical and block grants have successively become the standbys of public policy. Government has appropriated a large part of the field of private philanthropy and, more seriously, has begun to emulate and in that sense take over the function of philanthropy. In this process, philanthropy has lost leverage. And with depressed public spending, foundations have lost a leveraging influence they could earlier count on—the prospect that a demonstration grant would touch off governmental financing at larger scale.

Another challenge to the private sector and foundations is the process of regulation. We have clearly moved from business dominance over philanthropy to what is emerging as governmental dominance over philanthropy. Foundations are caught in the middle of this transition. They still have much of the value structure of the business community, but the role and ethic of the public and public control are expanding with great rapidity. This is partly a function of the complexity of our society: bureaucratization, large-scale corporate structure, ambitions and pretensions, [and] conspicuous budgets clearly induce the regulatory process.

But the drift toward governmental regulation is more than a

function of complexity. It also flows from the American penchant for fairness, equity, and equality, in our day growing ever stronger. We are witnessing a new age of proceduralization. We in the universities are facing this now. I must say that as one who has helped stimulate the movement in earlier incarnations and then suddenly become a dean, some of my populism has been chastened. On the other hand, I have watched the coming in of fresh air, dispelling the dense fog of whimsy and caprice that often dominates the academic process, because of these new if sometimes clumsy controls. The philanthropic sector is not far behind the universities in becoming subject to these controls. I went back to read a recent Council on Foundations publication, and noticed that about eight pages, or two-thirds of it, was dedicated to the fine points of regulations, IRS decisions, court decisions, etc. Very little of that was required reading when I stopped being a philanthropoid a decade ago.

Another challenge is the weak identity and self-image of foundations and of the third sector generally. There is little sense of presence—not as much as some of our prose would indicate. When public criticism mounts and attacks begin, we don't bark very loud, and I guess it may be because nobody fears our bite. But I think it may be even more because of public uncertainty over who we are. I welcome some of the controversy over philanthropy, even at the cost that it has meant, if only because as the public becomes a bit more informed we are forced to inform the public all the more.

Another factor is mixed values. Again, diversity comes to plague us; but more than that, the congeries of values seen in philanthropy give one a sense of mush. Sometimes one hears hard business principles, sometimes populist democratic ideals, sometimes rather religious expressions, sometimes vague aspirations of social reform. I don't want to become so simplistic as to say we should have a code of ethics or credo that describes our value structure; but something more coherent is called for if philanthropy is to establish more of a presence.

Another problem is philanthropy's preoccupation with and susceptibility to financial and political controls. This became painfully evident to me out of a recent teaching experience. For a course in ethics that I'm teaching, I went back to reading the Church Committee report on security, its final report having to do with foundations, as a matter of fact, the whole private sector and their vulnerability to intrusion by the CIA.[2] Well over 100 foundations have been involved; 50 percent of all grants over $10,000 in the international field not given by the "Big Three" (Rockefeller, Ford, and Carnegie) were involved with CIA expenditures and activities. This amounted to 10 percent of all grants over $10,000 across the board. In other words, as the Church Committee reported, the intrusion of the CIA into the field of philanthropy can be described "as nothing less than massive." I was not aware of that during the years that I practiced as a foundation bureaucrat, except as a sixth sense might have told me. The fact that the third sector could be so vulnerable must shake our feelings about the strength and viability and the future of philanthropy.

I am equally troubled in a far more subtle sense with the dichotomy between a personal and a public trust. What John Nason found was that foundation trustees tend to think of the money as "our money and nobody else's business," despite the efforts of the Council on Foundations to [correct] this feeling and despite the growing incidence of governmental regulation. We have not touched the bulk of foundations on this, let alone philanthropy at large. This is illustrated by the Council on Foundation's membership, which is less than 10 percent of all foundations in this country. We have a long way to go in educating philanthropy to the concept of a public trust.

Perhaps even more subtle is the preoccupation with money and the money function of philanthropy. Again, the question: "Who would come to you, and what would you do if you didn't have any money to give?" Reading the literature about foundations—inter-office memos, docket items, and so forth—one finds that despite the growing attention to program and purpose, philanthropy is still dominated by the process of exchanging money. The grant is the conspicuous action, and therefore the hallmark of a foundation. I

---

[2] In 1975, Senator Frank Church (D-Idaho, 1924–1989) was appointed chairman of the Select Committee to Study Governmental Operations with Respect to Intelligence Activities. The Church Committee investigated alleged abuses of power by the CIA and the FBI. In 1979, he was named chairman of the Senate Foreign Relations Committee.

wonder what you would do if suddenly you did not have to process grants, if your exclusive concern were thinking through society's needs and what (besides spending) could be done about them.

A less subtle preoccupation is with tax exemption. I wonder if philanthropy would have half those regulations if it were not associated with tax advantage. The radical question that I would have to ask in this context is, has philanthropy gained more or lost more by being associated with tax advantage, which has brought us into being but may well compromise our future? It is an excuse [for] regulation, it is an excuse for harassment, and more than that (as I have argued elsewhere) it has kept the third sector from having the full range of free speech. We have allowed Congress to condition the right of free speech because of tax advantage, so that (for instance) we can only speak our mind before legislatures and the public within certain specified constraints. In the world that I see coming, I see more and more the essential role of philanthropy as a countervailing and complementary force, not so much having to do with its money function as with its role in helping set the agenda for public consideration and debate.

A final set of problems in establishing more of a philanthropic presence are the diverging logics and imperatives that will govern each of the three sectors over the next generation—especially if one perceives how confining these logics become within the provincial concepts of nation-states and established social orders and what each must do, or feels it must do, in order to survive intact. Call to mind the case of the immigration problem along our own southern border, illustrative of the growing fluidity of massing populations and poverty worldwide. The logics of business are very insistent; it's a tough market out there, and companies are led to chase competitive returns on investment across national lines, and some-times across moral lines as well. Nations whose lines are crossed follow their own defensive and aggressive logics. In that environ-ment, I would argue that philanthropy—the third sector—needs all the more to assert a logic of its own: a more universalistic ethic [that] transcends the limitations of business and government and most likely will be increasingly in tension with both.

I am happy to see signs that philanthropy is helping give expression to a "third logic." With private support, the Club of

Rome[3] and economists Tinbergen and Leontief[4] are beginning to talk about the basic changes in the world order [that] will have to occur if we are going to keep any modicum of peace. We are in many ways at a time not dissimilar to that of the aristocracy before the French Revolution; the question is whether we can move swiftly enough in shaping a viable new order to avoid global violence. Philanthropy can be a powerful bridging influence, but not without distinguishing itself and its imperatives more clearly from those which—at least in the short run—control business and government. Frequently, the third sector will have to take some very tough positions [that] diverge from the value structures of its founders. This has to do with social justice and distribution. The challenge to the existing order is basically one involving a redistribution of resources; the emphasis is increasingly on social justice. Philanthropy [has] long [been] wedded to the existing pattern of resource distribution; it will not find it easy to challenge or change that pattern, or to work sympathetically with new constituencies.

Let me indicate another area where the tensions are going to be extraordinary—that is immigration. Stop to look at the world as a repository of six or seven billion people, as it shall be shortly, 80 percent of them below the line of poverty. Latin America, with

---

[3] The Club of Rome was established in 1968 as an international group of 100 scientists, economists, businessmen, civil servants, heads of state, and former heads of state who seek "to adopt a global perspective, to seek a deeper understanding of interactions within the tangle of contemporary problems, to suggest effective solutions, and to take a longer term perspective in studies than governments do," according to the Club's mission philosophy (published on the World Wide Web at http://www.clubofrome.org/cor_declaration.htm as of January 1997). Its members vow to devote a "significant proportion" of their time and talents to "helping to build societies that are more humane, more sustainable, more equitable, and more peaceful."

[4] Dutch economist Jan Tinbergen (1903–1994) awarded the Joint Nobel Prize in Economic Science in 1969, is credited with developing the first econometric models. Published *Income Distribution: Analysis and Policies* (1975). Russian-born Wassily Leontief (1906—?), awarded the Nobel Prize in Economics in 1973, advanced the theory of international trade and its empirical implementation. Publications include *Studies in the Structure of the American Economy* (1953) and, just prior to this speech, *The Future of the World Economy* (1977). Both economists were active in the study of input-output analysis.

growth rates over 3 percent, is one of those bulging reservoirs. Its accelerating overflow across the Rio Grande now accounts for most of the approximately 800,000 illegal immigrants sifting into the United States annually. If you have walked the streets of American cities, particularly in the coastal regions, you will find new populations accumulating. If you then think in a global way, you will see our cities as underutilized infrastructure for a world that has too many people and too few cities for them to live in. Mexico certainly doesn't have enough to absorb its urbanizing people. That's why the Mexican president reacted so apprehensively when President Carter indicated that he was going to close off immigration from Mexico to the United States; he knew the only other place his "surplus population" would move to was an already overwhelmed Mexico City. In contrast, our central cities are losing populations; even with deterioration and unemployment, they remain relatively attractive magnets for increasing millions of potential migrants from the impoverished Third World. I have seen it happening. I have gone back into the New Jersey cities that I knew so well ten years ago, and found population that I have never experienced before, languages that I did not know, and certainly cultures that I was unacquainted with.

There is [another] third world growing and on the move, a constituency philanthropy increasingly has to orient to, frequently alienated from the social and political sectors philanthropy has been aligned with. You can glimpse a local colony of that third world in the youth of our cities—40 percent of them unemployed and alienated.

We are living now with problems our economy and established order haven't solved. They have not grown enough opportunities for the children we have borne. That's the tragedy my generation has to account for. Youth is developing a kind of counterculture, and we are beginning to see illustrations of it around the world. I do not like to point with alarm, but I would say that spontaneous acts of violence—and some not so spontaneous—are going to be repeated more and more in our society. Recently one foundation commissioned a report, not yet released, on behavior patterns during the recent New York blackout. The pattern that study reveals is much different from the civil uprisings of the 1960s: the "rip-off" has replaced the cry for social justice. The preconditions for anarchy seem to be forming: a counterculture eating its way like an acid through the pretensions, the ideals, of the existing system.

A more attractive, but still challenging, quality of this developing "third world" is the free and growing spirit within us. Don't be misled by the currently conservative demeanor of today's college generation. If you read the book by David Ewing, *Freedom Inside the Organization*,[5] which describes the frustration in the corporate organization of people who want to live whole lives and exercise their rights, you sense again the power of that spirit within. Certainly that restiveness for self-expression is evident in the emerging Hispanic population within the United States. I encounter it among those enrolling, happily in increasing numbers, in graduate education at Harvard. They are spirits on the move. But they are struggling with ambivalence—a strong wish to succeed within the system and a reluctance to accept it, knowing what meager room and reward it has given their own community. They are wrestling with what political posture they ought to be taking; they have analyzed the Black "revolution" of the 1960s—which was partly productive and partly counterproductive. But they do not see themselves in quite that same mold. How does a young person with great sophistication about the realities, and great hopes for his or her future, perceive and deal with current social structures and participate with integrity? For me, this is a fascinating enterprise, and I welcome even the harder moments that go with it (being called a tool of the establishment is not one of my chosen experiences).

Another sense of growing value tensions, and of the need for an assertive third force, has come with my participation on the board of a multinational enterprise, the Van Leer Packaging Industries, whose net earnings flow wholly and directly into charitable activities. Its structure is unique, but the questions we're struggling with are generic—again, the respective roles of the three sectors. As you know, the rights of property (property in the sense of establishing dominion or control) are now diminishing. Rising social consciousness is nibbling away at those rights, particularly on the European

---

[5] New York: McGraw-Hill, 1977.

scene, where workers now have veto rights over corporate board appointments and where the socialist parties are beginning to develop their own philanthropies for job creation funded through a kind of excess profits—which in effect sluice corporate earnings directly into state-operated foundations. What this does, obviously, is to short-circuit private philanthropy, bypass the role of the third sector. In the short run, these developments threaten existing patterns of management and dominion in business, government, and philanthropy; certainly they challenge the novel way in which the Van Leer group has turned conventional capitalism on its head and run a business for the benefit of disadvantaged children rather than simply to turn a profit. Yet thinking beyond Van Leer, I wonder whether private philanthropy has thought itself creatively beyond the industrial era in which it was born, into a post-industrial era when the role and concepts of business and government—reading from present trends—will almost certainly be transformed.

I see this as a cutting edge for philanthropy, a question far more challenging than whether or not you have X amount of money or can maneuver around Y or Z regulations. The big foundations have begun addressing it; they should take the lead, because they—and the endowed foundations they represent—are the most secure and influential segment of the third sector. They have the capacity to help set a public agenda that responds to emerging circumstance and to the independent spirit within all of us that is searching for a restructured definition of issues, a new dimension in social thought.

Let me conclude with two specific suggestions. The first is to encourage the instinct for self-renewal within American philanthropy, an instinct I see expressed—imperfectly, no doubt—in the coalescence of gadflies who first formed the Donee Group[6] and then established the National Committee for Responsive Philanthropy. That group, I know, has the inherent fault of being claimants as well as critics. What I find disturbing is the tendency of established philanthropy to dismiss them rather than to pick up the cause of self-renewal and a more effective third sector which they are trying to represent.

---

[6] An outgrowth of the Filer Commission. See p. 283.

A second suggestion has to do with the internationalization of philanthropy. At this very moment, the Arabs have sent a delegation to Japan to compare notes with representatives of the Toyota Foundation and other philanthropies. The Japanese in recent years have moved quickly into the field; so far, their entry has been closely tied to corporate interests, and I suspect that's the experience the Arabs will be principally concerned with. But the essential logic of the third sector in modern society has not been lost on the Japanese; my quest—at least my hope—is that the notion of an independent third force will germinate and grow in that and other sections of the world. Those of you who have met with the Toyota Foundation will appreciate the speed and acumen with which they and other newcomers to philanthropy have comprehended its fundamental nature and social potential. It will not be easy in their culture to realize that potential. But there is a universal appeal in the nonmonetary values philanthropy represents—the notion of a third force dedicated to values [that] go beyond economic gain and political power.

Communicating just that on a global scale is the ultimate challenge of American philanthropy.

Ethics and Philanthropy

(Adapted from a presentation to the Associated
Grantmakers of Massachusetts, Inc., March 18, 1982)

*"I wonder whether giving in our tradition has
become an impersonal way of relieving ourselves of
responsibility for others rather than personally
accepting it."*

I'm counting, in this presentation, on your open-mindedness—an
open-mindedness that for better or worse seems to go with
philanthropy. At the Ford Foundation some years ago, one of my
colleagues explained what a philanthropoid was. "A philanthopoid,"
he said, "is like a monkey in a cage—present him with anything and
he'll consider it seriously."

Ethics and philanthropy—I'm not sure exactly why the topic
appealed to those who organized this meeting. The topic appealed
to me because ethics is the one course I've chosen to teach at the
Graduate School of Education. My feeling is that if deans are to teach
anything, they ought symbolically to deal with the ethical dimensions of the profession they represent.

Ethics, to a philosopher, is an arena for clear systematic thinking.
Ethics for a practitioner is something far more mercurial. When one
finds oneself in a real-life situation, sometimes it's almost impossible
to say with certainty that there is an ethical dilemma or dimension to
the case and even more difficult to prescribe how one should act in
that circumstance.

I want to deal today at case level with the question of ethics and
philanthropy. Let me start by saying that when you put two words
like ethics and philanthropy together, you're in trouble: each of them
resists definition, and when combined they can be totally elusive.

Take ethics first. Ethics is a study of what is "right." I put "right"

318

in quotation marks because when we talk about ethics, we talk about a sense in us that goes far beyond what is simply legal. Yes, we do have legislated ethics, codes of ethics. We also have laws that tell us how we can behave and not behave. But in our ambition to be ethical, we're expressing a sense that transcends what is lawful or even what may be socially acceptable. We are indeed stretching toward that seemingly innate, surely elusive ideal of acting nobly and of being judged as doing so, not least by ourselves. That constant urge keeps testing conventional measures, and over time— in any caring society—tends in an evolutionary way to raise the standards of behavior that have been codified in law or custom.

Next, philanthropy—also teasingly imprecise. Literally, as derived from the Greek, it means a love of humankind. It assumes that our actions as philanthropists stem from love and caring and not from some baser motives. Those baser motives (which are usually submerged in our public rhetoric) include self-interest, personal aggrandizement, power, a calculus of advantage like tax benefits, and in a subtle way professions of the public interest that carry a whiff of the egocentric. The latter is one of the vulnerabilities of professionalized philanthropy, where "the public interest" more and more has become a touchstone for determining whether one's actions and choices are proper, right and noble.

If one starts from the literal meaning of philanthropy, the interesting question arises as to whether we're knee-deep in some contradictions in terms. For example, is corporate philanthropy one such contradiction? Simply, the argument would go [that] corporate philanthropy historically has had to justify itself by demonstrating some benefit to the giver. If indeed philanthropy is a matter of altruism—a love and caring for other people—can the word philanthropy logically be applied to corporate giving?

Another possible contradiction is implicit in the concept of professional philanthropy, which over the last century has emerged as a recognizable career. Philanthropy originally was a one-to-one act of charitable giving. It is now practiced almost impersonally—in some cases by large bureaucracies—and by a code of behavior that frowns on becoming emotionally involved with its clientele. Dispassionate analysis is the hallmark of the trade, which is plied not by, but on behalf of, a now-distant donor. Can you be philanthropic and be dispassionate? Or does the love of human beings, which is a passion in itself, require a dimension of human feeling outside the reach of professional standards and bureaucratized donors?

Could it also be a contradiction in terms to talk about tax-induced giving? Is it giving if it's tax-induced? With modern philanthropy, both personal and corporate, now inextricably entwined in the tax system, we've taken to calculating with scientific precision how to induce giving. The Filer Commission was based on some very sophisticated analyses by economist Martin Feldstein of the philanthropic consequences and efficiency of present and proposed tax incentives. The question is, is that really philanthropy? Or are we measuring another motive than compassion?

It's interesting that philanthropists have never produced a code of ethics. It's one of the major professions without one; curiously, you're joined in that respect by philosophers. Could it be that both professions deem themselves so self-justifying that they don't need codes of ethics? Or is it simply that philanthropists are so diverse that there is no possibility of framing and enforcing common standards of behavior? That diversity certainly accounts for part of the Council on Foundations' historic reluctance to legislate and enforce a code of ethics for its "trade association." Instead, it has relied on persuasion and the force of heralded example; thus its featuring of pace-setting and best practices.

This gentler process of pace-setting from within the profession has been outstripped by two external pressures on philanthropy to raise its behavioral standards. One is a slow but steady accumulation of public feelings about how philanthropy ought to be practiced in an evolving democracy. The other is legislation [that] periodically crystallized those feelings, most commonly the rhythmic outbreaks of congressional criticism, from Walsh to Patman,[1] leading to legislated codes such as the Tax Reform Act of 1969. No accident that such a law was passed, or that its terms and tone were so punitive.

---

[1] Frank Walsh was chief counsel for the first congressional commission to investigate large U.S. foundations, including the Carnegie and Rockefeller foundations. After holding hearings in 1915, the Walsh Commission made a number of recommendations intended to protect the public interest which were never

A century's scan of philanthropy shows some significant differ-ences—and, I would argue, improvements—in the way it goes about its business. A code of ethics, if not yet explicit, is clearly evolving: a public, sometimes legislated, sometimes self-imposed, set of expectations about how philanthropists should behave. Recent historical essays etch the sharp contrast between the imperious style of the early benefactors (Carnegie, Rockefeller, et al.) and the studied social sensitivity of their modern counterparts. The magnates of those early days seldom bothered to delineate where business left off and philanthropy began—mostly, the two were carried on in the same offices. Fear of the law, and a sense of what's proper, nowadays would blow the whistle on such conduct.

Clearly, [there is] an evolving code of behavior. It may never become fixed or explicit. An argument can be made that an articulated code would stifle the freedom and discretion that are the essence of philanthropy, that an unwritten constitution capturing the gist rather than the exegesis of noble conduct is what we should be striving for. Whatever the form, I am convinced an evolutionary process is at work. Some indication of the agenda of issues being worked out can be gained by asking the following questions. You may disagree and want to add questions of your own. My purpose here is simply to crystallize and constructively to provoke.

Is there an ethical requirement to give, and if so, how much, and in what form?

We all know it's deep within most cultural and religious traditions to give—a concept rooted within Judaic, Christian, and Moslem religions. It's also a part of oriental cultures, although my sense is that the practice in China and Japan is more confined (to established

---

implemented. Congressman Wright Patman (D-Texas), chairman of the House Committee on Banking and Currency for forty years, waged an anti-foundation campaign during the early 1960s. He believed that wealthy east coast families exploited legal loopholes available to foundations in order to protect their fortunes, thus unfairly competing against emerging fortunes in the south. Ylvisaker often speculated that Patman's intense suspicion and contempt for the wealthy and their foundations stemmed from a childhood experience—Patman's father's small grocery store was forced out of business when a large east coast supermarket chain moved into his Texas hometown.

relationships) and is accompanied by a considered set of reciprocal obligations and responsibilities (e.g., the obligation one takes on in saving another person's life). I'll return to that sense of responsibility later. For the moment, let me add it's made me wonder whether giving in our tradition has become an impersonal way of relieving ourselves of responsibility for others rather than personally accepting it. A subtle but very important difference.

Granted the cultural heritage of a personal obligation to give, is that also an ethical imperative for corporations? A century ago, the answer was a definite No; as Britain's Lord Justice Bowen vehemently declared, "Charity has no place at the directors' table." Yet a bit later (1883), he relented, ruling that charity may have a place at the directors' table *if* it involved a direct benefit to the corporations, i.e., a demonstrable self-interest.

Bowen's dictum wedged an opening that others would progressively widen. Andrew Carnegie's homilies on the social obligations of wealth hastened the trend in the United States, setting an example for other heads of amassing corporate affluence.

During those formative years, it was hard to distinguish personal and corporate philanthropy. But not after enactment of the income tax, and in particular passage of the Tax Act of 1935 which explicitly allowed corporations to deduct 5 percent (now 10 percent) of pretax profits, in the form of charitable contributions. Corporate giving was now not only legitimate, it was to be encouraged by public policy. The state of Delaware—the legal home of a host of American corporations—acted in consort, acknowledging the propriety of giving in its charters of incorporation.

But Bowen's rule of a demonstrable self-interest still persisted as a hard-line restraint. Then came the softening interpretation by the New Jersey Supreme Court in the 1950s, not only affirming the right of a corporation to give general support to a university (Princeton), but declaring such support to be "a solemn duty." That decision was announced just as the excess profits tax of the Korean War period spawned a myriad of new corporate foundations; it opened for them a far broader range of charitable activity. Civil violence and social activism in the 1960s further accelerated corporate giving, in both scope and volume. Now it's commonly accepted that corporations *should* give—an obligation President Reagan has turned into an operational premise of a conservative administration. The requirement of a demonstrable self-interest remains, but has been relaxed into a Cheshire-cat smile by such socially sensitive corporations as Dayton-Hudson: "We serve our own interest by advancing the community's interest."

Giving in the general interest is finding its place in the corporate ethic. But not without challenge. It is still a leadership practice, growled at and begrudged by many a corporation. [Economist] Milton Friedman[2] remains an articulate skeptic. And an interesting theoretical argument has been raised by one Christopher Dukakis in his continuing opposition to AT&T's social contributions. They may, he contends, have been justified before the era when the federal government finally accepted its social responsibilities. But now that the feds are into social security, etc., corporations should stick to their immediate business.

However one feels about Dukakis's principle, President Reagan and his campaign of retrenchment seem to have dulled its practical edge. They've also placed corporations on the defensive, having to explain why they're *not* giving. So too have the spreading growth of the "5 percent" and "2 percent" clubs[3] and the tenacious pressures being brought by shareholders such as L. Wien of New York City, who is haunting annual meetings with his persistent cry for increased contributions.

The ethic of giving seems accepted. But there is still no consensus of how much or in what form. Tithing is still the rule for certain religious groups; Senator Kennedy's recent amendment to the tax laws has also set 10 percent as a seemingly impossible norm for corporations. Even the "5 percent club" is an exclusive one in the corporate sector; attempts to spread its membership have met with fierce resistance among those who see 1 percent or 2 percent as a proper target. Debate also continues about the form of giving, a

---

[2] Nobel laureate economist Milton Friedman objected to the use of corporate dollars for community purposes on the grounds that corporate executives had neither the knowledge nor the political license to make those decisions.

[3] The 5 percent and 2 percent clubs refer to corporations committed to contributing 5 percent and 2 percent of pretax net income to charitable organizations and causes.

debate symbolized in the contrast between Dayton-Hudson's emphasis on grants and Control Data's stress on contributed services and direct involvement.

Is there an ethical imperative for philanthropy not to take the easier way out?

The question has become far more insistent, and much harder to avoid, in this emerging era of triage, a time of hardening conditions and choices. Thousands of charitable agencies will be facing the prospect of going under; meanwhile, social needs accumulate— witness the growing number of homeless, a million Americans adrift on our streets. In that environment, is it ethical for an organized philanthropy to define its way out of those hard realities by declaring "safer" programs and priorities? Whether it will ever emerge as unethical to avoid those choices, God only knows. But I predict that we will get into a lot more public debate with questions raised about corporations, foundations, and individuals remaining aloof from the turbulence and trauma of contemporary social triage.

Is it ethical to sidestep public accountability?

For example, grantmakers have been required since 1969 to file [IRS Form] 990s with the federal government. But in an age of public accountability, that is a minimal obligation. What about annual reports, public meetings, equal access, open communications? Current expectations are that philanthropy should be public, reachable, communicative, and accountable.

Is it ethical in an age of democratization to continue self-perpetuating boards [that] may or may not reflect the various interests of society?

Within the Filer Commission that question was hotly debated— some insisting that boards should be open and representative, others contending that philanthropy is a private, independent affair and should not be subjected to such constraints. It was in the midst of that debate that the Donee Group emerged[4]—a harbinger, I think, of

---

[4] As the Filer Commission began its work, some were concerned that it was "too elitist" and that the concerns and work of more broad-based or smaller nonprofits

an emerging public expectation (if not yet an ethical imperative) that philanthropy in both its governance and its programming demonstrate that it is in touch with and responsive to a broad range of social issues and constituencies. In the face of that expectation, surely it will be hard to justify the easy money that has (less frequently now than in the past) flowed from philanthropy to friendly clients, financial trustees, and legal advisors.

How ethical is giving that stems from self-aggrandizement?

Philanthropy is the love of other people, not one's self. Yet one of the common behavior patterns in philanthropy is to seek recognition for the donor, whether a person, corporation, or foundation. There are subtle and not-so-subtle expressions of that motive, ranging from statues in the park to press releases designed for headlines.

How appropriate is it to use foundation grants to substitute for personal giving or to extend networks of control?

Robert Anderson of ARCO, one of the notable figures in corporate philanthropy, is now being questioned on why it was that nine out of fifteen grants and a major part of ARCO's giving last year [1981] went to charities on whose boards he served. (This and a number of other examples are drawn from a recent IRRC [Investor Responsibility Research Center] publication on corporate philanthropy.)

Considerations of equity, and in that sense of ethics, might also be raised when favorite causes and institutions are singled out for gifts by foundations whose trustees have a personal stake and might substitute that grant by a contribution of their own. Common examples are grants to schools and colleges [that] trustees and/or their families attended, grants made without an annotated programmatic rationale or competitive access and consideration for other potential recipients in the same category.

---

were likely to be overlooked. The commission then funded a separate, parallel investigation (the name Donee Group reflects the grant-receiving status of many smaller nonprofits) into issues important to such organizations. The Donee Group's report to the Filer Commission recommended—among other things—that Filer advocate open reporting by foundations and add to its membership representatives of smaller, minority-based and female-based nonprofits.

Now I'm walking on some territory that is extraordinarily sensitive. Charitable activity historically has always meant freedom to give with the added presumption that personal predilection, even whim and fancy, are a legitimate part of the game. But when wealth is translated into organized philanthropy with protected status in public policy, a new set of rules and expectations come into existence, and I detect a new ethical code barking at the traditional culture.

How legitimate is it to use philanthropy to buy goodwill?

What is to be said if a national retailing chain times its store openings with the announcement of gifts by its foundation to charities in those communities? A questionable use of philanthropy, or appropriate corporate and foundation behavior? What is to be said about Kellogg, which as a charitable program provides nutritional information to schools and features the eating of cereals? Or about Mobil, Exxon, ARCO, and Gulf, who together in 1980 brought 72 percent of the prime time of public broadcasting during the period when they were under attack for excess earnings?

What about Nestlé and its charitable financing of the Coordinating Center for Nutrition in Washington? That center has served to counter the criticism coming from the World Health Organization and representatives of the World Council on Churches—criticism focused on the advertising and sale of Nestlé products as substitutes for breastfeeding among Third World populations.

What about Freddie Richmond, congressman, industrialist, and philanthropist, who translated corporate profits into foundation grants spread generously through his congressional district?

What about the spreading support by corporate philanthropy for the teaching of "free enterprise" in American colleges and universities? Given the hostility that corporate leaders have sensed on the nation's campuses, that response is understandable. But is it an appropriate act of philanthropy, viewed either from the position of the corporate donor or of the university?

What about *Time* [Magazine]'s philanthropic investment through museums in the King Tut exhibition? Philanthropy or commercialization?

What obligations does one who gives have to one who receives?

This is the most fundamental of all ethical questions to be asked of philanthropy. It's also the most difficult; it admits of no easy answers. One might start by recalling the ancient Chinese admonition that in saving a person's life, one accepts a continuing responsibility.

If indeed giving involves an obligation, what's the nature of that ethical requirement? One more case in the ethics of power: the ethics of helping. The act of helping, implying the capacity to help, is an expression of power. The question is, does the exercise of that power become—explicitly, subtly, unintentionally—a process of manipulation and control, or a gift of autonomy, assurance of dignity, integrity and mutual respect?

Those are abstractions, and at that level none of us has difficulty choosing and expressing our values. But in the everyday of our grant negotiations, motive and effect tend to become hazy, and the route to ethical philanthropy obscured. Again some cases: two current situations in which the power of helping is being put to the test.

First, [there is] the financial predicament of universities now struggling to maintain their integrity while raising the money they need for research. Early in the 1970s, political animus—in one notable case voiced by President Nixon against the antiwar stance of Jerome Wiesner[5]—showed the vulnerability of heavy reliance on government for funding. Counterbalancing support has been sought from industry, now attracted by breakthroughs in biological and electronic technology. Movement of corporate grants toward university research labs has been swift and massive, in forms and under terms that have made many a scientist and academic administrator

---

[5] Jerome Wiesner (1915–1994) was a professor at MIT and served as its president in the 1970s. His early work on radar and electronic components used in atomic bomb testing greatly advanced military technology, but these experiences may have led to his pacifism later in life. As an advocate of nuclear arms control, Wiesner helped establish the U.S. Arms Control and Disarmament Agency and to restrict deployment of antiballistic missile systems. His efforts led to the 1963 Limited Nuclear Test Ban Treaty signed by the United States, the Soviet Union, and Great Britain.

fearful of flooding and erosion of the scholarly ethic. Sophistication in negotiating such support is also growing with encouraging rapidity. But there is still reason to wonder whether philanthropy emanating from and driven by the market will be able to balance its own imperatives with those which assure fair and open inquiry within the university.

The second theater for testing the sensitivity and spirit of philanthropy is the triage now forced upon the nonprofit world by recession and Reaganomics. Those who pay the piper can now easily call the tune; the temptation to dictate and direct will be enormous.

This is not to say that the helping hand should suddenly go limp—leverage and a firm lead are part of what philanthropy has to contribute—but to warn that arrogance is the occupational hazard and original sin of this profession. Irving Kristol was right in saying that not so long ago.[6]

Where I thought he was wrong was in not acknowledging his own—a case of the pot calling the kettle black. When I chided him for that, his winning response came quickly: "But Paul, I never pretended to the virtue of humility."

---

[6] Social critic Irving Kristol, known as the father of the neoconservative movement (he began as a socialist), has written essays and books on politics, economics, society, religion, culture, literature, education, and social values. In 1965, he founded the magazine *The Public Interest*, in part because he found contemporary conservative intellectual thought insufficiently analytical, too hostile to the realities of American politics, and too willing to ignore civic responsibility.

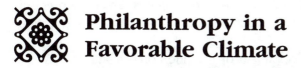 # Philanthropy in a Favorable Climate

(Presented to the Fifteenth Annual Meeting of the
Southeastern Council on Foundations, Sarasota, Florida,
November 8, 1984)

*"My concern is whether philanthropy may be
straying too far from its humanistic and altruistic
origins. The trend toward more professionalized
philanthropy has in most respects been a good
thing, but not when it stiffens into bureaucracy
and loses the spontaneity and compassion of the
one-to-one."*

Your immediate response to the title of this talk has to be "You must
be kidding!" And your disbelief would have some very substantial
bases. Government and the public sector these days are getting out
of the business you're in, namely social amelioration. This week's
election results give you little hope the double burden you're now
carrying will again be shared.

And you're undoubtedly drowning in applications, now that
you're becoming the remaining source. Applications to foundations
are now running 33 percent or more above past averages. You'll be
saying "No" to most of them—an unpleasant circumstance—and
what do I mean, "a favorable climate?"

Add to that the frustration you feel in tackling the world's
contemporary problems and all their baffling complexities with the
minimal resources you have at your command. Who, even a half a
century ago, would have believed that it would be up to the average
citizen and local philanthropies to comprehend and cope with
global futures? And this, Mr. Speaker, is a favorable climate?

To add to the bleakness, there's the deficit and the specter of
continuous scarcity and possibly renewed inflation. We know what

the inflation of the 1970s did to us—reducing our resources precisely at the time social needs accumulated and public contributions diminished.

So where does the optimism of my title come from?

Partly, I must admit, to offset the melancholy that comes with my being a Norwegian. I don't know what it is about the northern climes that makes Scots dour and Scandinavians melancholy. But I know it accounted for what was the worst speech I ever gave: to an audience of octogenarians years ago in Pennsylvania. Without thinking, I chose the topic "Life in the Year 2000." Afterwards, my wife told me it was the worst speech I had ever given—a judgment already evident from the audience's deadly silence. But my daughter, ever kind, comforted me by adding, "But, Dad, you made the year 2000 sound so awfully gloomy, they must have been happy they wouldn't be around."

I'm also mindful of the fact that pessimism is out and optimism is in. America's new pride of nation, the celebration of the Olympic victory, President Reagan's drumbeat of an ever-improving future, all have conspired to make this presentation upbeat.

But there's far better reason for the mood of my title. All things being relative, it's fair to ask, "Favorable compared to what?" And the answer for me rings clear: philanthropy's standing in America has improved considerably.

To gain perspective, let's take a quick look at American philanthropy through two previous fifteen-year periods. First, the period 1954 to 1969. In many respects, that seemed the heyday of foundations. Their number was burgeoning, horizons seemed unlimited, affluent governments seemed ready to pick up and universalize innovative projects [that] philanthropy set in motion. But to some it all seemed quixotic and sometimes ridiculous. Remember the famous *New Yorker* cartoon, showing a young man throwing dollars out the window, with a startled trustee coming upon him and calling out, "That's not the way we do it in the Ford Foundation, young man!"

The sudden affluence of that period was symbolized by the Ford Foundation. Planned in 1950 for an annual grant level of $20 million, it found itself by 1955 with an unspent accumulation of over half a billion dollars, and with a hostile Congress ready to penalize such accumulation. Those were some tense times in that foundation: trustees pressed hard on officers and staff to "unload" in some way that would both do good and do well by Congress and public opinion. The result was a massive and speedy set of grants, roughly half of the accumulation going to increase faculty salaries in private colleges, most of the other half going in surprise packages to delighted hospitals throughout the country—more to the point, in every Congressman's district. I can never forget the executive director of the American Hospital Association emerging from the Ford Foundation trustees' meeting, reaching in incredulous bliss for the telephone to inform his home office of the action—but also to complain that because of the raging snowstorm he was having trouble getting a train home. Over his shoulder came the soothing voice of the bemused trustees: "There, there, we'll buy you one."

The heyday of philanthropy? True, a nation that had long honored philanthropy without really knowing much about it, became newly excited about foundations, and foundations basked and became more ambitious. Seemingly, their entrepreneurial role had gained public acceptance. But had it, and to the degree it had, was that acceptance earned? Or bought?

Whatever, it was certainly paid for when the year 1969 rolled around. A volcanic explosion of distrust and resentment broke through the thin crust of acceptance and spilled its searing lava over the whole of philanthropy. The explosion had been building and partially venting throughout the period 1954 to 1969: first, a conservative Republican anger directed at the eastern Establishment that had nominated Eisenhower over Taft, an Establishment well represented in the board and staff of the Ford Foundation. Then Cox and Reece and McCarthy[1] and, throughout the years, [Congressman] Wright Patman with his smoldering dislike of the eastern moneyed. Patman's ire infected the hearings of the Ways and Means Committee,

---

[1] The Cox Committee of 1952 and the Reece Committee of 1953 investigated possible communist activities among foundations, although their mandates were originally to study interlocking control of foundations and foundation funds by certain families, corporations, and groups. This shift of focus was part of the national obsession with communism that was both fed and exploited by the "witch-hunting" activities of Wisconsin senator Joseph R. McCarthy.

and the result, as we all know and have lived with, was the punitive Tax Reform Act of 1969.

The fifteen years since 1969 brought us to the Congressional hearing of 1984. Their benign mood and the friendly Tax Act of 1984 are the measure of the difference in today's philanthropic circumstance and of the distance we have traveled. Congress and the public can now be said with confidence to have accepted philanthropy and the need to have it move assertively on the American scene.

Question is, have we now really earned that acceptance? In many ways, I would argue that we have.

First of all, we have reformed. Not entirely, and certainly not completely on our own. It took the Congress and [the] Tax Reform Act to point out how far we could stray from the ideals and standards of true philanthropy, and now we ought to change some of our behaviors. We were also prodded by the clientele we serve. The so-called Donee Group,[2] evolving into the National Committee for Responsive Philanthropy, documented a number of our shortcomings, and still remains as sort of a Jiminy Cricket chirping at our conscience.

But not all our reforms have come under pressure from the outside. Meetings like this show the force of improvement from within, and generally, the establishment and performance of the regional associations of grantmakers are symbolic of that instinct to self-reform. The Council on Foundations, haltingly at first and now aggressively and consistently, is ratcheting up the standards of philanthropic performance; its "Principles and Practices" are the measure of how far we have come.

We have also become more self-aware, and in that awareness have more clearly and self-confidently defined our place in society. The Filer Commission was symbolic. Created as an effort to avert "another 1969"—another assault on a philanthropy ill-prepared to explain or defend itself—the Filer Commission massively researched and then illuminated the role of foundations in American society. But it did more than that. It linked the donors with the donees in what was then strategically labeled the third, or independent, sector.

---

[2] See p. 283.

This newly named sector, symbolic of voluntarism and private initiative, took on meaning and strength hitherto neither articulated nor constitutionally recognized. In any future controversy, foundations would not stand alone; they would be an inseparable part of one of democracy's vital mechanisms and preserves.

Since 1969, we have also grown and diversified. Sadly, the birth rate of private foundations has fallen off (though some massive ones have been newly created: e.g., MacArthur, Getty, and soon Hughes.) But that decline has been offset by the accelerating growth of corporate, community, and public foundations. The last two categories of foundations, interestingly enough, represent a democratizing trend in philanthropy: community foundations being governed by at least a presumptively broader representation of social interests, and public foundations (technically not foundations but 501(c)(3) public charities) experimenting with new forms of governance and appealing to the market for the funds they then make available as grants. One could reasonably argue that in the growth of these two types of grantmaking institutions there is visible a trend toward philanthropy that is less elitist, closer to the market, more consistent with the democratic nature of our society. (Again, one has to recognize the influence of the Tax Reform Act of 1969, which in its distaste for elitist philanthropy created incentives for the establishment of both community and public foundations.)

Since 1969, foundations have also become more sophisticated and versatile. They have always given money; now they are explicitly and self-consciously doing far more than that. One could easily cite a dozen or more roles they play: technical assistants, program-related investors, lenders; insurers, conveners, gadflies, evaluators, incubators, partners, Good Housekeeping Seals of Approval.

As their activities have diversified, so have their social philosophies. Foundations in the past have been castigated simultaneously as being too liberal and too conservative—proof in itself that there have always been differences enough to make generalizations difficult. Recently, with the general American drift toward the right, conservatives have been much more aggressive in the use of foundations, in their own words trying to counterbalance a predominantly liberal tilt in philanthropy. To the extent this represents greater diversity among foundations, the trend is a healthy one. But to the extent it politicizes and polarizes philanthropy, it is a disturbing development.

Leadership in philanthropy is also diversifying and diffusing. We were vulnerable in 1969 partly because leadership had been concentrated in the "name" heads of the very big foundations; they became our spokespeople and the visible targets of hostile critics. There was not much contact either among these dominating figures nor with the world of the smaller foundations—a lack of alliance that made philanthropy all the more vulnerable. I can recall the efforts of Homer Wadsworth[3] and others to forge more of a linkage during the 1950s and 1960s; but their voices were not heard or listened to at the top. Since 1969, the situation has changed. Regional associations of grantmakers have sprung up around the country; the Council on Foundations and Independent Sector have become forceful instruments of cohesion, and a welcome flow of philanthropic leadership and energy has been bubbling up in all manner of places.

In these ways we've earned our greater acceptance—not least by becoming more socially sensitive and accountable. As I'll indicate in a moment, we still have a long way to go. But there's solid evidence we're trying: through experimentation in governance [that] gives broader representation, in better public reporting, in better relations with applicants and grantees. Arrogance—the occupational hazard of philanthropy—is now the chronic target of self-chastening addresses, two of them the major presentations at the 1984 annual conference of the Council on Foundations. But in our avid search for humility, we might remember the delicious comment of a social satirist: "Humility is an elusive quality; just when you think you've found it, you've lost it!"

We've also become far more politically adept. Compare the awkward response to the congressional hearings of 1969 with the sophistication and preparedness shown by both the Council [on Foundations] and Independent Sector in 1984.

---

[3] Homer Wadsworth (1913–1994) served as director and president of the Kansas City Association of Trusts and Foundations (1949–1974) and director of the Cleveland Foundation (1974–1984). Wadsworth's interest in promoting greater leadership among national philanthropic institutions inspired his work in developing both the Council on Foundations and Independent Sector.

To the degree described, we have earned the more favorable climate we now operate in. But mostly, let's admit, the change is a function of social circumstance: in these days, the philanthropy we represent is in greater demand—we're more needed, more wanted. We've become a vital part of the democratic system. My guess is that if we were to rewrite the American constitution today, at least some reference would be made to philanthropy (thus elevating it from the lower region of the Tax Code!), or at least to the independent sector. The tenth amendment, in its vague allusion to residual local and private rights, made room for the development of the sector; were a modern-day Jefferson to put his pen to paper again, I'm sure the reference would be more explicit.

The need we are filling is multiform. It begins with our present circumstance of scarcening resources, a circumstance in many respects recalling the Biblical account of Joseph and his interpretation of the Pharaoh's dream: a period of affluence to be followed by an era of shortage. Our funds can no longer be satirized as whimsical add-ons to a secure economy and public fisc; they are essential elements of survival and an essential stimulus to growth that are jealously sought after and monitored by a beleaguered society.

We also represent one facet of the contemporary social trend toward decentralization, the quest for some way of coping with a complexity and scale that transcend the capacity of any one locus of authority and initiative. One can see that trend globally, in the moves toward decentralization in the developed as well as in the developing nations, in capitalistic as well as socialistic societies. Certainly it became evident to those of us serving as the National Academy of Science's Commission on National Urban Policy, where we documented the forced entry of every American metropolis into an environment of intense global competition, with the concomitant need for each locality to struggle largely on its own to accommodate and survive.

I suspect there's a rhythm to these historic trends toward and away from centralization. Centralization, when there's certainty about solutions (witness the heyday of economic theorists, whether classical or Keynsian); decentralization when uncertainty prevails and the premium is on experimentation, exploration, and (not least) on avoiding final responsibility (witness the political advantage of President Reagan passing on the hot potatoes of current responsibility to the governors, to the mayors, to the private sector). Whatever the cause, these are times in America when the decision-making process is flattening out, and it's no accident that society would respect and nurture the more spontaneous, less constrained style of foundations.

But decentralization also contributes to particularism and the loss of a sense of the whole. Again one comes to cherish the potential of philanthropy to see and deal with things whole. General-purpose foundations are in the best position to realize this potential, being free to scan the whole range of human needs before stating their priorities. But even foundations with specified terms of reference have an opportunity to integrate [that] is given to few other institutions in society. Government is territorialized, so are business firms, so are most functional bodies. Again, one can understand why philanthropy is looked to these days with appreciation.

Philanthropy also represents a "movable dollar": flexible resources [that] can be reallocated with greater speed and fewer restrictions than almost any others publicly available—certainly compared with governmental expenditures which, as their level recedes, expose more and more hard rocks of fixed outlays.

Philanthropy is all the more appreciated for its explicit dedication to an integrity of process and a noble public purpose. What it aspires to is what a growingly suspicious, even cynical, public wants in its heart of hearts the more it is disillusioned by public scandal and private greed. Foundations, even when they have not earned it, somehow have come to stand for rationality amidst political harangue, a commitment to social justice at a time when minorities are outvoted, the children of the poor neglected, and the majority of us beginning to weary of the burden of being our brother's keeper. This week's election showed, if nothing else, that shouldering that burden governmentally is not a platform for electing a President. But still there is the American conscience, all the more grateful for the tradition of private philanthropy—a tradition constantly reminding us of philosopher John Rawls' definition of justice: "You arrive at it by looking at what should be done generally from the viewpoint of the weakest members of society." We can't expect many institutions

[that] are in the market for votes or dollars to abide by that imperative. But we can expect it of philanthropy.

So the social winds are in our favor. Can we fully justify the faith or fulfill the expectations now invested in us? I wouldn't ask the question unless I had some concerns as we now enter the third fifteen-year period stretching from a favorable congressional hearing to the uncertain horizon of the year 2000. And here are some of those concerns:

First, we haven't managed to spread the word of philanthropy very widely; there are far more potential donors in America than have become avid practitioners of the art. To cite a measure of that potential: the Forbes 400 wealthiest persons in America have twice the total assets of all foundations combined. Also, the rate of giving by the wealthiest has actually declined since the Reagan tax cuts and the diminished incentives (increased costs of giving) built into that legislation. Corporations are still contributing at the minimal rate of 1 percent of pretax profits. Think what the impact would be if the extent of giving from those sources were doubled.

Another set of concerns has to do with the mixing of motives in American philanthropy. Personal interest, whim, and aggrandizement play far more of a part in giving decisions than most of us would like to admit. I know this touches some raw nerves and sensitivities, but it's worth reminding ourselves more than occasionally that foundations are established to fulfill a public purpose, not simply to express or satisfy a personal idiosyncrasy. Another source of concern, already mentioned, is the seeming increase in philanthropy [that] reflects a partisan/politicized intent. The question of mixed motive is also fairly addressed to the giving of corporations. First, in the context of across-the-board corporate citizenship; corporations are now paying very little in the way of federal taxes, a fact sometimes conveniently obscured by the rising totals of their charitable contributions. Second, in the pattern of their gifts, which recently have featured "cause-related advertising" and the PR advantages of focusing on popular enterprises such as the restoration of the Statue of Liberty. There are always tradeoffs—on the favorable side, the stimulus to giving, on the questionable side, the redirection of giving from higher to lower priorities of social need and the subtle debasing of the motivation of philanthropy.

Nor are community foundations beyond a poke or two of probing concern. To maintain their standing as public charities, they are legislatively forced into a constant expansion of their asset base; along with this incentive, there's the familiar penchant for growing ever bigger. At what point does the urge to bigness overcome the commitment to purpose and quality? And as community foundations become larger, they become more of a factor in the exercise of power and in the play of local politics. Mayors—in the presence of steadily amassing local philanthropies—have been known to ask, "Who's the government in this community?"

Still another facet of philanthropy that invites concern is the too-easy way in which foundations can and ofttimes do define the public purpose which it is their legal requirement to serve. The requirement can be met simply by giving money to any one of the million or so eligible nonprofit organizations [that] already exist, or to one [that] any of us can easily create. There's virtue in that profusion, but there's also an easy escape from the rigors of a more serious and far-ranging assessment that this society needs from independent institutions that have been given the luxury and latitude of reasoned choice and the longer look. Pet charities, the favoring of friends, and safe havens of giving convert philanthropy into a matter more of prejudice and whimsy than of thought and judgment.

And have we made the governance of foundations too easily accessible to some, too difficult for others? It takes only a glance at the statistics on board composition to see how narrow a sampling of social diversity is represented; philanthropy is still a province of the elite. A question very few of us are prepared to raise and discuss is whether the governance of foundations—as in the case of family foundations—should be "inheritable." The question is not only sensitive; it's debatable. Some of our most effective philanthropies are those in which family and descendants are involved, showing both commitment and admirable social sensitivity. But should the right of governance be in every case earned rather than simply accorded by blood or the buddy system?

As John Nason found when he scanned the nation's philanthropic trustees, those who govern foundations have not scored very high— speaking generally rather than particularly—in meeting the test either of social breadth or "due diligence." In too many cases, philanthropy is operating in society's cozy corners and taking too casually the responsibilities of trusteeship.

My final concern is whether philanthropy may be straying too far from its humanistic and altruistic origins. The trend toward more professionalized philanthropy has in most respects been a good thing, but not when it stiffens into bureaucracy and loses the spontaneity and compassion of the one-to-one. We have also tended to identify philanthropy almost totally with money and the giving of money; but giving and philanthropy are far more than that, and are often spoiled by it. Another tendency has been toward "gentrification"; we start with a presumed focus on those of less advantage and end by serving the interests of the more privileged. We also sometimes stifle philanthropy by confining it to a world of privatism: "This is our money, and it's no one else's business but ours as to how we spend it."

You knew my genetic melancholy would break through. But even a listing of all these concerns shouldn't turn the happier philanthropic mood of 1984 into a gloomy forecast for the coming fifteen years. I'm convinced we've come a long way over the past thirty years, that we've learned how to self-correct, and that if the year 2000 is still a viable one for human society, philanthropy will have played a vital part in making it so.

The Spirit of Philanthropy and the Soul of Those Who Manage It

(Presented to the Thirty-Eighth Annual Conference of the Council on Foundations, Atlanta, Georgia, March 1987)

"Philanthropy is not just another institution. It stands for something distinctive and special, with a tradition and necessarily a spirit which represent to society the nobler motives of altruism and the more humane considerations so characteristically missing in the worlds of business and politics."

Stewardship is a term that is healthily disciplining, but it is also too passive: it does remind us of the specific trusts we have accepted, but it does not suggest the creative roles we inescapably play. We are stewards not merely of money, but of a tradition—a tradition [that] is still evolving. And that makes us accountable not only for what we preserve but for what we create.

I'd like to brood with you over both the custodial and the creative responsibilities of philanthropic managers.

I'll be making some generalizations that suffer all the liabilities of half-truths. Fair warning á la Robert Wood,[1] who once introduced me with the mischievous alert: "I want you to listen carefully to Paul Ylvisaker. He's always persuasive but not always right." Still, how else than by generalizing do we human beings communicate insights—or keep an audience awake?

---

[1] Robert C. Wood, a political scientist and MIT professor, served as secretary of Housing and Urban Development, and director of the Harvard-MIT Joint Center for Urban Studies. In addition to their shared interest in urban studies, Wood's tenure as president of the University of Massachusetts (1970–1977) and superintendent of Boston Public Schools (1978–1980) overlapped with Ylvisaker's tenure as dean of the Harvard Graduate School of Education (1972–1982).

Who are the managers of philanthropy? To start with, the seven or eight thousand who don't own the money but make their living giving it away (the "philanthropoids"), plus another nearly equal number of trustees who manage organized philanthropy without benefit—some would say, without burden—of paid staff, but essentially all responsible for discharging the fiduciary responsibilities involved in running foundations.

Even at that, we're talking about a meager fraction of Americans: only six out of 100,000 who are trustees of foundations, and only three out of 100,000 who are paid staff.

Philanthropy is not easy to generalize about, despite those meager numbers. There can't be a more esoteric human activity, nor one more extraordinarily diverse—especially given the vast assortment of trusts that exist and therefore of the responsibilities involved.

But it is not enough to take refuge in diversity. We have a name, and therefore an identity; we have a function, and therefore a set of personal and public responsibilities. In searching for the spirit of philanthropy, that quintessential that instructs us in how we should behave and what values we ought to symbolize, there are two traditions to explore.

First, that of charity, the older and better understood; it has become almost instinctive in ours and other cultures in its presuppositions if not always its practice. Its "pure theory" builds upon six elements:

1. Altruism, the subordination of self-interest.

2. Compassion and empathy as the best avenues to understanding.

3. Taking the perspective of "the least among us." John Rawls built this into his theory of justice: the just society is one which tests its actions by their impact on the condition of its least powerful members.

4. A readiness to affirm and to act alone.

5. A quest for a better human condition, sometimes in its sense of perfection reminiscent of the search for the Holy Grail.

6. Giving as a one-to-one human encounter in a microworld of personal relationships.

In juxtaposition to this tradition of charity, another has evolved, [which] we now call modern (organized) philanthropy. It has developed its own set of presumptions, adapted from and adapting to, another environment:

1. The environment in which it works is the one in which institutions, rather than individuals, are the key actors. We have moved from the world of the one-on-one to that of institutionalized interaction.

2. There is a separation of donor and beneficiary into a world of intermediaries. The original donor, if still involved, acts through trustees, who act through staff, who act through one or more layers of nonprofit agencies, who act through staff, who act through a filter of representatives of the class, or problems, ultimately being dealt with. And further distancing occurs with the growth of specialization.

3. A look past the immediate condition of persons to what we call root causes and systemic reform.

4. A tilt toward reason and dispassion as the best route to systemic understanding and change.

5. A consciousness of institutional image and self-concern, ranging from tax considerations and the explicit rationalization by corporations of self-interest in their charity, to the incessant search all of us are engaged in for a distinctive mission and focus.

6. A recognition of a public responsibility, with accompanying public disciplines and restraints—and the redirection of that search for the Holy Grail toward an even more elusive concept called the public interest.

7. A conscious engineering of power, not only through grants and leveraging but through processes such as convening in which the gift plays only a part. Also, an explicit recognition of playing a social role, not simply a personal one.

8. A shift from gift to negotiated contract. We do this to both provide discipline and an assurance of effectiveness by watching carefully the terms of the grant. We also, by that method, allow reciprocity and participation. It is not the Lady Bountiful, unilateral act, and therefore it is consistent with the nature of our time. But have the very words "gift" and "grant" become archaic? Think about the way you deal with applicants. It is a negotiated contract that we have come to, rather than a gift or grant.

9. A search for consensus in approach and resolution. Consensus

is an institutional imperative in our times, simply to minimize the friction generated by institutions moving through a crowding social and political environment.

10. A bias in favor of excellence and a meritocratic elite, both as justifications in themselves for philanthropy, but also as the preferred vehicle for helping the less advantaged.

Let's be clear: each of these elements has its own rationalizing logic. I am not putting these things down, but describing them. Each has made its own contribution to the evolving tradition of philanthropy. Without what they represent, charity could never have developed into the equilibrating and distinctive social force it has become. Charity could not have adapted to the social, economic, and political transformations that have taken place in modern society.

But the change has produced an institution and a profession with internal tensions, if not outright contradictions. Philanthropy has evolved, as Joseph Schumpeter[2] once analyzed capitalism to have evolved, to produce a routinization of progress. Good works in our time have become routine, which partly explains the paradox of organized philanthropy routinely turning out worthy grants with gray-flannel-suit regularity and rhetoric—just read all those foundation annual reports.

Have we moved from flesh-and-blood giving to dispassionate and depersonalized philanthropy?

Which of these two traditions—the charitable or the more recent—are we the custodians of? The answer is both. We are tested by how creatively we balance and resolve those contending logics and meld them into a concept and code of behavior that honor the imperatives of both traditions. This may seem, and partly is, just another version of the contemporary dilemma: how do we remain human in an institutional environment?

---

[2] Joseph Schumpeter (1883–1950) was a free-market economist and Harvard professor who originated the term "creative destruction" to describe how competition improves the economy even as it destroys obsolete firms and ideas. He believed that the strength of capitalism was the continuous appearance of new products and processes. He is credited with expanding the narrow scope of economics to include interdisciplinary dimensions of politics, history, and social science.

But it's not that; philanthropy is not just another institution. It stands for something distinctive and special, with a tradition and necessarily a spirit which represent to society the nobler motives of altruism and the more humane considerations so characteristically missing in the worlds of business and politics.

Each of us will find his or her own way of living with these tensions—each one's own resolution, each one's own way of contributing creatively to the evolving practice of philanthropy. But there are some guiding maxims and imperatives I would urge on you, though clearly they reflect my own biases and pieties. (You'll note there are eleven commandments. Anything to outdo Moses.)

1. Guard your own humanity. The first ethical commandment, taught to me by a distinguished professor of ethics, is to take care of yourself. This is not acting for number one; it means taking care of what you are or should be, so that you can radiate that out to others. If you lose your own soul—whether to arrogance, insensitivity, insecurity or the shield of impersonality—you diminish the spirit of philanthropy. The goal to aspire to is that you will be a distinguished human being who gives to the foundation as much an identity as you derive from it, and far more than the money you give or negotiate away. In a very real sense, you *are* philanthropy, even if you don't own the money.

2. Guard the soul of your own organization, even from your own pretensions. Those of you lucky enough to be part of an institution that has a soul know what a precious environment it is. It's a secure environment within which distinctive personalities complement rather than compete with each other; it's an open environment in which hierarchy is respected but not imposed, and where posturing and game-playing are unnecessary; it's an institution in which values are explicitly and easily discussed, and there is a consistency between values stated and values played out; it's an organization [that] demonstrates its humanity equally in its responsiveness to the needs and sensibilities of its external constituencies and in the care with which it nourishes and grows in its own personnel.

3. Be ready to speak out and act on your own on those hopefully rare occasions when principle is at stake or the unspoken needs to be aired.

4. Constantly assess your own motivation, whether what you're arguing for reflects your own power-drive and personal predilections or a measured evaluation of public need and foundation goals. This goes for trustees as well as staff, and ranges well beyond the more apparent realm of conflicts and interest.

5. Scan the whole gamut of your foundation's activities to make certain they are consistent with the goals and spirit of the philanthropic tradition. Are the values that peek through the back-page listing of your investments the same as those featured in the pious opening pages of your annual report? In your convening function, are you more intent on demonstrating influence than on catalyzing and releasing community energies?

Do your personnel policies and board compositions jibe with the affirmative action expectations directed at your applicants? Does the care with which you consider public needs and foundation policy match the exhaustive scrutiny you give to applicant proposals and budgetary attachments? Compile your own checklist of such questions; you'll find it an instructive and sometimes chastening exercise.

6. Constantly traverse the lengthening distance between the words used in foundation docket items and press releases and the ultimate impact and beneficiaries of the grants once made. Have the intended beneficiaries really benefited? Who are they, and how many of them are from among the least advantaged? Has the quest for a better human condition dissipated in the chase after some abstraction? Have verbalizations and the mere recital of good grants made substituted for demonstrable attainment of tangible goals?

7. Be willing to open the black box of philanthropy to share with others the mysteries of values and decision-making. They may seem disadvantageous to you as a protective mechanism, but in reality they're a breeding place for personal and institutional botulism. An anaerobic environment is not a healthy one for the spirit of philanthropy, nor for the soul of a manager.

Be ready and willing to mix with the community, and with those closer to real life than you are. Engage in dialogue with others who have legitimate interest in what you're doing and who may provoke you into insights that seclusion may have kept you from.

Consider another ethical commandment: always be ready to

explain publicly your decision and your reasons for your actions. Don't wind up your organization so tight that competing ideas can't filter through.

8. Never stop affirming. When you find your battery of hope, excitement, and even idealistic naiveté so drained that you don't let an applicant finish a presentation without pointing out why it can't be done, it's time you departed for another profession. Philanthropy builds on the hope of rising generations; it lights fires rather than snuffs them out.

9. Follow both routes to understanding, the compassionate as well as the analytical. No one can comprehend the universe who does not understand and care for the sparrow.

10. Don't ever lose your sense of outrage. Bill Bondurant *[Executive Director, Mary Reynolds Babcock Foundation, 1974–92]* can't forget, nor can I after he related it, the wondering comment of an applicant who looked about Bill's comfortable office and lifestyle: "How, Bill, do you keep your sense of outrage?" There has to be in all of us a moral thermostat that flips when we're confronted by suffering, injustice, inequality, or callous behavior.

11. Don't ever lose your sense of humor. Organized philanthropy so easily dulls into pretentious drabness, and we all need the revitalizing spark of a good laugh, mostly at ourselves.

My own chastening reminder is the memory of a cocktail party at which I, Mr. Big Bucks from the Ford Foundation, was pontificating to all within earshot. To make a point even more impressive, I paused to pick up an olive. But what my bad eyes had missed was that it was actually a cigar butt. Any of you who have ever tasted one knows the abrupt and ignominious end of that pious performance.

Philanthropy—in the degree to which it fulfills the aspiration of its spirit and tradition—is a rare element in our social firmament, a salt that cannot be allowed to lose its savor. It is a distinctive function that, like religion, relies eventually and essentially on its moral power.

We diminish that force when we get absorbed in a mistaken quest for power of another sort, be it money or social and political influence. Philanthropic influence derives more from spirit than from social positioning or monetary domination. The love of that money is undoubtedly the most corrupting element in the grantmaking enterprise.

There is enough of an alien spirit already attaching itself to philanthropy—self-interest being an ancient example and partisanship and political manipulation a more recent one—without our failing to recognize and honor the spirit and tradition of which we are stewards.

The power of organized philanthropy can indeed corrupt. But conducted in a humane spirit, and with soul, it can also ennoble.

I was once asked to work for Joe Clark, then mayor of Philadelphia. When I inquired of him what the job was, *really*, he thought a minute and replied, "To help fight the battle for my mind." It was an irresistible challenge.

But what I'd ask of someone about to join us as a foundation manager would be quite another dimension: "Help fight the battle for our soul."

Community and Community Foundations in the Next Century

(Excerpted from *An Agile Servant: Community Leadership by Community Foundations*, edited by Richard Magat)[1]

"The more global the foundation, the more it is attracted to the local; the more local the grantmaker, the stronger the urge to reach outward."

Community is a word of elastic meaning; its capacity to stretch has been challenged over the last century and will be tested even more dramatically during the next. The changing dimensions are not only geographical but include forces of diversity, social fragmentation, values, and shared interests.

The Geographic Dimension

The attraction of the local is so powerful that grassroots philanthropy will never lose its appeal, even as the territorial concept of community constantly expands.

The geographic stretching of community is actually a constant process, simultaneously moving in opposite directions: downward, to the individual neighborhood, and outward, to embrace the entire world and eventually (certainly with environmental concern) all of space. These polarities are magnetic in their attractions. One can draw from them almost a general rule: the more global the foundation, the more it is attracted to the local; the more local the grantmaker, the stronger the urge to reach outward.

---

[1] Washington, D.C.: The Council on Foundations and The Foundation Center, 1989.

What are the driving forces? There seem to be at least four. First is the expanding reality of what we call community. The stable environment we once knew as our neighborhood has dissolved into a fluid urban environment that melds imperceptibly at its edges into a region, a nation, and the world. Physical definitions are almost totally elusive, except as we mark them by imposed feelings of belongingness: Minneapolis-St. Paul are most clearly identified by who roots for the Twins and the Vikings; Boston, by the viewing area of the Celtics, the Red Sox, and the Patriots; New York and Los Angeles, by their televised and otherwise stereotyped images and lifestyles.

In this flowing world of indistinct boundaries, and with modern philanthropy assigned the task of finding generic solutions to root causes mostly lying beyond any local jurisdiction, it is hard to resist the drive toward enlarging territories.

The second and equally powerful force for expansion is financial: the greater potential of a larger territory for fundraising and asset building. This has undoubtedly prompted much of the recent movement toward regional and statewide community foundations, now accounting for [more than] 10 percent of the total number and rising. The outward movement of the Spokane Inland Northwest Community Foundation is but one example.

A third generating force [is] the vacuum that usually exists in the coverage of community foundations in adjacent, more rural, areas and regions beyond metropolitan boundaries. Nature abhors vacuums, and so do many human-made institutions. It is almost inevitable that existing community foundations would reach out to supply the missing philanthropic service.

It is a short step from such a lack to the fourth motivation for geographical expansion: the social necessity represented by community foundations, a bonding and leavening influence in modern society that only a private agency with flexible resources and public credibility can provide. Modern philanthropy has evolved as America's contribution to the theory and practice of constitutional democracy in an age when complexity and the demand for shared power have outstripped the capacity for governments to handle social problems on their own. Gradually, foundations have emerged from their purely charitable preserve to become an essential and recognized social process—in effect, a set of private legislatures allowing an autonomous determination and implementation of public needs and agendas.

Community foundations are the localized expression of what modern philanthropy has become and has to offer; and as such, they are coming to be everywhere in demand.

The Dimension of Diversity

Two great social movements have vastly expanded modern concepts of community, both in the United States and worldwide: migration and liberation.

World War II marked the explosive release of these two forces. Self-determination became the rallying cry of colonies everywhere; within a decade, it was echoed within industrialized nations as well, dramatically evidenced by the civil rights and women's liberations movements in the United States.

The war had also released another genie: the power to see a global world, over which there could be human movement on a massive scale. The result is the modern "community," an incredible potpourri of human beings from all kinds of cultures and places—as in London and Los Angeles [whose citizens speak] 100 or more languages—everywhere motivated by an intense desire for self-direction and survival. It is that kind of community, diverse and individualistic, to which community foundations are now trying to adapt.

But a cultural lag is evident. Boards and staff only minimally reflect their community's burgeoning diversity. And the distance remains (in some cases is growing) between a *status quo* perception of a homogeneous citizenry that once may have been, and the heterogeneous, self-determining mixture that has fast become the community of present and future reality.

The Dimensions of Fragmentation

Two other forces are tugging at the very notion of community: individualization and polarization. The rugged individualism that flourished on the frontier and gave the private sector the enviable strength and autonomy it now has, has inexorably extended itself into a ruling maxim: "Get government off my back and let me be." That elaborating syndrome has become, as de Tocqueville put it, "a habit of the heart"; and while it has extended the range of human freedom, it has also created a pervasive climate of individual isolation and aloneness, poignantly documented by Robert Bellah and his associates in *Habits of the Heart.*[2] Elemental social institutions—family, church, neighborhood—have all been eroded by this atomizing force; the "community" has become more of an ideal to be arduously fabricated than a reality to be assumed and counted upon. Simultaneously, the social cohesion that the concept of community calls up is further jeopardized by the recurrent tendency toward stratification. America's middle class, long the bulwark of its stable communities and its politics of equilibrium, is being magnetized in two opposing directions, the richer and the poorer, while at the same time it is being atomized.

The Dimension of Values

Some jagged fangs of adverse change and reaction are gnawing at that sense of a community of values, the noble truths of the Declaration of Independence and the Constitution, the common aspirations of successive waves of immigrants, the dominance of Judeo-Christian heritage, and the accumulating bonds of an achieving economy and national pride. One scarring bite has come with the rise of religious fundamentalism both here and abroad—an unyielding insistence on value uniformity, an unwillingness to tolerate diversity, a readiness to impose rather than arbitrate social solutions. Another has come from an ominous source wholly alien to accepted values—one to which there is no apparent bridge. Generically, it is known as "the criminal element," a counterculture built on a combination of violence and greed. The international drug cartels with their own treasuries and armed forces are one variant;

---

[2] *Habits of the Heart: Individualism and Commitment in American Life*, Robert N. Bellah, Richard Madsen, William M. Sullivan, Ann Swindler, Steven M. Tipton. University of California Press, Berkeley, 1985.

the emerging "corporate" street gangs of central cities like Detroit, with bulging bank accounts and armament of their own, are domestic equivalents. So are those now known as white-collar criminals, as well as those who take from the community without giving in return. All challenge the presumptions of community and if not contained could lead to an era of global hegemony of warlords.

The Dimension of Shared Interests

If neighbor no longer knows or interacts with neighbor, bonds are increasingly being formed with kindred, if distant, spirits. We reach out and touch them, by telephone, rapid travel, satellite, computer, fax, and every other medium of modern technology. In so many ways, the more distant, the closer; the closer, the more distant.

As one travels outward along this dimension, homogeneity displaces heterogeneity; we select our "neighbors," and it becomes easier to live in this community than in that of our actual residence.

Community foundations live with this depersonalized residue; the question is, to what extent have they, or will they, or can they, adapt to it or make something more of it? And will another form of community foundation emerge that fits and flows along this elusive dimension—community foundations of common interest rather than common place?

The Essential Role and Challenge of Community Foundations

Whatever territory they select, and whichever dimensions they move along, the essential role that community foundations play is that of making a community more of a community: to strengthen its sense of itself as a community, to help forge ties that bind, to assist in overcoming divisiveness while tempering the excesses of self-centeredness and escapism into isolating worlds beyond the humanizing discipline of personal interaction.

Community foundations have the distinguishing responsibility of supplying what philanthropy has to offer within a defined territory, however much that territory may enlarge and one's conception of community may expand. Their distinguishing structure—sometimes more, sometimes less—adds the burden and discipline of accountability.

What About That Future and [Community Foundations'] Likely Adaptation to It?

Community foundations will continue to be the fastest-growing sector of the foundation world.
The reasons are several. The most important is the role that philanthropy plays in an evolving and complicating society—a role now coming to be recognized even in the controlled economies and politics of the socialist world. Philanthropy symbolizes and releases the social energies that are only available when expressed spontaneously and autonomously.

Furthermore, the potential represented by community foundations is available to only a selected number of localities. They are not evenly spread, nor do they cover all the metropolitan areas and cities of a size that could benefit from such philanthropic resources. Greater proliferation and coverage can be expected. This will occur as the notion catches on that the generic concept of community foundations is relevant at different scales, from neighborhoods to regions and states, and for diversifying purposes and constituencies.

Another reason for continued, and probably accelerating, growth is the greater compatibility of community foundations with the democratic tradition of this and other modernized and modernizing nations. Congress, in the historic Tax Reform Act of 1969, recognized this distinctiveness by giving preferred status to these and other nonprofit institutions precisely because of their "publicness." They were separated out from private foundations, reflecting congressional respect for their greater accountability to the general public, their heavier reliance on public contributions and the discipline involved, and the assurance they give (with few exceptions) of governance less insulated from public influence than the closed and self-perpetuating boards of private foundations. For all these reasons, one can safely predict the continued and accelerating growth of community foundations well into the next century.

There will also be a proliferation of kinds of community foundations in the foreseeable future.

One can expect not only differing scales of operation, from neighborhood to region and state, but also different adaptations in form and style to diversifying constituencies, needs, and cultures.

This trend is already evident. In Washington, D.C., Cleveland, and Boston, secondary-school students have been organized to become "philanthropists" in their neighboring communities, first analyzing and ranking in priority the needs of those communities and then raising monies to dispense, along with the obligation to monitor and evaluate.

In that mode, neighborhoods—set in motion by what seems to be a new round of combating poverty, and imbued with the growing tradition of assertiveness and self-reliance—are likely to preempt the generic concept of community foundations, raising funds they will independently disburse. Not only neighborhoods but also communities of like-minded citizens of similar origin are operating independently. Prototypes can be found in the Haymarket Fund and similar funds being organized as public charities, systematically raising funds for distribution, and having an attachment to defined localities. Ethnic equivalents are also likely to appear and multiply, converting their historic analogues—the mutual aid societies—into modern counterparts of community foundations.

Similarly, those intent on solving such particular problems as drug addiction and crime in their locales may well develop focused grantmaking agencies, borrowing the community foundation format.

Community foundations, along with their kindred variants, will become more explicit and assertive about their generic philanthropic function.

In the social context of the next century, either community foundations will live up to their philanthropic responsibilities or they will wither and be discarded. It will not be an easy century. Globally, the pressures of exploding and impoverishing populations, together with a depleting and deteriorating environment, will demand a level of human creativity and a readiness for social change beyond anything yet exhibited by this or any other nation. The signs and beginnings are already in place. The nonprofits, already squeezed by government cutbacks, are besieged by accumulating social needs, as are their counterparts in the governmental sector. Mayors, long diffident toward the world of private giving, are now explicit in their rhetoric and in their planning about the essential role of private donations if city halls are to achieve any progress and partnership in their efforts at civic improvement and unity. So are their colleagues at the state and national levels—governors calling for public-private alliances in educational reform, President Bush evoking the helping spirit of "a thousand points of light."

Community foundations will find this demanding environment their world of everyday reality, the more so as formal institutions, dealing uncertainly with the restive tradition of shared power, will experience more and more roadblocks in their attempts to proceed multilaterally through consensus or unilaterally through authority.

A promising segment of local philanthropy gives evidence of being ready; one can see it conspicuously in the creative talent and programming of the very large community foundations, but also in the more diminutive ones that have discovered the many nonmonetary ways in which "small can be effective."

But all will not be sweetness, growth, and enlightenment. Undoubtedly some community foundations will fall by the wayside. One type of casualty will be those that fail to reach critical mass of funding and growth potential in the communities they serve.

There will also be casualties of competition. There are already somnolent community foundations that have not responded to developing trends and urgencies—yielding the initiative, and sometimes turf and survival, to more farsighted and assertive private foundations and other funders. Another source of competition stems from the large versus the small, usually the case in major urban and metropolitan areas where a centralized community foundation enjoys a territorial and fundraising advantage over smaller nearby colleges.

Competition also exists in the relationship between some community foundations and the United Way. Both are in the fundraising business, with similar interests in community betterment. The boundary marker of current funding, as against endowment funding, does indeed differentiate the two, but [it] tends in the heat of practice to crumble under obliterating traffic from both directions.

The prospect of philanthropy stepping out front and acting more assertively is a likely reason for other local friction. This might occur as conventional charities lose some of their advantage in funding patterns of some community foundations that favor less traditional or more grassroots organizations, and equally with new agencies and programs vying aggressively for a bigger share of the funding pie.

Lastly, community foundations will face the probability of a plethora of new grantmakers adopting the same format and even the label. There are, after all, no restrictions on how many community foundations can operate in the same geographic area. Boston, for instance, has three community foundations within the metropolitan area and another two within hailing distance. Each bears the name of a different municipality, but there is definite overlap in the areas they serve. Another variant is the ethnic community fund.

Philanthropy in general, community foundations included, will be inviting targets for public attention and increased regulation.

Foundations—fortunately and unfortunately—have been surprisingly insulated from informed and consistent public scrutiny. But with philanthropy entering a period of increasing social significance, one can expect a more intense focusing of public attention on what foundations are doing and how they are doing it. The notoriety of the Buck Trust case in Marin County, California, may exaggerate what philanthropic life in the future may be like, but it foreshadows some of the turbulence that lies ahead.[3] Certainly the wakening interest of the press, of scholars and educators, and of state attorneys general and legislatures are omens of an environment to come.

Community foundations, because of their "publicness," are in a better position than private foundations to endure in this environment and to retain their cherished attributes of independence and flexibility. Their increasing exposure to the public eye, however, will

---

[3] In a 1986 settlement, a judge removed from the San Francisco Foundation the $400-million-plus Buck Trust. The deceased donor had earmarked the funds for use in Marin County; the San Francisco Foundation tried unsuccessfully to modify the restriction.

make certain of their characteristics (such as slowness to respond and initiate, and insulation from the social diversity of their communities) more vulnerable to criticism and to appeals for more public control.

Giving in the United States is likely to rise. If indeed it does, community foundations will be among the principal beneficiaries.

While there are conflicting trends, the greater probability is that private giving in this country will grow significantly. The mood favors what is voluntary rather than compulsory, and as social needs expand, giving of time and money is likely to follow.

Individual giving is also becoming more cautious, more pragmatic, more favorable to what is known and close at hand. That is much to the advantage of community enterprises and foundations. Their further edge is that they afford larger givers favored tax status, smaller givers the efficiencies of combining lesser gifts into larger endeavors.

Giving clearly will never match the rising level of public need. Nonetheless, predictable gains will substantially assist community foundations in fulfilling the role the coming century will assign them.

The community foundations model is adaptable in other countries as well, and is likely to spread internationally.

Interest in community foundations has been expressed by a number of non-Americans; it seems compatible with a variety of cultures. The naturalness [of the idea] and its affinity with the long tradition of mutual aid societies are congruent with experience everywhere, not least the emerging formation of private foundations within the Soviet Union. That the notion of community foundations is already taking hold in Japan, Britain, Canada, and elsewhere is further confirmation of the adaptability of the format.

Futures are hard to predict, and likely scenarios can diverge widely, depending upon a bewildering variety of forces and the volatility of their interplay. What has been written here flows from a relatively optimistic reading of social tea leaves. It does not take much of a Pollyanna, however, to conclude from the record of community foundations over the past seventy-five years that, as a class, they have performed effectively and have become an increasingly vital force on the American scene. Nor is it a flight from reality to see their flowering, along with [that of] philanthropy in general, as a fundamental process needed for the flexibility, independence, and creativity they represent.

Whether they are as strategically positioned as this essay suggests, or as prepared as they might be to realize their potential, may be arguable. What is beyond question, one might reasonably conclude, is the logic that has brought them into being and embedded them as habits of the American heart.

Small Can Be Effective

(An occasional paper for the Council on Foundations,
April 1989)

*"Foundations do not need a lot of money to be
effective. If, indeed, they were to exploit only a
fraction of the strategies available to them, their
individual and collective impact on American life
would be vastly and beneficially expanded."*

When people think, talk or write about foundations, almost
invariably they have in mind the large and very large philanthropies,
starting and usually ending with the Fords, Rockefellers, Carnegies,
and MacArthurs. Rarely will they be focusing on any or all of the
small foundations [that] actually [make up] the overwhelming mass
of grantmakers in the United States. Twenty-three thousand of the
total of twenty-five thousand foundations in the U.S. have assets of
less than $10 million (arbitrarily chosen here are an approximate
indicator of what could reasonably be classified as a "small
foundation"). Bear in mind that a number of "pass-through"
foundations have little or no assets but actually give away sizable
sums and can hardly be classified as small foundations.

The Council on Foundations has commissioned this essay in the
belief that more attention should be paid to the workings of these
smaller philanthropies, as well as to their contributions. All too little
is known about them, but it is doubtful in the climate of rising
demand for philanthropic funding and growing sophistication of
applicants that they will remain invisible or unnoticed. Concern has
already been expressed that increased scrutiny at both state and
federal levels might well focus on actual and alleged shortcomings in
this sector.

But the Council's interest is more on the positive side. There is
vast potential in small-scale philanthropy, and this is a time when

that potential needs to be fully released. The dollars held by small foundations, individually and collectively, are a precious resource in a society trying to meet burgeoning needs with the increasingly scarce public funds.

Moreover, it is the Council's fundamental belief that the *creative* use of foundation moneys rather than their size and scale constitutes the real potential of philanthropy—"small can be effective." This monograph, then, is an appeal for creativity, and an attempt to illustrate how small foundations have been and can be both creative and effective.

What is a Small Foundation?
Some Further Benchmarks

In addition to assets size, small foundations might be distinguished by two other criteria: *size of annual grants* and *size of staffs*. Both indicators are arbitrary and approximate.

Foundations [that] award an annual total of $1 million or less can reasonably be classified as small. Similarly, foundations with five or less paid staff might be thought of as being small. But there are always exceptions that plague any attempt to classify or generalize. For example, the Alden Trust of Worcester, Massachusetts, has over $50 million in assets [and] awards more than $1 million annually, but operates without staff: its trustees handle all the normal grantmaking operations.

So it's probably best to deal in approximates, and with a pervading sense of relativity. Small compared to what? To the Ford Foundation with its billions in assets, its hundreds of millions in annual grants, its scores of professional staff?

In the final analysis, to paraphrase a Supreme Court Justice, you know a small foundation when you feel you are one.

The Function of Foundations: Three Traditions

Before answering the question of how small foundations can be effective, one needs to go back to some basics: What are the great traditions within which foundations, large and small, move and have their being? Essentially, there are three:

The oldest and most widely practiced and understood is *charity*.

In its simplest form, it is a one-to-one transaction between two parties—one more affluent sharing resources with one more needy, a classic example being the Good Samaritan.

A second and equally ancient tradition is *patronage*, the identification and nurturing of talent. Originally practiced by kings and nobles, the tradition has given us the masters and masterpieces of art, sculpture, and music. In its modern form, it is represented by fellowships, such as the Guggenheim and MacArthur awards, and by direct support of cultural and educational enterprises.

The third great tradition is modern *philanthropy*, only a century old and still evolving. It emerged with the massive fortunes of Andrew Carnegie, John D. Rockefeller, and their kindred barons; it took on the structured character and law of the corporate world and associated itself with the outlook and professionalism of organized science. It dedicated itself to finding systemic solutions to underlying causes of poverty and other social ills, and over time has become a recognized social process—in effect, a set of private legislatures defining public problems, setting goals and priorities, and allocating resources toward general solutions.

Imbedded as we are in the immediacies of that evolution, we perhaps do not fully appreciate the role that foundations are allowed—and increasingly are expected—to play in American society. We have, in effect, been given a "hunting license" as private organizations to participate in what has conventionally been thought of as exclusively a public/governmental domain. And what is even more significant, this is becoming a global development: societies everywhere, growing in diversity and complexity, have become aware that government alone cannot release the energies and potential of their citizenry without giving room for spontaneous private initiatives. Even the Soviet Union is now encouraging the formation of private foundations.

Modern Philanthropy:
The Challenge to Foundation Creativity

Philanthropy in its contemporary form has grown explosively in its potential for social influence and creativity. It now has a multitude of ways in which it can be an effective and generative force for human betterment.

These generic functions of modern philanthropy can be listed under five general headings: financial, the catalytic role of philanthropy, the conceptualizing role of philanthropy, the critical function of philanthropy, and the community-building role of philanthropy. The following enumeration illustrates the range and variety of the devices by which foundations, whatever their size, can exercise and maximize their effectiveness. Only a few directly involve the transmission of money—which in itself gives an answer to that provocative, if somewhat mischievous, question: "Who would come to see you if you didn't have any (or much) money?"

Financial: Support Functions of Philanthropy

1. *Grantmaking.* Notice how in our times the concept of giving (the older charitable mode), and even the word, have given way to the modernized term of grantmaking. Actually, the process has become one of negotiated contracts, in which two parties, the donor and the donee, at least in theory agree on the terms of the exchange. Implicit in this exchange is the equality of the two parties, although there is still the hangover from former days of the superior position of the grantor, and hence the oft-cited occupational hazard of arrogance. But if we were explicitly to recognize the "democratization" of an elite institution, we would be practicing the equality of exchange in which money from one party secures the services of another on mutually acceptable terms.

It is in this kind of negotiation that philanthropy at any scale can and should ensure both its effectiveness and its credibility. In being credible, it will be all the more effective—and in making the adjustment to modern thought, it will demonstrate its creativity.

2. *Lending.* Granting money is only one way of extending financial support. A foundation can also lend, and by that device stretch its resources. Lending may be done at below-market or even at no interest, accepting higher risk while not depleting a foundation's financial capacity. Lending has proved an effective way, for example, of covering revenue shortages, often experienced by social service agencies whose cash flow position has become temporarily precarious.

3. *Insuring.* Another means of providing financial assistance is re-insuring commercial loans extended by banks or other sources to

non-profit agencies. Again, it allows foundations to be of assistance without diminishing their financial capacity.

4. *Investing.* The past decades have added still another device to a foundation's repertoire: program-related investments. Once thought to violate the doctrine of prudence, such investments—out of the foundation's corpus and usually at below-market rates of interest—are now generally accepted and increasingly practiced. Again, they enable a foundation to stretch its resources without depleting them.

Another significant use of investments is to make an ethical statement. By screening its own investments through criteria that are socially and environmentally sensitive, a foundation can ensure not only that its own programmatic and financial goals are congruent, but also that its example may have an impact on other sectors of the general public.

The Catalytic Role of Philanthropy

5. *Initiating.* Foundations often diminish their effectiveness by remaining passive, waiting for others to propose while hanging back themselves. Even small foundations can become pro-active, taking initiatives that stimulate others to act.

6. *Accelerating.* Social action is usually a slow process. Foundations by stepping in can speed up the process, acting as "society's passing gear." A notable example of this came when then-Governor Terry Sanford created the North Carolina Fund through the help of local foundations. The fund made it possible for minorities to participate in decisions and programs [that] speeded the adoption and experimentation of a rich variety of solutions to the state's long-festering social problems.

7. *Leveraging.* Small foundations are particularly at a disadvantage, not having enough money to fund larger ventures. But they can leverage their funds by bringing other resources into play.

8. *Collaborating and partnering.* Leveraging usually involves collaborating with others in joint grantmaking—another development in modern philanthropy [that] is picking up speed. A relevant case in point are the educational partnerships spreading across the country. Small foundations are conspicuous in school reform, maximizing their own energies, resources, and creativity.

9. *Convening.* One other mode of foundation activity that has

come into vogue is that of bringing together several sectors of the community with a common concern. Convening can be done with or without a financial outlay, but it does require credibility and trust. Foundations are a natural in this role. They are usually viewed as nonpartisan, a trusted meeting ground for divergent interests, and their functioning in this role can often have spectacular results. The Fund for the City of New York specializes in this activity. It holds "no-agenda lunches" where both public and private agencies can meet and discuss what's on their minds, regularly resulting in new approaches and joint ventures. It can be one of the most creative— and least expensive—forms of philanthropy, ideally suited to small foundations and their limited means.

The Conceptualizing Role of Philanthropy

10. *Analyzing.* Foundations are well known for the research they do and the fact-finding and analyses they finance. The role is at once valuable [and] mostly uncontroversial, and need not be expensive. And it need not in every case be complex or sophisticated, often requiring only some time, asking the right questions, and searching in the right places. Subjects for small foundations cover the whole range of community problems, [from] assembling data on the incidence of specific diseases to examining the import of demographic changes.

11. *Defining and redefining.* In a rapidly changing society, one of the most valuable processes is taking a new or another look at issues that have long been, shortly will [be], or should be on the public agenda. There is too often a lag in public perception and recognition; foundations can play an effective part in defining and redefining those issues through research, analyses, conferences, seminars, publicity, or simply reporting their own considerations and grant results.

12. *Focusing.* Again, in setting their own priorities for grantmaking, foundations of whatever size can extent a powerful influence on how nonprofits and public agencies concentrate their own energies and objectives. This is a further argument for foundations clarifying their goals and publicly stating/reporting what they hope to accomplish.

13. *Inventing and testing.* A more familiar part of philanthropy's

thinking function is that of devising new programs, new approaches, and new solutions. Innovation and experimentation early on became synonymous with the modern foundation. Two of our most ingenious solutions to serious social problems came from the pioneering efforts of very small foundations: the practice of painting white lines on the outside edges of roads and highways, radically reducing accident and mortality rates, and the use of lasers to limit the ravages of diabetic retinopathy, saving the residual vision of millions in this and other countries.

The Critical Function of Philanthropy

14. *Commenting.* Foundations, by their reluctance to speak out and their uneven record of public reporting, have all too often passed up what is one of their readiest and least expensive opportunities to be of influence. They have the freedom and the platform not only to inform the public of what they stand for and have done, but to comment on the state of the community they serve and on the needs they see as not being fulfilled. Small foundations in general are particularly remiss. The infrequency of their public reporting and their seclusion from public awareness have bound them in knots of their own tying.

15. *Approving and disapproving.* Foundations, small as well as large, carry their own "Good Housekeeping Seal of Approval." Given the public trust and confidence accorded to them, they are looked to as symbols of what has been disinterestedly judged as favorable or not favorable, promising or not promising, a risk worth or not worth taking. The use of that symbol is one to be exercised and guarded with the greatest of care and with the willingness to be explicit about both purpose and criteria.

16. *Advocating.* Brian O'Connell of Independent Sector has stated his belief that advocacy is the most powerful and precious of the roles of foundations and nonprofits. But it is hardly the most popular. One has to be willing to live with controversy. Small foundations willing to engage in it, either directly or through grantees, will obviously have to assess the risks, but they should also know of the potential rewards.

17. *Gadflying, or serving as social conscience.* This is the "prophetic" role, which foundations at any scale can choose to play.

They can do it through sponsored studies, commissions, and reports; or through statements and actions of their own. In recent years, small foundations throughout the United States have stirred the conscience of their communities on such topics as hunger, homelessness, AIDS—not to mention such nagging constants as civil rights and environmental protection.

The Community-Building Role of Philanthropy

18. *Bonding/unifying*. De Tocqueville more than a century ago noted a virtue in the new nation that might well become its fatal flaw: individualism leading perhaps ultimately to the fragmentation of community. It is a theme recently picked up again by Robert Bellah and his associates, in their volume *Habits of the Heart*.[1] And for me, it was etched memorably in a friendly argument with Fei Xiao Tong, the noted Chinese anthropologist. "You," he amiably charged, "are the White Devil. You symbolize undisciplined individualism. You define human potential in terms of what an individual can accomplish on his/her own, regardless of whether or not that accomplishment is to the benefit or to the detriment of that person's community."

Strengthening both the sense of community and the tradition of community service may well be the first obligation of foundations, whatever their size. [This is] an obligation that goes along with the rare privilege given philanthropy: the freedom to decide privately the means by which the goal of community building is to be accomplished.

19. *Balancing*. Building a community requires conscious efforts simultaneously at diversifying and equalizing, an essay in social balancing to ensure that disparities and polarization do not get out of hand. Even small foundations can make a difference simply in what they say, how they act, and what they do. Choosing trustees and staff who reflect diverse backgrounds and interests is powerfully symbolic; making certain that grantees are similarly reflective, seeking out and being accessible to people and agencies struggling

---

[1] *Habits of the Heart: Individualism and Commitment in American Life*, Robert N. Bellah, Richard Madsen, William M. Sullivan, Ann Swindler, Steven M. Tipton. University of California Press, Berkeley, 1985.

at the margin are ways of helping a community achieve a healthy balance.

20. *Leading.* Foundations have no alternative but to accept the leadership position their command of flexible resources places them in. They will lead even when passive and silent; the only question is whether they will recognize and accept the responsibilities of their advantaged position. A foundation is a public trust; it is not simply a private prerogative, to be maintained as a private sanctuary and for private purposes. Why else the tax advantages accorded them by a public [that] expects public benefit in return?

Vast Room for Creativity

By now, it should be evident that foundations do not need a lot of money to be effective; within the twenty generic functions of modern philanthropy, they have all the room they need to be creative. If, indeed, they were to exploit only a fraction of the strategies available to them, their individual and collective impact on American life would be vastly and beneficially expanded. This nation needs what foundations at any scale have to offer; public awareness and expectancy are fast rising.

It might well be worth the effort if trustees and staff were to review their grants and activities to determine which and how many of the twenty generic functions they have engaged in.

Examples of Small Foundation Creativity

Examples of creativity have been scattered throughout the preceding pages; it may be helpful to identify a few more. These are but a sampling of the myriad instances where the generative potential of small foundations has been realized.

The Edward P. Hazen Foundation has distinguished itself over two generations as a powerfully leavening influence both on the American scene and in the philanthropic community. [Although it was] originally a family foundation, its board has for some time been composed of non–family members representing a wide diversity of gender, race, and occupational background. With [foundation] assets of less than $10 million, its grants have been consistently well-considered and often pioneering: for example, its earlier work in values, and its more recent nurturing of a minority scholar (Ron Edmonds) whose work touched off the Effective Schools movement in the United States. The foundation has also risked the calculated decision to invest a considerable part of its income in employing a succession of extraordinarily competent staff, whose personal influence has matched in many ways that of the foundation's program grants.

The Henry C. Frick Educational Commission of Pittsburgh, with assets under $5 million, has for nearly a century been a generative force in that community. With a board of trustees of eleven members representing such areas as finance, law, education, business, and community leadership, the fund has served not simply as a grantmaker but also as a program developer, catalyst, broker, and convener. It has carefully focused its activities, concentrating currently on the alarming turnover of principals and superintendents (in the process initiating the development of a Principal's Academy), on early childhood, and on problems such as teen pregnancy [and] drug and alcohol abuse.

A dramatic example of what a very small foundation can accomplish came with establishment this past year of the Dan and Inez Wood Fairfax Fund within the Southern Education Foundation. Created by Jean and Betty Fairfax in honor of their parents, the Fund will award college scholarships to black high school students in Phoenix, Arizona, who have persevered through graduation. The original asset contribution was $125,000, an endowment [that] is expected to grow modestly over the next seven years. It stands as a stimulating example of what minority donors of limited means can accomplish with a well-conceived contribution.

The Albert Kunstadter Family Foundation of New York city, with assets of less than $3 million, has decided that its grants should focus on critical operating needs of a very wide variety of nonprofit organizations; the range of recipients extends from minority educational ventures to agencies working on international development and security. In doing so, the foundation has carved out its own niche: a flexible response at critical times in the life of an organization that has proved its worth. These timely grants rarely exceed $5,000; most are between $2,000 [and] $3,000.

Finally, the Peninsula Community Foundation of Burlingame,

California, it has assets of less than $5 million; it grants range in size from $50 to $75,000, with the average between $5,000 to $20,000. It has displayed remarkable ingenuity (and parsimony) in its response to local needs. To illustrate:

- [It has] created, and with local business support maintained, a community resource library of funding sources and a training seminar for those seeking funding.

- In working with local corporations, [it has] set up a distribution center for the free disposition of computers, furniture, and other supplies to local nonprofit agencies.

- [It has] provided a convening and coordinating point for staff and public and private agencies working on teenage pregnancy [and] for several dance companies.

- [It has] initiated (at a total cost of $250) a get-together of the local constabulary and youngsters with cars and motorcycles, dissolving tensions and leading to the holding of a very popular rally and concourse.

- Along with other local funding sources, [it has] established a program of internships [that] adds college volunteers to the staffing potential of local nonprofits.

As Bill Somerville, [the Peninsula Community Foundation's] executive director, notes, "the challenge lies in how creative one can be with limited resources. Small foundations should be low-budget operations, but this has nothing to do with how flexible and responsive they can be. . . . The San Francisco Foundation is a limousine, and the Peninsula Community Foundation is a motor scooter. We both carry people; they can carry more, but we can take the corners quicker."

Family Foundations: High Risk, High Reward

(Published in *Family Business Review*, Winter 1990)[1]

"Foundations are a remarkable human invention. They provide private persons a free-wheeling opportunity to be socially and publicly influential. Without having to meet the tests either of the market or the ballot box, private persons can independently determine what the needs of society are and how best to go about meeting them."

A (married-into) member of a sizable family foundation recently commented somewhat sardonically, somewhat ruefully, "Building a foundation on the fragile relationships that characterize any family is a precarious enterprise, but the returns are worth the risk and all the tensions that go with it."

What are the attractions, what are the risks, what are the payoffs? Are the ecstasies of success worth the sometimes agonies of the effort?

The attractions: foundations are a remarkable human invention. They provide private persons a free-wheeling opportunity to be socially and publicly influential. Without having to meet the tests either of the market or the ballot box, private persons can independently determine what the needs of society are and how best to go about meeting them. The range of choice is almost infinite: health, education, science, human services; the cause of women, children, minorities, the poor, both at home and abroad; all the arts, community betterment, technological advance, immediate

---

[1] Vol. III, No. 4. Reprinted with permission from the Family Firm Institute. Copyright Family Firm Institute Inc. For use by the Council on Foundations. All rights reserved.

amelioration or fundamental and long-range reform—indeed every-thing but direct engagement in politics, and even that arena can be touched through research, education, and advocacy.

Over long years of evolution, foundations have emerged from their origin in charity to being globally recognized as an essential social institution. Modern societies have grown incredibly complex, no longer susceptible to simple ideologies, centralized governance, or single outlets for human energy and creativity. A pluralistic network of for-profit, nonprofit, and public agencies, sometimes working cohesively and sometimes competitively, is required to sustain the accumulating weight of human needs and potential. [It is] no accident that as American society has become more complex, the role of foundations has become more essential and appreciated. No accident, either, that foundations are spontaneously and dramatically emerging around the globe, even in the formerly rigid societies of Japan, the Soviet Union, and eastern Europe.

Private wealth has always been influential. But when it is transformed into a foundation, it takes on another image and coloration, no longer simply the expression of personal whim and ego but the credibility of a considered evaluation of community welfare that is the expectation—if not always the record—of modern philanthropy.

If the institution of private philanthropy is a remarkable social invention, its availability to families is equally remarkable. Society has offered families what is in effect a permit to engage indepen-dently in matters otherwise thought to be the public's business. Philanthropy becomes a legitimate and ennobling process, elevating the accident of kinship into the loftier realm of civic participation and responsibility. The often narrowing confines of individual giving open into the broadening vistas of social concern.

The risks, the hazards: succeeding in a family business or succeeding into a family fortune does not transpose easily into successfully operating a family foundation. Family businesses and fortunes are usually disciplined by the bottom line and hierarchical, often patriarchal, management; family fortunes sooner or later become divided or inherited into individualized control.

Foundations, with a single corpus and collective decision-making, are quite another proposition. They not only invite an intensifying stress on tensions already evident among family members, but intrude yet another dimension of differences—those that arise from the subjectivity inherent in determining social needs and priorities. There are few if any certain guidelines in deciding which social needs to focus on, which instrumentalities to work through, which criteria to adopt for judging success.

In that murky environment, family tensions can flare up and consume, existing differences exaggerate into factions and sometimes feuds. Governance can become an anguishing issue: in the first generation, how to overcome the tendency to bow obsequiously to the founding donor; in subsequent generations, how to include a spreading avalanche of family members without being exclusive or overwhelmed.

Distinguishing personal from social priorities is yet another hazard. To what extent should family obligations be expressed in foundation giving—obligations either imposed by the legal or felt need to honor the founder's charitable interests, or intruded by individual family wishes to give to favored charities? [This is] complicated often by the presence of surviving advisers to the original donor with dominating memories of what the founder wanted. What has to be remembered throughout and above all is the public purpose [that] the foundation is obliged to honor, the governing phase in society's permit to transform private wealth into a tax-favored and socially credible institution. The price is a commitment to go beyond personal whim and advantage to an equitable and serious consideration of social need.

That is the acquired ethic of a family member turned foundation trustee.

At the nuts-and-bolts level, there are obviously other risks, hazards, and difficulties. Forming a private foundation is no longer something that can be done by amateurs. Government regulations have increased along with public recognition; sophisticated legal, managerial, and financial advice is essential. There are regulatory no-no's contained in both federal and state legislation, some that carry civil and even criminal sanctions. Professional ethics and standards have also elaborated, subtly insinuating themselves into public expectations of philanthropic performance. And while smaller family foundations can often operate with ingenuity and effectiveness, increasing size carries with it the necessity of adding competent staff and advice. Not least [is] the inevitability of becoming sensitive to the growing attention [that] the public is giving to the role of foundations and to their performance. The day of sequestered philanthropy, of foundations acting quietly and non-responsively in the shadows, is waning, if not already over.

The rewards: the returns on a family investment in philanthropy are—or can be—extremely high, both internally and externally. Well executed, a family [foundation] can achieve the cohesion that comes with a sense of higher purpose and cooperative effort. Family members report an excitement and fulfillment going far beyond what they had known simply being blooded (often bloodied) members of a tribe. The educational experience involved in assessing public needs and evaluating grant proposals is incomparable, and can be extraordinarily bonding.

Externally, the rewards are also considerable. Society honors those who practice philanthropy, and the families who have kept the faith and held together have achieved public standing almost as an aristocracy: the Rockefellers, the Babcocks, the Nords, the Woods, the Gunds, the Heinzes, are simply suggestive of the potential for distinction that family foundations have bestowed. And in an age of family disintegration and lack of social role models, the potential for public appreciation is incalculable.

What Makes For An Effective Family Foundation?

There are a plethora of ways in which an effective family foundation gets started. One is by a founding donor with an infectious sense of social commitment, in turn transmitted through his/her family and successive generations. Others can vary from the opposite extreme of a fortune left by someone of minimal interest in philanthropy, but whose progeny and/or trusted advisors somehow ignite the spark and passion of social conscience. Sooner or later what binds these disparate examples together is an accumulating tradition of serving a worthy cause, along with some other common elements.

One is the willingness to argue through to agreement an explicit set of goals and objectives for the foundation: both a mission statement and a more focused bill of particulars that can guide applicants, staff, and trustees. This may be made moot by the trust's specification of purpose; but even when the charter is restrictive rather than general, enough room for argument exists to make the process of consensus-building essential.

Another, perhaps more arguable, ingredient has to do with professional staff. Many a successful family foundation, usually the smaller, has managed without such help, relying entirely on trustees and/or the designation of a family member to handle the day-to-day necessities of grantmaking. (One Massachusetts trust has successfully challenged this rule by relying solely on trustees to administer an endowment of over fifty million dollars.) Professional staffing does involve some almost inevitable delicacies and sensitivities, centering on board-staff relations and the eternal questions of how much power to delegate and whose money it really is. But certainly as size and scale increase, the need for professional staff becomes more essential and insistent, requiring a search for persons who combine competence with family sensitivity and compatibility—which has not prevented some foundations from finding persons with that potential within the family itself.

Not as arguable is the need for family trustees to be willing to work hard at the job. Giving away money—as many a donor has found—is not easy; doing it intelligently requires long hours of sifting priorities, sorting through proposals, learning to know the fields in which the foundation has expressed interest, getting to know the applicants and their circumstance, sensing who has the talent and which projects hold promise. The due diligence that is exacted from corporate boards has an even more exacting analogue in the obligations of foundation trustees.

This makes the selection of trustees extremely crucial. Within the family, selection can be as delicate as it is crucial. Boards are very rarely large enough to include every potentially eligible offspring; winnowing that longer list implies exclusion. And when exclusion is based on the mercurial criteria of competence and commitment, choices can be explosive. Families have tried to deal with the problem in many ways: from arbitrary fiat, to rotation, to determination of interest, to careful training and mentoring of younger family and oncoming generations. The more effective foundations have taken the selection process seriously, using rotation to spread participation and providing ample opportunities for learning the art and obligations of successful grantmaking.

An often divisive question is whether a family foundation would be well advised to invite the participation of nonfamily trustees. There are weighty arguments and examples on both sides, but the inclusion of outsiders has much to recommend it. Internal family dissension tends to soften and disappear in the presence of respected "guests at the dinner table"; the level of discussion and debate is elevated, especially with the participation of credible outsiders with experience in philanthropy and knowledge of the subjects being attended to. Numbers are not as important as simple presence; the catalytic effect of nonfamily trustees is the essential value.

A final question is whether an effective family foundation is forever. Not all foundations have survived through later generations, or even the first; some have been dissolved; some have broken into separate philanthropies, each presided over by conflicted family members; others have seen the influence—even the presence—of family disappear over time in favor of nonfamily appointments. It has even and provocatively been argued that family foundations should be subject to a sunset requirement, converting at some point into a more public institution, with or without retaining the family name.

But there is something distinctive and precious about family foundations that suggests they should remain as they are: a unique opportunity for families to make and leave their mark on the society around them, to share with others the fortune they have enjoyed and the creative energies they so often possess.

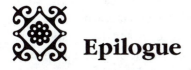 **Epilogue**

Writing about Paul Ylvisaker in the past tense when he is so presently with me is a challenging, humbling and heart-wrenching task. For those who knew him, we simultaneously mourn his loss at the same time we feel his presence in our lives and in our work. This book is about that person. It encapsulates that presence through speeches that were once scrawled on the back of an envelope, a testimony to a man who was forever challenging his own thinking by rewriting and editing until the moment he walked up to a podium.

The writings in this volume convey a sense of Paul's journey to make meaning of his life. These speeches and writings allow you to see his hopefulness, his anguish, his belief in the human heart. Every word is about him and what mattered to him. His probing intellect seemed always to be used in service of others whether it was as college professor or university dean, mentor, colleague, corporate or foundation trustee, government official, grantmaker, neighbor, brother, father, husband, or friend. No matter what street he walked down, people stopped him. What was it about this man that we so loved and admired? Was it his intellect, his wit and charm, his wise counsel, his character, his faith in life?

The events of his life, the professional positions and the people in his life, tell a lustrous story. The messages in his words give texture to the meaning of this story—the story of an outstanding public servant and a thoughtful Christian who had an uncommon and challenging conversation with God. And while he came to be identified with the institutions with which he was affiliated and the positions he held, it is the roles he played that transcend organizational affiliation for which he will be remembered—student of life, wise counselor, public servant, patriot, teacher. That role, as teacher, was his most satisfying.

Paul gave of himself to so many. Everyone was worthwhile.

Nothing was inconsequential. I recall Ginny Esposito saying, after she returned from reviewing Paul's archive at Harvard University, that in just one small file Paul had saved notes from speeches ranging from the United Nations to a high school graduation to a women's garden club in the United Kingdom. He was interested in people, all kinds of people. And he was interested and perplexed by life itself. I once attended a speech Paul gave to an arts and education group in Boston in which he expressed his awe about the artistic and creative power of life when he said, "It's really an incredible thing to be born a human being."

Those of us who shared the profession and the passion of philanthropy with him, see Paul as a transitional generational icon, representing the past, present, and timeless values of philanthropy. Imagine an Ylvisaker symbol as a human pyramid—a multi-generational, multi-colored group of people, all entangled with one another, with those at the summit reaching for all. Paul inspired his grantmaking colleagues, as he did his students of every discipline, to explore the critical human issues of the day and the values, virtues, and skills needed to address them. He gathered his students around him and encouraged them to learn from, argue with, and care for each other.

This book ultimately will realize its importance not in how it helps those who knew him, but in how it introduces new generations—those who may share his professional interests to his contributions. Paul himself would have resisted this publication as a memorial tribute alone. Where he would see value and, I believe, take some pride in this book, is in the hope that new audiences—new students—might see it as a means to make meaning of their lives and experience his joy in serving others.

I hope that readers of this volume come away with two important impressions about the life and work of Paul Ylvisaker. First, that living a meaningful and productive life has a great deal to do with who you are and how you make meaning of life, what your values are, where you place passion, to whom and what you extend your compassion and how you use your life to benefit and serve others.

Second, that Paul had a deft understanding of the synergistic relationship between individuals and institutions. The power of institutions to shape individual identity and the power of individuals to create institutions of value and purpose. As this book attests, he spent most of his life working with and through institutions—private, public, and not-for-profit—all the while challenging them to serve both their authoritative and moral purpose. Today, when many Americans feel comfortable in distancing themselves from institutions, public institutions especially, he would remind us of the high costs such disassociation exacts from the nation's political, social, economic, educational, and philanthropic institutions. For Paul Ylvisaker believed in the power of institutions to challenge and shape individual lives and, most importantly, the role of the individuals to create institutions that reflect the best of our intentions and humanity.

As someone who shared his professional interests in several kinds of institutions—state government, philanthropic, and educational institutions particularly—I understand the need to have each field continually revitalized and reshaped by new forces and new generations. And as these new generations take their place, it is essential that the young and the veterans alike remember the seeds planted by those who have gone before and understand the legacy with which they have been entrusted. Thank you, Paul.

Wendy D. Puriefoy
Washington, D.C.

Wendy Puriefoy was a program officer at The Boston Foundation, a community foundation, when she met Paul Ylvisaker, then a member of the foundation's Board of Directors. She worked in Massachusetts state government, and now shares his commitment to public education by serving as president of the Public Education Network, a coalition of local education funds and initiatives throughout the United States.

Message from the Funders

The chance to write about Paul Ylvisaker brings back a rush of memories of Swarthmore College in 1948, when he was a young Assistant Professor of Political Science and I was an even younger Dean of Men. Many years later, as the director of the Nordson Foundation and the Lorain County Community Foundation, I invited Paul to Cleveland to speak to my trustees.

He set out westward from Boston by plane, but since he was his own secretary (not one of his skills) he wound up in Dayton. Discovering his error, he rushed over to the ticket counter and charmed the agent, who caught the Boston-Dayton pilots as they walked by, and explained Paul's predicament. The pilots were so taken with him that they worked out a scheme to carry him as a gloriously singular passenger on a dead-head run to Pittsburgh, whence he would be whisked by a luggage tugger across the tarmac to a revving-up plane that would get him to Cleveland in the nick of time. His talk was a smash!

Paul became an important source of inspiration and guidance for the trustees of the foundation. He covered the basics, cautioned delay in arriving at a focus for granting, urged taking some chances in grant decisions, made suggestions about collaborative granting, warned of problems that plague many family foundations, and examined other opportunities and problems characteristic of a number of foundations. What he said was sensible and important, grounded by experience and informed insight.

How he said it was equally important. Acceptance and retention was greatly enhanced by his style, energy, sparkle and gentle humor. Paul Ylvisaker was a complete, first-class package: brain, knowledge, judgment, idealistic conviction, personality, and unobtrusive performing skills.

When the Nord family learned of this book, they knew they had found a way to fulfill their desire to honor Paul for his willingness to share his hopes for philanthropy with them. They still cite his advice more than six years later and credit him for much of the joy and fulfillment they have found in participating in the Nord Family Foundation. It is a pleasure and privilege for them to share his inspiration with you.

Jeptha J. Carrell
Oberlin, Ohio

Jeptha J. Carrell, a former Swarthmore College colleague of Paul Ylvisaker, is the former director of the Nordson Foundation, the Lorain County Community Foundation and the Nord Family Foundation.

Index